The Benefits of Public Art

The polemics of permanent art in public places

Sara Selwood

POLICY STUDIES INSTITUTE
London

PUBLISHING

The publishing imprint of the independent
POLICY STUDIES INSTITUTE
100 Park Village East, London NW1 3SR
Telephone: 0171 468 0468   Fax: 0171 388 0914

© Policy Studies Institute 1995

ISBN 0 85374 608 7

PSI Research Report 770

A CIP catalogue record of this book is available from the British Library.

1 2 3 4 5 6 7 8 9

PSI publications are available from
BEBC Distribution Ltd
P O Box 1496, Poole, Dorset, BH12 3YD

Books will normally be despatched within 24 hours. Cheques should be
made payable to BEBC Distribution Ltd.

Credit card and telephone/fax orders may be placed on the following
freephone numbers:

FREEPHONE: 0800 262260
FREEFAX: 0800 262266

Booktrade representation (UK & Eire):
Broadcast Books Services
24 De Montfort Road, London SW16 1LW
Telephone: 0181 677 5129

PSI subscriptions are available from PSI's subscription agent
Carfax Publishing Company Ltd
P O Box 25, Abingdon, Oxford OX14 3UE

Laserset by Policy Studies Institute
Printed in Great Britain by Latimer Trend and Co. Ltd

To my parents

Contents

Illustrations

Henry Moore, *The Arch*, Kensington Gardens, Royal Borough of Kensington and Chelsea

Art at Broadgate, London Borough of Hackney and the City of London

Art in Centenary Square, Birmingham

Abbreviations

ABSA	Association of Business Sponsorship of the Arts
ACGB	Arts Council of Great Britain *
BMBC	Barnsley Metropolitan Borough Council
BC	Borough Council
BSIS	Business Sponsorship Incentive Scheme
CARE	Community Action in Rural Environment
CBD	Central Business District
CC	County Council
COSLA	Convention of Scottish Local Authorities
DNH	Department of National Heritage
DE	Department of Employment
DES	Department of Education and Science
DOE	Department of the Environment
DT	Department of Transport
DTI	Department of Trade and Industry
DC	District Council
ERDF	European Regional Development Foundation
GLA	Greater London Arts
ICC	International Convention Centre
LAB	London Arts Board
LB	London Borough of
MC	Metropolitan Council
MBC	Metropolitan Borough Council
MDC	Metropolitan District Council
MSC	Manpower Services Commission
OAL	Office of Arts and Libraries

PSI   Policy Studies Institute

PAF   Public Art Forum

RAA   Regional Arts Association **

RAB   Regional Arts Board **

RSGB   Research Surveys of Great Britain

RB   Royal Borough of

RTPI   Royal Town Planning Institute

SCAT   Sheffield Contemporary Arts Trust

SOM   Skidmore, Owings and Merrill

UDC   Urban Development Corporation

UDG   Urban Development Grant

UDP   Unitary Development Plan

WAWP   Works of Art Working Party

Note

*   Unless otherwise stated, The Arts Council refers to The Arts Council of Great Britain, which became The Arts Council of England in April 1994.

** Regional Arts Associations (RAAs) ceased to exist in 1991 when they became Regional Arts Boards (RABs).

Acknowledgements

I should like to thank the members of the Steering Committee: Caroline Foxhall and Felicity Harvest, West Midlands Arts; Alan Haydon, former-ly of the Arts Council of Great Britain; Caroline Taylor, Yorkshire and Humberside Arts; Amanda King and Pru Robey, London Arts Board; Sandra Percival, PADT; David Perry, British Railways Board; Robert Hutchison, formerly Head of Arts Research at PSI, and Paul Filmer, Goldsmiths College, who edited the text. My conclusions are not necess-arily reflective of their views.

I would also like to thank all those members of the public who responded to our surveys. Individuals who participated in the focus groups, answered questionnaires, discussed the case studies and sent me unpublished material are too numerous to mention here, but are listed in the report itself. Many of those involved in the case studies, commented on the draft. Most of their comments have been incorporated in this revised version.

Tim Eastop, formerly of the London Borough of Hammersmith and Fulham and Paul Swales of Sheffield City Council, were both consistently and generously informative.

Finally, I am grateful to my colleagues: Diana Irving at Art & Society; at PSI, Lydia Maher, who analysed the returns from the survey of local authority Chief Executives and Jeremy Eckstein; to Russell Southwood and, last but not least, Bob Jarvis, who originally suggested I undertake some kind of research into public art.

Sponsors

Arts Council of England (formerly of Great Britain)
Railway Community Network (formerly British Railways Board, Community Unit)
London Arts Board
Yorkshire & Humberside Arts Board
West Midlands Arts Board

Executive summary

Rationale

Expansive claims are made for public art. It is credited with being a cultural investment vital to the economic recovery of many cities, contributing to local distinctiveness and cultural tourism, increasing the use of open spaces, humanising the built environment, encouraging residents to take greater pride in their locality and creating employment and confidence among various communities.

The objectives of this enquiry are to consider the perceived social, cultural and political benefits of public art, to examine whom it benefits and how, and to ask what implications its findings have for the future promotion of public art.

Background

The statistics available suggest that there was a steady increase in the growth of public art in Britain during the 1980s, and that it was predominantly commissioned in the public sector. The majority of local authorities with public art policies were in the metropolitan areas. Projects often involved partnerships, in particular between bodies in the public sector.

The burgeoning of public art happened for various reasons. Foremost among these was the scale of state investment in areas of urban deprivation and incentives to the private sector. These created opportunities for the development of arts in urban areas through community programmes, the cultural industries and high-profile prestige projects.

These opportunities were only conceivable because attitudes towards the arts had changed. Whereas the arts were previously assumed to occupy a separate realm to that of material production and economic activity, they were now regarded as an important economic sector which sustained employment, provided training opportunities and contributed to economic regeneration in a wider sense. Public art was both a highly visible and symbolic manifestation of that thinking.

The Arts Council had supported the display of art in public places since its foundation in the late 1940s. The priorities it promoted were generally those of the artists and the art itself, rather than those of the public. However by the 1980s arts funding bodies' attitudes towards arts development and public art had changed considerably in response to shifts in the political, social and economic order. Arts funding was frequently justified in economic terms and the need to create greater parity between the provision in London and the regions was acknowledged. So was the need to expand audiences for the arts – both numerically and in terms of target groups (including rural populations) – to support non-traditional art forms, evaluate projects and acknowledge the interests of the market. These concerns were widely promoted, as arts funding bodies assumed roles as advocates.

The bureaucratic infrastructure for public art was thus influenced both directly and indirectly by government policies and arts funding agencies. In formal terms, the arts funding agencies pump-primed specialist officer posts in local authorities, supported the growth of public art agencies, campaigned for the adoption of public art policies, including Percent for Art, contributed to the development of planning documents, provided training, and sought to encourage private sector interest in public art.

In pragmatic terms several constituencies have an interest in public art in addition to arts funding bodies. They are categorised as those overtly involved in public art commissions, members of the artistic community and members of the public. 'Leaders of local opinion' are included within the latter group. Each of these constituencies' interests are, in many respects, different. They have given rise to various contradictions and dilemmas implicit in attitudes towards the commissioning, siting and reception of public art.

The commissioning of public art, for example, raises issues about the contribution of public art to public good; whether public art necessarily constitutes good art; if working in or for the public realm necessitates compromising the artistic integrity of the artist; whether public art is an environmental improver; what the nature of its relationship to the built environment is; what contributions artists have to offer over and above those of other professionals, and whether public art is educational and if so, in what ways?

The processes by which public art is commissioned and sited similarly raise sets of questions: who should be responsible for taking the lead in commissioning public art; does it constitute a form of professional development; is it best administered by public art agencies or local authority officers; what criteria should commissions meet; should public art be subject to public consultation; would competition between artists raise standards; does the siting of public art in the public realm influence the processes of private patronage; are committees capable of making artistic decisions; who should be publicly accountable for public art and is Percent for Art 'a good thing'?

Finally, the reception of public art begs questions such as: what factors affect the reception of public art; in what sense can it be 'owned' by the public and by whose standards should it be judged?

These issues are exemplified in seven case studies drawn from examples of permanent works of public art commissioned and sited between 1978 and 1991. The conditions of each case study are markedly different – their commissioners, objectives, funding, administration, location, aesthetic and target audience, etc. The following conclusions, however, were made on the basis of the similarities between them.

Observations drawn from the case studies

The relationship intended between works of public art and the public was rarely articulated. The majority of case studies were described as for the wider community who were, by definition, geographically defined. However this may not in itself constitute a sufficient basis upon which to forge a relationship between public art and its audiences. Some of the case studies referred to particular groups within the community, highlighting the interests of one group over and above those of another. Professional interests prevailed among the case studies. It was comparatively rare for those not professionally engaged in the visual arts to be involved in their initiation and management.

The public was usually assigned a relatively passive role in respect of the case studies. They were more likely to be informed about proposed commissions than consulted. Indeed, the processes by which the public might be consulted about public art works are not highly or formally developed. The intentions for the case studies were rarely formally articulated. Although conceived in the public interest, they inevitably serve numerous interests, in particular those of the groups most directly involved, but the parameters of the professional relationships between those directly involved in the case studies and the lines of responsibility between them were not always clear.

Whatever their reputation or experience, the value of artists' involvement was taken as 'a given'. Several artists whose work constituted the case studies were self-selecting in that they had been involved in the initiation of the projects themselves. Others were invited or selected through limited competitions.

There appears to be a functional relationship between the scale of a purchaser's or commissioner's aspirations for the work, the size of the budget and the status and reputation of the artist. However, it did not follow that the scale of the fee and the value to the public of the work produced were related.

The majority of case studies were formalised by agreements between the artists, funders and agents. In some cases a brief for the work was also agreed. The existence of agreements did not necessarily prevent matters from going wrong. The final appearance of a commissioned work might constitute a matter of dispute; maintenance clauses were not always respected. In the majority of cases, the theme, content and appearance of works were proposed by the artist and artistic autonomy was generally considered to be of major importance by all those constituencies involved. Distinctions between the commissioning of a work, its patronage or sponsorship were rarely considered. On the basis of the case studies examined, the public sector appears less likely than the private sector to intervene in the production of works.

Artists were not usually instrumental in determining the sites for commissioned works. Nevertheless, their own initiation of projects tended to be in response to particular sites. The majority of case studies were site-specific in that the works were conceived for and determined by particularities of the location. Few, if any, of the case studies conceived as discrete works dominate their contexts.

There was little consistency about the granting of planning permission. Some case studies were granted permission; others did not go to planning committee. By definition, the granting of planning consent carries certain implications including the authority's endorsement of the work.

Public response was generally considered part of the complete public art process. However, the paradigms by which the case studies were judged by the public were not necessary consonant with those of the groups overtly involved in their promotion. The public's attitude tended to have a symbiotic relationship with media coverage. However the received wisdom of professionals is that the public may grow to appreciate public art works in the long-term on the basis of familiarity and that the burgeoning of public art will contribute towards the creation of new audiences for art. We found no evidence to support this. Little information about the public art works studied was available to the public.

None of the case studies had been formally evaluated by those involved. The specific criteria according to which they might have been evaluated were rarely identified as such. Of those objectives cited, some were self-fulfilling. These were more likely to do with administrative processes than art *per se*. Assertions about the qualities of projects were often made in the short-term and on the basis of visible evidence. Sometimes little distinction was made between the aspirations for and the actual impact of works studied. Claims made for public art were infrequently substantiated.

Many of the dilemmas which characterise the case studies reflect the tensions which typify the relationship between Modernism and the promotion of contemporary art in the public realm. These are manifest in the contradictory interests of artists and the public; between the conception of art in public places, community art and art developed in consultation with the public; arguments for and against public consultation; attitudes towards compromise and artistic integrity; the assumption that art speaks for itself as opposed to needing interpretation; the difficulties implicit in conceiving of art as a public service; the notion that public art is unmeasurable and so on.

Policy issues and recommendations

These address matters pertinent to the range of professional interests represented in the field of public art and could be implemented in both the public and private sectors through conditions of funding.

Intentions and accountability
There should be a greater openness as to how decisions are made, who makes them and for what reasons.

The intentions, conditions and values which inform the funding, commissioning, siting and reception of a work of public art should be clearly articulated and agreed at the outset as should the respective roles and responsibilities of all those overtly involved.

These intentions should represent the criteria against which individual public art works are evaluated and should determine the methodology and timescale of that evaluation.

Professional development

Those involved in funding, promoting and production of public art not only need to understand what is required of them, but what to anticipate from other constituencies involved. Gaps in their knowledge and understanding should be filled by professional development.

Consultation

Where appropriate, the commissioning of permanent works of public art – in particular by the public sector – should be subject to consultation.

Agreements

All commissions should be subject to legally binding agreements and briefs which protect all parties involved. They should serve to make maintenance clauses more widely respected; to define the anticipated life of the work and responsibilities to it and clarify any details pertaining to consultation and evaluation.

Information and interpretation

It should be requisite for information about public art works to be made accessible to the public.

Evaluation

Formal evaluation and the monitoring of projects in the short, medium and long-term should be carried out by funders or other responsible bodies. The outcomes of such evaluations should be used to inform subsequent work by those involved. Where possible the funding of public art projects within the public sector should be contingent upon evaluations of previous projects by those involved. It is likely that evaluations will contribute to respect for public art and its development in the future.

Introduction

Rationale

> A renaissance of sorts is taking place in the relationship between artists and the general public; a renaissance in which local authorities are playing an increasingly large part and diverse, if sometimes discreet role. It is, without overstating the case, an evolution which is returning art and artists to the service of the people; an evolution which appears poised to enter a high renaissance of achievement of cultural and economic benefit to all (Eric Moody, Introduction, *The Public Art Report*, Public Art Forum, 1990).

Much is surmised about the development of public art in Britain during the past fifteen years, but relatively little is known about its impact. There are no comprehensive sets of statistics available at local or national levels which might enable us to describe authoritatively how much public art there is, assess the scale of the public art economy or draw comparisons between the public art commissioned at particular times, in particular places or by the public or private sectors. Nor have there been any attempts to judge the quality of contemporary public art.

Yet since the late 1970s, despite the recession, interest in public art and the scale of local, regional and national commitments to it have grown substantially. Contemporary public art has assumed an increasingly visible presence throughout Britain. Numbers of commissions have been generated by the public and private sectors. Local authorities in England, Scotland and Wales are increasingly adopting public art policies. Colleges have established public art courses or courses with a public art component. Numerous agencies have grown up to promote it, and many artists regard its practice as a legitimate way to earn their living. At a time when research suggests that arts audiences tend to come from social groupings AB and C1 and have a higher than average household income (MSS Marketing Research 1993) it is perhaps not surprising that the artistic constituency believes that public art might reach the 'vast numbers of people who never visit galleries' (Selwood 1992:22).

Expansive claims are made for public art. It is credited with being a cultural investment, vital to the economic recovery of many cities. It is

said to contribute to local distinctiveness; attract companies and investment; feature in cultural tourism; add to land values; create employment;
increase the use of open spaces; reduce wear and tear on buildings and
lower levels of vandalism. Conceivably as a response to preoccupations
with architecture and the environment it is supposed to humanise and
otherwise improve the environment; bring about safer areas and encourage greater care of areas by residents whose pride in their locality has
increased (Public Art Consultancy Team 1990:25). In 1988 the Cabinet
Office endorsed its contribution to urban regeneration (Cabinet Office
1988:25). Five years later, the Secretary of State for National Heritage
emphasised that the arts could help deal with 'the problems of unemployment and alienation in our inner cities' as well as contributing to the
creation of a classless and tolerant society' (DNH 1993).

Given the lack of evidence about the impact of public art in Britain,
it appears that many organisations in the public and private sectors
promote public art and commit resources to it largely on the basis of
traditional, social conventions.

However by the end of the 1980s some of the constituencies involved
in funding and promoting public art were beginning to consider whether
they should adopt a more critical, if not strategic, approach to public art.
According to the Director of the Scottish Arts Council:

> It is probably fair to say that our attitude towards art in public spaces has
> changed with regard to the nature and scope of the projects/organisations we
> now support. When there was very little development in this area... we were
> naturally keen to assist whenever possible and were not unduly concerned by
> opportunities or commissions which sprang up through opportunism rather
> than anything else. However, now that this whole area is far more diverse and
> widely practised, we are keen to encourage developments which occur within
> some sort of strategy/context (Appendix 5, p. 343).

Several local authorities were also beginning to question their own
promotion of public art, and felt that the time had come to develop

> new understanding of the true scope and function of public art and the link
> between cultural and economic regeneration (Roberts and Salter 1992:8).

And there are those in the corporate sector, such as David Perry of
British Rail who

still feel exposed. There is a lack of confidence within the industry that a) we should be doing it and b) that we are competent to make the final selection.

Critics on both sides of the Atlantic similarly questioned the development of public art. According to the American critic Patricia Phillips, while public art had 'filled a perceived void in cultural production' it continues to 'operate in a critical vacuum (1993:6). Others (see, for example, Walker 1989 and Dormer 1992) have asked what good public art does. In 1984, a Professor of Government examined the public funding of the visual arts, including art in public places, from the standpoint of its benefits to individuals and the public interest (Banfield 1984). Three years later, Stalker and Glymour went so far as to propose that

> public contemporary sculpture does little or nothing to enhance the quality of life generally... Whatever legitimacy there is to government support of such displays derives from the tradition of serving the special interests of a very limited group of citizens. But this justification is overwhelmed by the fact that publicly displayed contemporary sculpture causes significant offence and harm, and does so in a way that intrudes repeatedly into peoples' normal living routines (1987: 334).

In many respects the British tradition of commissioning art for public places was characterised by the Victorians. Their provision of what we might now refer to as public art was premised on the notion that it was essentially ennobling. The 1841 House of Commons' Select Committee appointed 'to enquire into the state of the National Monuments and Works of Art in ... Public Edifices', for example, was concerned that these should contribute to 'moral and intellectual improvement for the People'. Similar aspirations informed the funding of other cultural amenities in the public realm, such as the new museums, libraries and parks. They were intended to have an enlightening and therefore 'civilising' effect, to strengthen local ties and serve as a means of diffusing social tensions (Conway 1991). Galleries reflected civic aspirations, regional prosperity and the nobility of private benefaction. Parks were peppered with statues, buildings, drinking fountains and sundials which commemorated royal visits, celebrated the achievements of local heroes and promoted local and national pride.

It goes without saying that more than a century later there are substantial differences between art, the concept of the public realm and the attitudes of those promoting public art and the public. Public art no longer predominantly comprises memorials and monuments to people, events and common aspirations. When it attempts to do so its meaning is often inescapably imbued with conspicuous ironies, as the plaster *Goddess of Democracy* erected in Tiananmen Square, Saddam Hussein's monument to the Iran-Iraq War, the *Victory Arch* in Baghdad and, nearer home, *Bomber Harris* demonstrated. As Robert Melville observed in 1954, 'the significant statuary of our time' is unlike that of our Victorian predecessors, in that it 'serves no sacred, commemorative or symbolic purpose and has practically no validity as architectural decoration'. Artists now conventionally make their own work for public places. Perhaps, as Phillips suggested, 'it is the questions and the controversies that art raises that can consolidate an audience of citizens'(1993:9).

Art is also credited as playing a part in urban, as opposed to civic, improvement. Whatever their strategies, urban theorists assume that the modern city is open to improvement, albeit maintaining or intensifying urban densities, or decentralising and creating low-density cities. Either way, art is regarded as an accessory to, if not an integral part of, the planning process (see Sudjic 1993).

It is also the case that, in recent years, public art has been assumed to have economic benefits. However, attempts to quantify these are unsubstantiated and fraught with difficulties. Several writers have expressed doubts about the rhetoric of the economic impact of cultural policy on urban regeneration, which often embraces public art programmes (see Booth and Bloye (1993) for example). With respect to public art in particular, the University of Westminster found that the commercial benefits of public art in private developments are irrevocably linked to other factors.

> Investment in public art is worthwhile in the medium to long-term in commercial office developments. Developments endowed with art installations as part of their overall image profile are likely, provided factors of rent, location and quality of accommodation are equal, to have a competitive edge over their rivals (Roberts, Marsh and Salter 1993:52).

Public art appears to have had little impact on the art market. Despite the boom in the mid-1980s and the fact that gallery art came to represent what the critic, Thomas Crowe referred to as the 'irreplaceable status indicator' (Crow 1986:19) members of the art trade consulted during the course of research for this report suggested that works of public art appear to have limited commodity value (see Appendices 1, p. 273 and 2, p. 280).

Indeed, as Gordon Hughes suggested in his critique of John Myerscough's report on *The Economic Importance of the Arts in Britain* (PSI 1988), attempts to measure the arts in terms of their success in the market are flawed both methodologically and intellectually, and their results exaggerated (Hughes 1989). Like Sir Alan Peacock and Samuel Cameron (1991), he disputed the validity of Myerscough's use of certain types of information in building up a picture of the economic value of the arts. Consideration of ancillary expenditure, for example, assumed that such expenditure would not otherwise have taken place. Doubts were also cast on the use of multipliers and cost-benefit analysis, particularly where spending on the arts might be off-set by losses elsewhere in the economy. Myerscough was also criticised on the basis of his conclusions and recommendations being counterfactual: they appeared to have been intended to present the potential benefits that would accrue from additional public expenditure on the arts. Subsequent research has cast doubts about the effectiveness of using public subsidy to pump prime other economic activities – at least in the short-term (see Loftman and Nevin 1992).

Furthermore, Hughes questioned the value of measuring the economic value of the arts *per se*. It would, he writes, 'be both odd and unconvincing if the strongest argument for public spending on the arts relied upon its employment impact', rather than its other, less tangible, benefits.

Hughes identified three ways in which the non-market value of the arts might be assessed, largely based on analyses of environmental problems. The first referred to the arts' option values. People place a value on the opportunity to enjoy artistic activities, even if they choose not to take advantage of that option at given times. Second, Hughes proposed that the benefits of the arts could be considered in respect to the externalities or spillover benefits which they generate. These apply to the whole of society, and are not determined by the values placed on the activities by those directly engaged in experiencing them. Third, the arts can be regarded as comprising merit goods – goods or services whose consumption is thought to be desirable for the community as a whole, regardless of whether individuals choose to consume them of their own free will. It is often argued that people harbour prejudices about the arts and only place a higher value on artistic activities after exposure to them. The case Hughes constructs clearly applies to public art and it informs the nature of the present enquiry.

Objectives

The primary objectives of this enquiry are to consider the perceived social, cultural and political benefits of public art, to examine whom it benefits and how, and to consider the issues arising from it. In that sense, this enquiry is essentially polemical. It is intended to contribute to the evaluation and formulation of public policy in respect of public art. It is not intended to serve as a manual on the commissioning or funding of public art.

Readership

The Benefits of Public Art is addressed to those who commission and promote public art including local authorities, developers and other corporate investors and partners from the private sector; public art agencies; funding agencies including the Arts Council of England and the Regional Arts Boards, private foundations and the Department of National Heritage.

Definitions

Public art is notoriously ill-defined. It is often regarded as synonymous with 'sculpture in the open air' althoughthe critic Lawrence Alloway, for example, maintained it took 'more than an outdoor site to make sculpture public' (Forgey 1980:86). It has been said to include 'any object bought or commissioned from a person who considers themselves to be an artist or a craftsperson' (Roberts, Marsh and Salter 1993:7). It may be 'produced for, and owned by, the community' (Apgar 1992:24) whether the community actively participates in its creation, or remains passive. It may can be located in relatively inaccessible places such as schools, hospitals and even 'private places' (Roberts, Marsh and Salter 1993). In this respect, it might be more accurately located in an ideological public realm, rather than the physical spaces of the 'public sphere'. It may represent a 'funding' category, since its source of funding may be what defines it as art, as opposed to street furniture; it may represent an aspect of marketing – 'it can put your place on the map' or ' reinforce a sense of place'. It is also often said to improve the environment. It may be the product of state intervention and corporate investment. The objects it produces may refer to self-conscious avant-gardism or heritage culture. Its relationship to its context is equally variable: it might be 'packet art', 'parachuted in' or 'site-specific'. It may ultimately represent a battleground between the artist's freedom of expression, and the public's right to choose.

These characteristics imply a public art that is permanent, static and object-based. However, public art does not necessarily require any of these qualities. It may comprise artists working as members of design teams, festivals, performances, carnivals, firework displays, fellowships or exchanges. It might be defined as political intervention – such as Krzystof Wodiczko's projection of a swastika onto the front of South Africa House, Trafalgar Square. It may constitute physical resources – galleries and museums, studios, spaces for temporary exhibitions, foundries, material banks. It might be an educational process – workshops, artists working on site or in residence, discussions, talks, seminars and conferences. It might not even be manifest in the form of the visual arts. It might comprise combined-arts projects, multi-media events or literature (Public Art Consultancy Team 1990:81-3), such as Poems on the Underground. It can embrace interests as varied as broadcasting, landscaping and tree planting (Appendix 3, p. 299).

The taxonomies according to which public art is categorised are equally confusing. Some employ concepts of form, function and constituencies of interest to describe public art: 'Permanent commissions', 'Time-Based and Temporary Commissions', 'Arts Provision and Resources', 'Community and Educational Involvement' (Public Art Consultancy Team 1990:81-3). Others emphasise place and time – past, present and future: 'Historic American Public Sculpture', 'Contemporary Monuments and Memorials', 'New Directions in Public Art', 'Places with a Past', 'Arts in Public Spaces', 'Place as Art', 'Sculpture Parks', 'Art in Public Transit' and so on (Art on File 1993).

In writing this report, we have adopted an exclusive, as opposed to an inclusive, working definition. The report concentrates specifically on permanent, static and object-based works sited in public places rather than transient manifestations. Research suggests that the majority of public art commissions are permanent. Although a considerable amount of temporary work has been promoted since the late 1970s, we believe

7

that to include permanent and temporary works would cause the enquiry to become too general. Attitudes to passing events, as opposed to physical fixtures, are ultimately determined by memory rather than renewable familiarity. Focusing on permanent works enabled us to ask specific questions about the value of public art as an investment and to consider whether the meaning of specific pieces, if not attitudes towards them, might have changed over the years. We required that each piece studied should have been in place for no less than 18 months at the time of research. This enquiry focuses, in particular, on public art produced since 1977, when the last Labour Government introduced its urban policy. Urban regeneration substantially contributed to the conditions in which much public art developed in Britain.

Our working definition of public art is also restricted to work which is freely, physically accessible to the public. It does not refer to art which, although sited in the public domain, may only be 'semi-public' in that access is inhibited or otherwise intended for a restricted audience. There are, therefore, no references to artworks commissioned within the National Health Service, to the work of artists in residence in schools or community centres, to work in office buildings or shopping malls locked after closing time. Thus in the context of one of the case studies – Centenary Square and the International Convention Centre, Birmingham – there is no detailed discussion about the murals inside the ICC which are only visible to concert and conference goers and some other users of the building, or those sufficiently motivated to request access.

Difficulties are inevitably implied by the use of language pertaining to public art – the implications of the term 'public art', for example. This is used throughout the report in preference to 'art in public places'. It deliberately refers to art intended for the public, created by the public or sited in spaces, which although not publicly owned are nevertheless intended for public use. The term carries overtly social and civic nuances. 'Art in public places', on the other hand, is used to specifically refer to art, which may not have been intended primarily for the public benefit.

The use of other words in public art parlance, such as 'community' and 'public', also suggest particular ideological positions. 'Public', for example, is often used as a metaphor for an anonymous mass, credited with imagined attributes and attitudes, whose interests stand in direct contradiction to those of the self-asserting individual – in this context, the artist or the art professional. 'Community' expresses particular kinds of social relations, distinct from those of the state or society. Community art has a distinctly polemical edge. Like community politics it involves direct action, local organisation and working directly with the people (see Williams 1988).

The report

The report is organised in three parts:

Part 1 Background to public art in Britain since 1977 and the issues arising from its dissemination
Part 1 is divided into two chapters. The first considers the political, economic and cultural conditions within which public art developed. It considers how the expansion of public expenditure on urban regeneration and the policies of arts funding agencies contributed towards the infrastructure for public art, and how public art is disseminated. The second chapter considers issues raised by the production and siting of public art works, in particular the conflicts and dilemmas which characterise different constituencies' attitudes towards public art – their intentions, their involvement in its commissioning and siting and its reception. The issues are those raised by interviewees and focus group participants during the course of research. Many of the points raised are considered in greater detail in the case studies.

Part 2 Case studies
This part of the report examines seven case studies situated in three regions – London, the West Midlands and Yorkshire & Humberside. Although they are not intended to represent a comprehensive sample of public art works, they have been selected to indicate different sets of intentions for public art, the various processes by which commissions are realised and the ways in which they are received.

They represent major trends in commissioning and patronage, corporate, community, local, national and international aspirations and a range of artistic interests. Some were initiated by artists; in other cases artists were invited or entered limited competitions. In some instances the artists were involved early on in a new development. They also demonstrate a range of functions ascribed to public art and a variety of forms in which public art is cast, such as sculpture, architectural embellishment, street furniture, etc. They include representational and abstract works, those that are skill-based or primarily conceptual, those that are autonomous decorative and functional. Some are solitary commissions and others comprise clusters of works commissioned or otherwise acquired within the context of a unified strategy or physical location. The case studies are located in private and publicly owned spaces. Some are in designated priority areas. Each case study has different constituencies, including local residents, the working population and tourists, and each impacts differently on the environment, the public, the artistic community and its investors themselves. The fact that the majority of case studies focus on sculptural works largely reflects their preponderance among public art in Britain.

In London the two case studies are *The Arch* in Kensington Gardens in the Royal Borough of Kensington and Chelsea and the various sculptures sited in the public spaces at Broadgate which, at the time of research, crossed the boundary between the London Borough of Hackney and the City of London. In the West Midlands they include the works in Centenary Square, Birmingham and the painting of the shops in Smethwick High Street, Sandwell. In Yorkshire & Humberside, the three case studies are *The Chantreyland Sculpture Trail*, Graves Park, Sheffield, the *Silkstone Heritage Stones*, Silkstone, Bradford and *A Light Wave* at Westgate Station, Wakefield.

Unlike many works of public art around the country, those examined as case studies are in a reasonable, if not good state of repair. Issues of maintenance may consequently not be examined as closely as the selection of other works as case studies might have warranted.

Part 3 Implications and conclusions
By reference to the general political, cultural and economic conditions within which public art has developed in Britain and to the specific intentions, processes and impact of the case studies, the report finally considers the implications of these findings for the future development of public art and artists' contributions to the public realm.

Appendices

The Appendices contain lists of those consulted during the course of research and the schedules, questionnaires and topic guides used for surveys, focus groups and structured interviews. Detailed analyses of the majority of surveys carried out are also provided.

The Appendices also contain an edited transcript of an interview with Richard Serra, one of the artists commissioned at Broadgate. The interview has been reproduced partly because of the controversial nature of Serra's work and partly because it raises many issues pertaining to current practices of public art promotion, such as the introduction of the artist at an early stage of development, the work of public art as subject to planning control, as serving particular functions other than affirming corporate ideology and the relationship between the artist's and the commissioners' intentions.

Sources

Given the wide ranging objectives of this research, it necessarily draws on three main sources of information. First, it refers to the critical literature on public art, in particular that published in Britain since 1977. The second source comprises the available facts about public art and the context within which it developed in Britain. This draws on extant research, in particular the Public Art Forum's *Public Art Report* (1990), the returns of which were reanalysed, and the University of Westminster's *Public Art in Private Places* (Roberts, Marsh and Salter 1993), in addition to that carried out for this report. It goes without saying that comparisons between different surveys are, at best circumstantial. They cover different geographic areas, and are based on different definitions of public art. The third source used comprises recorded opinions and attitudes towards public art – public art in general and the case studies in particular.

Opinions about public art in general

These were mainly collected through surveys, focus groups and in-depth interviews. They included surveys of the chief executives of local authorities in London, West Midlands and Yorkshire & Humberside; specialist public art and Percent for Art officers employed by local authorities; public art agencies; arts funding bodies; art dealers and auction houses; town artists; art colleges and universities with courses on the practice and administration of public art; planning courses and public art agencies. Focus groups were organised with members of the business community, and with 'leaders of local opinion' and the 'artistic community' in each of the three regions. In-depth interviews were also held with planners and architects.

Some of those whose opinions were sought were self-selecting in that they responded to notices in the professional press. Others were specifically invited to contribute. These researches provided background material for Chapter 2 in particular. Unacknowledged quotations are usually derived from such sources.

Case studies

Surveys and structured interviews relating to the case studies were carried out across the four main constituencies of interest – the local public; leaders of local opinion; those overtly interested in the case studies and the artistic community.

1. Those overtly interested in the case studies
Interviews with those overtly interested in the case studies (such as local authority officials, developers, public art agencies and artists) were the first to be carried out. These took the form of personal interviews. Acknowledged quotations are usually derived from such sources. The matrix according to which all these interviews were based is reproduced in Appendix 2, p. 277. The findings of those in-depth interviews determined the form in which the case studies are presented.

2 and 3. Leaders of local opinion and the artistic community
Focus groups comprising 'leaders of local opinion' were held in the three regions in which the artworks studied are situated. Those invited included teachers, senior local government officers, business managers, planners, architects, academics, representatives of the media and administrators not directly involved in the case studies, but involved in the development of national and regional strategies for public art. These groups were primarily intended to discuss the political frameworks within which public art is promoted. These groups prompted discussions which raised issues pertinent to public art in general and the case studies in particular.

Focus groups comprising the artistic community were also held in each region. Those invited included artists, arts consultants, those involved in training artists to work in public and arts promoters. These groups were intended to discuss the processes through which public art works are brought to fruition, including the criteria required of their commissioning and their relationship to local communities.

The two sets of regional focus groups, those with the 'leaders of local opinion' and 'the artistic community', were based on a shared agenda. This focused in particular on issues pertaining to commissioning, siting, public consultation and the funding of public art. The full topic guide is reproduced in Appendix 2, p.279. Another focus group discussion was held with representatives of corporate sector (Appendix 2, p. 278). Contributions from these sources are also acknowledged.

4. The public

Each of the public artworks studied had, by definition, a different public. Their attitudes were sought in various ways. Opinions aired at the time the works being studied were sited, were gathered through documented correspondence to newspapers and radio phone-ins. Detailed consideration was given to the question of how attitudes were formed, not least by the media.

In the cases of the two largest studies, Broadgate and Centenary Square, the respective tenants and users of the Convention Centre were surveyed (Appendix 2, pp. 290-293). For Broadgate, an existing survey was also reanalysed (Hall 1992). For other case studies, short interviews were held with random samples of passers by (Appendix 2, pp. 286-289). In all cases opinions were invited through posters in libraries and notices in local papers.

Methodological approaches

The published research on public art in Britain has, to date, been quantitative. Organisations do not conventionally apply performance measurements to public art (see, for example, the Arts Business, 1991). There is no body of research into attitudes towards public art upon which our investigations might have been based.

The primary research for this report – finding out about people's attitudes towards public art at first hand, as opposed to drawing on secondary, or existing research – relates to methods employed in the exploration of meanings and values that people attach to landscapes, nature and places (see Harrison and Burgess 1988) and methods employed in visitor studies in museums and art galleries. These largely derive from anthropological, sociological and educational approaches. While there are substantial differences between the intentions of people visiting such institutions and those who, often accidentally, encounter public art, certain procedures employed in visitor studies can nevertheless be adapted in studying attitudes towards public art.

There are no universally agreed canons about researching attitudes towards the visual arts. Contemporary work in the field of visitor studies reflects different sets of interests. Its practice may focus on processes of evaluation or research, different subjects of enquiry – what the exhibit does to visitors, as opposed to what visitors do to the exhibit – and the relative merits of objective or subjective approaches (see Bicknell and Farmelo 1993).

Evaluation essentially seeks to 'assess the worth or value of things' (Miles et al 1988:127). It can be used to judge projects against norms of targets, to see if something works, to match the intentions with the end result. In the field of visitor studies, evaluation may be used to examine the relationship between the visitors and the exhibit in terms of affective and cognitive measures: is the message getting through and what did people understand by it? Research, on the other hand, encompasses evaluations to develop generalisations.

The case studies in this report constitute evaluations in so far as they compare the intentions for the commissions with the work's impact on the public. However, the attitudes which informed the commissioning or siting of the case studies do not necessarily easily lend themselves to this type of investigation. As Henry Moore is reported to have said of one of his monumental figures erected in front of the UNESCO buildings in Paris in 1958, he intended it to mean whatever anyone wanted it to mean.

The research for this report employs both objective and subjective approaches, and renders up quantitative and qualitative information. Objectivity espoused to what researchers refer to as 'positivism'

would appear to mean a belief in the existence and availability of objective facts, and above all in the possibility of explaining the said facts by means of an objective and testable theory, not itself essentially linked to any one culture, observer or mood (Miles 1993:29).

Surveys carried out for this report have produced objective facts about public art, such as the number of local authorities with policies, the numbers who implement those policies, and so on. However, as described above, we also sought to find out about the cultural and social significance of public art through focus group discussions and in-depth interviews. Such techniques are based on the approaches of interpretative sociologies and media studies, and have been described as repudiating

> objectivity as such ... objective truth is to be replaced by hermeneutic truth. Hermeneutic truth respects the subjectivity both of the object of the inquiry and of the inquirer, and even of the reader or listener (Miles 1993:29).

Subjective approaches reveal how individuals perceive things and how they give meanings to experiences. Their knowledge may be based 'less on the nature of the object, than on the manner and context in which it is experienced'(Roberts, L. 1993:99). Such approaches also emphasise what people bring to their 'readings', the 'symbolic value' they attribute to things (Willis 1990), or their 'cultural imaginings'. These:

> are imaginative in that they involve creative interaction between visitors and the exhibition; and they are cultural in that these interactions are influenced by all kinds of expectations and ideas (Macdonald 1993:77).

References to the Introduction

Apgar, Garry, 'Redrawing the Boundaries of Public Art', *Sculpture*, May-June, 1992.

Art on File, USA and Public Art Development Trust, UK, *Art on File International: Colour Slides of Public Art, Architecture, Landscape Architecture and Urban Design*, 1993.

The Arts Business Ltd, *Measuring the Arts. Practical Use of Performance Measurement in the Arts and Entertainment Sector*, 1991.

Banfield, Edward C., *The Democratic Muse. Visual Arts and the Public Interest*, Basic Books Inc, New York, 1984.

Bianchini, Franco and Parkinson, Michael (eds), *Cultural Policy and Urban Regeneration: The West European Experience*, Manchester University Press, 1993.

Bicknell, Sandra and Farmelo, Graham (eds), *Museum visitor studies in the 90s*, The Science Museum, 1993.

Booth, Peter and Bloye, Robin, 'See Glasgow, see Culture' in Bianchini and Parkinson (1993).

Cabinet Office, *Action for Cities*, Cabinet Office, Department of the Environment and the Department of Trade and Industry, 1988.

Carey, John, *The Intellectuals and the Masses: Pride and Prejudice among the Literary Intelligentsia 1880-1939*, Faber & Faber, 1992.

Conway, Hazel, *People's Parks: The Design and Development of Victorian Parks in Britain*, Cambridge University Press, 1991.

Crow, Thomas, 'The Return of Hank Herron', *Endgame: Reference and Simulation in Recent Painting and Sculpture*, The Institute of Contemporary Art, Boston, 1986.

Department of National Heritage, 'Peter Brooke calls for greater access to arts, sport and heritage', press release, DNH, 28.6.1993.

Degmore, E., *The Experience of Public Art in Urban Settings*, PhD dissertation, City University of New York (unpublished) 1987.

Dormer, Peter, 'Lipstick on the face of a gorilla', *The Independent*, 9.9.1992.

Forgey, Benjamin, 'It Takes More Than an Outdoor Site to Make Sculpture Public', *ARTnews*, September 1980.

Hall, James, 'Lust for Rust', *The Guardian*, 25.9.1992.

Harrison, Carolyn and Burgess, Jacqueline, 'Qualitative Research on Open Space Policy', *The Planner*, November, 1988.

Hughes, Gordon, 'Measuring the Economic Value of the Arts', *Policy Studies*, vol 9, no 3, Spring 1989.

Israel, T., *The Art in the Environment Experience: Reactions to Public Murals in England*, PhD dissertation, City University of New York (unpublished) 1988.

Loftman, Patrick and Nevin, Brendan, *Urban Regeneration and Social Equality: A Case Study of Birmingham 1986-1992*. Research Paper no 8. Faculty of the Built Environment, University of Central England in Birmingham, 1992.

MSS Marketing Research Ltd, *Arts 93: Audiences, Attitudes and Sponsorship*, Clerical Medical and ABSA, 1993.

Macdonald, Sharon, 'The enigma of the visitor sphinx', in Bicknell and Farmelo, 1993.

Melville, Robert, 'Henry Moore and the Siting of Public Sculpture', *Architectural Review*, vol 115, no 686, February 1954.

Miles, R.S., Alt, R.S., Alt, M.B., Gosling, D.C., Lewis, B.N. and Tout, A.F., *The Design of Educational Exhibits*, Unwin Hyman, 1988.

Miles, Roger, 'Grasping the greased pig: evaluation of educational exhibits', in Bicknell and Farmelo, 1993.

Moody, Eric, 'Introduction', *Public Art Forum*, 1990.

Mulgan, Geoff, The Public Service Ethos and Public Libraries, *Comedia Working Paper 6: The Future of the Public Library Service*, 1993.

Peacock, Sir Alan and Cameron, Dr Samuel, 'The Socio-Economic Effects of the Arts', *Discussion Document 4, National Arts & Media Strategy*, Arts Council of Great Britain, 1991.

Phillips, Patricia, *Public Art – The New Agenda*. Transcript of the keynote address at a one day conference organised by The University of Westminster, November 1993.

Public Art Consultancy Team, *The Strategy for Public Art in Cardiff Bay*, Cardiff Bay Development Corporation, 1990.

Public Art Forum, *Public Art Report*, 1990.

Roberts, Lisa C., 'Analysing (and intuiting) the affective domain', in Bicknell and Farmelo, 1993.

Roberts, Marion and Salter, Miffa 'Planning for Arts Sake', *Planning*, no 966, May 1992.

Roberts, Marion, Marsh, Chris and Salter, Miffa, *Public Art in Private Places: Commercial Benefits and Public Policy*, University of Westminster, 1993.

Stalker, Douglas and Glymour, Clark, 'The Malignant Object: Thoughts on Public Sculpture', Glazer and Ilea (eds), *The Public Face of Architecture: Civic Culture and Public Spaces*, The Free Press, 1987.

Selwood, Sara, 'Art in Public', Susan Jones (ed.), *Art in Public: What, why and how?*, AN Publications, 1992.

Sudjic, Deyan, *The 100 Mile City*, Flamingo, 1993.

Walker, John A., 'Public Art is Good for You', *Art Monthly*, October 1989.

Williams, Raymond, *Keywords: A Vocabulary of Culture and Society*, Fontana Press, 1988.

Willis, Paul, *Moving Culture: An enquiry into the cultural activities of young people*, Calouste Gulbenkian Foundation, London, 1990.

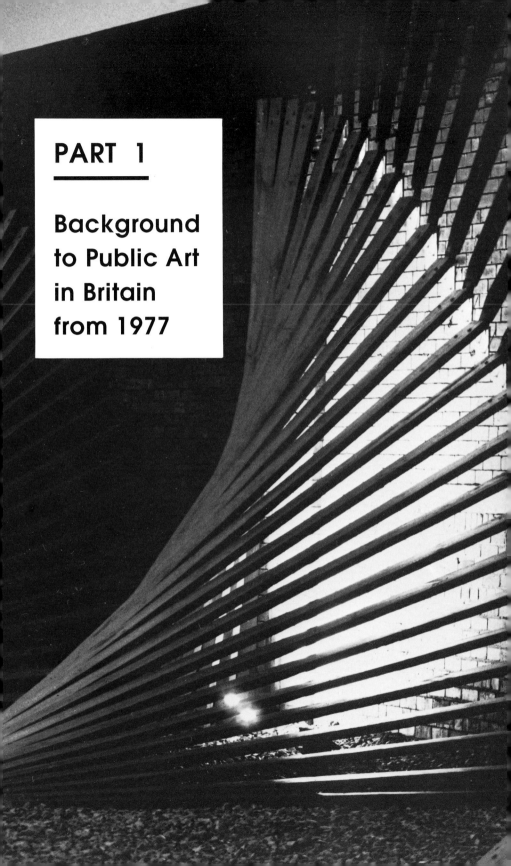

PART 1

Background
to Public Art
in Britain
from 1977

Introduction

The statistics available suggest that there was a steady rate in the growth of public art in Britain during the 1980s. In 1984, it was estimated that there were 550 works by 195 modern sculptors scattered around Great Britain (Strachen 1984). Between 1984 and 1988, 124 local authorities in England, Scotland and Wales commissioned 433 works including sculptures, murals, environmental improvements, glasswork, mosaics, textiles (Public Art Forum 1990). In 1993, it was estimated that over 750 'public art installations' had been provided in the last decade and that taking into account the commissioning habits of health authorities, institutions of higher education and major landowners such as British Rail, there might be as many as 3,000-4,000 works of public art in England and Wales (Roberts, Marsh and Salter 1993).

There is also clear evidence to suggest that much of public art is generated by the public sector. On the basis of research carried out for this report, it has been estimated that the public sector generates over three times as much public art as the private sector (Appendix 3, p. 294). The majority of local authorities which commission public art – nearly 60 per cent – do so in partnerships with the public and private sectors; 35 per cent with the public sector, 38 per cent with the private sector, 37 per cent with both (Appendix 3, p. 299). Public Art Forum's 1988 survey found much the same. Although it found that single local authority departments were often successful in attracting small scale sponsorships from local companies, they more consistently attracted co-funding from the public sector – other local authority departments, other authorities, RAAs, development corporations and the MSC, as well as different authorities.

We also know that the majority of local authorities with public art policies are in metropolitan areas – London Boroughs, City Councils and Metropolitan Borough Councils (Appendix 3, p. 294).

These facts alone give rise to certain questions which are examined in Part 1 – why public art developed during the 1980s, why it is predominantly a public sector interest and why it became the focus of partnerships.

1 The political, economic and cultural background

Central government frameworks

The decay at the heart of Britain's cities is one of the biggest challenges faced by government. Successive administrations have tried to reverse the trends. The aims have been to support and stimulate environmental renewal, to encourage new jobs and give the residents a better quality of life and new hope (Peter Wilmott and Robert Hutchison (eds) *Urban Trends 1*, 1992).

In 1977 the then Labour government published a white paper entitled *Policy for the Inner Cities*. It was followed in 1978 by the *Inner Urban Areas Act*. The two documents contained the first comprehensive policy statement to acknowledge the inner cities as a definable and cohesive problem. Labour's urban programme prioritised particular cities and parts of cities needing support for regeneration. Its intention was to prevent higher unemployment, deteriorating housing and a decline in public services. The measures it introduced were essentially social, premised on the notion of state investment and directed towards the needs of the community as a whole.

At the same time the Arts Study Group of the National Executive of the Labour Party produced a report entitled *The Arts and the People* (1977), which proposed that the arts could help develop a sense of community. This ambition was fully consistent with the Labour government's policy for the inner cities; indeed it was predicated on the notion of making available Urban Aid Programme funding to local authorities to encourage community-based activities. These might contribute to unified neighbourhoods, help overcome the neglect and alienation felt in deprived areas, and ultimately the crime and vandalism which, it was supposed, were contingent upon them.

In many respects these proposals recalled post-War attitudes towards the use of art in the reconstruction of bombed cities and the planning of the new towns and the development of artists' placements and town artist posts (see Gibberd 1973). According to the planner, Walter Bor, in the mid-1950s the London County Council committed a very small percentage of its budgets to installing works of art in its construction of flats and schools. By the 1960s the idea of town artists gained momentum. Victor Pasmore worked as a consultant with the architectural team designing Peterlee New Town between 1954 and 1977. David Harding was appointed Town Artist in Glenrothes in 1968. His brief was to 'contribute creatively' to the built environment of the town (Petherbridge 1979:125). At the *People and Cities* conference held in Coventry in 1966, it was proposed that the sculptor, working in conjunction with the planner and the architect, was responsible for 'expressing the meaning of the city' (Biggs 1984:32). The Artists Placement Group, established that same year, evolved a system of placing artists in various constituencies – industry, government and local communities so that 'they can bring their creative viewpoints to bear on problems, often previously unidentified' (Petherbridge 1979:127).

On coming to power in 1979, the Conservative Party was faced with soaring unemployment (it rose from 1.1 million in 1979 to over 3 million in 1986) and acute problems in the inner cities, which exploded in the riots of the early 1980s. Successive Conservative administrations expanded the programme of urban aid inherited from Labour, investing heavily in deprived areas through local authorities. Despite their concern to cut public expenditure, between 1976/77 and 1984/5 funds available to local government from the urban programme increased from £30 million to £348 million. By 1990/91 total government spending on inner cities exceeded £892 million.

The Conservative government's urban policy was substantially different to Labour's, in that it was essentially economic rather than social, directed at the needs of the individual rather than society and premised on the notion that urban regeneration would be led by the private sector rather than state funding. The government devised various pump--priming schemes intended to attract private investment or 'partnerships'. Mainstream urban programme funding was largely directed towards helping new businesses and providing training for employment.

The urban programme that evolved during the successive Conservative administrations was complex, having been funded by different departments, in particular the then Departments of the Environment (DOE), Trade & Industry (DTI), Employment (DE) and Education & Science (DES) and continually subject to changing policies. In 1989 the

Audit Commission referred to the government's support programme as a 'patchwork quilt'. It is described briefly here because certain aspects of it were fundamental in creating the conditions in which public art developed.

In 1987, the government discontinued support of the 150 authorities which had received funding under the 'traditional urban programme'. They concentrated resources on the 57 areas identified as the most deprived in England, together with proportionate numbers for Scotland and Wales. These new urban programme areas were selected on the basis of an official deprivation score applied to the findings of the 1981 census. Indicators of deprivation included unemployment, overcrowding, amenities, ethnic composition, single parents and pensioners.

In 1988 the various initiatives of the urban programme were brought together under the umbrella of *Action for Cities*. They included Urban Programme and Derelict Land Grants; designated Enterprise Zones and Simplified Planning Zones encouraged development through a combination of the relaxation of planning controls and tax incentives. Other initiatives included the establishment of such agencies as the Training Agency, which assumed responsibilities for training and business programmes.

Urban funding itself was largely channelled through local authorities in priority areas and, from 1981, through the Urban Development Corporations (UDCs). These were local quangos set up for a limited period to perform specific functions with respect to the regeneration of specified areas. They assumed statutory powers, most notably pertaining to planning. The first UDCs were established in Docklands and Merseyside. Nine more followed in other priority areas, including the Black Country and Sheffield, in 1987 and 1992. UDCs are due to be wound up in the mid-1990s.

In 1991 the government announced City Challenge, which transformed the way in which local authorities approached local urban regeneration. Under City Challenge authorities in priority areas, in partnership with the public and private sectors, were invited to bid competitively. Criteria for bids included consultation with local communities.

In November 1992 the government announced a reduction in its spending for the next two to three years. The end of that period will mark the final demise of the scheme (Dix 1993:6-8).

Funds for urban regeneration were also available through other funding agencies and professional associations. European funds were committed to what the DTI designated as Assisted Areas. Although conditions of that funding changed, it mainly benefited urban communities, areas of industrial decline, training and the long-term unemployed. Other bodies such as the Civic Trust, English Heritage, Royal Institute of British Architects, the National Heritage Memorial Fund and Business in the Community provided resources for environmental regeneration and training (Keens et al 1989:87).

The arts in the service of urban policy

The combination of state investment in areas of urban deprivation and the incentives offered to the private sector created opportunities for the development of the arts. According to one Regional Arts Board's spokesperson, it successfully put the arts 'on planners' and developers' agendas' (Dix 1993:8). Indeed, the Cabinet Office's document *Action for Cities*, (1988) endorsed the arts' contribution to urban regeneration. Paul Collard's report on *Arts in the Inner Cities* commissioned by the Office and Arts and Libraries (OAL) in 1987, identified arts developments in priority areas as falling into three distinct categories: outreach and community programmes, cultural industries, and prestige art projects. However, in order for the arts to be regarded as pragmatically contributing to the regeneration of the inner cities, perceptions of them had to change.

In the 1960s and early 1970s the arts – in particular the visual arts – were commonly perceived as occupying a realm separate from, and often actively opposed to, the realm of material production and economic activity. They were subsidised on the grounds of their possessing inherent values – life enhancing qualities – which are fundamentally opposed to, if not threatened by, commercial forces. In that sense arts funding was predicated on notions of artistic 'originality' and 'excellence'. It was assumed that the need for these values was universal, uncontaminated by questions of class, gender and race, and that it could not, by definition, be satisfied by the market. As Nicholas Garnham observed in 'Concepts of Culture' (1987), this ideology attributed a 'special and central status'

> to the creative artist whose aspirations and values, seen as stemming from some unfathomable and unquestionable source of genius, inspiration or talent, are the source of cultural value. The result of placing artists at the centre

of the cultural universe has not been to shower them with gold, for artistic poverty is itself an ideologically potent element in this view of culture, but to define the policy problem as one of finding audiences for their work, rather than vice versa. When audiences cannot be found, at least at a price and in a quantity which will support the creative activity, the market is blamed and the gap filled by subsidy (Garnham 1987:23).

By the early 1980s the state support of an arts policy which pertained to a narrow range of activities and a narrow audience, and had only a marginal impact on the consumption of cultural commodities and services, became increasingly politically, economically and culturally necessary to justify. Not only were most people's cultural needs and aspirations supplied by the market, but the massive growth of cultural and media studies had shifted the parameters of what could be considered worthy of critical attention. Popular culture could be taken as seriously as high art and equally legitimately funded.

That thinking was reinforced by the mobilization of the concept of the 'cultural industries' in the mid-1980s. The cultural industries – social practices whose primary purpose was the transmission of meaning – newspapers, periodical and book publishing, record companies, commercial sports organisations and so on, were conceived as functioning in a wholly different way to the conventionally subsidised arts in that they actively contribute to the economy and create employment by intervening 'through' rather than 'against the market'. The concept of the cultural industries also potentially refuted the assumption that quantity and quality were mutually exclusive.

By the mid to late-1980s both the Left and the Right subscribed to the view that the arts could be ideologically and administratively grounded in economic and social 'realities'. This view was given considerable weight by John Myerscough's independent research into *The Economic Importance of the Arts in Britain* (1988). He presented the arts as a major contributor to the economy, and claimed that they stimulated tourism, contributed to urban renewal, were a major export earner, and employed substantial numbers of people.

These were precisely the kind of arguments used to support the funding of public art and the concept of the received arts contributing to the vitality of cities (see, for example, Bianchini et al 1988) and their marketing. In much the same way that the Mayfest and the events organised during its year as European City of Culture (1990), such as

Peter Brooks' *Mahabharata*, contributed to changing the popular image of Glasgow – exemplified in the 1989 slogan, 'Glasgow's Miles Better' – so the National Museum of Photography, Film and Television and the Alhambra contributed to Bradford's image; the National Exhibition Centre, Centenary Square, the International Convention Centre, the City of Birmingham Symphony Orchestra and the relocated Birmingham Royal Ballet to Birmingham's image, and the Architectural Enhancement Programme to Swansea's. These kinds of initiatives were typical of developments elsewhere in Europe and North America (see Glasgow City Council 1992; Griffiths 1993).

In the context of the city conceived as a cultural entity (Bianchini and Parkinson 1993), not only was cultural provision perceived as a continuum across both the public and private sectors, but the arts were assumed to be a valid form of training and capable of 'sustaining employment' and 'a cost-effective means of job creation'. Arts-based training for employment attracted considerable government investment. At its peak (1986/87) the Community Programme administered by the Manpower Services Commission (MSC) and funded by the DE under *Action for Cities*, generated 6,751 authorised places on 359 projects classified under a 'cultural' heading. The cost of the programme was estimated at £24 million. The arts received other government funds through the NHS, the Home Office's Section 11 funding, and the DOE. In many areas the DOE, DE and DTI provided more by way of arts funding than the RAAs and local authorities together. In 1987, for example, MSC funding for the arts in Merseyside was reported to have exceeded that of Merseyside Arts and Liverpool City Council combined (Collard 1988:12).

Public art, in particular, was employed in various capacities – as symbols of cities' identities, as the object of MSC schemes, as contributing to a safer environment and to the health service and, perhaps most conspicuously, as a feature at Garden Festivals which the DOE funded between 1984 and 1992 to stimulate investment in and regenerate those areas scarred by the abandonment of manufacturing industries. Garden festivals were characterised by the reclamation of derelict land – the removal and camouflaging of waste land and industrial debris – to secure long-term redevelopment, provide a focus for regional promotion and celebrate urban renewal.

It was no coincidence that public art should have flourished at the same time that privatization was being encouraged. According to wri-

ters on both sides of the Atlantic, one effect of privatism was to diminish
the scope of the public realm

> As governments rely on private enterprise, public property decreases in
> favour of privately owned property. It became harder and harder for citizens
> to find means to communicate with other citizens. Only the wealthy may find
> effective communication possible (Justice Thurgood Marshall cited by
> Kowinski 1982. See also Sennett 1970 and 1977; Pawley 1974, Bianchini et al
> 1988 and Punter 1990).

Public art in private places provides one such means of communication, albeit symbolic. Significantly, many of the awards available for
public art in Britain have been won by private initiatives. These include
the Capital & County Art and Work Awards, which since 1985 have
sought 'to encourage the use of art to create pleasant and stimulating
atmospheres in which to work'. The Royal Society of the Arts and the
DOE's Art for Architecture Awards (established in 1990) encourage the
integration of works of art and craft into new and refurbished buildings
at the planning stage. The RTPI's Jubilee Cup Awards for planning
achievement have been awarded to developments which feature public
art and which were considered to have revitalised the area, refurbished
redundant land, produced economic, environmental and social benefits,
provided a high quality environment, buildings, work places, leisure
areas and contributed to the transport infrastructure as well as having
improved the image of the place – in short 'created a civilised environment'. The Arts Council/British Gas Awards Working for Cities was
launched in 1991 'to encourage and reward arts developments in Britain's
inner cities'.

Arts in rural areas

In much the same way that the arts were employed in the regeneration
of urban areas, they were also considered appropriate in respect of rural
development.

Brian McLaughlin's unpublished report on rural deprivation commissioned by the DOE in 1985 showed that considerable numbers of
people in the rural areas were suffering levels of deprivation equal to, if
not exceeding, those experienced in urban areas. His subsequent writings, and those of others, have highlighted the effects of the social and
economic restructuring of rural Britain, such as the erosion of jobs in

traditional labour markets such as agriculture and mining; the effects of privatised public transport prioritising the most profitable routes; the repopulation of rural areas by a more affluent population and its impact on the housing market; the introduction of new wealth and different values to rural areas and the development of tourism and related industries (see McLaughlin 1991; Mason and Taylor 1990; Scottish Development Agency 1990; Archbishops' Commission 1990).

The nature of the changes affecting rural communities inevitably raised questions about their identity. According to McLaughlin, for example, the articulate and generally affluent in-migrants – people 'there from choice' – have a vested interest in preserving the image of the rural idyll: 'For them, the sanitised countryside is the ideal habitat and increasingly they are working towards that objective by means of effective participation in pressure group politics and/or through local democratic networks' (see also Hewison 1993).

Whereas the Urban Programme focused on priority areas, the Rural Development Commission identified Rural Development Areas for economic and social programmes. And, from the mid-1980s onwards arts organisations, arts funding agencies and rural and countryside agencies – often in partnership – increasingly promoted the arts in rural areas. As in urban areas, the arts were perceived as having a part to play in 'interpreting' the environment and 'improving the lot of country people, particularly in the key areas of self-determination and reaffirming local distinctiveness' (Johnson 1991A: 3).

However, the conditions according to which the arts are promoted in rural areas are, in many ways, different to those in urban areas. The amateur arts have more importance in rural areas (Hutchison and Feist 1991); conventional wisdom dictates that arts activities will only flourish in rural areas where enthusiastic individuals or groups supply the necessary back up; they should relate to the life of the community; projects often work on a longer time-scale; they assume a particular significance – 'every event is an occasion in a rural community'. According to one arts funder, 'the key message is: help rural communities to have access to opportunities they want and help rural communities to help themselves' (Stote 1989).

Common Ground's projects, for example, are fundamentally concerned with the values people attach to their own places, 'surmounting the old stereotypes of planning law and politics' (Common Ground,

1990). The organisation which was formed in 1983, works 'to encourage new ways of looking at the world to excite people into remembering the richness of the commonplace and the value of the everyday, to savour the symbolism with which we have endowed nature, to revalue our emotional engagement with places and all that they mean to us and to go on to become actively involved in their care' (see also Relph 1976). Common Ground's projects include books, sculptures, paintings, exhibitions and events. They are funded by a variety of sources not all of which are identified with the arts – such as the Countryside Commission, Nature Conservancy Council, the World Wide Fund for Nature. *The Parish Maps* project, for example, encourages local people to recognise, enjoy, respect and protect local landmarks; *New Milestones* is about what places mean to the people who live there and about how to express that through sculpture. *Trees, Wood and the Green Man* was intended 'to heighten awareness of tress and wood by stressing their cultural, spiritual and aesthetic value leading to a wider concern and practical caring'. It includes the *Save our Orchards* campaign, *Tree Dressing Day* and *Apple Day*. *Local Distinctiveness* addresses the variety of buildings, landscapes, people, wild life and cultural associations being lost.

Rural agencies similarly use the arts as a means to achieve their overall ambitions. Between 1987/88, the Woodland Trust, a national charity concerned with the conservation of broadleaved trees and woodland, collaborated with Common Ground and RAAs, to commission seats and resting places in selected Trust woods which would 'widen our appreciation of trees and woods and most importantly, enhance the distinctive character of each place'.

The Countryside Commission 'works to conserve and enhance the beauty of the English Countryside' and to 'ensure that people are aware of opportunities for recreation in the countryside and have the confidence, ability and understanding to enjoy it' (Countryside Commission 1992). It has funded a variety of arts projects within the context of its existing programme, such as tree dressing and various projects initiated by Common Ground and an arts officer post for Thames Chase Community Forest.

Forest Enterprise, as part of the Forestry Commission, manages the forests owned by the nation. Part of its brief is to provide recreational opportunities. Grizedale Forest, Exeter Forest and the Forest of Dean all contain sculpture projects. These are perceived as attracting new visitors:

'Keen outdoor types can enjoy contemporary art with their healthy walks while a new audience is introduced to the forest in the shape of art lovers who come to see the sculptures' (Paul Burke cited in *Forest Life* (8) March 1992). They were also intended to 'open visitors' eyes to the hints of history, sense of awe and magic, above all to the sense of beauty of a living and productive environment' (Martin 1990).

Arts funding and development frameworks

The attitude of arts funding bodies towards public art – or, more precisely, the Arts Council's attitude to art in public places – differed in many respects to those of central government. These differences are considered here, not least because they inform what appear to be inconsistencies in contemporary public art practice.

When it was founded in 1946, the Arts Council inherited the dual objectives of the Council for the Encouragement of Music and the Arts (CEMA). These were to promote the arts as part of people's daily lives and to support professional artists. But, as a former Secretary General observed

> Almost from its beginnings, an ideological conflict underpinned the theory and practice and public funding for the arts. Serious efforts were made to encourage a holistic approach to cultural policy – but gradually the interest of the public as audience, reader or spectator took over that of the public as doer, maker or participant (Everitt 1992:6).

In 1945, Maynard Keynes, the first Chairman of the Arts Council and former Chairman of CEMA, perceived the support of the artist as the primary function of the Council.

> Everyone, I fancy, recognises that the work of the artist in all its aspects is, of its nature, individual and free, undisciplined, unregimented, uncontrolled. The artist walks where the breath of the spirit blows him. He cannot be told his direction. He does not know it himself (cited in Pearson 1982:55).

He regarded it as 'the task of an official body' to 'give courage, confidence and opportunity' to the artist, and worried lest support of what he patronisingly referred to as the welfare side, 'was to be developed at the expense of the artistic side and standards generally' (Everitt 1992). The Council's programme to disseminate the arts to sites of popular culture such as holiday camps, works' canteens, factories, shops and schools was subsequently shortlived. Between 1965 and 1984, it prioritised 'housing the arts' in separate buildings.

Yet the Arts Council consistently promoted sculpture in the most accessible places, such as in public parks and in the landscape (considered to be the 'natural' location for sculptures to be seen), in the built environment and at festivals. It never had a specific funding category for public art, as such, but directly funded it under various headings – from 1977/9 as 'Works of Art for Public Buildings'; from 1979/80, 'Art in Public Sites' and from 1985/6, 'Art in Public Places'. During those years, the visual arts department specifically sought to encourage both the public and private sectors to invest in public art – indeed, it gave grants to development corporations, London Transport, British Rail, health authorities, universities and local authorities, as well as Sainsbury's, Sun Life Association, London Life Assurance and Alloy and Metal Stockholders to encourage the commissioning of works.

In supporting art in 'the open air' the Arts Council's primary objective had been to serve the artists and the art itself. The audience was less of a priority than the fact that the open air provided 'a test of sculptural quality' (Melville 1954:88).

> Inside a public gallery, limitations of space and artificially constant light sometimes lessen the full impact and enjoyment of a piece of sculpture ... Limitations of light and restrictions of site can be overcome when a piece of sculpture is placed out of doors ... In all instances, the actual physical setting of the work is never fixed; it changes, not only as the spectator alters his distance and view point, but also with the variations in the play of light. The relationships between sculpture, space, light, background and spectator become capable of infinite permutations; and in their constant interplay the work achieves its fullest effect (Pickvance 1960).

In the post-War years, the Arts Council, like other public bodies, reinforced notions of artistic autonomy. For example the London County Council, a major promoter of public art after the War, as a matter of policy made no attempt to dictate what it thought suitable for commissions for schools. Each chosen artist, once granted the approval of a 'client committee', produced whatever he or she considered appropriate. That 'freedom' extended to artists' commissions for the private sector. In executing 'Meridian' for John Lewis, Oxford Street, London, Barbara Hepworth reputedly abandoned the proposal that the work 'should express the idea of the firm's partnership' as too restrictive of her 'creative impulses'. She decided that the figure should represent an exercise in 'pure form' designed as an aesthetic embellishment for the building. The credibility attached to the maintenance of artistic integrity persisted well into the 1970s and beyond. In 1972, the sculptor, William Tucker, who selected some exhibitions for the Arts Council, could confidently describe the making and appreciation of sculpture as

> a fundamentally private activity; and if ... it reenters the public world, it does so in its own terms, to transform and take possession of that world: the public opportunity extends, gives breadth and air, to the private vision (Tucker 1975).

He believed that work selected for display in the public realm needed 'neither apology nor justification'. Its aspiration should be 'to stand free' and 'remain inconvenient, obtrusive – a challenge to facile and conventional views of history and aesthetic' (Tucker 1975).

Exhibiting works in the open merely increased their potential audience.

> Exhibitions held in the open air have two great advantages over those held in galleries. An outdoor site will invariably attract more people if only because on a fine afternoon they have decided to take some fresh air and the exhibition provides a focal point in the park. People also go into public parks and gardens without any of the prejudices which they might have when stepping into a building which houses only works of art and is dedicated to instructing as well as pleasing (Dempsey 1967).

In general it was the audiences who were expected to make concessions to the artists, not *vice versa*. Interpretation was rarely provided. In the late 1940s, arts organisations had no qualms in explaining that the work they showed called for 'a wide tolerance and understanding on the part of the visitor' and that they – the visitor – would be rewarded by 'a fuller appreciation' (Tomlinson 1948). Some twenty years later the Arts Council still maintained that 'an openness of mind is all one needs' (Dempsey 1967).

In the 1980s the Arts Council supported the display of work in public places which was often 'difficult' or 'inaccessible'. Its support of live art, installations and site-specific work often took it 'beyond the constraints of the gallery'.

However, the Arts Council's attitude to the relationship between art sited in public places and the public was beginning to change. This reflected shifts in its overall policy – partly prompted by the government's calls for private investment in the arts and for the Arts Council to be more publicly accountable, and partly by the Council's own attempts to expand audiences for the arts, and develop resources and support for the arts. The Regional Arts Associations (RAAs) similarly redefined their role.

One change was in the Arts Council's attitude to the relationship between culture and economics. Following the publication of the Government's *The Arts are Your Business* (1980), the Council increasingly justified funding the arts in terms of their financial benefits. This is reflected in the titles of its own publications – *The Great British Success Story* (1983), *Partnerships* (1984) and *Better Business in the Arts* (1988). Between 1988 and 1991 parts of the Arts Council's allocation from the Office of Arts and Libraries (OAL) were specifically earmarked for enhancement funding at the behest of the Minister. This was to encourage arts organisations to become more financially enterprising, improve their commercial management skills, strengthen their long-term financial bases by increasing their earnings and develop a sustained and reliable income from the private sector. In many respects this complemented the Government's Business Sponsorship Incentive Scheme (BSIS), initiated in 1984 and administered through the Association for Business Sponsorship in the Arts (ABSA). BSIS was designed to foster the private sponsorship of the arts through the incentive of matching funding.

Economic arguments also contributed – in the general sense – to the introduction of professional, academic and vocational training for arts professionals in particular, to the development of public art courses. The first, an M.Phil in Public Art and Design, was established in 1985 at The Duncan of Jordanstone College of Art & Design. At the time of our research, there were at least 19 fine art courses which include public art as an area of study at graduate or post-graduate level (see Jones 1992:156). Other courses refer to it in the context of architecture, planning and art administration. Various aspects of public art can thus be studied – Art in Social Context, Art and its Audiences, Environmental Art, Art as Environment, Site Specific Sculpture, Fine Art and Critical Studies, Interdisciplinary Studies in Art & Architecture, Art in Architecture and Curating and Commissioning Contemporary Art. Despite the introduction of art and design as statutory subjects and a history of initiatives which had linked art, design and environmental education from the early

1970s (see Adams 1989 and Stone 1989), public art appears to have had relatively little impact on the National Curriculum.

A second change in Arts Council policy was its expansion of funding to the regions. After the closure of its regional offices in the mid- to late 1950s, the Council single-mindedly focused its support on London, 'a great artistic metropolis, a place to visit and wonder at'. It was only after the publication of a government White Paper, *A Policy for the Arts – the First Steps* (1965), that the regional arts associations and, subsequently, local authorities' support for arts developed. In many respects this broke the Arts Council's cultural monopoly. Concepts of 'diffusion', 'local' and 'regional' challenged the Arts Council's maintenance of what it cast as the 'national' art and culture, conceived within the terms of a received tradition and judged by standards of 'excellence' (Pearson 1989:62).

The antagonism between the Arts Council and the regional agencies during that period was marked, as the fortunes of the *Peter Stuyvesant Foundation City Sculpture Project*, which the Council grant-aided as a regional public art initiative, suggests. Seven contemporary sculptures were placed in cities throughout England in the hope that the works would find permanent homes. Its organisers failed to consult any of the RAAs or the local authorities. Not one sculpture remained in place, several were destroyed, and worries that cities would be embarrassed persisted for many years (for example, Chapter 5, p. 128).

It was not until the late 1970s that the Council's regional policy began to change. In his report on the *Support for the Arts in England and Wales* (1976), Lord Redcliffe-Maud observed that despite the 'flowering of professionalism in the arts ... large areas of Britain constitute a Third World of underdevelopment and deprivation in all the arts and crafts.' In order to reach a 'wider circle' of audiences, he recommended increased funding and the 'judicious mixing of national and local finance'.

> We must look to local elected councils at district and county level to become the chief art patrons of the long-term future, developing a comprehensive service as part of the main fabric of local development (1976:25).

In 1980 the Arts Council and the RAAs published the self-explanatory declaration of intent, *Towards a Better Relationship*. The Council's ten year development strategy, known as *The Glory of the Garden* (1984), proposed a more equitable geographic distribution of its expenditure and the support of regional 'centres of excellence'. At the same time it increased the value of its grants to the RAAs. In 1985 it devolved £250,000 to the RAAs to assist public art commissions, expecting that these would 'yield' £3 million of matching funding (ACGB November 1990:2.4). Arts 2000, launched in 1990 and topped up in 1993, designated different cities in the UK 'cities of culture' as part of a general attempt to refurbish the 'cultural fabric of the nation'. This new relationship between the Arts Council, the RAAs and the local authorities was crucial to the development of public art.

A third change to affect the Arts Council comprised extending access to the arts provision. This necessitated the arts funding bodies targeting different constituencies of interest and expanding the range of work they supported.

In the 1970s this embraced 'community arts'. Community artists typically pitted themselves against the conventional institutions of the commercial and subsidised art worlds and sought to create art 'outside the gallery' where it would be both physically and cognitively accessible to the local 'community'. According to the Greenwich Mural Workshop (undated), the initiative for this primarily came from artists, many of whom had been fine arts trained. They envisaged the development of art as being through a collaboration with ordinary people. An understanding of their work would not be premised on specific competencies or inculcated through formal education.

The development of community art projects coincided with and complemented the development of communities involvement in planning, architectural and refurbishment schemes. The artists often cast themselves in the role of 'animaters' working with, and on behalf of sections of the public. Such projects enabled artists to undermine the traditional distinctions between audiences and themselves.'For the artist, it was the opportunity to prove that they were artisans with a definite place in society' (Greenwich Mural Workshop, undated). The *Art into Landscape* and *Art for Whom?* exhibitions at the Serpentine Gallery and *Art for Society* at the Whitechapel Gallery in the late 1970s, reinforced the notions of art as 'both socially and aesthetically relevant' and of artists' having 'responsibilities to society'.

Many such community projects – the painting of murals in particular – took place in what the government classified as deprived areas. Greenwich Mural Workshop's book, *Murals in London since 1971*, traced some 341 murals, of which 196 were located in the 10 most deprived urban authorities in the country.

The Arts Council remained fundamentally resistant to such initiatives. As the country entered a period of financial restraint towards the end of the 1970s, it wound up its brief for community arts and opted to concentrate on what in its terms unarguably constituted art, leaving community art, which it associated with participatory activities, social and educational work, to be financed by other government resources such as Urban Aid.

However by the mid-1980s, under the political pressure of the new social movements – the black arts lobby in particular (for example, Owusu 1986) – there were changes. The Arts Council and the RAAs developed initiatives for minority groups which were intended to redress the traditional bias of gender, race and class and the divisions imposed between amateurs and professionals. The discussion papers written for the *National Arts & Media Strategy* (1991) suggest something of the range of the diversity of the constituencies vying for the recognition of their needs: youth arts, community arts, folk arts, Cypriot culture, amateur arts, arts in rural areas, arts and disabilities and women in the arts. It was in this climate that the Council affiliated, as opposed to disassociated, itself with work promoted in 'non-art' contexts, including art employed in urban regeneration.

The demands for cultural diversity and cultural equity were not merely about parity of funding, but definitions of culture. The relativism promulgated by each constituency of interest undermined traditional notions of excellence in the arts and rendered questionable judgements as to whether one activity was qualitatively 'better' than another. Combined with the government's demands for accountability in the public sector, this plurality of interests encouraged the Arts Council – like other arts funding bodies – to become more concerned with who was being served by the arts, and what they thought of them – what was the public's attitude towards public funding of the arts; do they personally value them; do they benefit the places they live and work in, and their quality of life. Reports published by arts funding bodies included GLA's two surveys on the arts in London, *A Qualitative Research Study* and a *Survey of Attitudes of Users and Non-Users* (both 1990), the results of the Arts Council's *Survey of Arts and Cultural Activities in Great Britain* (RSGB 1991) and its *Research into Contemporary Visual Arts* (Robb 1992), and *Arts 93: Audiences, Attitudes and Sponsorship* (ABSA 1993).

A fourth change to effect the Arts Council was closer to home. In 1987 the Serpentine Gallery, previously run by the Arts Council became independent with its own Board of Trustees. In 1988 the running of the Hayward Gallery was devolved to the newly set up South Bank Board which was also charged with managing the National Touring Exhibition Service and the Arts Council Collection on behalf of the Arts Council.

Following the devolution of some of its clients to the regions, from 1987, the visual arts department of the Arts Council effectively ceased funding certain activities directly and cast itself in an advocacy role.

All four shifts in policy – the need to increase income to the arts from the private sector, to create more equitable regional provision and greater access to the arts and redefine its role – combined to inform the Arts Council's attitude towards arts development in general and public art in particular. Similar conditions influenced the RAAs. Indeed that aspect of their work concerned with development assumed such importance by the mid-1980s that several RAAs referred to themselves as development agencies. Within the prevailing financial climate, art funding organisations had to do more than simply fund the arts. They had to foster its development through planning and the provision of support, resources and incentives and consolidate their relationship with constituencies as varied as central government, local authorities, UDCs, the private sector, environmental groups and the artistic community.

That consolidation is exemplified in the Arts Council's two campaigns of 1988, Percent for Art and An Urban Renaissance. The objectives of An Urban Renaissance were essentially didactic. It sought to promote awareness of 'the substantial contribution of the arts to the revitalisation of our inner cities'.

> They are ... essential ingredients in the mix of cultural, environmental and recreational amenities which reinforce economic growth and development. They attract tourism and the jobs it brings. More importantly they serve as the main catalyst for the wholesale regeneration of an area. They provide focal points for community pride and identity. Equally importantly, they make a contribution in bringing together communities which might otherwise be divided:

> The Arts create a spirit of optimism – the 'can do' attitude essential to developing the 'enterprise culture' this Government hopes to bring to deprived areas. Inner city economic stagnation is a downward spiral. Failure breeds on failure, people lose confidence in their ability to succeed and

consequently their will to try. The arts provide a means of breaking this spiral and helping people believe in themselves and their community again.

According to Lord Palumbo, Chairman of the Arts Council from 1988-1994, the key to that success lies in 'partnership – between individuals, arts organisations, local authorities and private companies'. And it was through public art that the partnerships between these diverse constituencies were most publicly celebrated.

The infrastructure for public art

The conditions according to which public art is commissioned were largely developed by the national and regional arts funding bodies – the Arts Council of Great Britain, the Scottish and Welsh Arts Councils and the RABs. All the arts funding bodies described their primary objective as being to support the infrastructure for public art (Appendix 5, p.334). In practice they pump-primed specialist public art officer posts in local authorities, advocated and campaigned for their adoption of public art policies – in particular, Percent for Art – contributed to their City Challenge bids and UDPs, provided training and professional development for artists and administrators and, to a greater or lesser extent, encouraged the private sector to commission art. They also supported the growth of the public art agencies, which the Arts Council's Percent for Art Steering Group praised as 'one of the success stories of the visual arts in the past decade' (ACGB November 1990:17.2).

The impact of government policy on some arts funding organisations' programmes is perhaps best exemplified by the London Arts Board's Arts Challenge (1993/94). Its stated objectives were

> to create opportunities to support regionally significant/model projects for professional artists to contribute to the conception, planning, design and implementation of major schemes to improve the urban environment and contribute to urban renewal (LAB 1993). Successful schemes might include 'the involvement of an artist ... in a design team approach to a major Town Centre improvements scheme'; their involvement in 'a major housing project' or 'in the reclamation of derelict land for community use.' It was also expected that LAB's financial support would 'lever in other sources of significant funding from both public and private sectors'.

Public art agencies

In 1993 membership of Public Arts Forum, a national association which promotes knowledge, understanding and appreciation of art in public places, included representatives from some 20 public art agencies. PSI's survey of 13 of the agencies which promote permanent works as opposed to temporary events or artists' placements (Appendix 1, p. 272) suggested that the majority were established during the 1980s – over half between 1983 and 1987. Most are constituted as charities and receive project or annual revenue funding from arts funding agencies. The rest of their income generally comprises commissioning and consultancy fees, sales, grants from trusts and foundations and sponsorships – hence their description as 'hybrids of the public and private sector' (ACGB November 1990:17.2). Only one agency surveyed was entirely self-supporting.

It has not been possible to compare the financial operation of various public art agencies on the basis of their annual reports, not least because they employ different accounting categories. However, there appears to be considerable disparity between different agencies' operations. One agency's accounts, for example, (for the years ending 1986, 1989 and 1991) indicate that between 8-12 per cent of the organisation's total expenditure was committed to wages, salaries and contributions, with 78-82 per cent committed to artists, researchers and direct project expenditure. Between 1990 and 1992, another agency's accounts shows that between 48-58 per cent of the organisation's total expenditure was committed to salaries and contributions. In 1992, artists' fees and expenses are indicated as representing 8 per cent of its total expenditure. That agency raises a substantial part of its income from commissions. During that period 48-55 per cent of its income was derived from fees earned and between 22-43 per cent of its income derived from 'unrestricted grants', 'restricted grants' and awards and donations.

As 'hybrids of the public and private sectors' public art agencies are able to take advantage of assistance available to arts organisations through various funding bodies. Public Arts Commissions Agency, for example, won an Incentive Funding Award from the Arts Council in March 1990, an ABSA award for a commercial commission in 1991 and assistance from Price Waterhouse under the West Midlands Business in the Arts Scheme the same year.

Many subsidised public art agencies have, or have had, a close working relationship with their RABs. Indeed, several directors of subsidised public art agencies were formally employed by the RAAs. At the time of research, seven out of the ten English RABs had either devolved their commissioning services to public art agencies or created new ones. Their missions largely reflect the interests of the art establishment.

The majority describe their primary function as being to promote art and create opportunities for artists. The needs of the community, education, the environment and the provision of an advisory or management service are secondary. While it was never intended to represent the interests of the constituency, *The Strategy for Public Art in Cardiff Bay* (Public Art Consultancy Team 1990), preparing for the redevelopment of the city by a consortium of public art consultants, articulates many of the assumptions and conventional wisdom upon which the promotion of public art is based. The Public Art Consultancy Team included the Directors of the Public Art Commissions Agency, Art in Partnership, Public Art Development Trust and the Welsh Sculpture Trust.

Its Strategy for Cardiff was predicated on ideas which straddle modernism and the concept of the cultural industries. It promotes the contributions that visual arts consultants and artists in particular, might make to urban regeneration in general. The former are described as holding the 'key' to 'achieving and maintaining a high quality programme', the latter, as having usually 'spearheaded the process of urban regeneration ... central to the successful marketing of a city's cultural image'. Artists' professional involvement is regarded as a significant factor in determining the commercial, environmental and cultural success of building programmes and regenerative schemes; their early involvement in projects is said to result in 'a greater harmony between artworks and their settings.' Residencies by artists in community settings are an 'extraordinarily successful means of creating firm relationships between artists and the public'. The Strategy calls for the presentation of opportunities for artists to present 'radical and innovatory' schemes – qualities often regarded by the arts sector as synonymous with excellence.

The Strategy also credits the objects of public art with a wealth of attributes: as a cultural investment, vital to the economic recovery of many cities; as capable of attracting companies and investment to places; as a feature of cultural tourism; as adding to land values; creating employment; increasing the use of open spaces; reducing wear and tear on buildings and levels of vandalism; humanising environments; bringing about safer areas and encouraging greater care of areas by residents whose pride in their locality has increased.

The missions of public art agencies have been informed by such views consistently. They seldom change. One agency, established in the early 1980s and now offering a commissions service to the private sector, reported having changed its priorities 'as the employment of public art agents working for art boards, local authorities and health services had taken over in public areas'. Subsidised agencies are unlikely to do more than 'refocus' their activities, extend their geographic remit or take on more art forms. As one agency Director put it, he was 'convinced that our original premise was correct'. One significant factor which has affected the work of the agencies, not least in respect of increasing awareness of public art, prompting more commissions and thereby extending its infrastructure, is Percent for Art. Even though Percent for Art is not necessarily concerned with public art – it can apply to elements inaccessible to the public – it has become closely associated with it (Appendix 3, p. 319).

Percent for Art
The Arts Council launched the Percent for Art campaign in 1988, although it had been considering Percent since the late 1970s. Like An Urban Renaissance, it emphasised the contribution of the visual arts to urban regeneration. According to Luke Rittner, then Secretary General of the Arts Council, Percent echoed government policy precisely.

> Percent for Art applied to the strategies outlined in 'Action for Cities' could transform the climate for investment while improving the urban environment (Rittner 1988).

However its primary objective was to secure practical opportunities for artists and craftspeople to

> transform the built environment and ensure greater opportunities for collaboration of artists and crafts people in the building process and offer the prospect of more attractive buildings and open spaces in Britain (ACGB November 1990:3).

It sought to do this by ensuring that a proportion of the capital cost of buildings and environment schemes is set aside for commissions by artists and craftspeople.

The Arts Council's campaign was based on European and American precedents – schemes in which Percent for Art is levied under statutory legislation on particular types of building and developments. (see, for example, ACGB 1991; Power 1991-2; Eisenberg 1990). Although the Council consistently supported the idea of legislation (ACGB November 1990:3 and ACGB 1993:113), it did not regard the 1980s as the time to introduce a restriction on the free use of capital, make what might be seen to be more demands of the public purse or increase public sector borrowing. In the event, the campaign did not lobby for a mandatory scheme but disseminated information and sought to persuade bodies to adopt Percent policies voluntarily. In 1988 the Arts Council established a Percent for Art Steering Group, in association with the Council of Regional Arts Associations, the Welsh and Scottish Arts Councils and the Crafts Council, which was wound up in 1994, having achieved its aims. In 1991 it published *Percent for Art: A Review* intended as guidance for all those involved in commissioning art and craft for public places. By July 1990, it had spent some £32,000 on Percent for Art since 1988 by way of encouraging developers through 'education and example', and was

> already committed to spending £30,000 over the next three years to support the creation of new posts in four local authorities aimed at introducing the Percent for Art policy within the planning system. The Council is meeting half the costs of these posts (Luce 1990).

The *Report* of The Percent for Art Steering Group identified the constituencies which might potentially employ Percent for Art – local authorities, UDCs, government departments and private sector developers. It also recommended various ways in which Percent might be implemented. These included the mandatory application of Percent for Art to all public building schemes and public works with a contract price over £3 million, sponsored by local authorities, government departments and executive agencies. The government should issue planning guidance advocating Percent for Art to local authorities, instruct UDCs to adopt Percent policies and implement such policies itself within the capital programme of the National Health Service. The Arts Council and the Crafts Council should make incentive awards to private sector developments, devote increased resources to developing the infrastructure of Percent for Art management and produce practical guidance. The Royal Fine Art Commission should include Percent for Art in its considerations.

Percent for Art should also be formally introduced into continuing professional development for architects and joint courses be established for
architects, artists, craftspeople.

The appeal of the Percent for Art principle varied according to its
target constituencies. The UDCs, for example, were legally obliged to
provide a 'visually attractive environment'. Institutional investors were
another target. According to an Arts Council spokesman, towards the
end of the 1980s, not only was the construction of £30 billion of new
properties planned, but these would 'alter the appearance of Britain
faster than at anytime since the Victorian era'. Property developers might
adopt Percent for Art because it would 'add value by virtue of distinctive
artifacts and the creation of a high quality public environment for buildings'. Assuming that public art comprises good design, and that good
design equals good business, value would presumably take effect by
granting developers a competitive edge over their rivals. Several developers had already taken a lead. The *Report* cites Capital and Counties,
Stanhope Properties PLC, Speyhawk PLC, Lynton P&R (now BAA)
(ACGB November 1990:8.3). In their Strategy for Cardiff Bay, the Public
Art Consultancy Team referred to 'an incentive package' designed to
encourage the private sector's commitment to Percent for Art. The advantages it listed are relevant here. 'Specific incentives' include tax relief
on charitable donations and sponsorship, inclusion in the publicity for
the public art programme, and access to grants including the Business
Sponsorship Incentive Scheme. 'General incentives' include the opportunity to contribute to the quality of the company's offices and the wider
environment, investment in the land and business value of the area, and
to take advantage of maintenance and conservation schemes and to join
a local 'patrons of art scheme' (Public Art Consultancy Team 1990:43-7).

Local authorities
Local authorities support the arts for a variety of reasons. According to
the Audit Commission, they want to promote artistic excellence, enhance
the quality of life for local residents by facilitating the provision of a
broader range of activities than that which the commercial market could
support and to promote social cohesion. The creation of a flourishing
artistic environment is perceived as benefitting the local economy by
attracting tourists and day trippers on the one hand and investment on
the other, as companies seek locations to provide a congenial working

environment. The arts are also regarded as part of the cultural heritage of the locality (Audit Commission 1991). None of these social, economic or cultural ambitions are restricted to arts, recreation, leisure or community activities. They inform authorities' other functions, in particular planning and development.

Although they have no statutory obligation to provide financial support, local authorities came to assume an increasingly important role in the funding of the arts, particularly after the upper limits for their spending were removed in the *Local Government Act* of 1972. Following the abolition of the metropolitan counties in 1986, the government imposed limits on local authorities' expenditure, especially in 'high spending authorities', which were often those in deprived areas most in need of environmental improvements. A combination of problems with collecting poll tax, charge capping, proposals for compulsory competitive tendering and the diminution of their education budgets affected authorities' spending. Faced with increasing pressure on their statutory provision of education, health and social services, cuts almost inevitably took effect on annual revenue commitments in the areas of the arts, recreation and leisure.

The Percent for Art campaign was, in many respects, timely. According to one local authority public art officer

> It ... fulfilled a useful function in the debate ... and has encouraged many, both in the public and private sector, to think analytically about our environment and embark upon arts-led projects which have had social as well as artistic benefits (Appendix 3, p. 329).

According to research into Percent for Art policies carried out by West Midlands Arts, authorities perceived Percent as a mechanism which would enable them to increase public access to, and awareness of, visual arts, improve the environment, stimulate the local economy and develop positive identities for different areas of the borough (Appendix 3, p. 294). Authorities adopt Percent for Art for other reasons. It may attract money to the arts from other budgets, improve the quality of life in the community, break down barriers between art and architecture by the 'proper integration of the artworks at development stage', 'assist the Council in fulfilling its City strategy'. One officer described how it might enable the authority to apply for other sources of funding and professional recognition 'for example, the Arts for Architecture Award, administered by the Royal Society for Arts and Department of the Environment'. Many of these aspirations were reinforced by the criteria demanded of Unitary Development Plans (UDPs) and City Challenge bids which authorities had to produce in the early 1990s (Appendix 3, p. 299).

Although, as our research found, as many as 36 per cent of authorities which commission public art have no policy, and some implement Percent for Art without a policy, the Percent for Art campaign stimulated a number of local authorities to adopt public art policies. In 1990, on the basis of research carried out in 1988, Public Art Forum's (PAF) returns showed that six per cent of authorities in England, Scotland and Wales had public art policies. By comparison, in 1993, the University of Westminster estimated that 42 per cent of local authorities in England and Wales had public art policies. Thirty seven per cent of local authorities in the three regions surveyed by PSI have public art policies.

The number of local authorities with Percent for Art policies also increased. In 1988, PAF found that 2.5 per cent of authorities had adopted Percent for Art policies. The *Report* of the Percent for Art Steering Group (1990) registered 40 local authorities, UDCs and agencies in England, Scotland and Wales 'understood to have adopted Percent for Art at committee level, in local plans or building policies'. The Arts Council's *Annual Report* of 1990/91 stated that 50 authorities and two UDCs had committed to Percent, in other words 10 per cent of all authorities. In 1991, two RABs which researched the public art provision in their regions, suggested a higher percentage: West Midlands Arts' survey revealed that 22 per cent of those authorities in its region which responded had adopted Percent for Art policies; Eastern Arts, 18 per cent. PSI found that 28 per cent of the authorities it surveyed had adopted Percent policies.

The majority of local authorities with public art and Percent for Art policies are in the metropolitan boroughs. The University of Westminster estimated that 50 per cent of the London boroughs with public art policies had adopted Percent for Art, as had over one third of metropolitan districts. All metropolitan boroughs had heard of Percent for Art.

The number of authorities considering adopting Percent policies is also up. PAF's returns identified 4.5 per cent of authorities. Three years later, both West Midlands Arts and Eastern Arts suggested 22 per cent were considering Percent for Art policies.

Public art and Percent for Art policies feature in a wide range of statutory and strategic development and planning documents which often reflect the idiosyncrasies of individual authorities. These include local plans, draft city plans, economic plans, draft UDPs, major planning briefs, marketing packages for sale of land, 106 agreements (ACGB 1991:59) and annual reports. One authority cited its City Strategy for Leisure. Sixty one per cent of authorities with public art policies state them in the UDPs. Fifty eight per cent of these statements refer to Percent for Art policies (see Horstman undated).

The majority of local authorities' Percent policies, like their public art policies 'cover anything'. One authority described its approach as embracing

i)   the purchase, design and production of art and craft works on and off the site of the development, refurbishment or landscaping scheme

ii)   the promotion and development of projects including exhibitions of proposed public art works, artists residencies in design teams, communities and schools and presentation to developers, architects and landscape designers

iii) the provision of arts facilities eg. artists' studios

iv)   the commissioning of both permanent and temporary artworks.

Others have considered the principle of pooling, whereby the percentage raised on the capital costs of development is allocated towards the agency or Trust responsible for promoting public art in a given area. This allows the monies accrued to be used to respond to local public initiatives as opposed to possibly private, development-led work. According to the Public Art Consultancy Team pooling allows 'greater flexibility and a more strategic approach to the commissioning process' (1990:16). It might provide funding for complete buildings, such as the Museum of Modern Art in Los Angeles, USA, or, as one of the local authority public art officers surveyed suggested, provide 'an answer to the Council's shrinking funds'.

In practice, public art and Percent for Art commissions are more restricted than these aspirations might imply. They often pertain to permanent, usually site-specific works. In this, they reflect public art practices in general. Some 50 per cent of authorities' commissions pertain to environmental features, and approximately 30 per cent to statues and sculptures. Furthermore, many authorities have policies which they do not implement. PSI found that 32 per cent of policies were not implemented (Appendix 3, p. 299).

The most frequently cited reasons for policies not being implemented are the lack of financial resources (in particular, the decline in private sector investments and the downturn in the construction industry), the lack of specialist staff and it being 'too early' since their adoption of a policy, or in terms of their thinking about public art. These are also reasons why authorities do not adopt policies. However, PSI's analysis of those authorities which commissioned the most art in London, West Midlands and Yorkshire & Humberside shows that budgets and specialist staff are not necessary requirements for local authorities' commissioning of art. The lack of written strategies describing the processes by which an authority might go about commissioning work may, however, be a contributory factor. Few authorities have such strategies.

Local authorities' public art officers
If the Percent for Art campaign encouraged local authorities to adopt public art and Percent for Art policies, it also encouraged them to employ public art agencies and, in some cases, to appoint their own public art officers. Their jobs are usually created in the wake of the authority's adoption of a Percent for Art policy or its general desire to improve and enhance the built environment (Appendix 3, p. 319). By 1993 as many as 21 per cent of local authorities were employing specialist public art officers or agencies.

At the time of research, PAF's membership included eleven specialist public art officers (among them, one Percent for Art officer) employed by local authorities. Like public art agencies, local authority public art posts are often funded by a combination of local authority and arts funding, sponsorships and self-generated income, which includes fees from Percent for Art commissions. Some posts depend on partnership funding. One, for example, is funded by a partnership between the Arts Council and three local authority departments – Planning Works, Building Services and Arts Department.

Public art officers' job descriptions are wide ranging. They include the advocacy and promotion of policy; the initiation, negotiation and management of projects; communication; fund raising and the promotion of place. One officer described responding to schemes arising though the planning process, and pro-actively initiating schemes by commissioning ideas for areas under redevelopment. Like the public art agencies, they work across both the public and private sectors. Authorities may also employ artists or designers on a long-term rather than a freelance basis. In some authorities – for example, in Dudley and Sandwell at the time of our research – the functions of the Town Artists included initiating, in some cases commissioning and executing public art projects. (Since then Sandwell has lost its Town Artist and Dudley has a Public Art Resource Unit).

Public art policies inevitably reflect the interests of the departments within which the officers are located, even if – as one officer described – this is subject to policy which, as a 'corporate effort', is continually debated. Of those surveyed, officers report to departments as varied as Cultural Policies in the Arts & Museums Division of Leisure Services Department; a City Arts Team in the Directorate of Leisure, Tourism and Amenities, and the Planning Division of a Department of Land and Planning. Although local authority commissions reflect local authority strategies such as 'environmental improvements', 'entertainment and cultural facilities', 'conservation and design', 'community needs and services', 'arts and tourism' and 'tourism and leisure'.

The majority of public art works are commissioned by planning departments and are concerned with 'environmental improvements'. As 'environmental features' they include permanent fixtures – street furniture, decorations, embellishments, paving, features, landmarks (Appendix 3, p. 299). These are often referred to as art, not least because of planners' aspirations for those objects to transcend the norm, because they lend a sense of 'authenticity' to place or because of the degree of craftsmanship or skill displayed in the design or manufacture of those objects – qualities popularly regarded as indicating quality in art.

Other infrastructures

Given the diversity of interests represented in its promotion, it is perhaps not surprising that public art is not regarded as belonging exclusively to the domain of the arts. As one local councillor suggested, 'there would be some advantage in taking it out of the current arts infrastructure'. In many respects, public art has come to serve other purposes than those of either the arts or urban regeneration.

Environmental bodies such as the Countryside Commission, the Groundwork Trust, English Nature, the Nature Conservancy Council and the Forestry Commission have for example, over the years directly and indirectly funded projects which include, if not focus on, public art. But whereas arts organisations prioritise the promotion of art objects and the creation of opportunities for artists, these organisations use art to further environmental interpretation.

2   Conflicting interests and dilemmas

The divergent interests of the constituencies involved in public art and the absence of an agreed definition of public art inevitably give rise to contradictions about the intentions for public art, the processes involved in its commissioning and siting and its reception. These conflicting interests not only inform how public art is perceived but how it is judged. Some of the resulting dilemmas are discussed in the following paragraphs.

The issues discussed are those raised by participants in the various focus groups, interviews and surveys carried out as part of the research for this report (Appendices 1-3). They also draw on the current literature. Many of the points raised are developed in the seven case studies which comprise Part 2.

Intentions

Public art as public good vs public art as good art
Gerald Rothman of the property company, Olympia & York Canary Wharf Ltd, suggested that

> the patronage of public art is a humanising and civilising endeavour which, in my view, comes primarily into the category of 'goodness being its own reward'.

Yet 'the assumption ... that public art is somehow good for new buildings and good for all of us' is, according to the critic Peter Dormer (1992), 'a wholemeal notion that is at best vague and at worst patronising'. Andrew Brighton, goes one step further. He proposes that the concept of 'public good' is, by definition, incompatible with art.

> Public art is an oxymoron ... the arguments for it are often implicitly hostile to serious art. In the age of mass culture, art is art by not being mass culture. The history of modern art is the history of works that hold off assimilation into entertainment: it calls for all kinds of attention unlike mass culture; it requires reflective effort, and sometimes uncommon knowledge, if we are to make sense of it. The conventions of public culture, of entertainment, news,

51

commercial design and advertising, provide the harmonics in which art makes discord and difference. To this degree at least, art is a critical and dissenting activity (Brighton 1993: 42).

Distinctions between aspirations for public art as a public good and as 'serious art', inform certain of the case studies – *the Arch* in Kensington Gardens and the Art at Broadgate (respectively p. 80 and p. 96).

Public art as an environmental improver

Francis Tibbald's presidential address to the British Royal Town Planning Institute in 1988, emphasised the threatening consequences of certain types of private developments in the inner cities. He feared that London in particular was

> drifting towards a '1984 – style' dirty, threatening public environment with travel almost impossible and with countless people living in the streets – but with a few incongruous splendid set pieces, like escapist islands in a sea of pollution. In short, an environment of private affluence and public squalor, and with no effective means of controlling it.

He called for a new agenda which would 'elevate the needs and aspirations of ordinary people above a combination of rampant profiteering ... and arrogant professional individualism'.

Other writers have also commented on the effects of contemporary city-building. In *The Conscience of the Eye* (1990), for example, the American Richard Sennett, remarks how developments tend

> to wall off the differences between people, assuming that these differences are more likely to be mutually threatening than mutually stimulating. What we make in the urban realm are therefore bland, neutralising spaces, spaces which remove the threat of social contact; street walls faced in sheets of plate glass, highways that cut off poor neighbourhoods from the rest of the city, dormitory housing developments (1990: xii).

As suggested in Chapter 1 public art is generally intended to contribute to the eradication of that sense of threat by enhancing the built environment. Its benefits are presumed to permeate throughout the community, if not somehow unify it. There is little, if any, questioning of what David Harvey refers to as the 'illusions' created by 'the mobilization of the spectacle' (1989:273), or the desirability of what the American writer Grady Clay referred to as the 'unlocking or translating an urban situation to its inhabitants or visitors' (1973:180).

In practice, the debate about art as an environmental improver tends to focus on narrower, more parochial issues such as the relationship between the major protagonists.

Public art and architecture: assimilation vs integration
One way in which art is supposed to contribute to the environment is as embellishment to individual buildings. In so far as artists are called upon to *decorate* buildings, they are regarded as belonging to the tradition of artisans or craftspeople. In practice, however, they may lack the skills, experience or the attitude required. According to the architect, Theo Crosby:

> The whole problem comes from the intellectualisation of art and architecture ... In the past, the architect and artist were protected by a degree of ignorance – their sources were the workshop tradition and very modest inputs from outside – usually as a demonstration of skill.

Architects are also reputed to be reluctant to collaborate with artists. This state of affairs is described in the Art and Architecture Manifesto of 1989.

> Art & Architecture came into being to heal a broken visual culture. This culture was broken apart in the aesthetic struggles of the first decades of this century. Before that time, there was no architecture which did not have a contribution from artists: sculptors, painters, weavers, carvers of ornament and a host of craftsmen and women in every medium whose images enhanced and completed the building.

> Instead, our generation had inherited, and is still largely dedicated to making, an environment in great part of naked buildings and the bleak spaces which surround them. This was the inevitable result of an aesthetic movement which considered architecture to be an art form in its own right, an art form moreover that was conceptual and abstract. In this conceptual and abstract art form, ornament was said to be a crime and the artist seen as superfluous.

> Artists were soon forced out of an increasingly reductive building process as architects searched for a 'pure' or 'style-less' style. In parallel with that of the pure architect, the prestige of the 'pure' or gallery artist rose to heights that made the production not just of humble items of everyday use but even a grand scheme of decoration for a major building seem a lowly, even a demeaning activity.

> What our generation has so painfully discovered is not that 'less is more' but

that less is less, less of all those innumerable interventions that made the built environments of previous generations truly civilised.

Such reflexes beg the question, whether it is the function of art to 'humanise' buildings, to make them somehow better, to serve as what the architect Norman Foster referred to as, 'lipstick on the face of the gorilla'?

The premise that a work of art might, as the sculptor Richard Deacon suggested 'validate' a development, 'give it moral stature', has been regarded as contentious for some time. Some 30 years ago, such sculptors as Henry Moore and Hubert Dalwood objected to the idea that 'sculpture can be brought in to provide a veneer of culture to a building'. To them, this represented 'the humiliating subservience of the sculptor to the architect' (Calvorcaressi, 1981:135). At that time, discussion about the relationship between art and architecture focused on the concept of 'assimilation' – the absorption of art into architecture. The current debate has shifted to the question of 'integration' – art as a necessary component of the whole.

Art which is integral, or at least complementary to its surroundings, is conventionally regarded as somehow more desirable than that which is added on, 'implanted' or 'detached'. This is precisely what informs the recruiting of artists into design teams, as exemplified in the artist Tess Jaray's work with the design team on Centenary Square (p. 128). According to Andy Kerr, an engineer who also employed her to work on the redesign of Wakefield Cathederal precinct

> Our philosophy was that the design of anything covers the whole spectrum ranging from practical things at one end to aesthetics at the other. All these are equal components to the total design ... We felt we were well endowed at the practical end, we wanted something to balance it at the other end. Hence, Tess was invited. But she was invited right from the very start. We felt that we didn't want a bolt on – to add a bit of sculpture – we wanted the art to be an integrated part of the whole scheme.

Attitudes to art conceived in contradiction to the architecture, or competing with it, are less clear as the example of Richard Serra's work at Broadgate (p. 96) suggests.

But in what sense might art be integral to architecture? Financially, as part of the overall costs of a development or formally, as part of the aesthetic or cognitive processes?

Art which is integral is often regarded as decorative. But as decoration it may not be considered to be art. 'People perceive objects as art, not decorative schemes'. Serra describes works that appear as decor or embellishment as

> just badges of corporate awareness. For the most part they don't enter into any controversy at all, because – why bother? They're harmless, and in that sense they're almost useless as art. To tell you the truth – a lot of applied art and decoration is being bandied about as what's needed. It masquerades under the guise of art for the people (Appendix 6, p. 345).

In some contexts artists' contributions may be redundant. On the one hand, the architecture itself may be regarded as art 'in which case there is no need for [additional] art'. As the artist Mike Stubbs proposed, some people would 'much rather have good buildings, good design and good architecture than bad buildings with bits of public art at the base of them.' On the other hand, as Serra pointed out, architects may well produce their own 'art' objects.

> What you have in the USA is architects who, rather than giving the percent to painters and sculptors, take it upon themselves to interact with the needs of what they think ought to be presented to the public ... Serious sculptors are denied the possibility of those interventions because the architects are coopting the money ... that parades as post-modernist signature for context (Appendix 6, p. 345).

The working relationships between different professional groups, the power, control and, conversely, the loss of autonomy vested in them, are discussed in relation to the commissions for Centenary Square (p. 128) in particular (see also Campbell and Cruikshank, 1986).

Artists' contributions

One might ask what artists can contribute to the built environment over and above architects, landscape architects and designers? What, for instance, distinguishes a bollard designed by an artist from that of an architect or an industrial designer? Some of the planners interviewed professed not to have thought about it. Their thinking was often uncritical. They presumed that public art is something produced by 'a person who consider[s] themselves to be an artist or a craftsperson' (Roberts, Marsh and Salter, 1993:7) and that 'by definition, an engineer is incapable of producing art'. They accept the notion that 'public art projects, because of their nature as a 'one-off', tend to allow more freedom of expression than a programme of traditional landscape improvements'. A distinguishing feature of 'art' might be that it possesses an unusually high degree of craftsmanship or skill, which is popularly regarded as indicating quality. But this excludes art which deliberately flaunts such expectations. It is maintained that art lends a sense of 'authenticity' to place, as in the case of the Silkstone Heritage Stones (p. 204). But what if the art in one place resembles that in another as in the case of Henry Moore's work in cities all over the world?

Public art and education

Not all public art projects include formal education programmes (unlike the case studies of Smethwick High Street (p. 164), Chantreyland Sculpture Trail (p. 185) and Westgate Station (p. 214), yet public art is often cited as an educational resource. 'Why would anyone want to promote public art unless it was educational?' Despite the inherent paternalism implied – 'it is presuming a lot to educate people' – the question remains: 'if public art is educational, in what does that educational component consist?'

The educational function of public art is described in various ways. It may, as the art historian Chris Bailey suggested, be intended 'to enable' and 'empower' the community.

> If there is an education process going on there, then it is of the kind that says that what people need to know more about is themselves ... There is also another kind of education ... which says that there is a substantive and normative art practice which more people ought to see. Because they don't see it in galleries, it should come out of galleries and be put onto the streets. Public art is ... doing both of these.

A commonly cited aspiration for public art is that it should 'raise levels of awareness','challenge people's preconceptions', persuade people 'to recognise that art is a healthy activity in life; not a luxury, but a basic need' or encourage them to give artists 'a role in society'. It could be intended to make the public 'think about a particular issue'. Precisely what the issue might be is less frequently articulated than the imperative that they should think.

Even the public expression of dislike of a particular work is sometimes construed as beneficial. In the case of the art in Centenary Square (p. 128), for example, the Director of the public art agency involved asserted that 'controversy is all to the good if it makes people think and talk'. Such arguments are commonly cited with respect to works of art in general. The Arts Council, for example, quoted the American, Doris Freeman, to similar effect in its publication *Percent for Art: A review*.

> Many works of art provoke scattered grumbling and protests, but this may in itself be a good thing, for the art therefore fulfils one of its functions by encouraging the exchange of ideas and the elicitation of responses and reactions (ACGB 1991:21).

Few other fields of endeavour are defended by such rhetoric.

If public art is inherently educational, it follows that the artist is, in some sense, regarded as an educator even if educating the public is not necessarily a conscious priority. Some are more concerned with their own agendas, as the following statements suggest.

> I do public commissions to enable me to work in the studio on other things (Sally Freshwater).

> I'm working quite selfishly. It's not campaigning on my part. I'd like to look at things that give me a *frisson*, speak about my experience. Maybe I'm the sole consumer. If it resonates with anyone else out there – great! (Helen Chadwick, talking on the BBC in 1992).

> For me, to work in a public space is incidental. I am not trying to reach a public, as it were. I am trying to develop my work in interesting spaces. They happen, generally, to be in public, but that's not the main consideration. The main consideration is to develop my work and to hopefully be able to communicate whatever I am working on at the time to an audience.

> If there is a problem, it should really be for the public to be talking about art more and to understand it more, than for the artist to approach the public ... (Daniel Santisi).

According to some people who work in the visual arts, works by artists primarily concerned with their own development are of 'more value' to the public precisely because they are 'difficult' and 'stretch the public aesthetically and intellectually'. Indeed their very strength is said to reside in the fact that they are 'challenging'.

Public art and artistic integrity

Artists' desire to realise the 'artistic integrity' of works designed for the public realm may represent a point of contention. One curator who

57

develops projects for public places denied, for example. having any interest

> in commissioning projects which have at their base the need not to displease ... On the contrary ... they have to be prepared to displease (Lingwood 1990:152).

This view is endorsed by many artists.

> Community art severely compromises an artist to make something very simple which isn't simple, and perhaps fail on that level (Daniel Santisi).

It is commonly held within certain artistic constituencies, that the public sector should support artistic activities *per se*, whether or not they are understood or appreciated by the public. Public and private sectors may be motivated by a sense of philanthropy. However representatives from the corporate sector who participated in focus group discussions articulated more pragmatic concerns. David Perry regards British Rail's investment in art as a 'business resource'; Gordon Edington, BAA, perceives art as contributing to customer care.

> The sculptures at Stanstead are designed to make the passengers' journey through the terminal a more uplifting one (*The Independent*, 11.9.1993).

Commissioners in the corporate sector might opt for an art which is 'conducive' – what Crosby refers to as 'good, ordinary art'.

> A perfectly decent piece – very comfortable and reasonable. Give it a pat as you go by. You can't ask for more.

Such statements represent an anathema to the notion of art being anti-commercial and unbound by materialist culture. Some 50 years ago the critic Clement Greenberg observed that 'the avant-garde was tied to the bourgeoisie with an umbilical cord of gold'. Certain coteries of the art world still find that unpalatable – David Batchelor, for example, writing in the art press in 1992 about the art at Docklands.

> Docklands and contemporary art are not terms which chime in my mind with a great deal of resonance: more of a dull thud. The two terms do not sit together comfortably. Rather the opposite. They suggest either a non-relationship or an antagonistic relationship – they point in different or opposed directions. No major surprises here: after all 'Docklands' has become a cipher for a certain kind of culture, one which has defined itself in part though the negation of just those values ... we associate with art. The Docklands Development Corporation, and the jewel in its crown, Olympia & York's Canary Wharf

Development, is as close as you can get to a physical embodiment of the spirit of modern Conservatism. Can good art come out of such a bad place? ... It can't. If art could only grow out in amorally hygienic culture, there would be no art. But then, some cultures are more barren than others. A better question would be: has the work made for Docklands succeeded? Does it count as a contribution to the tradition of critique and dissent? (Batchelor 1992:8.)

Andrew Brighton (1993), similarly regards the bureaucratisation of public art as a force for the bad.

The antagonism between the art world and 'the hand that feeds it' is, however, in many respects mutual. Brighton purports that in the private sector, 'the disjuncture between the art and audience has a function: it adds value'(1993). However, such potential antagonism produces a different effect in the public sector. Local authorities may, for example, feel obliged to prioritise the interests of the public good in general and the rate payers in particular, over those of the artistic community. As David Patmore, Director of Arts, Sheffield City Council, observed

what is aesthetically acceptable to the art world may not be consonant with the consumers ... I don't think you can avoid the politics of art, and I think that there is a case to be made for taking public art, or the animation of public art, out of the accepted infrastructure.

Processes

The processes by which public art is commissioned and sited – its selection and administration – inevitably reflect the different interests and aspirations of the constituencies involved.

The initiation of public art projects and professional training.
The majority of case studies examined in this report were initiated by artists. But the fact that the other professional groups involved in public art – planners, architects and developers – consider it their prerogative to initiate public art projects is reported to make artists feel displaced: 'not enough opportunities are artist-led', 'it must be possible for an artist to initiate suggestions'.

Architects regard themselves as ideally placed to commission work because they have 'a whole view of the process'. But since the time and space available to them is limited due to their contractual relationship with clients and the physical boundaries of the site, it could be argued that the wider responsibilities for public art 'must be planners'.'

Planners are, by definition, familiar with 'the underlying structure and ethos' of the place (Hillman 1990:21).

> planning is very apposite. It deals with the hard edged problems of getting buildings built and bits of the city developed (Patmore).

Planners' statutory involvement with public art is determined by Acts of Parliament and planning policy guidance issued by the Department of the Environment. These cover areas such as aesthetic control, design considerations and planning gain – all of which pertain to permanently sited public art.

The DOE's *Planning Policy Guidance* (1992: Annex A6) states that planners should focus on 'encouraging good design rather than stifling experiment, originality or initiative'. However there has been considerable debate as to whether they should interfere in design matters, particularly those that involve architects and whether they should actively participate in design matters (for example Pour, 1992; Jarvis, 1992).

The Royal Town Planning Institute merely proposes that planners should be 'competent' in 'aesthetic dimensions and design awareness' (1991:2). During the focus group discussions, architects and planners commented on their own lack of training for commissioning public art. Bob Jarvis, School of Land Management and Planning, South Bank University, for example, says

> unfortunately the [planning] profession ... is completely inadequate to deal with it at the moment. So [if it were to be planners] it would not be the planning profession as it is now – but the planning profession which understands public space ... and which involves a relationship with architects, users of that space and all sorts of people ... Unfortunately, those sorts of planners don't really exist.

Crosby described architectural education as similarly inadequate.

> In architectural colleges, the words 'beauty', 'convenience' and 'comfort' are never mentioned. Something has to change.

For such professional groups as architects and planners, working with artists may constitute a form of professional development.

> Art in the environment: mural painting and street sculpture is not my main concern ... Rather, I am interested in ways in which the artist's perception of

the environment can help us sharpen up our own, better equip us to see potential for improvement, and overcome [a training that leaves us lacking in confidence in dealing with aesthetic matters] (Taylor 1991:6).

This argument is often put forward by the visual arts constituency. Vivien Lovell, the Director of Public Art Commissions Agency, for example, regards the value of artists contributing to the design process as residing in

their free thinking, lateral approach to design problems [and], daring to challenge the banal, which comprises so much of the current environment (*The Independent*, 11.9.1992).

Lovell considers potential commissioners as another group which sometimes needs 'educating'.

A great deal could be done in terms of educating or providing information to clients in the public sector and the private sectors on the subject of funding different types of public art activity.

This, of course, may have more to do with marketing than education. Perry described 'educating' commissioners as a matter 'of changing hearts and minds by encouraging them to take [public art] on board as part of what they do anyway'.

The issue of artists' training was hardly touched on, although Crosby maintained that 'the radical thing that has to change is ... art education itself'.

Public art agencies and public art officers
Public art agencies and public art officers employed by local authorities comprise another professional constituency involved in the commissioning and siting of public art. They are largely associated with 'encouraging awareness' of public art and promoting the interests of artists, managing and advising on projects for the private sector and bringing a 'freshness' of approach to each project.

The focus group discussions which contributed to this research tended to focus on local authorities' arts officers. Councillors and officers who participated in the discussions regarded employing their own public art specialists as advantageous, particularly with respect to local projects. This is because they are, by definition, closely associated with the public interest.

They know more about the wishes of local groups ... Agencies cannot have understandings, interests of local community so close to heart. That comes through working in it for a long time:

Successful bids have to do with particular zeitgeist of particular areas. They need to be sensitive to that. Being on the ground scores:

They may also be able to seize opportunities faster. They are there when the planning applications come through the door.

The commissioning of public art is, however, not restricted to employed professionals. Although it is rare, members of the public themselves commission works designed to be sited in public places – as in the case of the Silkstone Heritage Stones Project (p. 204).

Criteria for commissioning public art: the artist's interests vs those of the public

Commissions weighted towards the interests of artists might, for example, be awarded for reasons such as their 'attachment to the place' (for example the Art in Centenary Square, p. 128). They may also be intended to create opportunities for young or inexperienced artists (Chantreyland Sculpture Trail, p. 185).

Commissions might, alternatively, not be oriented to artists but predicated on briefs

which address the public's needs in terms of the space and the siting. Some of them are functional needs, like sitting and eating a sandwich. There are also symbolic public needs. Questions of public meanings and the space which planners and urban designers are starting to address can be as appropriate to public art as they are to writing briefs for architects and developers. It is an area not particularly explored. If it is work that is expected to have some kind of public interest, then I would have thought that it was in the interests of all the involved bodies to start to investigate those sorts of processes (Jarvis).

In these circumstances, certain sorts of art may be regarded as more appropriate than others – as in 'we could have a more 'challenging' piece in the cultural industries quarter than in front of the new Courts.' But in what might that appropriateness comprise? Should artist's so-called 'freedom of expression' be constrained? Can the subject matter of public art be conceived to reflect the common interests or shared aspirations of local communities or the non-specific regional, national or 'international' public? Can a work of public art be understood on various levels – 'be all things to all people'?

If public art is intended for the public, should its commissioning be a democratic process characterised by a plurality of voices? Or is voting undesirable because it 'reduces art to the lowest common denominator'? If public debate and consultation are desirable, should the public be consulted about every piece of public art to be erected or just some? What should that consultation entail? Should it be systematic – based on representative samples, like market research; or should it be random? Might not informing the public, as one Director of a public art agency suggested, justifiably be termed 'consultation?'

On a practical level, how can the public be consulted in a city centre which has no sense of community and which people generally 'want to get away [from] as quickly as possible'? Do people even want to be consulted? David Blackburn, one of the Directors of Rosehaugh Stanhope Developments, the company that built Broadgate, observed

> It is generally assumed that the public has a right to a major say on all issues of architecture ... the public doesn't regard itself as part of the process of public art.

Are people sufficiently aware of their environment to make sound judgements? 'Do they know enough to be consulted?' Can they, as some planners asked, 'read drawings sufficiently well to anticipate how things will be'? or is the act of consultation synonymous with education? Should such decisions be regarded as the responsibility of elected councillors and officers, as in the case of Centenary Square (Manser 1980). Do committee decisions inevitably lead to artistic compromises and, if so, are these necessarily a bad thing?

Perhaps more to the point, does public opinion influence the outcome of public art commissions? Is consultation, as it is alleged, 'little more than a sham'?

There appear to be differences between public and private sector commissioning. Is the private sector obliged to respond to the public's wishes? Edington doubted it.

> I don't know how you balance the views of two groups of different opinion. Do you provide them with a chocolate box? I think you should you keep the courage of your convictions.

Conceivably commissioning might be best left to a single visionary individual. 'The best way for art to be commissioned is by a dictator.'

Is risk a desirable element in the commissioning of public art? Commissioning processes are often designed to cut risks. Liaison committees, for example, comprise people concerned with different aspects of a business and 'provide a wide view of opinion and give the selection a certain credibility'. According to Blackburn

> If you don't start off by acknowledging that you have to take these into account, you'll be very lucky if you don't end up with a disaster of some sort.

If 'closed competitions', restricted to certain artists, result in safe, predictable outcomes, are open competitions preferable in that they 'sharpen awareness and overcome predicability', or are competitions only as good as the people judging them?

Public art, interpretation and accountability

It is sometimes construed as exciting for people to come to an understanding of particular works on their own or through 'word of mouth'. But it is also the case that

> unless you know ... there's no way you can work out what the art is about.

Dave Kennedy of Bradford Council, whose work enables young people to work on public art projects, described wanting

> to read about these things that I can see – who did it, when it was done, what it's about. We ought to tell people. We do it for nature trails and other parts of the environment. I'm sure we could do better ... There's nothing wrong with interpretation outside.

The general tendency not to provide labels for works in public places has been described as 'an inverse form of snobbery'. However, it may be part of a wider problem about responsibility and accountability.

> There is little discussion about accountability. It is still missing from the debate ... There is a tendency to keep kinds of aesthetic judgement especially, very private ... Even where people will talk about everything else, like budgets, they still won't talk about why they chose this rather than that, and that is an essential part of the process. It's very important to think that someone thought it was worth doing (Bailey).

Some of the professional groups involved are evidently reluctant to commit themselves. The DOE's *Planning Guidance*, for example, advises planners not to

> impose their tastes on developments simply because they believe them to be superior. Developers should not be compelled to conform to the fashion of the moment at the expense of individuality, originality or traditional styles. Nor should they be asked to adopt designs which are unpopular with their customers (ACGB Nov 1990: 5.5). Their concern may lie with whether works of public art harm the 'the visual amenities' (see Planning Inspectorate 1992).

Art administrators are also disinclined to participate in public debates about the quality or relative successes of public art works. Antonia Payne, former Director of the Ikon Gallery, Birmingham, observed

> because one knows that there are so many occasions where that would be highly damaging. One is in the ridiculous position of feeling constrained not to declare publicly one's negative value judgements about much public art.

And yet, precisely

> because public art is so much to do with negotiation between a variety of individuals ... it is terribly easy for everybody to pass the buck:

> Someone has to take responsibility for decisions, and they have to be visibly accountable ... With a lot of public art this is not the case. We, the public, are presented with an object and we actually don't have any idea at all of the ideologies that underpinned the choices ... [or] the situation within which decisions were being made:

> I'm not sure ... how it can happen – but the point at which I feel public art is no longer tenable is the point at which no one is visibly taking responsibility for the works that are there ... It is the most depressing situation because, for want of any visible critical rigour and debate, some very uninteresting art is being got away with ... That seems to be unacceptable.

Crosby agreed. He thought that 'the building client must take the blame and the kudos. A regiment of arts officers and public art consultants only pass the buck'.

Public art and Percent for Art

Several public art officers whose authorities had adopted Percent for Art policies, expressed doubts about its efficacy, particularly with regard to the private sector (Appendix 3, p. 319).

The concept of Percent for Art is viewed with suspicion by many District Planning Officers ... as a policy which will put developers off moving into their area.

Although the Art at Broadgate was funded according to a percent principle, many developers are antagonistic to the idea of mandatory Percent for Art, 'Why should we undertake this experiment in arts funding?' (ACGB Nov 1990:8.1). Even leading private sector commissioners regard it as having drawbacks. Edington, for one, perceives it as 'debasing the whole process', and Blackburn insists that

you don't want to force people to stick things on their buildings to comply with just another bit of the regulations:

Far worse ... is the risk that you develop a whole technique of identifying things ... as art when they're not ... That accounts for a certain part of your percentage ... They reconstruct their cost plans so that they can break out the art element of every single aspect.

The workings of Percent for Art are far from straightforward. Percentages are sometimes calculated in retrospect. The paradigm of one per cent of the capital costs promoted by the Arts Council is rarely adhered to. In practice, authorities negotiate at different points in the development process for what they can get. Flexibility is essential in reaching voluntary agreements. One public art officer reported securing percentages for various projects ranging from 0.25 per cent to five per cent. Some view the target of one per cent as too high, 'not a realistic proposition for many schemes'; others perceive it as too low: 'an infinitesimal amount'. Authorities have to be pragmatic.

In difficult times we negotiate for what we deem to be a reasonable contribution ... These negotiations concentrate on the amount of money rather than on a percentage basis:

Achieving what is appropriate is more desirable than a percentage sought for the sake of it:

As a policy we encourage Percent for Art as one component of achieving a better environment. The amount of money to be spent, as a percentage of the capital costs is not discussed, as we are only interested in the visual impact the development will have.

It is rare for an authority to implement Percent for Art without adopting a policy (as in the case of Birmingham). Many local authorities have difficulties in effectively administering the Percent for Art policies they have. Few officers employ formal strategies. Procedural difficulties may inhibit pooling, 'it would be difficult to persuade developers of the benefits'. Others doubt that Percent for Art will attract the financial self-sufficiency anticipated.

A major concern voiced by public art officers is the prospective quality of the work produced. A *Daily Telegraph* leader, written in response to the Arts Council's campaign, articulated a similar opinion.

> We live in the present, an era of unsettled aesthetic values ... The very notion that ... a statutory one per cent could be spent on their products – that a fixed figure buys work of lasting importance – is grossly Philistine ... What confidence can we have in the taste of many local authorities ... Before capitulating to the enthusiasts, the Arts Council should consider what such a commitment could do for its own reputation ('Artless Dodge', *The Daily Telegraph*, 1.3.1988).

If Percent for Art, as officers feared, generates 'too much permanent public art', temporary projects might be preferable in preventing cities becoming 'over crowded'; the focus could shift away from art to 'environmental contributions' and public art works could be 'deaccessioned'. But whereas people are used to demolishing buildings, works of public art tend not to be removed. 'It's only a matter of time.' More often public art works are left unmaintained and neglected – contributing to environmental squalor rather than improvement.

One public art officer surveyed believed that 'Percent for Art has had its day'. Another considered that 'too much rides on Percent for Art rather than the more general ... public art'.

One misnomer is that Percent for Art is synonymous with art in public places. Some £550,000 was committed to Percent for Art at Quarry House, the new headquarters of the Departments of Health and Social Security at Leeds. This constituted one per cent of the total cost of £55 million. At the time of research, with the exception of external works, these were reported as not freely accessible to the people of Leeds (Renton and Lacey 1993). Should public money be spent on art which, in that sense, is not public?

Reception

The ways in which public art is received raise issues about its meaning, its assimilation into the social and physical environments in which it is placed, its 'ownership' by the community and judgements about its quality.

Criteria according to which public art is judged

According to Councillor Pye of Sheffield City Council

> Most successful pieces work on several levels. Their meaning can be unravelled according to the degree of interest of those who are consuming it.

The meanings attributed to public art may be triggered by factors which do not necessarily pertain to artists' intentions for the works, their formal or aesthetic qualities, but to extra-aesthetic characteristics such as the context in which the work is sited, the manner of its introduction to the community, the circumstances of its siting, whether it appears to constitute value for money, objections to the moral or political values it represents, what the papers say, whether it adheres to artistic or other conventions or whether it is regarded as 'art' (see *Art-Language* 1969:7-8; Atkinson 1970:6). Works commissioned for places which have little or no tradition of showing contemporary art may, for example, meet with prejudices against art perpetrated by people worried about 'being had'. The critic, Mary Sara, maintains that

> people aren't worried about it being art, if they like it:

> The most successful pieces of public art are what the public doesn't see, they walk across it or lean up against it. They don't know it's art ... If it is appropriately sited, the feeling is that it always should have been there.

Brighton (1993) speculates that what constitutes a 'genuine' public art, may have little to do with art conventions.

> Just off the London Road, on the outskirts of Oxford, a shark's body and tail stand twenty feet above the roofs of an ordinary street. Its head appears to have smashed through into the attic of a house.

> The artist, John Buckley's *'trompe l'oeil'* assemblage of house and shark has been neglected by art critics and rarely cited with enthusiasm by public art agencies and advocates. Ironically, it is one of the few examples of genuinely public art we have. It is not just art placed in a public place ... offering little meaning or pleasure for those who encounter it. Buckley's assemblage works

in familiar conventions. This is the shark as seen in 'Jaws', and the house is a house. There is no insider-dealing on offer for the art-initiated eye. It offers no aestheticist *frisson* and has no significant visual relationship with past or current art.

A sense of 'ownership' is also conventionally deemed an important aspect of the public's appreciation of public art. Common sense suggests that this accrues from the work having been in place for some time – 'people grow to own the sculptures'. Yet, neither familiarity with nor affection for works of public art are consonant with their perceived qualities. In the case of the appeal against the refusal of a planning permission for Buckley's, *The Shark*, the Secretary of State for the Environment did not hold that public opinion added weight to the case in favour of the work (Planning Inspectorate 1992). People also

recognise poor quality. Some early projects where the community created their own art resulted in some very poor quality art. They were the first to recognise that (Sara).

Yet in the focus group discussions few participants were reluctant to make judgements about quality – even when they were in the position of committing public subsidy to it. As one local councillor put it

Quality has to be decided by the customer. If the customer perceives the product as being of quality, then it is of quality irrespective of what everyone else says.

Such ambivalence may be in response to the notion that 'there is a real danger of creating a professional priesthood which determines what is quality and what is not'. Consensus may carry more weight than authority – as in 'that piece is universally abhorred'. One constituency's attitude may be granted little respect by another. Within the artistic community, for example, it is comparatively rare for the artist or the agency to be blamed for the failings of particular commissions. If the public is unappreciative of a work, the artistic community may dismiss them as 'ignorant', 'philistine' or 'visually illiterate'. There is, as Richard Deacon observed, an apparent lack of transfer between the kind of skills used in looking at television and advertising and looking at the built environment.

Responsibility for forming judgments is a product of the education system ... but ultimately the 'artistic community' does have a major input into the visual education of society.

References to Part 1

ABSA, *An Overall Total for Business Sponsorship of the Arts During 1990/91*, Association of Business Sponsorship of the Arts, 1991.

ABSA, *Arts 93: Audiences, Attidtudes and Sponsorship*, Association of Business Sponsorship of the Arts, 1993.

ACGB, *Percent for Art. Report of a Steering Group established by the Arts Council of Great Britain with the Council of Regional Arts Associations, the Welsh and the Scottish Arts Councils*, 1990.

ACGB, *Percent for Art: a review*, Arts Council of Great Britain, 1991.

ACGB, *A Creative Future: the Way Forward for the Arts, Crafts and Media in England*, Coordinated by the Arts Council of Great Britain on behalf of the English Arts Funding System, HMSO, 1993.

Adams, Eileen, *Learning to See*, Royal Fine Art Commission, 1989.

Archbishop's Commission, *Faith in the Countryside, The Report of the Archbishops Commission in Rural Areas*, 1990.

Art-Language. The Journal of Conceptual Art, 'Introduction', May 1969.

Association of District Councils, *Towards Unitary Authorities: Arts and Entertainment* (undated).

Atkinson, Terry, 'Concerning Interpretation of the Bainbridge/Hurrell Models', *Art-Language. The Journal of Conceptual Art*, February 1970.

Audit Commission, *Local Authorities, Entertainment and the Arts*, HMSO, 1991.

Batchelor, David, 'Under the Canary', *Frieze*, 5, 1992.

BBC, *Outing Art*, BBC2, 1992.

Bianchini, Franco, Fisher, Mark, Montgomery, John and Worpole, Ken, *City Centres, City Cultures. The Role of the Arts in the Revitalization of Towns and Cities*, Centre for Local Economic Strategies, 1988.

Bianchini, Franco and Parkinson, Michael (eds), *Cultural Policy and Urban Regeneration: The West European Experience*, Manchester University Press, 1993.

Biggs, Louis, 'Open Air Sculpture', Davies, Peter and Knipe, Anthony (eds), *A Sense of Place*, Coelfrith Press, 1984.

Booth, Peter and Bloye, Robin, 'See Glasgow, see Culture' in Bianchini and Parkinson, 1993.

Brighton, Andrew, 'Philistine Piety and Public Art', *Modern Painters*, 1993.

Calvorcaressi, Richard, 'Public Sculpture in the 50s' in Nairne and Serota, 1981.

Campbell, Robert and Cruikshank, Jeffrey, 'Art in Architecture', *Places* 3, no 2, 1986.

Clay, Grady, *Close-Up. How to read the American city*, Pall Mall Press, 1973.

Collard, Paul, *Arts in Inner Cities*, The Office of Arts and Libraries (unpublished), 1988.

Common Ground, *An Introduction to the deeds and thoughts of Common Ground*, 1990.

Countryside Commission, *Enjoying the Countryside: Policies for People*, 1992.

Dempsey, Andrew, 'Introduction', *Outdoor Sculpture*, Arts Council of Great Britain, 1967.

Department of the Environment and the Welsh Office, *Town & Country Planning Act 1971: Planning Gain*, DOE Circular 22/83, 1983.

Department of the Environment and the Welsh Office, *Aesthetic Control*, DOE Circular 31/85, 1985.

Department of the Environment and the Welsh Office, *Planning and Compensation Act 1991: Planning Obligations*, DOE Circular 16/91, 1991.

Department of Environment and the Welsh Office, *Planning Policy Guidance: General Policy and Principles*, HMSO, March 1992.

Dix, Gill, *Resources for Urban Areas: historical and current context*. Briefing paper 003. Policy and Planning Unit, Arts Council of England, 1993.

Dormer, Peter, 'Lipstick on the face of a gorilla', *The Independent*, 1992.

Eisenberg, Barry, 'Percent for Art Update', *Sculpture*, 1990.

Everitt, Anthony, 'Homage to the arts'. *The Insider*, no 13, 1992.

Garnham, Nicholas, 'Concepts of Culture: Public Policy and the Cultural Industries', reprinted in *Cultural Studies 1*, 1987.

Gibberd, Sir Frederick, *Sculpture in Harlow*, Harlow Development Corporation, 1973.

Glasgow City Council, *The 1990 Story: Glasgow, Cultural Capital of Europe*, 1992.

Greenwich Mural Workshop, *Murals in London Since 1971*, (undated).

Griffiths, Ron, 'The Politics of Cultural Policy in Urban Regeneration Strategies', *Policy and Politics 21*, no 1, 1993.

Harvey, David (ed.), *The Urban Experience*, John Hopkins University Press, 1989.

Hewison, Robert, 'Field of Dreams', *The Sunday Times: The Culture*, 1993.

Hillman, J., *Planning for Beauty: the case for design guidelines*, HMSO, 1990.

Horstman, J. Jean, *Creating Space. Unitary Development Plans and the Arts, Culture and Entertainment*, London Arts Board, (undated).

Hutchison, Robert and Feist, Andrew, *Amateur Arts in the UK: The PSI Survey of Amateur Arts and Crafts in the UK*, Policy Studies Institute, 1991.

Jarvis, Bob, 'The Lost Art of Town Planning', *Urban Design Quarterly*, 1992.

Johnson, Diana, *Pride of Place: The Arts in Rural Areas*, Arts Development Association, 1991.

Jones, Sue (ed.), *Art in Public: What, why and how?*, AN Publications, 1992.

Keens, William, Owens, Pam, Salvadori, Danni and Williams, Jennifer (eds), 'Funding Mechanisms', *Arts and the Changing City: An Agenda for Urban Regeneration*, British American Arts Association, 1989.

King, Angela and Clifford, Sue, *Introduction to the Deeds and Thoughts of Common Ground*, 1990.

Kowinski, W.S., *The Malling of America*, William Morrow, 1982.

Lingwood, James (ed.), *New Works for Different Places: TSWA Four Cities Project*, TSWA, 1990.

London Arts Board Funding Programmes, *Arts Challenge*, (Programme 22), 1993/4.

Luce, Richard, *Hansard*, 1990.

Manser, M., 'An excuse for lousy buildings', *Journal of the Royal Institute of British Architects*, 83, no.9, 1980.

Martin, Rupert, *The Sculpted Forest*, Redcliffe Press, 1990.

Mason, Sara and Taylor, Rhys, *Tackling Deprivation in Rural Areas*, Calouste Gulbenkian Foundation/ACRE, 1990.

McLaughlin, Brian, Opening address to the *Pride of Place Conference*, Johnson, 1991.

Melville, Robert, 'Henry Moore and the Siting of Public Sculpture', *Architectural Review*, 115 no. 686, 1954.

Moreland, Joanna, *New Milestones*, Common Ground, 1988.

Nairne, Sandy and Serota, Nicholas, *British Sculpture in the Twentieth Century*, Whitechapel Art Gallery, 1981.

Owusu, Kwesi, *The Struggle for Black Arts in Britain*, Comedia, 1986.

Pawley, Martin, *The Private Future*, Thames and Hudson, 1974.

Pearson, Nicholas M., *The State and the Visual Arts. A discussion of State Intervention in the Visual Arts in Britain*, Open University Press, 1982.

Petherbridge, Deanna, 'The Town Artist Experiment'. *Architectural Review*, 1979.

Petherbridge, Deanna, 'Writing on the Wall', *The Independent*, 1991.

Pickvance, Ronald, 'Introduction', *Contemporary British Sculpture*, Arts Council of Great Britain, 1960.

Planning Inspectorate, *Retention of a Public Sculpture "Untitled 1986" ("The Shark")*, Ref. APP/G3110/A/91/184337, 21 May 1992.

Pour, Ali Mandani, 'Design Control and Design Teaching: Problems and Perspectives', *Urban Design Quarterly*, 1992.

Power, Gary, 'Percent for Art', *Art Monthly*, 1991-2.

Projects Environment in association with the Groundwork Foundation, *Arts and the Environment: The Groundwork Experience*, 1991.

Public Art Consultancy Team, *The Strategy for Public Art in Cardiff Bay*, Cardiff Bay Development Corporation, 1990.

Public Art Forum, *The Public Art Report: Local Authority Commissions for Art in Public Places*, 1990.

Punter, John V., 'The Privatisation of the Public Realm', *Planning, Practice and Research 5 (3) 9*, 1990.

Redcliffe-Maud, Lord, *Support for the Arts in England and Wales*, Calouste Gulbenkian Foundation, 1976.

Relph, E., *Place and Placelessness*, Dion, 1976.

Renton, Alex and Lacey, Hester, 'Bureaucrats stay in the pink', *Independent on Sunday*, 1993.

Research Survey of Great Britain, *Report on a Survey on Arts and Cultural Activities in Great Britain*, Arts Council of Great Britain, 1991.

Rittner, Luke, 'A mite to make the arts mighty', *The Guardian*, 1988.

Robb, Denis, *Results of Research into the Contemporary Visual Arts*, Arts Council of Great Britain, 1992.

Roberts, Marion, Marsh, Chris and Salter, Miffa, *Public Art in Private Places: Commercial Benefits and Public Policy*, University of Westminster, 1993.

Royal Town Planning Institute, *The Education of Planners: Policy Statement and General Guidance for Academic Institutions Offering Initial Professional Education in Planning*, RTPI, 1991.

Scottish Development Agency, *Rural Development in Scotland: A Review of Trends and Issues*, 1990.

Sennett, Richard, *The Use of Disorder*, Penguin, 1970.

Sennett, Richard, *The Fall of Public Man*, Cambridge University Press, 1977.

Sennett, Richard, *The Conscience of the Eye: The Design and Social Life of Cities*, Faber & Faber, 1990.

Stote, Sally, *Think Rural: A Report for the Arts Council on Art in Rural Areas*, Arts Council of Great Britain, 1989.

Stone, David, 'The Islington Schools Environment Project', Miles, Malcom, *Art for Public Places: Critical Essays*, Winchester School of Art Press, 1989.

Strachan, W.J., *Open Air Sculpture in Britain*, Zwemmer and Tate Gallery Publications, 1984.

Taylor, Michael, 'The Art of the Environment', *The Planner*, 1991.

Tomlinson, R.R., 'Introducing the Sculpture Exhibition', *Open Air Exhibition of Sculpture*, County Hall, 1948.

Tucker, William, 'Notes on sculpture, public sculpture and patronage', *Art International 183*, no. 940, 1972.

Tucker, William, 'Introduction', *The Condition of Sculpture: A Selection of Recent Sculpture by Younger British and Foreign Artists*, Arts Council of Great Britain, 1975.

Willmott, Peter and Hutchison, Robert, (eds), *Urban Trends 1, A report on Britain's Deprived Areas*, Policy Studies Institute, 1992.

Woodland Trust, Country Seats in our Woods, (undated).

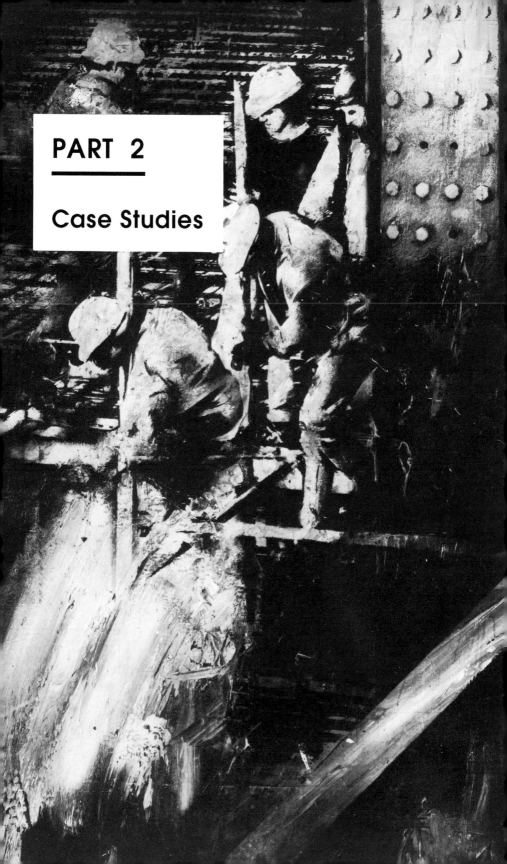

PART 2

Case Studies

3 Introduction and rationale for selecting the case studies

Selection

The seven case studies were selected to suggest the diversity of permanent art works sited in public places. They represent a range of intentions for public art, different processes involved in its commissioning and siting and ways in which it is received. They also raise a series of issues. The permutations are enormous and the case studies cannot, therefore, be easily categorised.

The case studies themselves represent different sets of interests – those of central and local government, the community, local artistic, business and other special interest groups. Their concerns are reflected in the function, the funding and the siting of the works.

Intentions for the works vary. One originally formed part of a tribute to the artist; another represented a desire on the part of a local authority to support the work of artists 'beyond the gallery'. Others were part of wider ambitions – often to contribute to the revitalisation and regeneration of a specific area; create a sense of place or an identity for a new development, celebrate local distinctiveness or attract tenants.

One was initiated by private, as opposed to public sector agencies; another came about as the result of a local newspaper campaign. Several were originated by the artists themselves.

The works chosen as case studies were funded by a range of public and private sector institutions, although the majority were paid for by partnerships dominated by the public sector. Some, located in areas of high deprivation, received urban programme monies. By comparison, one case study was funded by rural agencies. Two of the case studies – one private, the other in the public sector – were funded through Percent for Art. Another was a gift by the artist to the State. It involved no financial transactions.

The costs involved in commissioning and siting the case studies ranged from a few thousand pounds to several million.

Details of case studies' administration also varied. One was funded, commissioned and managed by a private property company, another by a local community group. Several involved partnerships forged between various parties – among them an artists' group, British Rail, various local authority departments, art galleries and public art agencies.

All but one of the case studies are urban. They occupy spaces ranging from a private office development to civic squares, parks and a high street.

Some are specifically about the history of the place where they are sited. The rural case study, for example, is a memorial to children drowned in a flash flood in a local mine. Others, such as the Art at Broadgate (p. 96) make no reference to the history of the site whatsoever.

The majority of the case studies comprise free standing sculptures. This reflects the general tendency of public art. Several fulfil specific functions as street furniture, paving, bollards and architectural embellishment.

Some comprise solitary commissions, but most form clusters of works which may or may not have been conceived as part of an overall strategy. Most are one-offs and site-specific; others include multiples which can be seen in other places elsewhere in the world. The authorship of the works represents another variant. Some are by internationally renowned artists. Moore was known as 'the world's greatest living sculptor'; others counted among the 'Top 100 Contemporary Artists' listings. The case studies also include younger, less experienced artists who may have worked with the local communities.

Not all the works were necessarily executed by the artist. One was carved by Italian stonemasons, one was cast in a German steel mill, another painted by local contractors.

Last but not least, the case studies are intended for different constituencies – the parish, local residents and workers, shoppers, dog walkers, tourists, the business community, conference delegates and so on. All the case studies were intended to have local appeal. Some aspired to national and international audiences.

Presentation

The seven case studies are presented in a way which is intended to allow comparisons to be drawn between them. Each account is written in a narrative, divided into three sections. These describe the origination of the artwork or artworks, different constituencies' expectations of them, the processes according to which they were commissioned and sited, the kind of impact they have had. The following questions were asked of each:

Background
How did the work come to be there? What prompted its commission? Who was involved in the conception of the commission and how? For whom was the work intended? How was the work funded? Where does final responsibility lie? What did the different constituencies hope to gain from the commission? What informed those aspirations? What roles were ascribed to the work's public?

Processes
How were decisions made about the theme, contents and appearance of the work? On what basis were the artists selected? What was the nature of their personal engagement or commitment to the project? Whose values was the work to express? In what sense was the work considered specifically relevant to its location? How were decisions made about the siting of the work? How was it introduced to the public? What steps were taken to ensure that the criteria of the funding bodies were met?

Impact
Has the work been evaluated? If so, by whom and how? How has it informed the subsequent work of any of those involved? (Appendix 2, p. 277).

How has the work or works impacted on the public? Have the different constituencies' opinions towards the work shifted? If so, in what ways? What symbolic values does the work hold for different constituencies? Has the question of deaccessioning been raised? If so, why?

Research

As described in the Introduction, structured interviews relating to the case studies were carried out among those overtly involved in the case studies. The opinions of the local publics, leaders of local opinion and the artistic community were sought through surveys and focus group discussions.

4 London

The Arch
Kensington Gardens, Royal Borough of Kensington and Chelsea

Background
According to his patron, Sir Kenneth Clark, then Director of the National Gallery, Henry Moore was 'the greatest living sculptor'. The promotion of his work and the making of his national and international reputation owed much to the Arts Council and the British Council respectively. It was therefore fitting that *The Arch* should have originally been sited in Kensington Gardens by the Arts Council as part of its celebration of the artist's 80th birthday. Like the other sculptures displayed in that exhibition, *The Arch* was only intended to be there temporarily. However during the course of the exhibition, the *Evening Standard* newspaper mounted a campaign to keep one of Moore's sculptures permanently in the park.

The exhibition, *Henry Moore at the Serpentine: 80th Birthday Exhibition of Recent Carvings and Bronzes*, was held at the Serpentine Gallery, then run by the Arts Council of Great Britain. It was open between 22 July and 8 October, 1978.

The tribute at the Serpentine was only one of several celebrations mounted in London that year. These included *Henry Moore The Carver: An Eightieth Birthday Tribute* at Fischer Fine Art and *Henry Moore: 80th Birthday Exhibition of Graphic Work* at the Curwen Gallery. The Tate had two exhibitions, *The Henry Moore Gift*, which showed works Moore had given them to augment pieces already in the collection, and *The Drawings of Henry Moore*, a major retrospective of 260 works which came to London via Canada and Japan. Over the summer, the only galleries showing modern art that were open at the Tate were those containing Moores.

The largest birthday exhibition in the country was organised by Michael Diamond at Cartwright Hall, Bradford some 20 miles from Castleford, the artist's birthplace. It contained over 200 works. The Henry Moore Foundation has records of some 15 other birthday exhibitions

Henry Moore, *The Arch*, 1980, © The Henry Moore Foundation

which took place in USA, Switzerland, Venezuela, Japan, Germany, Spain and Norway.

The exhibition at the Serpentine focused on carvings and bronzes made during the previous decade since the 70th birthday exhibition at the Tate Gallery. Little of that work had been seen in Britain. Much was on a large scale and was meant to be placed outside. (As described in Chapter 1 on p. 31, the Arts Council had championed the display of sculptures 'in the open air' since the late 1940s.) There had never been a predominantly open-air exhibition of Moore's work in London and the Arts Council considered such an exhibition would be the most appropriate way to celebrate the artist's birthday. According to the press release the Serpentine Gallery and the surrounding park would provide 'an ideal setting for the work of this artist who has always preferred his sculpture to be seen outdoors in the landscape'. The use of Kensington Gardens necessitated the Gallery collaborating with the Department of the Environment (DOE), then responsible for the Royal Parks.

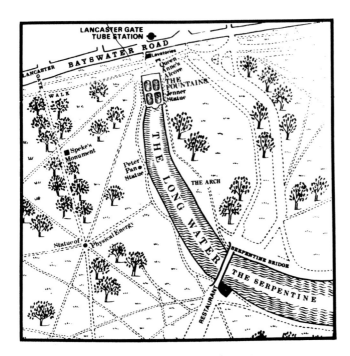

Map showing
the location of
The Arch taken
from the press
release issued by
the Serpentine
Gallery
announcing its
unveiling,
October 1980
© South Bank
Centre

The DOE was particularly sympathetic towards the project. In 1977, prompted by the artist the late Dame Elizabeth Frink, it had set up a Committee on Sculpture in the Royal Parks. Its objective was to show works loaned by contemporary artists in the Royal Parks which might not be shown elsewhere. It was intended to interest people who would not normally visit galleries. As Baroness Birk, then Parliamentary Under-Secretary of State, Department of the Environment, responsible for the Royal Parks, put it,'the idea was to fix their eye in a different way'. The committee had no funding for purchases. Transport and siting were covered by the Architect for Palaces and works were insured through Government indemnity.

There was never any doubt by members of the DOE's committee, or the Arts Council, about the value of showing works of art in public places. As Sir Robert Marshall, Second Permanent Secretary at the DOE who chaired the committee, and Lady Birk both recalled, 'it was simply taken for granted that it was a good thing. It never occurred to us to question it'.

Moore's presence in public places in London
At the time of the exhibition, there were already nine sculptures by Moore on permanent display in public places in London. They were sited on or by both public and private properties: *West Wind* (1928-29) at St James's Underground Station; *Time-Life Screen* (1952-53) Time-Life Building, Bond Street; *Three Standing Figures* (1947-48) Battersea Park, London Borough of Wandsworth; *Two Piece Reclining Figure No 1* (1959) Chelsea School of Art; *Knife Edge Two Piece* (1962-65) Abington Street Gardens, Westminster; *Locking Piece* (1963-64) Tate Gallery and *Sundial* (1965-66) Times Newspapers, Blackfriars, which was subsequently sold to IBM, Brussels. The Greater London Council (GLC) had sited two sculptures on modern housing estates in an attempt to 'humanise' them: *Draped Seated Woman* (1957-58) Stifford Estate, London Borough of Tower Hamlets and *Two Piece Reclining Figure No 3* (1961) Brandon Estate, London Borough of Southwark. Sculptures by Moore were also temporarily sited on the lawns of the Tate Gallery during the summer.

At that time, the preponderance of sculptures by the artist in London was such that William Feaver, the art critic for *The Observer* noted, 'you can't go far in London without bumping into a Henry Moore'(16.7.78). By the time W.J. Strachan compiled his guide, *Open Air Sculpture* in 1984, there were 45 Moores in Britain, which accounted for over eight per cent of works by modern sculptors in public places.

During the exhibition at the Serpentine, Henry Moore was in the process of considering a suggestion by Sir Robert Marshall that one of his major pieces should be sited in Greenwich Park. Moore liked the idea and selected *Large Standing Figure: Knife Edge* (1961), which was loaned by the Henry Moore Foundation. Marshall's intention was 'to show the work of a great artist in a great place'. Greenwich was also a focus for his and the artist's social interests as a site where the 'rich community of Blackheath met the poorer community of Tower Hamlets'.

Sculptures in Kensington Gardens
By the time the Moores came to be sited in Kensington Gardens, albeit temporarily, there were already several permanent sculptures on view to the public.

The Gardens had been open to the public – or more specifically members of the public who were not soldiers, sailors or servants – since George II's time. His move to Buckingham Palace meant that Kensington

Palace was no longer a principal Royal residence and in subsequent years the park opened full time.

The sculptures in Kensington Gardens date from 1858. Conforming to Victorian conventions, the majority are memorials. They include the statue of the scientist *Edward Jenner* by W Calder-Marshall; the memorial to the explorer John Hanning Speke (1866); *The Albert Memorial* (1872), *Queen Victoria* (1893) and a bronze cast of G.F. Watt's *Physical Energy* (1907), which was originally designed for the Cecil Rhodes Memorial on Table Mountain, Cape Town. The Gardens also contain George Frampton's *Peter Pan* (1912). With the exception of *The Albert Memorial*, a gift of Queen Victoria, and *Physical Energy*, purchased by the Ministry of Works, all these works were paid for by public subscription. Other features include the various fountains in the Italian Gardens and the *Elfin Oak*, a stump from Richmond Park set up in 1928 and carved by the artist Ivor Innes with gnomes, elves and goblins.

Processes

Nine of Moore's sculptures were sited around Kensington Gardens by the exhibition's organisers. The majority were bronzes. *The Arch* was made of white fibreglass. It was sited along Longwater where it had what *The Times* 'Diary' described as 'the noblest prospect in London'. It stood directly opposite Watt's *Physical Energy*, sited on a rise on the other side of the Serpentine.

The fibreglass *Arch* was specifically made for exhibition purposes. It was originally intended for the British Council's exhibition of the artist's work in Florence in 1972, where it became a popular landmark for bridal couples having their photographs taken.

The subject of *The Arch* had already occupied Moore for some ten years. Other versions of the sculpture are sited all over the world – the maquette, the working model and the large bronze. The *Maquette for Large Torso: Arch* of 1962 (height 11cm, cast in a bronze edition of 9+1 in 1971). *Large Torso: Arch*, 1962-63 (height 199.5 cm) was cast in a bronze edition of 7+1. Casts are at the Museum of Modern Art, New York; Societa Assicuratrice Industriale, Turin; the University Art Gallery and Museum, Stanford and the Nelson-Atkins Museum, Kansas City. A large bronze 580cm version of *The Arch*, identical to the fibreglass and travertine carving, was cast in 1979-80 in an edition of 3+1. Casts are at the Cleo

The Arch, 1980, seen across Longwater © The Henry Moore Foundation

Rogers Memorial Library Plaza, Columbus, Indiana; the Sonja Henies og Niels Onstads Stiftelser, Høvikodden; the City Museum of Contemporary Art, Hiroshima and the Henry Moore Foundation. The production of limited multiple editions of the same work in different sizes is typical of Moore's working practice.

Interpretation
At the time of the exhibition, the Serpentine – like many other galleries – had no formal education programme as such, although it occasionally organised talks. The Arts Council had historically maintained that art should 'speak' to people directly. However, with the artist's help and encouragement, the Serpentine built a replica of Moore's maquette studio in the South Gallery. It was full of the artist's source material – such as bones and shells – displayed together with what the Director of the Serpentine, Sue Grayson, described as a 'few well chosen words from Moore's autobiographical writings'. The juxtapositions between these and the maquettes 'explained much better than anything else could have,

the ideas behind his work – that's what set the exhibition apart'. Two BBC videos about the artist and his work were also rented and shown during the period of the exhibition.

It was thus left to the exhibition catalogue to describe the Arts Council's, or rather the curators', attitudes towards the artist's work, to suggest the reasons for mounting the exhibition and explain what interests the work might hold for the public. According to Grayson, the exhibition catalogue sold out in about six weeks. A second, revised edition contained photographs of the replica of the artist's maquette studio.

The Introduction to the catalogue was written by David Sylvester, who had curated exhibitions and written about Henry Moore since the early 1950s, including the 70th birthday exhibition at the Tate Gallery. Sylvester was also closely associated with both the Arts Council and Serpentine Gallery itself, as guest curator and panel member. Some 15 years after the exhibition, he remained attached to the Serpentine Gallery in the capacity of a Trustee.

In his preamble to the catalogue, Sylvester wrote that it was 'impossible to generalise comprehensively about the nature of Moore's achievement in the period covered'. But he nevertheless offered several possible interpretations of the work – in particular, that it upheld the European sculptural tradition and that it represented universal, elemental experiences.

Referring back to a statement that the artist had made some 40 years previously in 1937, Sylvester proposed that Moore's 'mission'

> was to restore to European sculpture a traditional richness that had gone bad, had therefore to be sacrificed during a period of purification, but now had to be recovered.

He also believed that the works shown in the exhibition revealed a dominant preoccupation – one which Moore had himself described in the early 1960s.

> One of the things I would like to think my sculpture has is a force, is a strength, is a life, a vitality from inside it, so that you have a sense that the form is pressing from inside trying to burst or trying to give off the strength from inside itself, rather than having something which is shaped from outside and stopped (ACGB 1978).

According to Sylvester, Moore was increasingly preoccupied with 'tactile ... and motor sensations'.

> These sculptures show forth the experience of running one's hands over a body – and into a body ... And they show forth what is experienced in using one's body, feeling one's skin stretching tautly ... feeling the muscles tighten.

> There can be a marvellous uncertainty about what part is involved. And Moore's haptic metaphors are resonant with ambiguities.

> It all has to do, in a way, with sculpting like a blind man ... there is a still more universal, elemental sense of a blind, helpless need to live and to touch. Sculpture as expressive as this of the primacy of the tactile celebrates the fact that, whether we make love with the lights off or the lights on, the crucial contact happens in the dark (ACGB 1978).

It was presumably one of the intentions of the exhibition to demonstrate this and the newspaper correspondence columns of the time reflect similar sensibilities towards the work as those raised in Sylvester's catalogue essay.

The fact that people were allowed to touch the sculptures elicited positive responses and gave scope for them to appreciate the sculptures' tactile qualities. A registered blind person who wrote to the *Evening Standard*, for example, described Moore's work as offering 'one of the most moving and tactile experiences'. A correspondent to *The Times* (17.11.1978) described the works' sensual, existential and transcendent qualities.

> Have you not ever felt under your hand the vibrance of cold bronze or the vigorous undulation of smooth stone? No, you cannot see the grandeur of this enormous sculpture. Enormous in time and space.

> We see in Moore's work, the expression of mind through the acute perception of experience. Elemental beauty – love, mind, isolation, gaiety and overall truth. And with godlike craft, there, larger than life, almost nonchalantly like the hills – they ARE.

One characteristic of the exhibition frequently documented in the press was of children climbing over the sculptures. Moore endorsed this activity. It created a stark contrast with the conditions of display at the Tate Gallery where no one was allowed to even touch his work. One *Evening Standard* reader described the pleasure children took in sculptures they 'were actually able to touch'. An appreciation of the sculptures by a school child (aged seven) was published, presumably to make the point that the value of the works was so elemental that they appealed to the innocent, natural and untutored eye.

Several members of the public who were moved to write to the papers about the exhibition expressed a preference for experiencing art 'out in the open air', as opposed to its being 'hidden away in some claustro-phobic corner of a museum'. The designer of a 1968 exhibition of Moore's work at the Tate Gallery wrote to *The Times* to emphasise 'how much light from the open sky benefited such sculptures'. It was also argued that if Turner and Constable needed special museums, 'Moore needs a park'.

Writers to *The Times* and the *Kensington Post* focused on the respect due to Moore's status as the 'greatest living sculptor'. This not only certified the quality of his work, but legitimised the requirement that they should be kept for the public's benefit; 'the whole world knows Henry Moore'; 'Henry Moore is a member of the Order of Merit and a Compan-ion of Honour and consequently affects two of the nation's three highest honours.'

Dissenting voices proposed that to honour Henry Moore by a perma-nent memorial erected in his own lifetime would be to 'risk future vicissitudes in taste' – an argument which had previously been employed by the artistic community in their objections to the Wilson Government's offer of £200,000 to house Henry Moore's donations to the Tate in 1967. One correspondent, who pronounced himself a 'philistine', was unim-pressed 'by modern fashions in sculpture ... We remember the story of the emperor's clothes' and remain unmoved by the 'pressure from avant-gardistes'.

Differences in people's attitudes towards Moore's work were typified by his conflicting reputations: Moore as a respected member of the establishment and Moore as an 'avant-gardist'. As William Feaver pointed out in his *Observer* review of the exhibition (16.7.1978), the artist had

> virtually reestablished sculpture as something other than memorial statues and portrait busts. He also took over from Epstein as the chief laughing stock. Moore-ish holed sculpture became the longest running Modern Art joke.

Other members of the public most notably, dog walkers and regular park users – local residents – were less than enthusiastic. (Their reactions to *The Arch* recalled those provoked by Nicholas Munroe's blue *More-*

B Wiseman, Cartoon from the *New Yorker*, 3 November 1951 © *New Yorker*

cambe and Wise some years earlier.) This constituency particularly objected to the fact that the Serpentine's Director was reported to have said that they had come to love the work.

> Even regular park users who thought of [the sculptures] as hostile presences at first, have come round to accepting them and saying that they would be sorry to see them go ('Let's keep the Henry Moores', *Evening Standard* (10.10.1978).

This group formed so vocal a lobby that one leading supporter of the works referred to the 'apparent absence of public support' for the plan to keep the sculptures. One local resident, writing in the *Standard*, for example, felt

> for many years now we have walked round the Serpentine every morning ... far from agreeing that 'the bronzes fuse into the landscape' ... we feel most strongly that our early walk which we greatly enjoy has been very largely spoilt by the repeated shocks of those incongruous and grotesque sculptures.

> Who are these people who have given them 'such an enthusiastic response'? We haven't met one. We deplore the expense involved in creating them temporarily, let alone the enormous cost of buying them to clutter up the Gardens for ever, and nobody we know feels otherwise.

> I very much hope your campaign won't have misled people into thinking that they are unique in their dislike of the sculptures and that therefore they must be wrong (17.10.1978).

The sentiments of other writers to the newspaper were much the same.

Who are these Londoners who respond with such enthusiasm to the Henry Moore sculptures?

I am a regular dog walker in that area and I have not met one! Crude, vulgar and incomprehensible are the only words to describe these blots on the local landscape, and the sooner such monstrous objects are removed the better (17.10.1978).

"That reminds me, dear—did you remember the sandwiches?"

Fougasse, Cartoon from *Punch*, 27 June 1951 Reproduced by permission of *Punch*

The works were often described as 'grotesque' and 'objectionable'. Some considered they made an invidious comparison to the 'exquisite statue of *Peter Pan* and the little animals. It is by these that children and tourists pause in admiration.' One *Standard* reader thought it was 'not without significance, perhaps, that ... dogs can and do behave on them exactly as they please.' To Moore's detractors, children's use of the sculptures as playthings also confirmed their lack of artistic value.

Although the works were all based on natural forms, they were considered by some to be totally inappropriate for the 'natural' environment – 'an affront to the human, ornithological and horticultural life of the park'. Joanna Drew, then Director of Art at the Arts Council, recalled that subsequent plans to establish a 'sculpture park' were frustrated by everyone agreeing that 'this would frighten the ducks'. *The Arch*, which one writer described as a 'gigantic croquet hoop', was said to 'disfigure the North Bank'. Several correspondents expressed the desire for 'our delightful Kensington Gardens to go back to its own natural beauty'. But, as one correspondent to *The Times* noted, there was little that was natural about the park which was artificially landscaped. He was convinced that the presence of the sculptures in Kensington Gardens was

> contrary to the original Bridgemen design, where art was intended to imitate nature. Had he wanted sculptures in the park, he would have included them in his original plan (25.11.1978).

The campaign to keep the Moores

Some 120,000 people visited the Serpentine, over twice the number as saw the Henry Moore birthday exhibition in Bradford and over three times as many as had attended the Serpentine's most popular exhibition to date, photographs by Andre Kersetz. The Director of the Serpentine estimated that thousands more saw the sculptures in the park without going into the Gallery itself.

Press coverage undoubtedly contributed to the popularity of the exhibition. It also influenced perceptions of the exhibition and attitudes towards the work. Within three weeks of the exhibition opening, two letters had appeared in *The Times* requesting *The Arch* and one of the other sculptures shown in the park to remain as permanent fixtures. It was proposed that there should be a public subscription to buy one of the works for Kensington Gardens. The idea that the works should stay came to dominate public attitudes towards them. This was especially the case after 10 October, two days after the exhibition had closed, when the *Standard* ran an editorial initiating a campaign for the works in the park to be left permanently.

> Let the authorities take their courage in both hands and leave them all. They have created at the Serpentine a brilliant and accessible monument to our greatest artist. Let it prove to be a lasting one.

> Write to the *Standard* and tell us what you think. We shall publish the best letters and forward all of them to the Department for the Environment ('Let's keep the Henry Moores', 10.10.1978).

According to Simon Jenkins, then Editor of the *Evening Standard*, 'it seemed like a good idea at the time.'

As a result of the enormous public interest the works had aroused, towards the end of the exhibition it was agreed by the Arts Council and the DOE that five sculptures would stay in the park for longer than had been planned. Arrangements had already been made for three sculptures to go on permanent display elsewhere – two to the German Federal Chancellory and one to Dallas, Texas.

On 11 October the artist, whom the *Daily Express* (29.7.1978) described as the 'highest individual earner' in the British art world, announced that he would rather make a donation than have the public pay to keep his work

as everyone knows I do all right now and I'd rather give something.

I'm very pleased about the interest everyone has shown in the exhibition and I appreciate it enormously. When I think of 30 or 40 years ago and the terrible time Epstein had there's no doubt that public attitudes to sculpture have changed so much ... (Henry Moore Memento Offer', *Evening Standard*, 11.11.1978).

Within a week of the exhibition closing, the Prime Minister, James Callaghan, who had known Moore since the 1940s, visited the sculptures that remained in the park accompanied by the artist. Photographs of the two men together appeared in the *Standard* the same day – 13 October, the last day of the Tory Party conference. By his own account, Callaghan played a part in cementing Moore's international reputation in that he was

instrumental in bringing Moore together with Helmut Schmidt, who had long admired his work, with the result that after some negotiations, a remarkable example of Henry Moore's sculpture stands outside the German Chancellory.

Sue Grayson recalls that the matter of Henry Moore's work being permanently sited was settled over a lunch at Downing Street at which Simon Jenkins was also present. Within the month, Lady Birk wrote to *The Times* describing her optimism 'that some work by Henry Moore will find a permanent home in the Royal Park'.

The issue of Moore's sculptures becoming a permanent fixture continued to feature in the correspondence columns of the *Evening Standard* and *The Times* until the end of November. The letters, including those written in response to the *Standard*'s appeal, reveal a divergence of opinion both for and against the sculptures staying. Indeed, as one *Kensington Post* reader observed, the controversy over the Moores recalled the furore that had taken place 50 years earlier after Stanley Baldwin unveiled Jacob Epstein's *Rima* in Hyde Park, a memorial plaque to the naturalist W.H. Hudson. He thought this 'tame' by comparison with the Moores.

By 10 November the *Standard* confirmed that a 'recast' of *The Arch* had been earmarked as a permanent feature of Kensington Gardens. The choice of that particular piece seems to have been determined by various factors. Lady Birk believed that DOE's request for a fibreglass, as opposed to a bronze sculpture, was relatively modest. It was at Moore's insistence that a marble version was cut. Whereas stone and bronze versions had been made of other sculptures by him, *The Arch* had never been manufactured in stone. The choice also reflected a preference for what David Mitchinson, Curator of the Henry Moore Foundation, described as a more classical, monumental piece suited to the landscaping of the park and which from a distance resembles a folly.

The marble is based on the fibreglass version, which was sent to the quarry at Querceta, Italy, as a model for the masons to work from. There are no extant records of when the fibreglass version was removed from the park. The DOE, as the owners of the work, were responsible for the sculpture's installation. They, or rather the Department of National Heritage, remain responsible for its maintenance and indemnity. The Foundation paid for the carving of the sculpture and the cost of transport from Italy. The Serpentine Gallery liaised with the DOE and the Henry Moore Foundation.

The travertine version of *The Arch* was erected in autumn 1980. It was deliberately timed to take place out of the mating and nesting seasons so that it would not be subject to the objections of local bird lovers. It was sited set back from the path, behind a fence. This prevents the sculpture being touched, protects the surface and makes it harder to see where the slabs of marble join. By definition, it also mitigates against the public experiencing the sculpture's tactile value, its scale or fully experiencing its relationship to its surroundings.

The fibreglass *Arch* has subsequently been shown in Madrid and Lisbon in 1981; Hong Kong, Tokyo and Fukuoka in 1986. It has been at the Yorkshire Sculpture Park since 1987, which is now associated with the largest display of Moore's work in Britain.

Impact

None of those overtly involved in the production or the siting of *The Arch* evaluated its impact, either at the time of its erection or subsequently. However, the popularity of the exhibition and the level of interest it aroused was reported to have given an impetus to the work of the Sculpture Park Committee, provoking plans for what the Standard referred to as 'blossoming of sculptures in parks all over London' to take place the following Spring. Until then the committee's activities had been restricted to Regents Park and Hyde Park. According to Lady Birk they would be

> branching out into some of the other parks. I would really like to see sculptures in parks like Richmond and Bushey ... The idea of having outdoor sculpture, particularly in the parks, is really catching on (*Evening Standard*, 10.11.1978).

In the event, that optimism was short lived. The committee was disbanded in 1979 by Norman St John Stevas, Minister for the Arts, during the first term of the newly elected Conservative Government.

It could be that one effect of Moore's ordering of the travertine marble version of *The Arch* for the DOE was to contribute to his own reputation. Some critics, including William Feaver, believe that the artist's place in the establishment was maintained, if not partly secured, by his strategic donations to art institutions and government agencies of works to be displayed in public sites around the world (Channel 4, 1993). In 1977, only the year before the Serpentine's 80th birthday tribute, the artist had established the Henry Moore Foundation specifically to encourage the public appreciation of his work and the fine arts practices in which he was engaged – sculpture, drawing and print making. The Henry Moore Sculpture Trust, part of the Henry Moore Foundation, for example, supported the Chantreyland Sculpture Trail, (p. 185). Many of the Foundation's Trustees are drawn from institutions which supported Moore's career. Current post holders include Lord Goodman, formerly Chairman of the Arts Council and Joanna Drew, under whose Directorship of the Visual Arts Department the 80th birthday exhibition was mounted.

The paucity of response by the public in the correspondence columns of the newspapers to the arrival of the marble version of *The Arch* suggests that popular interest in the matter had waned during the two years since the original controversy started. The *Evening Standard* published one letter a week after Michael Heseltine, as Secretary of State for the Envi-

ronment, had unveiled the sculpture on 1 October 1980. It simply proposed that 'Mr Moore's monstrosity should be closeted in the Tate
Gallery where it belongs'.

Some 15 years later, a random survey of 60 park users one weekday
lunchtime for this report suggested that reactions to the sculpture remain
mixed (Appendix 2, p. 286). The sample was made up of roughly equal
numbers of regular and non-regular park users, including tourists, and
roughly equal numbers of people under and over 50 years old. (It does
not represent a cross-section of park users since workers and joggers were
loath to stop, and the profile of park visitors may change at weekends.)
The most frequently cited reason for interviewees' presence in the park
was to walk – some with children or dogs: to spend time there, relax, get
some fresh air, have lunch or feed the ducks and squirrels. Although
nearly 70 per cent of those interviewed professed to like art, two specified
that this did not include modern art. None were intending to visit the
Serpentine Gallery, which was open at the time interviews were being
carried out.

Over 80 per cent of the sample noticed *The Arch*. In their words, it was
'hard to miss', 'intrusive', 'different'. They had become conscious of it
'because it's there', because of its 'size and shape' or because it was 'ugly'
or 'not very good'. Conversely, others had noticed it because it was
'interesting', 'beautifully done', 'because it's by Henry Moore'. One was
curious and had 'wondered why it was there'. About half the sample
knew it was by Henry Moore, although 40 per cent doubted that knowing
who the artist was would affect what they thought about it. None
suggested that their perception of it had been affected by knowing who
the artist was. One interviewee observed that she had enjoyed it without
knowing who the artist was.

People's reflections about the work tended to refer to its context. It
was described as 'enhancing the gardens', 'it goes nicely with the shapes
in the park', 'frames the landscape', 'spoils the view of the sunset'. It was
also compared to other sculptures in the park. People preferred *Peter Pan*,
or expressed their like or dislike of *The Arch* by comparison to the
'equestrian statue'. One interviewee thought there were 'not enough
sculptures for people to look and wonder at'. People attached some
importance to the fact that the sculpture stimulated them to use their
imagination. It was described as 'uplifting', and more often identified

with other things – 'a woman's pelvis', 'the bottom half of a human body', 'giant legs', 'a modern version of a gate'.

There was a sense that *The Arch* was not for the regular park users: 'The sculpture is more for tourists than for locals. None of my friends notice the sculptures'. One assumed it was there to 'serve a good purpose' but did not elaborate; another decided to 'look more closely next time'. It would appear that regular park users aged over 50 were the least appreciative of it, implying that people do not necessarily come to appreciate public art through familiarity.

Art at Broadgate
Hackney and the City of London 1986-1994

Background
The Act of Parliament for the redevelopment of the Liverpool Street Station received Royal Ascent in April 1983. The British Rail Board had proposed financing improvements to the station by the building of over one million square feet of offices on a ten acre site above and around it. The site, which surrounds the station on three sides, encompassed the old Broad Street Station. It comprised a declining railway system, shops and car park. The original designs for the new station proposed the radical, wholesale removal of the 19th century buildings. However, these plans aroused considerable opposition, largely mobilised by conservationists and were refused planning permission.

In response to the controversy, British Rail invited new proposals for the site and appointed Broadgate Properties PLC (formerly Rosehaugh Stanhope Developments PLC) from a shortlist of eight developers. Rosehaugh Stanhope Developments, as its name suggests, was formed by the partnership of Rosehaugh and Stanhope – two of the UK's premier property development companies. The reconstruction of the station itself was designed by British Rail's Architecture & Design Group, which incorporated and extended the 19th century buildings and design features. The Master Plan for Broadgate was drawn up for Broadgate Properties by Arup Associates, an internationally renowned architectural practice.

From the outset, the developers and architects were concerned to avoid the ghetto-ising effect of some corporate developments, what

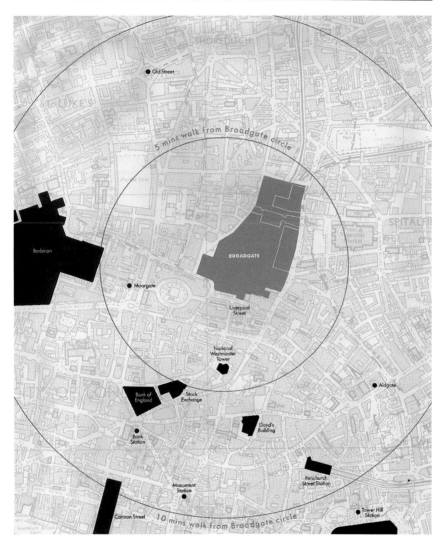

Map showing the location of public art works at Broadgate from *Broadgate: A Working Guide*, DEGW for Broadgate Properties, 1989

William H. Whyte referred to as 'the urban fortresses' whose 'distinguishing characteristic is self-containment' (Whyte 1988). Arup Associates conceived of Broadgate as 'an opportunity to create a major new part of the City – in its widest sense – as opposed to just building some new office blocks.' The design was generated by patterns of movement of people coming to the site from Liverpool Street and the surrounding area. It was intended to create a network of streets and three new public squares which would connect the development with the fabric of the City.

Construction started in 1986. Broadgate was planned in 14 Phases. Arup Associates worked on Phases 1-4, which were completed between December 1986 and July 1988; Skidmore, Owings and Merrill (SOM), the Chicago-based, worldwide architectural practice which was employed at Canary Wharf, designed Phases 5-14. Phases 5-11 were completed between October 1988 and July 1991 and Phase 14 in November 1991. Broadgate's completion was marked by the Queen's visit in December 1991.

Planning authorities

Plans for Broadgate had to comply with the criteria of two local planning authorities whose boundaries ran through the site – the Corporation of London (to the east) and Hackney (to the west). They are respectively one of the richest and one of the most deprived boroughs in Britain. Both serve radically different constituencies of interest.

During the 1980s the Corporation of the City of London deliberately encouraged new building. The deregulation of financial controls (1982) had increased the City's importance in respect to world markets. The Corporation's concern to attract new developments was such that, given the physical constraints of the Square Mile, it encouraged developers to build over roads and railways. The impetus to attract development to the City was further spurred by the simultaneous development of Canary Wharf in the Enterprise Zone created on the Isle of Dogs – less than five miles away.

According to Peter Wynne Rees, City Planning Officer, Corporation of London, the City's planning priorities are directed towards 'the well being of the financial community'. Whereas some 4,000 people live in the Square Mile, over a quarter of a million people work there. The Corporation's interest in Broadgate was essentially fourfold: having refused planning permission for the original scheme, it wanted to ensure the satisfactory restoration and redevelopment of Liverpool Street Station; it required the development of an efficient transport interchange which would not have a detrimental effect on listed buildings; it wanted to improve the shopping and services in the area and it wanted to ensure the 'permeability' of the site and the creation of public open spaces.

Whereas Broadgate was only one of several large scale developments to be built in the City during the 1980s, it represented a watershed for Hackney. It was the first substantial commercial development to take place within the borough. Its earliest phases were built almost wholly within the borough's boundaries. According to Ray Michael, Director of Environmental Services, London Borough of Hackney, Broadgate was important in that it promised to change people's perceptions of Hackney.

> We were concerned it should be a special development, not just a series of rent slabs, so right from the start, it was part of the planning brief that it should develop a character that contributed more to the area than just pure employment in the office blocks.

The positive aspects of Broadgate's relationship to the borough were symbolised by the Hackney Gate to the estate, opened by the Mayor. Its proximity to the coat of arms of the City of London suggests that Broadgate broke through the traditional separation of the respective boroughs' financial and cultural identities.

Hackney had several requirements of Broadgate, most of which were met through planning gain. They included the construction of public spaces.

> We were concerned that there should be public spaces that would generate activity and interest, rather than people coming in, doing a day's work and going off again. There was a need for shops, pubs and cafes. We were also very keen to establish some kind of performance space (Michael).

The borough was also concerned that training would be provided for Hackney residents, partly to improve their opportunities for employment and partly to

> attempt to integrate Hackney residents into working with the financial sector. As a local authority we were keen to promote that. Broadgate Properties were willing partners (Michael).

Hackney also acquired a railway viaduct between Dalston and Broad Street from British Rail, which would allow the borough to provide premises for small businesses at a low cost and control the environment along the one and a half miles of railway track and which might, in the future, enable them to improve the borough's transport network.(At the time of research, they were discussing the possibility of extending the East London Line to Dalston with London Underground.) Hackney also required Broadgate Properties to repave and surface the streets around the site, and replace existing street furniture, thereby improving the general environment.

Neither planning authority was explicitly concerned with, or prioritised, the provision of public art in their planning agreements. As Michael observed

> What is interesting about the public art at Broadgate is that it was developer-led.

Broadgate Properties: Research & Development

From 1985 Broadgate Properties commissioned a series of reports which not only ensured the cost effectiveness of the construction of the development, but enabled the company to anticipate, if not match, the needs of tenants.

> Stanhope's strategy is to add value to its developments through research on the requirements of buildings users, intelligent and attractive design, efficient, innovative and safe construction and prudent financing, all yielding quality and value for money. The intention is to minimise the risks involved by development, assuring that tenants will select Stanhope's buildings despite choice on the market (Stanhope undated: 28).

As a result of research into North American building methods, Broadgate was built at an average of 2.5 times the weekly rate of building than the average construction in USA and UK in 1986 (Stanhope undated:7). It required a highly skilled and motivated workforce.

Research also showed that international banking companies could not be accommodated in refurbished old buildings and that immediate physical proximity to the Bank of England and the Stock Exchange was no longer a major priority. However, large clear trading floors (up to 50,000 square feet) with high performance mechanical, electrical and telecommunications services were essential requirements. Buildings needed to accommodate miles of cabling and provide air-conditioning, power and lighting. These technological needs would inevitably inform the design and construction of the building. The prototype referred to was Number 1 Finsbury Avenue, situated on the corner of the Broadgate site, which Arup Associates had designed for Rosehaugh Greycoat Estates Ltd. (Greycoat's Managing Director, Stuart Lipton subsequently formed Stanhope Properties PLC.)

Broadgate Properties' research also showed that if foreign banks and financial services were to locate in the City – as opposed to Frankfurt, Brussels or the Isle of Dogs – it needed an alternative to 'rent slabs'. It required buildings with strong architectural identity situated in agreeable and well maintained surroundings, with a sense of place.

It was fundamental to the planning of Broadgate that it functioned as a public space. The estate was planned around three open spaces, the only public squares to be built in the City this century. Vehicular circulation was planned below ground, leaving the new areas free for pedestrians. Although Broadgate is, strictly speaking, a private estate, signs invite the public in to use the shops and leisure facilities, to partake of the entertainments, use the space for recreation and to enjoy the trees and water feature. In winter the circular Arena in Broadgate Square is flooded and frozen to make an ice rink. In the summer (between May and September) there is a programme of free live entertainment. This concept was also based on European and North American examples. As Roger Whiteman of SOM, observed, the investment required to build those spaces has produced considerable returns.

It was in this context that art was introduced into the estate. David Blackburn, Development Director, Rosehaugh Stanhope Developments recalled

> We regarded Broadgate as an extremely unattractive site that had associations that were far from positive in the minds of many people. We had to create a place that would be successful, attracting tenants to go there; making it profitable for us doing it, and making it attractive for people to work in and pass through ... Art was only one element of that totality [along with] architecture, open spaces – all creating the general environment.

Works of art at Broadgate were intended to unite the estate.

> ... they're on the outside, the streets, in the spaces, they go into the entrance halls, they go into the tenants spaces ... really what we're interested in, in a way, is not the building, it's the spaces between the building. These make cities (Lipton cited in BBC 1993).

Art has also been used at Broadgate to other ends. In 1989, Stuart Lipton commissioned Robert Mason, an artist whose studio at Shoreditch was near the site, to paint a single picture 'based on the redevelopment' for Stanhope's offices. In the event, Mason spent 15 months on site and produced some 150 paintings and prints in collaboration with the photo-

Robert Mason,
Phase II: Rainy Day,
1989 Collection:
Stanhope plc
© The artist and
Stanhope plc

grapher, Edward Woodman. Both his work and his presence on site is said to have contributed to the close working relationships between construction teams during the building of the estate.

Mason's intention was to express 'the commitment, skills and dedication of the workforce'. He worked during day and night shifts, attended site and union meetings. The work he produced included some 90 portraits of workers, managers, planners and developers and dramatic scenes drawn from such viewpoints as the tops of cranes, the sewers and the ventilation shafts.

According to the artist

The work was of great interest to the workers – who were regular visitors to my studio. A number own pictures and their friendship continues to this day. They attend exhibitions of these and subsequent paintings.

Works completed during Mason's residency were given to individuals, hung in the various buildings and UCATT union headquarters. Prints were given to each of the trade contractors.

Arts events have also been used at Broadgate to attract people into its spaces and to give Broadgate 'a sense of its place in the local and international community'. During the 1991/92 season of events, publicised in the monthly 'Broadgate Live' leaflet, installations and performance art events were programmed alongside jazz, new music, performances by students and local artists, the City of London festival, street theatre, new circus and live relays from the Olympics.

Processes

Permanent works of public art at Broadgate
At the time of writing, there were some 24 works in Broadgate's public and semi-public spaces, which include Broadgate Club and the lobbies of particular buildings. Thirteen permanent works are sited in Broadgate's public spaces. Of those, two thirds were commissioned, the rest, purchased. They include sculptures, a 'window drawing', ornamental gates and a 'water feature'. The last major art work, Bruce McLean's _Eye-I_, was completed in 1994. Neither the decorative paving and the seating designed by the architects, nor the signage by Pentagram are referred to in Broadgate Properties's list of artworks at Broadgate.

No public art agency was employed. Commissions are issued by Broadgate Properties directly to the artists and their agents. The development team is responsible for managing the commissions, liaising with the artists and architects, transporting and physically installing the works. Schedules are monitored by the Broadgate Properties project manager. The works are maintained by Broadgate Estates.

Both architectural practices employed at Broadgate had prior experience of working with artists. Both are multi-disciplinary practices, and employ various specialisms required in the construction of major developments such as civil and civic engineers. Arup Associates regard

Works commissioned for the public spaces at Broadgate

Richard Serra	*Fulcrum* 1987, bronze	Octagon	Phase 3
Alan Evans	*Ornamental Gates*	Sun St entrance	Phase 4
Michael Craig Martin	*Globe & Umbrella Window Drawing*	Bishopsgate	Phase 8
Fernando Botero	*Broadgate Venus* 1990, bronze	Exchange Sq	Phase 9/10
J Gardy Artigas	*Tiled Fountain* ceramic	West Wing	Phase 11
Xavier Corbero	*The Broad Family* basalt	Exchange Sq	Phase 11
Stephen Cox (consultant)	*Water Feature*	Exchange Sq	Phase 11
Bruce McLean	*Eye-I*	Pindar Place	Phase 14

Works purchased for the public spaces at Broadgate

George Segal	*Rush Hour* 1983/87, bronze	Finsbury Ave Sq	Phase 1
Jacques Lipchitz	*Bellerophon Taming Pegasus* 1966, bronze	Pavillion	Phase 2
Barry Flanagan	*Leaping Hare on Crescent & Bell* bronze	Broadgate Sq	Phase 4
Stephen Cox	*Ganapathi & Davi* stone	Sun St roundabout	Phase 4
J Gardy Artigas	*Bronze planters*	Hackney Gate	Phase 5

collaborating with artists as an extension of their multi-disciplinary practice. Each architectural practice discussed certain proposals with artists while their own designs were still on the drawing board.

Funding

The permanent artworks at Broadgate were funded by a percent mechanism – inspired by American and European models. The budget allocated for art amounted to £6 million, one per cent of £600 million construction costs at the time of planning agreements (1984/1985). Percent for Art was used as a device to secure funds within the overall budgets. Sums were allocated for different Phases of the development and covered the commissioning, purchasing and enabling costs – planning details, engineering, transport, insurance etc.

BROADGATE

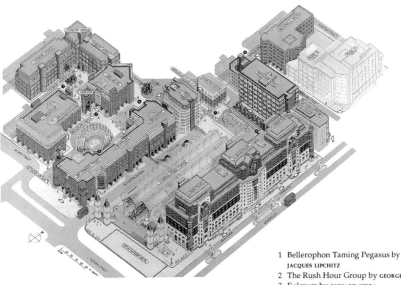

Broadgate: Visitors Map showing locations of public art works © Wordsearch

1 Bellerophon Taming Pegasus by JACQUES LIPCHITZ
2 The Rush Hour Group by GEORGE SEGAL
3 Fulcrum by RICHARD SERRA
4 Ganapathi & Davi by STEPHEN COX
5 Leaping Hare on Crescent & Bell by BARRY FLANAGAN
6 Broadgate Venus by FERNANDO BOTERO
7 The Broad Family by XAVIER CORBERO
8 Tiled Fountain by JOAN ARTIGAS
9 Ornamental Gates by ALAN EVANS

Interpretation and dissemination

In 1992 Broadgate Properties produced a guide to the Art at Broadgate, which comprises a map of the estate showing the location of art works and giving details of how access could be gained to those in semi-public sites. It also contained an introduction to the works by the critic Marina Vaizey, a photograph and a description of each piece.

Siting, selection and commissioning

The original master plan for Broadgate drawn up by Arup Associates indicated locations for the proposed artworks. Decisions about the theme, contents and appearance of each work were made phase by phase. The range of the art works at Broadgate was always intended to be catholic.

Two of the Directors of Broadgate Properties, Stuart Lipton and David Blackburn, are personally interested in contemporary art. Both collect. David Blackburn is a Trustee of Art & Architecture, an organisation which exists to promote the relationship between the two. Lipton is involved with the fine arts and housing the arts. He advised on the building of the Sainsbury Wing at the National Gallery (1985-91), the Sackler Galleries at the Royal Academy (1988-91) and the new opera house at Glyndebourne. He has been a Trustee of the Whitechapel Art Gallery and on the Advisory Board of the Royal Academy since 1987 and is a Commissioner of the Royal Fine Art Commission.

The selection of works involved the two Directors, both sets of architects, and advisors including Nicholas Serota, Director of the Tate Gallery and the Contemporary Art Society. Tenants of pre-let buildings and those whose offices would be particularly close to works, were also involved to the extent of endorsing choices. However, as Blackburn stressed, final responsibility for the works lay with the company itself.

> We were not concerned with customers or shareholders, the art was no more relevant a consideration than any other aspect of the business. The job of people running a business is to run it in the way they think is right, having regard to the interests of their shareholders and customers, but they are not going to be second guessed, or feel they have to justify themselves in a different way with respect to art decisions.

The methods by which pieces were selected varied. There were often several proposals for each location. The Directors sometimes commissioned work from particular artists and on other occasions they invited artists to submit proposals. Some would be developed, others not. Broadgate Properties and its architects found potential artists through exhibition catalogues, magazines, gallery and studio visits. Cox's *Ganapathi & Davi*, for example, was first seen at the Bath Festival, 1988 and purchased for a specific site. Sometimes the Contemporary Art Society brought paintings to Broadgate for works to be selected *in situ* for the lobbies of various buildings.

Lipton is reported to maintain that 'good architecture equals good business'. 'Good' art was similarly perceived as an investment. Many of the artists whose work is represented at Broadgate are internationally known. The Americans George Segal and Richard Serra, and the British artists Stephen Cox and Bruce McLean all appeared in Dr Willi Bongard's 'Kunst Atlas' and 'Kunst Kompass' – a series of periodical features, which between 1971 and 1985 regularly charted the shifting fortunes of a 'top 100 contemporary artists'. (Sol Lewitt and Jim Dine, whose work is displayed in lobbies at Broadgate also appeared in Bongard's lists.)

Briefs and contracts
The briefs and contracts issued by Broadgate Properties to artists are highly specific. As with any other contractor these are intended to ensure that Broadgate Properties's criteria are met.

As Barry Winfield, Project Director for Broadgate Properties, who has been involved in the briefing and development of many of the works, explained that the company was interested in works which might stretch or 'challenge' people's attitudes to art. Although 'absolutely open to ideas' the company would not commission works which might be construed as political or promoting causes, sexual or moral. In the words of one of the artists, Richard Serra, there was 'no aesthetic agenda'.

Contracts were only issued by Broadgate Properties at maquette stage. This ensured that

> we knew exactly what we were getting. There's a motto at Skidmore, Owings and Merrill that there should never be any surprises (Whiteman).

A contract and schedule agreed between Broadgate Properties and a commissioned artist is reproduced in Appendix 7, p. 348.

Fulcrum by Richard Serra

The major work commissioned for Phases 1-4 was Richard Serra's *Fulcrum*, placed at the Liverpool Street/Eldon Street entrance to the development. The guide to the *Art at Broadgate* (Rosehaugh Stanhope Developments 1992:9) describes the work as 'a tower, or sentinel' which 'acts as a remarkable pivot for the Broadgate environment'.

Richard Serra, born in San Francisco in 1939 of half-Spanish, half-Jewish parentage, is one of the most controversial and respected sculptors of today. There are several of his sculptures in Paris and other major cities in Europe and America. He has worked in lead, concrete and stone but most characteristically in steel and cor-ten steel. His weighty pieces, using these industrial and building materials, are totally abstract and usually about balance, lightness, air and vast vistas – although they sometimes indicate shelter as well and are often indicative of boundaries and walls. *Fulcrum* (1986-7) is Serra's only public art work in Britain to date.

Background

Serra was approached by Lipton, who had seen an exhibition of his work at the prestigious Saatchi Gallery, London, where Blackburn's wife worked. The exhibition ran from September 1986 to July 1987. The fact that Serra's work was shown at Saatchi's was in itself significant. The Gallery exhibits works exclusively drawn from Charles Saatchi's collection of contemporary art. When the gallery opened in 1985, the collection was hailed as the 'greatest body of contemporary art ever assembled'. It was detailed in a four volume catalogue entitled *The Art of Our Time*, which retailed for £100. The gallery came to be regarded as a barometer of fashionable taste. Although private, the collection is sometimes thought of as having acquired national status.

It is indicative of the high esteem with which Serra's work is regarded in the London art world that from the end of September 1992 to the middle of January 1993 (when the research for this report was in progress), the entire space of the central Duveen Sculpture Gallery at the Tate was cleared to exhibit one work by him. The Director of the Tate was one of the advisors for the art at Broadgate.

Like other manifestations of minimalism, Serra's work characteristically reveals no mark of the artist's hand. It is often produced by industrial processes. It has been suggested that such works are

Richard Serra, *Fulcrum*, 1987 © Sara Selwood

essentially only regarded as works of art in the context of a disclosure in which they stood as compelling proof of the unfolding of a certain historical inevitability. Lay spectators only recognise such objects as art (when, or if they do so) because they are located within the legitimising contexts of the gallery and museum, installed by curators and dealers in thrall (Chave 1990: 45).

Serra's work is often determined by the nature of the space within which it is sited and for which it has been made. The works are typically large and heavy, and installed with no visible support. The display of the artist's so-called 'prop' pieces in museums has been described as threatening.

The paradigmatic relationship between work and spectator in Serra's art is that between bully and victim, as his work tends to treat the viewer's welfare with contempt. This work not only looks dangerous, it is dangerous: The 'prop pieces' in museums are often roped off or alarmed and sometimes, especially in the process of installation and de-installation, they fall and injure or even (on one occasion) kill (Chave 1990: 58).

Serra's work is thus often characterised as 'macho, overbearing, oppressive'. As he conceded:

if one is conceiving a piece for a public place ... one has to consider the traffic flow, but not necessarily worry about the indigenous community, and get caught up in the politics of the site (Chave 1990:58).

To have commissioned Serra to produce a work for a private development in 1987 represented some risk on the part of Broadgate Properties. Serra has the reputation for being uncompromising and was, therefore, unlikely to create an affirmative work which would comply with conventional standards of corporate embellishment. More specifically, at the time of the Broadgate commission, the case of *Titled Arc* was being heard in the New York Federal Courts following a citizens action to have it removed. This substantially contributed to the mythology of the artist's work being popularly disliked.

Tilted Arc was commissioned for the square between the federal building and courthouse in Manhattan. The artist's intention was that it should 'encompass the people who walk on the plaza in its volume ... After the piece is created the space will be understood primarily as a function of the sculpture' (Serra cited in Storr 1985: 92). Following its installation in 1981, the work was greeted with marked hostility, manifest in letters to the media and a petition signed by 1,300 employees of the complex demanding its removal. People objected to being involuntarily involved and condemned 'to lead emptier lives' (Joseph Liebman, attorney at the International Trade Office, cited in Weyergraf-Serra 1991). Testimony at the hearing suggested that the working population of the offices in whose plaza it was sited, found *Titled Arc* intrusive, not to say totalitarian.

> I didn't expect to hear the arrogant position that art justified interference with the simple joys of human activity in a plaza. It's not a great plaza by international standards, but it is a small refuge for people who ride to work in steel containers, work in sealed rooms and breathe recycled air all day. Is it the purpose of art in pubic places to seal off a route of escape, to stress the absence of joy and hope?' ('Transcript: The Storm in the Plaza, excerpts from the General Services Administration hearing on the *Tilted Arc*, *Harpers*, July 1985, cited by Chave 1990: 59-86)

In stark contrast the artist's assertion was that the work exerted a 'beginning, civilising effort'.

The commission

At the time Lipton approached Serra, according to the artist

> Broadgate had just begun. They didn't really know exactly how the art was going to be placed, or where. They asked me to come in at the very initial stages and talk with people from Arup.

Serra initially visited the site when the frame and cladding for two of the buildings had been erected and the space between them had been designed, but the site itself was still 'mud'. The artist and architect agreed on the siting for the piece, and the nature of the physical relationship between the sculpture and the buildings.

> There was one walk down area they wanted to make either five, six, seven or eight sided, adjacent to the opening of the rink, where they thought it would be possible to make a sculptural inclusion. They asked me if I thought it would be possible to work there.

> We talked about campanile and we talked about how sculptures and artifacts of those kinds had functioned in piazzas and at the ends of intersections or whatever. I came to the conclusion that the piece needed a certain height – 40 feet or so, or higher; it needed a certain width; it needed the potential to collect people and act as a conduit, a place where people could walk into or locate, meet or gather.

The title of the work derives from the function Serra describes. A fulcrum is literally the point at which a lever gets a purchase, against which it turns or is supported. Broadgate Properties required the work to serve as a 'central beacon', to punctuate the entrance to the site, articulate the flow of movement in and out and open up the different vistas.

The artist also wanted to allow other possibilities for the work.

> It also needed to present art as art. Not just to be subservient to some projected populist notion of satisfying or enhancing or decoration or being used as application.

One of his intentions for the work was that 'in some sense it exposes the quality – good or bad – of the buildings'. This essentially critical characteristic was something which the commissioners accepted without demur.

> To tell you the truth, these people were very open in that they had no misconceptions about what a work of art ought to be. They didn't tell me that I had to satisfy an aesthetic agenda – so to speak – which I thought was fairly liberated on their part. Nor did it seem to me that they were interested in having a work of art function as a [symbol] of their liberalism. The work wasn't going to be coopted by the context.

> There really was a possibility of making a piece of work as art and having people reflect on sculpture as sculpture and think about the continuity of what sculpture was and what possibilities might become. Broadgate Properties had its own artistic ambitions for the work.

Blackburn, who particularly admired Serra, believed it was going to be a very important piece of art.

> We had an opportunity of bringing this to London and to Broadgate.

Commissioning Serra represented a way of Broadgate Properties displaying its own metal. According to Blackburn.

> I didn't for a moment imagine that it would yield dividends for us in the short-term, but I did feel that it would contribute very significantly to the perception of the whole place over a period of time. I could have gone for something that in the short-term would have been more successful, attractive, acclaimed and which might, quite frankly, have done as much for creating the image of Broadgate as that sculpture.

But he felt that

> There is a real space for somebody who has the courage of his own convictions and doesn't have to justify everything in a very formalistic or commercial way ... not to say he is losing sight of those.

Peter Foggo, who led the Arup Associates team, professed to have had 'no idea' of what Serra would do until the artist produced a maquette. The work proposed comprised five leaning sheets of oxidized cor-ten steel, so arranged as to turn through their height. In the event, there were few objections to Serra's proposal.

> We went ahead and proposed a piece 55 feet high with five plates, which you can enter into. We presented a model of one inch to a foot, in other words 55 inches. We talked to all the engineers, developers and architects. It had to pass their board. As I recall, the only alteration they asked was that the openings to walk into the volume, which is probably about 24 feet across and that you can collect in, were about three and half feet and we opened it up to about five feet. That was the only objection they had. They thought that if the entrances were too tight the piece would be too claustrophobic. They were worried about who knows what – molestations, or whatever. That seemed something I could live with. We opened it up to five feet.

The steel plates which the work comprises were constructed in Germany and installed by Serra and his team. Since the work itself, which weighs some 240 tons was unwelded, Arups constructed a sunken conical base for it. The work was installed prior to paving.

Serra was the only artist to be commissioned at Broadgate at this stage of the development. Although Stanhope's described the relationship between the artist and architect as close, according to Foggo communication between Serra and Arups was 'slight' and was carried out via the artist's agent. Foggo's philosophy was not to interfere with the artwork. By the same token, he expected the artist to treat his work with similar regard.

Introduction to the public

The installation of the major works at Broadgate were conventionally marked by an unveiling ceremony and a party to which members of the art world, press and tenants were invited. Workers, tenants and the local authorities were kept in touch through the regular Broadgate newsletter.

Planning authorities

The site for Phases 1-4 runs across the Hackney and City of London boundary and the two planning authorities met to consult.

Lipton regarded both planning authorities as 'helpful, pleased to have public art and welcomed it'. The authorities themselves described processing the planning applications for the artworks in the 'most low key manner'. Adhering to the principles of planning guidance, neither wanted to impose judgements on matters of artistic taste. Rees for example, says

> I listen to avant-garde string quartets in the privacy of my own home, but I wouldn't wish to thrust them on everybody. I'm quite happy, and indeed thrilled, that you can have pop music channels and the light music channels broadcasting music for every taste ... (cited in BBC 1993).

Michael's attitude was much the same.

> We had a role in that we were asked for our views and to comment on the intended pieces of art. I suppose we could have insisted on some kind of formal decision, but we felt it was not a planning or a local authority function to ... comment on the actual quality or the content ... or to execute any degree of censorship ... Although one can have a viewpoint about particular pieces of art, I don't subscribe to the view that there should be an institutional right or wrong for this kind of thing. Otherwise, I would have been very wary about the Richard Serra ... I didn't want my view to be a significant part of it.

In respect of planning legislation, Hackney would only have carried out a public consultation about the work if there was a resident population in the vicinity.

Rees emphasised that it was not his committee's place to be involved in 'matters of taste. Their concern is with matters of safety and siting'. With respect to the art works in Exchange Square, which falls within the City's boundaries, they were concerned with the precise locations and scale of particular works. Blackburn's recollection was that they expressed considerably more criticisms of what was proposed than Hackney.

Impact and evaluation

Objectives
To summarise, aspirations for Broadgate ranged from the general to the specific. The two planning authorities' needs were essentially pragmatic. The City needed to attract new developments. It also wanted an efficient transport interchange, the creation of public open spaces, better shops and services. Hackney similarly wanted public spaces that would generate interest, shops, pubs and cafes and some kind of performance space. The borough was also concerned that training would be provided for its residents.

Broadgate Properties aspired for Broadgate to become a major new part of the City, in the widest sense. It wanted to attract tenants, have people want to work in and visit the estate and ultimately to make a profit.

However, as Martin Pawley the architectural writer observed, Lipton prefers to talk about art and architecture than 'what he really knows about [and] what he brought to the City of London ... fast building' (BBC 1993). Lipton describes his ambition as wanting to 'ensure the quality of the space between buildings'. Art, he believed, is 'integral' to that, in

> enhancing the nature of the environment, providing scale, humanity and the *genus loci* that is the fundamental ingredient of successful urban design (Rosehaugh Stanhope Developments 1992).

> We put pieces of art all around Broadgate because art is part of life's activity and yes, we enjoy it. I think people enjoy it (Lipton, cited in BBC 1993).

Broadgate Properties had other artistic ambitions. The Serra represented a opportunity for the company to commission 'a very important piece of art', which would create an image of Broadgate. In this case, if not in all the others, the artist had his own agenda. Serra wanted to present 'art as art ... not just to be subservient to some projected populist notion of ... decoration'.

Fulfilment of objectives
Many of these objectives for Broadgate were satisfied as a matter of course. The planning authorities got an efficient transport interchange, with a reconstructed Liverpool Street Station and bus station. Public open spaces, better shops, services and a performance space were provided.

Although there has been no recent analysis of audiences at the Broadgate events, Hackney residents are doubtless among them. At the time of research, the borough was looking to organise a 'Hackney Festival', which would involve activities on the estate and 'hopefully bring people from other parts of Hackney to Broadgate'. Hackney also benefitted by what Michael described as 'a significant training programme'. This included construction training, employment incentives, arrangements for schools to use the ice rink and assistance in other areas. Over and above that, the borough was able to levy a Business Rate on those companies operating out of Broadgate. However, the subsequent introduction of the National Non-Domestic Rate has removed that direct benefit from Broadgate.

Corporation of London
In respect of the Corporation of London, Broadgate appears to have been a model development. In its Unitary Development Plan (UDP) (deposited, November 1991) the City adopted the following objectives 'to improve the provision, attractiveness and accessibility of open space'and to 'encourage the incorporation of art and art works into the urban scene, in appropriate locations'. Noting the increasing popularity of informal events, such as those associated with the City Festival (hosted at Broadgate), the Corporation also committed itself to continuing 'to support the provision of art, cultural and entertainment facilities and to encourage further provision by other organisations'.

Broadgate's success reflects well on the City. Between 1987 and 1992 it won 31 awards from bodies concerned with architecture, construction, planning and art. The latter include a commendation by Art & Work Awards (1990) and the ACGB/ British Gas Working for Cities Award (1991). These awards in general and the RTPI Jubilee Cup for Planning Achievement (1992) in particular, suggest that the City's planners are regarded as 'having done a good job' and that they are ultimately contributing to making the area attractive to business.

Hackney
Broadgate's impact on Hackney has been very different.

> Broadgate's relationship to Hackney culture is minimal. It is very much an outlay of the authority. I don't think it has had any significant impact on the lives of the majority of Hackney residents, although hopefully a number of

Hackney residents work in Broadgate in various capacities and they benefit from the whole of the development including the public art.

It is probably seen as a one-off isolated part of the borough which has a totally different character to the other areas of Hackney. However, it remains our aim to try to strengthen the relationship and make Broadgate a springboard for the arts and culture of the borough (Michael).

Hackney's official relationship with Broadgate was expected to change after April 1994. This is when the authorities' boundaries were revised and Broadgate became part of the City. Hackney will still benefit financially from Broadgate – albeit indirectly. Under the Rate Equalisation Scheme the City has to render up 90 per cent of its rates for redistribution to other boroughs.

Broadgate may have impacted on Hackney's own plans for the development of the borough in other ways. It may have partly influenced the authority's adoption of a Percent for Art policy as outlined in its UDP and the integration of public art into its City Challenge bid for which they received substantial support from Broadgate Properties Project Directors. However, Hackney's approach to public art, which involves 'working with the community', is unlike that employed at Broadgate.

Broadgate Properties
Broadgate is generally agreed to have been a considerable success for Broadgate Properties, as its awards suggest.

In financial terms, that success could be said to have been manifest in the effectiveness of the formula which Broadgate Properties devised to make Broadgate appeal to tenants. Lettings were well in hand before Mrs Thatcher turned the first clod of earth on the construction site in 1986. International bankers, insurance and related companies were among the first tenants to occupy Broadgate. Seven years later, at the time of this research, Exchange House was fully occupied and Broadgate had an overall occupancy rate of 97 per cent. This is significant at a time when, it was said (BBC 1993) one in five offices in the City was empty and other major developments such as Minster Court, Albany Gate and America Square remained partly vacant.

Broadgate's survival during the recession makes a marked contrast with Olympia & York's development of Canary Wharf which collapsed in 1992 and the individual fortunes of both Rosehaugh and Stanhope.

Between September 1991 and 1992 Stanhope's shares took a drop of over £100 million. In December 1992, Rosehaugh went into receivership. There has been considerable investment in Broadgate and lenders are naturally concerned to ensure the success of the development. In December 1992, Broadgate Properties's 53 banks agreed to a five year refinancing structure for Broadgate. Reporting the event, the *Estates Times* described Broadgate Properties as 'one of the biggest successes in the corporate property finance sector' and Broadgate as 'the best property development in the world'.

The revision of the City's boundaries in 1994 to embrace the whole of Broadgate may further increase its value and conceivably its desirability.

Since Broadgate, Broadgate Properties have developed a four acre site in the City at Ludgate, which was completed in 1992. Like Broadgate it was a collaboration with the British Rail Property Board and employed SOM as one of two teams of architects. Like Broadgate, Ludgate is centred around a public square, Fleet Place. It also features numerous public art works including examples by Bruce McLean and Stephen Cox – artists whose work is at Broadgate.

Impact and assessment of art at Broadgate

What benefits have accrued from the art at Broadgate? Has it enhanced the nature of the environment and the economic and social success of the development? Has it contributed to the image of the estate?

At the time of writing, Broadgate Properties had commissioned two evaluations of Broadgate. Although neither refer to the permanent art works directly, they nevertheless describe attitudes towards the environment of which they form a part.

The first evaluation was *A Post-Occupancy Evaluation of One Broadgate and Five Other Buildings*, commissioned in 1988 from the consultants, DEGW. It reported that one of the best features of Broadgate was its external image. Tenants and their employees liked the image of the development which they reported as being very impressive to clients. 'The planting is excellent, the ambience pleasant, quiet and relaxing.' The artworks and fountains in the reception area, were mentioned as contributing elements.

The second evaluation, *Broadgate Spaces: Life in Public Places* focused on the use of public spaces in the Broadgate development. Commissioned from Professor Bill Hillier at the Unit for Architectural Studies, Bartlett School of Architecture and Planning, it was written between October 1989 and January 1990, by which time Phases 1-4 were occupied, the retail outlets let, the ice rink open and at least five major artworks in place: Segal's *Rush Hour*, Lipchitz's, *Bellerophon Taming Pegasus*, Serra's *Fulcrum*, Flanagan's *Leaping Hare* and Evan's *Ornamental Gates*.

The aim of the report was to see how successful Broadgate had been in bringing life to public spaces, how far that success was due to design and how improvements might be made. It focused on the two squares which were in use at the time – Finsbury Avenue Square and Broadgate Square.

Hillier's criteria for success included the more or less continuous movement in the public spaces through the working day, with sufficient levels of people present during the evenings and the weekends to prevent the spaces looking empty. He recorded levels of informal activity such as sitting, eating, drinking and talking in the main spaces. The report also considered how levels of activity in the spaces were increased by 'attractors' – organised events, performances, shops, restaurants and so on.

The study revealed that Broadgate's were the best used public open spaces in and around the City of London. More people stopped there to eat, drink, talk, or watch the world go by than in any other open space. During a sample period in June 1989, a series of one minute counts showed an average of nearly 500 people stopped in Broadgate Square and over 150 in Finsbury Avenue Square.

According to Hillier, an average of over 80 per cent of people spending time, as opposed to simply passing through Broadgate's open spaces, came from outside the estate. Broadgate's success as a open space was not, therefore, dependent upon its occupants, but upon people who deliberately chose to spend time there. Indeed, the majority walked about quarter of a mile on average to get there, further than to any other space in the City. There was no discernable 'ghetto' effect. Hillier's team believed that this would attract potential tenants to the development.

Hillier and his team attributed much of this success to the design of the development, in particular Broadgate's spatial integration into the surrounding area. The planting of semi-mature trees contributed to this by implying that the estate was a well established part of the City. Rees described the landscaping as granting the development a certain kind of 'credibility'.

However, both Brian Carter of Arup Associates and Hackney's Director of Environmental Services, believe that the success of Broadgate's spaces could also be attributed to the high quality of maintenance by Broadgate Estates, who manage the site and to the 'creative management' of their events programme.

A postal survey of the Broadgate tenants, carried out in March 1993 for this report, reinforced Hillier's findings. Tenants were unanimous in their appreciation of the ambience of the public spaces, which were regarded as one of the best aspects of Broadgate. The most commonly cited preferences were for the open spaces, including the water feature, the terraces and the seating, which gave respondents a 'feeling of freedom' and 'relaxation'. However, less than 30 per cent regarded the general ambience of the public spaces, in which the public art is sited, as having influenced their tenancy. In most cases this was determined by the location of the estate. Other contributing factors, in order of diminishing importance, were the design and construction of the offices; business opportunities and transport (Appendix 4, p. 331).

The events programme has been assessed twice: once in 1992, in a report about the impact of the programme by a specialist arts officer employed between 1991 and 1992 and subsequently in a survey of the tenants carried out by Broadgate Estates. Although neither assumed a relationship between the live events and the permanent works, several issues raised in respect of the former nevertheless pertain to the latter.

Despite Broadgate Properties's desire to attract the public from outside the estate, the programme is primarily intended for the tenants. It is funded primarily by sponsorship with some managerial costs borne by the service charge and promoted through the in-house publications, *Broadgate Live* (which has been published monthly between May and September since 1992) and *Broadgate Broadsheet*. This provides information about what is happening on the estate, in the shops, what entertainments are taking place, details about the creche, etc. There is significant press coverage of events at Broadgate.

The objectives of the events programme are much the same as those for the public art – to contribute to the establishment of a 'unique arts space in London', to give Broadgate a sense of its place in the local and international community' and to enhance Broadgate's artistic reputation. The 1992 season, in particular, was intended to provide 'accessible, lively and immediately appealing' experiences as well as those that might be 'less overtly popular' and challenging. Like the public art, it was intended to cater for catholic tastes. Jenni Walwin, then Events Coordinator, maintained that

> Arts events, if they are successful, should change perceptions, uproot prejudices and excite the audience into new ways of thinking. Arts should not be confused with entertainment – a good work of art does not always make its audience happy (Walwin 1992A).

> Appreciation of art is largely about personal taste and clearly not every event pleases the whole audience but on the whole audiences ... have been good. It may be that more overtly popular work will have to be programmed ... if the tenants needs rather than artistic endeavour are to be paramount (Walwin 1992B).

Events organised during the 1992 season were supported by outside agencies, such as the Arts Council, the British Council, the Indian High Commission, Phillips and the British Rail Property Board and included collaborations with venues in Hackney and the City of London Festival. Concerts were broadcast live from Broadgate by Radio 3. Despite the considerable popularity of such events as the jazz seasons, the relay of the Olympics via a giant screen and others, Broadgate Estates found that about 75 per cent of the tenants who responded to its survey disliked the performance art events – 'too avant garde' or 'didn't see the art in it at all'. There have been significant changes since. According to Winfield ' a very sensible, if not a perfect balance of interests are catered for.'

Artworks

In his examination of the public spaces at Broadgate, Hillier made no reference to the artworks. This implies that they were not considered as something which would specifically attract people to the estate, influence their movement through the squares or encourage them to stay.

Lipton has, however, referred to putting pieces of art around Broadgate for the sake of people's 'enjoyment'. As Blackburn remarked, they are also considered to contribute specifically to Broadgate's reputation. The Serra is a case in point.

> We knew that the vast majority of people's attitude to Serra would be negative. What has been provided is something which makes a mark for Broadgate. Broadgate is identified with art. It is recognised as important (Blackburn).

Blackburn maintains that the art works are strategically useful. Chairmen of international companies like to feel their offices are housed in prestigious surroundings.

> It's difficult to prove, but it has got to be correct ... art accelerates business processes ... it has given us a competitive advantage.

Andrew Congreve, Managing Partner of Herbert Smith, an international law practice based in Exchange House, confirms that there is a specific relationship between the image that his company wants to project and that of the building it occupies.

> Well, its a very strong building, a very impressive building. We, I think, have a reputation of being a fairly tough firm. We have a substantial litigation practice ... are very committed to our clients and I believe that the building and its character does reflect much of what the firm stands for (BBC 1993; see also Roberts *et al* 1993).

Several of the photographs of the Herbert Smith partners which appear in its brochures were taken against the backdrop of the artworks at Broadgate.

It is significant that given the 'forward looking' image Broadgate and the companies which occupy it wish to promote, none of the artworks commissioned refer to the history of the site. It served as a Roman burial place, the location of the hospital of St Mary of Bethlehem (Bedlam), Elizabethan gardens and, of course, Broad Street Station (Rosehaugh Stanhope Developments and the British Railways Board 1991).

Other artworks associated with Broadgate have been used more explicitly in promoting the development and the companies associated with it. In 1990 Rosehaugh Stanhope Developments published a book, *Broadgate: Paintings and Drawings 1989-1990* by Robert Mason, having already published sets of reproductions. The company benefits from Mason's Broadgate images having been exhibited at the Guildhall, City of London, the Yale Centre for British Art, Newhaven, USA, and at various venues in Sweden. Mason's images of the estate under construction have been used to promote Ashurst Morris Crisp and Miller Construction, one of the companies contracted at Broadgate.

Reception of the works
Despite the catholic selection of art works at Broadgate, Blackburn expressed disappointment at the general lack of critical reaction to the

George Segal,
Rush Hour, 1983/1987
© Sara Selwood

works on the estate. He is in no doubt that people prefer the more 'realistic pieces' on a human scale. Indeed, the majority of people interviewed in a survey for *The Guardian* in September 1992 expressed a preference for the figurative works, in particular Barry Flanagan's *Leaping Hare on Crescent and Bell* and George Segal's *Rush Hour*. They appreciated them because they found them 'pleasant to look at', 'appropriate', 'familiar', 'life-like', not leaving 'too much to the imagination', 'in the right place' – generally affirmative qualities. But not everyone is so convinced. As one of the office workers interviewed by Dalya Alberge of *The Independent* newspaper put it: 'The hare brightens things up, but

Fernando Botero, *Broadgate Venus*, 1990
© Wordsearch

what's it supposed to be? If it's art, it should mean something' (Alberge 1990).

Respondents to a PSI survey of Broadgate tenants, also preferred the figurative works – Botero's, *Broadgate Venus*, works by Segal and Flanagan, Corbero's *The Broad Family* as well as the water-feature in Exchange Square.

The Segal was particularly appreciated for its 'life-like' qualities. Respondents referred to it as 'the people' and 'the commuters'. They found it 'relevant' largely because it related to their own experience. 'Just how I feel sometimes', 'it mirrors bustling commuters', 'it captures so precisely the look of people on their way to work'. It is used as a photo-point. Oddly one respondent who found it 'very pleasing' referred to it as 'the downtrodden'.

Barry Flanagan, *Leaping Hare on Crescent and Bell*, 1988
© Wordsearch

Xavier Corbero, *The Broad Family*
© Wordsearch

Botero's work at Broadgate attracted a divergent range of opinion. It was referred to as 'the big Bhudda' and 'the fat lady'. It reminded one respondent of '17th century Old Masters'. However, the sheer size of the sculpture and its 'fatness' captured most people's attention. Those who liked it, appreciated its sensual qualities – 'voluptuous, wonderful', 'she reminds me of my childhood sweetheart'. One woman particularly liked it because 'it makes everyone sitting nearby feel slim'. But it was more disliked than liked. Respondents were quite categorical about their feelings towards the sculpture. Some found it 'gross', 'somewhat repulsive', 'quite revolting' and 'awful. It cannot be avoided, an unpleasant feature.'

The Corbero, Flanagan and the water feature provoked least comment. *The Broad Family* was enjoyed for its humour, 'the feet poking out from under one of the blocks'. The water-feature was deemed 'relaxing' and 'peaceful'. Flanagan's *Leaping Hare* gave people the 'feeling of movement' and it was liked because of its 'original theme and design' and because 'it's not as abstract as most of the sculptures at Broadgate'.

One of Broadgate's intentions had been to provoke reactions. Serra's *Fulcrum* provoked more extreme reactions than any of the other pieces at Broadgate, not least because it appears to be the most visible work at Broadgate. Several people interviewed by *The Guardian* regarded it as a focal point and used it as a meeting place. Many were unaware of there being any other artworks on the estate.

Over 40 per cent of *The Guardian's* interviewees believed that the work should be removed. One interviewee asserted that the work had been imposed upon the public. A substantial number described it as a rusty mess, scrap, a waste of materials which had no meaning. One interviewee commented that the steel could have been 'put to better use', while another speculated that the money could have been spent on 'more worthwhile causes'. 'I haven't taken too much notice of it. It isn't up to much, is it?' 'I just walk past it'.

Among the respondents to the PSI survey, none expressed a liking for the Serra work, although one thought it was of a 'good scale'. Some appeared to have difficulty in referring to it as a sculpture. They alluded to as an 'item', 'boiler plates', 'slabs of steel'. Several objected to the rust. 'It looks a mess', 'I would have [the sheets] sand blasted and painted'. Others found it 'out of keeping with the general positivism of Broadgate'.

Criticism generally revealed that the work was disliked for its disaffirmative qualities. Some interviewees thought that the sculpture was conceived in contempt of British Rail and Broadgate. Others perceived its size, its domination of the space around it, its 'inappropriateness' and the marked contrast between its formal qualities and those of the buildings as strengths. Some interpreted it as an ironic statement on the vast and immoveable power of the City, a commentary on the harshness of capitalism and the limited future of the Broadgate development. These readings are reinforced by what is coyly referred to as its 'squalid' state and passers by contributing to its 'corrosion'. (The use of the sculpture as a urinal was presumably facilitated by Serra's opening up the entrances to the work at the insistence of the commissioners.)

Works on the side of the estate furthest away from Liverpool Street, that is Cox's *Ganapathi & Davi*, Evans' *Ornamental Gates* and Artigas', *Tiled*

Fountain, attracted no comments at all in the PSI survey. This may reflect their relative lack of visibility. In the case of the Evans and the Artigas, lack of comment may be indicative of people's uncertainty about whether ornamental embellishments constitute 'art' and should be referred to in a survey about such artworks.

Those with an overt interest in the works tended to disagree with popular opinion. From a personal point of view Rees, for one, regarded the most admired works at Broadgate as representing the 'agony of blandness'.

> They tend to the plaster duck end of the market – like any number of sculpted herons. I wonder if it doesn't to some extent devalue the coinage.

For his part Serra found much of the art at Broadgate 'conventional work that was already ascertained as being of a certain quality', essentially decorative.

> You could ... say that some pieces in their size or character are insignificant, because you could pass them by and you wouldn't worry about them. They are not going to present any problem to anyone.

Neither architect interviewed expressed a preference for works which could be said to 'humanise' their buildings. Nor were they taken by the notion of art as decoration or art which integrated with their buildings. They most admired works which formally contrasted with their buildings. The Serra was the most admired in this context.

5   West Midlands

Art in Centenary Square, Birmingham 1988-1991

Background

Centenary Square provides the setting for several of Birmingham's most important civic buildings – the International Convention Centre (ICC), the Hall of Memory, the Repertory Theatre, the Registry Office and Baskerville House. It functions as an outdoor space for exhibitions and events, such as New Year celebrations and as a pedestrian route to the city centre. The Square's discerning characteristics are its paving, street furniture, fountain and freestanding sculptures – all of which were designed by artists. In the context of this enquiry, the public art programme for Centenary Square and the ICC was the largest such public sector scheme in the UK between 1987 and 1991, and it was the first Percent for Art scheme to be implemented by a local authority for a major building development. The art in Centenary Square is the subject of this case study.

The City's plans for a civic centre and public square at the city end of Broad Street date back to the 1930s. These were halted by the advent of the Second World War. It was not until the early 1980s that the downturn of the West Midland's economy prompted new proposals. These bore no relation to the City's previous plans.

From the late 18th century the region's economy was dominated by manufacturing industries, hence Birmingham's identification as 'the City of a Thousand Trades' and the West Midlands as 'the workshop of the world'. In the 1870s Joseph Chamberlain began a major programme of social welfare in Birmingham. This included slum clearance and civic building, and contributed to its reputation as 'the best governed city in the world' (Upton 1991:24).

A century later, Birmingham suffered acute and accelerated decline. Between 1971 and 1983 employment in the city fell by 29 per cent. The City Council, together with other institutions in the city, saw an urgent need to revitalise its economy by levering in private sector resources, improving business confidence and creating much needed jobs. It sought to nurture service sector investment within Birmingham's Central Business District (CBD), in particular the development of business tourism. This required enhancing Birmingham's image, marketing it as a 'place', and promoting the quality of life the city had to offer – in short developing what its Council's officers describe as a 'feel good factor'.

> At the heart of this strategy is the focus of public and private investment in the city's CBD through the development of prestige projects. Four projects provide the centre-piece of Birmingham's strategy: The International Convention Centre, the Indoor National Arena, the Brindleyplace market-place development and the Hyatt Hotel. These projects, together with civic boosterism initiatives such as the 1992 Olympic bid campaign and the Birmingham Super Prix (an annual automobile race), form part of the City Council's attempt to create and promote a new national and international image for Birmingham (Loftman and Nevin, 1992:6).

Birmingham also needed to compete with the municipal entrepreneurial spirit of other cities in the same position (see Bianchini, 1991). There was political consensus about these aspirations for Birmingham. They were originally supported by the Conservative-led Council of 1983/84 and subsequently by Labour.

The City Council's vision for Birmingham was partly inspired by its development of the National Exhibition Centre (NEC) which opened in 1976. This successfully attracted business to Birmingham, prompted growth in the city's infrastructure – the motorway, rail and air links – and ultimately inspired confidence in the place itself. NEC marketing and management identified scope for further expansion in the field of business tourism, particularly in the area of conventions and trade launches. Their thinking was indebted to the examples of American cities such as Baltimore, which had similar histories of a declining manufacturing base and had adopted urban regeneration models based on privatism – 'an ideology which emphasises the supremacy of private sector solutions to the problems of urban areas'.

> Advocates of this kind of model of regeneration justify massive public sector expenditure on the development of prestige projects on the basis that they are directly linked to the well-being of all city residents, that all sections of the community will share the benefits which accrue and that the costs of the development will not be borne by the poor (Loftman and Nevin, 1992:6).

In 1983 the City Council commissioned a feasibility study into the building of a convention centre adjacent to the city centre. It examined the impact of the proposed facilities from both the point of view of the worldwide market and the regional economy. According to Geoff Wright, Head of City Centre Planning, the key to the scheme was a European Regional Development Funding (ERDF) grant. Birmingham's 1984 application to the European Fund anticipated that an International Convention Centre (ICC) would increase investment in the region by up to £40 million per annum, create 600 jobs during the most intense period of construction, 2,000 within the completed centre itself and indirectly stimulate a further 10,000. (The ICC's target was 150,000 delegate days within the first year, with an average delegate spending £130 per day.) According to a survey of Birmingham based businesses carried out in 1990, the majority believed the ICC, more than any other development in Birmingham, would affect the future image of the city (Bostock, 1990).

Confirmation of European funding was announced in January 1986. The President of the European Commission, Jacques Delors, laid the foundation stone of the ICC later that year. The ERDF grant for the Convention Centre was £49.75 million. The majority of the £180 million costs of the Convention Centre came from stock issues by NEC Ltd, the company which owns and manages the National Exhibition Centre. Although NEC is constituted as a private company, its Directors are City Councillors and the City its guarantor. By the mid-late 1980s NEC was running at profit, and reinvesting in the city.

The ICC, designed by the Convention Centre Partnership (the Percy Thomas Partnership and the Renton Howard Wood Levin Partnership) comprises 11 halls on a 6.7 acre site, among which is Symphony Hall, the home of the Birmingham Symphony Orchestra. The ICC was officially opened by the Queen in June 1991.

Once the ERDF application had been made, the City Council identified sites adjoining the ICC for related developments. The Broad Street Redevelopment Area (BSRA), situated between the city centre and the commercial developments at Five Ways to the West, was one of the largest areas of decline in the city. Ladywood, its neighbouring residential district, had an unemployment rate well above the city average. In 1990 it was 20 per cent compared with 11 per cent elsewhere in Birmingham. The post-War construction of the Inner Ring Road in the 1950s had separated Broad Street from the main commercial areas of central Birm-

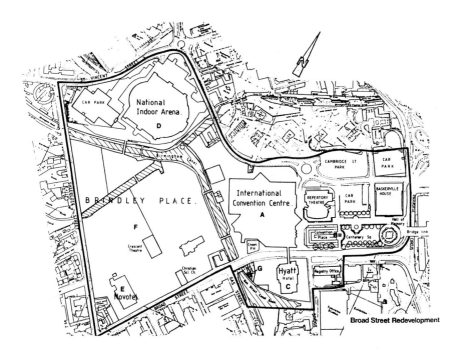

Map showing the Broad Street Redevelopment Area from the *Broad Street Redevelopment Area: Factpack* © Department of Planning and Architecture, Birmingham City Council, 1992

ingham. Apart from the theatre and the registry office there was little to draw people to the area. One of the planning objectives was to bring new activity into the area. The Council had originally decided to pave a small area outside the Repertory Theatre. This eventually developed into the proposal for a large public space outside the ICC.

Birmingham City Council (BCC) already owned some of the land identified for redevelopment including Bingley Hall, built in 1851 as the first purpose built exhibition space in Britain. Its site is now occupied by the ICC. The City compulsorily purchased the remaining buildings in 1984, sought permissions for listed building consent and road closures, and made an outline planning application. Its investment in the ICC, the £57 million National Indoor Arena, the £31 million Hyatt Hotel and Novotel Hotels and the environment of the BSRA set the scene for the final phase of BSRA. Plans for Brindleyplace, a £250 million private sector development include specialist retailing outlets, leisure attractions, canal-side bars and restaurants and offices, hotels, the first UK Omnimax Cinema and the National Aquarium, parking and quality urban spaces. The developers Rosehaugh commissioned Terry Farrell & Company to produce an urban design master plan. The scheme has, however, been delayed due to uncertainty in the property market. Canals also provide a focus for BSRA as visitor attractions. A group of canal-side listed buildings are being retained and refurbished for mixed use.

Given that Birmingham's future prosperity was perceived as linked to its city centre, the City invested in a series of planning studies and produced strategies. These were intended to transform the city's image from that of a concrete jungle dominated by the Inner Ring Road, and to encourage activity within the city centre. They included *The Highbury Initiative* (1988 and 1989) and a report on *Pedestrian Movement and Open Space Framework* (LDR/HLN, 1988). The subsequent City Centre Strategy, embodied within the Birmingham Unitary Development Plan (placed on deposit in 1991), sought to make the city centre highly accessible.

> A better city centre must be attractive and draw people into it. It must not be a place from which people at 5.00 or 6.00 return home. The strategic aim is to create a 24 hour, seven day a week city centre. That is why the strategy is underpinned by the twin considerations of good transport and the creation of an environment which is stimulating, pleasurable, safe and comfortable (BCC undated A: 5).

The Highbury Initiative also proposed engaging the business community in future plans for the development of the city, building partnerships and thereby generating confidence in Birmingham.

Birmingham's ambitions necessitated that the civic spaces be improved and key streets pedestrianised. Anticipating increased activity in the city centre, the Strategy proposed extending the central areas towards the Middle Ring Road. It also planned for Birmingham to build on its distinctiveness by promoting separate quarters around the central core – the Convention Centre Quarter, the Science Park Quarter, Warwick Bar/ Digbeth, the Chinese Quarter, the Media Quarter, the Jewellery Quarter, the Gun Quarter and the Aston Triangle. Better access should be provided between them, especially for pedestrians and particularly across the Inner Ring Road. The Strategy also stipulated that the city's neglected canal network should be integrated into the life of the city centre.

These aspirations led to the revision of the road network and the creation of a wide pedestrian bridge across a lowered ring road linking to the city core. Proposals for Centenary Square not only provided Birmingham with a civic space but formed part of a pedestrian route across the Inner Ring Road, creating a new east/west axis across the city, taking in Paradise Forum, Victoria Square, Chamberlain Square and New Street and various civic cultural amenities – Symphony Hall, the Repertory Theatre, the Library and the Museum and Art Gallery.

Centenary Square also developed from plans to create a space outside the ICC. The Council originally intended to pave a small area outside the Repertory Theatre. This eventually developed into proposals for a large public space outside the ICC. According to one of the city's officers, there is no public space comparable to Centenary Square in the public domain in Britain. It hosts a variety of events, ranging from civic celebrations such as firework displays and New Year's Eve, to promotional events organised by charities and commercial interests.

Although less than ten per cent of the Birmingham based businesses surveyed in 1990 thought that culture and the arts would affect the future image of the city (Bostock 1990), the City Council regarded the development of Birmingham's cultural amenities and resources as vital to the city's 'renaissance' (see, for example, BBC 1993; Turner cited in ICC undated). Thus, the ICC embraced Symphony Hall. (The City of Birmingham Symphony Orchestra led by Simon Rattle serves as its cultural ambassador worldwide (Bianchini 1991).) The city successfully attracted arts organisations such as the Sadlers Wells Royal Ballet (renamed, the Birmingham Royal Ballet), the D'Oyly Carte Opera and Ronnie Scott's. It also established a Media Development Agency and launched new festivals of jazz, literature, cinema and TV.

The visual arts were similarly employed to contribute to Birmingham's new image. Like the city's other cultural amenities, they were intended to serve the residents and its international constituency. According to Sir Richard Knowles, former Leader of the Council, 'the only interests that works in public spaces should express are those of the people who use those spaces'. The Council positively encouraged arts developments in 'informal, non-venue and outdoor settings, to bring people who would not otherwise choose to seek out the arts into contact with them' (BCC undated C). The Head of City Centre Planning also emphasised that the introduction of public art into the city centre was intended to broaden the contact between art and the public and to 'adopt design references which relate to the history and diverse cultural mix of our city'. Although he regards public art as benefiting 'the context of broader strategies for environmental change and an enhanced role for the city centre as a business centre for the region within Europe', Wright also stresses Birmingham's cultural role as 'the focal point for the people of the city and region'.

> So far as I am concerned it is the sight of the people of Birmingham taking pictures of each other in their new city squares that underpins the economic aspirations.

Thus the public art programme was intended to provide landmarks, contribute to environmental enhancement schemes and symbolise the city's aspirational 'international status'. The City Council maintained that the design of its buildings, squares and open spaces are a hallmark of its prosperity. Consequently investment in art was associated with investment 'for a successful future' (ICC/BCC undated). Centenary Square was a major element in that planning.

Processes

Birmingham, like many British industrial cities, has a heritage of civic and monumental sculptures commissioned during a period of rapid growth in the 19th century. It includes building decorations, such as those on the Victoria Law Courts, and statues of figures of national and local significance, Queen Victoria, Lord Nelson and Joseph Chamberlain.

Some of the public art commissioned in the later part of this century fulfils similar functions. They include William Bloye's gilded bronze statue of the industrial pioneers, *Boulton, Watt and Murdoch* (1956), William Pye's *Peace Sculpture*, originally commissioned as a memorial to those killed by enemy bombing in Small Heath (1984) and Vincent Woropay's *Wattilisk*, commemorating James Watt, for the New Crown Courts (1988).

From the late 1950s onwards the City Council commissioned a number of works associated with planning achievements. J.R. Thomas's *Hebe* was created to commemorate the start of the Inner Ring Road (1957), Kenneth Budd's mosaics at Holloway Circus, St Chads Circus and Manzoni Gardens, William Mitchell's mosaic at Colmore Circus and Robert Clatworthy's relief sculptures at the Bull Ring.

The rate at which Birmingham commissioned public art accelerated dramatically from the mid- to late 1980s with the construction of the ICC and the mobilisation of the concept of the city's cultural 'renaissance'. Between 1989 and 1992, some 40 public art projects were completed in the city, ranging from those costing a few hundred pounds to one costing £275,000.

In the late 1980s and early 1990s the emphasis of Birmingham's civic public art shifted to its large city schemes – its squares in particular. These included the art in the new Centenary Square, Anthony Gormley's *Iron Man*, Dhruva Mistry's water sculpture, *The River*, flanked by two sphinx-like 'guardians' in the redesigned Victoria Square and Siobhan Coppinger's sculpture of Thomas Attwood, a 19th century reformer and MP, in Chamberlain Square.

Public art policy
In recent years Birmingham's policy for public art has been essentially implicit in that

> it supports the promotion of public art as good planning practice, bringing cultural, environmental, educational and economic benefits to new development and to the community at large.

The city has no formal statement as such regarding its public art policy. However its Unitary Development Plan (1993), describes how

> in order to add variety to the visual environment, the Local Planning Authority will, in appropriate cases, encourage the provision of new works of art as part of schemes of development and will have regard to the contribution made by any such works to the appearance of the scheme and to the amenities of the area. This approach will be of particular importance in the case of major projects in prominent locations. In 1991, when Centenary Square opened, Birmingham's public art policy effectively comprised four strands:

1. In 1987 the NEC/ICC Committee had agreed a Percent for Art policy for the ICC. According to this one per cent of the original capital budget for ICC was allocated to the commissioning of works of art.

2. In April 1989, the Arts, Culture and Economy (ACE) Sub-Committee of Birmingham City Council agreed a formal statement with regard to its Public Art Policy: where appropriate, artists would be commissioned to

work with officer designer teams on environmental enhancement schemes. The amount spent would be determined by the needs of the scheme rather than by an arbitrary financial equation. As a member of the project design team, rather than an independent contractor, the artist's work would be likely to be appropriate to the nature of the scheme.

3. In 1989, the Public Art Commissions Agency (PACA), a public art agency based in the West Midlands, initiated and the ACE Sub-Committee endorsed the post of Inner City Public Art Officer. The post was founded jointly by the Economic Development Committee and the Calouste Gulbenkian Foundation, and was based at PACA.

4. In 1990, the ACE Sub-Committee approved recommending the use of the planning process to encourage a greater involvement in public art in the part of private sector architects and developers.

Implementation

In practice, several departments are involved in commissioning works, including the Museums and Art Gallery, Planning and Architecture, Libraries, Engineers and Recreation. However overall responsibility for public art falls to the Museums and Art Gallery. They own the works in the ICC and Centenary Square, insure them in respect of public liability and maintain them. The ICC holds its own maintenance budgets. The paving and street furniture in Centenary Square comes under the responsibility of the Planning Department. By 1993 the city had a £100,000 budget for public art, £90,000 for maintenance and £10,000 for new works. Budgets for commissions are created by involving artists in the capital development projects of other departments.

At the time of research for this report the city employed two specialist public art officers to serve its public art programme. The Public Art Conservator (full-time) assisted with the general management of the public art programme (contracts, budgets, etc), was responsible for maintenance of public art in the city (including monuments, fountains and clocks) and for ensuring the quality of materials, structures and maintenance schedules for all new commissions. (This officer retired in March 1994 and will not be replaced.) The Public Art Officer (appointed in 1990) is also Assistant Keeper of Fine Art. She manages all new public art projects – where appropriate via the Public Art Commissions Agency – and is responsible for the commissioning and interpretation and marketing related to public art.

The City also employs the public art agency, PACA, to carry out the project management of many individual council schemes to contracts, policies and procedures set down by the City Council. It also carries out strategic and feasibility studies as commissioned by the City Council. PACA has provided the city with 'specialist advice and facilities in a new and unfamiliar area of activity'.

Centenary Square and Percent for Art
The works in Centenary Square and the ICC were administered as part of the same public art programme. Although they represent different sets of interest within Birmingham's public art policy, most of the works in Centenary Square, including Tess Jaray's design of the paving and the street furniture, Tom Lomax's *Spirit of Enterprise* and David Patten's *Monument to John Baskerville – Industry and Genius*, were funded through the Planning Committee. Jaray was appointed as a member of the City Council design team on the advice of PACA. Raymond Mason's *Forward* and Ron Haselden's *Birdlife* at the entrance to the ICC were funded under the Percent for Art Scheme adopted by the NEC/ICC. Roderick Tye's *Battle of the Gods and the Giants*, on the canal-side entrance to the Mall, was sponsored.

When plans were initially mooted for the ICC in 1982, before the viability study was complete, Michael Diamond, Director of Birmingham City Museums & Art Gallery, recommended Percent for Art commitment from the City – some six years ahead of the Arts Council's Percent for Art campaign.

This commitment was confirmed until 1987. The Council was willing to comply with this initiative, having already committed two per cent to 'special features'. Diamond himself had a long standing interest in contemporary sculpture. He had organised the major eightieth birthday exhibition for Henry Moore at Cartwright Hall, Bradford and was the first Chairman of both the Yorkshire Sculpture Park and PACA.

PACA's press release, announcing the opening of the ICC, credits its own personnel as being 'instrumental in convincing Birmingham City Council to apply the Percentage for Art principle in the first place'. Vivien Lovell, Director of PACA, was also involved in the programme from the start. In 1983, as Deputy Director of the Ikon Gallery, she had made a slide presentation about public art's potential role in Birmingham to David Franks, the planner in charge of the ICC, and Colin Hough of the

Chief Executive's department. Lovell recalls that neither officer knew that Diamond had secured commitment for Percent for Art at the ICC. Franks had, however, pencilled in two per cent for 'special features' and agreed that one per cent should be allocated to art. Her own contact with the project developed through 1987 when, as Public Art Officer for West Midlands Arts, she had further meetings with the City Council. PACA carried out a preliminary feasibility study and in December 1987, two months after the organisation was set up, it was commissioned – in its own words – to 'organise every aspect of the Public Art Programme from selection through to installation of the various works of art'.

In 1983, after the Percent for Art principle was initially agreed, the total cost of the ICC was estimated as being in the region of £80 million. The percentage allocated for art was £800,000. This was subsequently reduced to £740,000 as £60,000 had to be found for a creche. In the event the costs of the development escalated substantially. The final cost of the ICC was about £180 million. What had been one per cent was therefore reduced to 0.44 per cent. A further £200,000 was raised by PACA in commercial sponsorship. Sponsors included the National Westminster Bank plc, Ingersoll Publications and its subsidiaries, the Birmingham Post and Mail, Douglas Holdings plc, Pinsent & Co, Sign Specialists and the Convention Centre Partnerships. The scheme was also supported by a Business Sponsorship Incentive Scheme award.

In order to oversee the public art programme, a Works of Art Working Party (WAWP) was set up. It comprised councillors from the two major parties, the Director of the Museums and Art Gallery, an Assistant Chief Executive of the Birmingham City Council, the ICC Project Manager and representatives of the Architects to the ICC, the Arts Council and PACA. The users of the building could not be represented since the building did not come into use until after the programme was complete. PACA's suggestion that local residents' associations be appointed to the WAWP was rejected as the Council maintained that its councillors were the people's elected representatives. The public itself was not involved in the selection of works for Centenary Square although maquettes for all the pieces were shown at Baskerville House during the City's application for planning permission. The exclusion of West Midlands Arts on the Working Party was indicative of tensions which existed at the time between the City Council and the Regional Arts Association.

Selection and commissioning

The selection of artists for ICC and Centenary Square was deliberately eclectic. It represented the range of interests recommended by PACA in its report to the WAWP of January 1988 and included

> Functional and non-functional works of art; a balance of regional, national and international artists; a balance of work in terms of style, subject matter, media, technique; work which reflects the most creative expression of contemporary artists; work which reflects the multicultural nature of the city and the uniqueness of Birmingham.

Diamond describes the programme as developing 'incrementally over time ... there was no way in which we could have anticipated what opportunities might have arisen.' The sites for the major pieces emerged as options during the design process. The committee selected those they preferred. The types of work required were also identified: Centenary Square, for example, was to have a central sculpture, a water feature, iron work, seating, a large area of paving, a green space and planting. The required pedestrian route through the Square also determined aspects of its overall design. Raymond Mason's work had originally been proposed when it was thought that Centenary Square would consist only of the area in front of the Repertory Theatre. When the concept of the enlarged Centenary Square was developed, 'it became clear to everyone that the right place for a major sculpture was where it now sits' (Diamond).

Briefs for each publicly funded piece were agreed by the WAWP. An example of the brief for *Forward* for Centenary Square can be found in Appendix 7, p. 356. In broad terms, the briefs dealt with the impact the pieces were intended to have on the public, their durability, requirements for their safety, maintenance and the materials to be used. This appears to have been the limit of the City's intervention. According to Knowles, the City's only criteria were that work should be of

> the highest possible quality and appropriate to the site concerned. We would not dream of imposing our views with regard to such things as subject matter or style, which emerge naturally from the commissioning process. We hope that what we do is intellectually accessible to most people ... The only interest that works in public spaces should express are those of the people who use those places. There are spin-offs, such as the encouragement of local talent, but these are of no value unless the piece does something to stimulate the space for the people that use it.

Given that PACA was not contracted until the end of 1987, there was insufficient time to organise competitions for the selection of artists for the major pieces in Centenary Square as had been intended. In 1988 Jaray, Mason, Haselden and Petherbridge were all invited to make works. Patten's commission came about as a result of his own initiative to PACA and was subsequently approved by the WAWP. A limited competition was, however, organised for the fountain. This was won by Tom Lomax. Although an international open competition for the proposed Canalside Sculpture Trail was agreed, in the event it did not take place. A limited competition was also held for a major glass art work which was won by Alexander Beleschenko.

In the case of Centenary Square, the public art works were introduced to the public through the application for planning permission and exhibitions. *New Meanings for City Sites*, which contained maquettes for all the works, was mounted by PACA at Birmingham Museums and Art Gallery three weeks before the Square itself opened. Masons's maquette and related drawings had already been shown at the Museums and Art Gallery in 1989 in his retrospective exhibition. A version of Patten's

Raymond
Mason,
Forward,
1988-1991
© Birmingham
City Council

Baskerville piece, together with related materials, was shown at the Ikon Gallery, Birmingham (1989) and in its touring exhibition, *Approaches to Public Art* (1989-90).

Mason, who had been born about a mile from the site of his sculpture, was directly commissioned by Birmingham City Council to create a monumental sculpture for Centenary Square. According to Lovell the WAWP had asked PACA to put forward a shortlist of artists for an invited competition. They nevertheless chose to invite Mason rather than hold a competition 'one of the reasons being that the members wanted Birmingham to offer Mason his first UK commission'.

Mason's proposal was based on a maquette he had exhibited at Birmingham Art Gallery that year. According to the artist the theme of the work was

> the city, its citizens and its advance in time, thus the title *Forward*, the city motto. It would necessarily be a composition of multiple figures. I wished to remind Birmingham folk that at one moment in history, Birmingham, first manufacturing city in the world, was unique. The slope of the sculpture descends in diminishing scale through the 19th century, with its industrial workers and craftsmen, to disappear into the mists of smoke and time. Seen from the back the acceleration of size aptly faces the new Convention Centre and the future.

> This image of the all-red brick city necessarily implies polychrome. Thus the material utilised would be synthetic resin – polyester and fibre glass, the ideal support for polyurethane paint.

Mason described the commission as having came about as a result 'the personal interest of Vivien Lovell of the public art agency and Evelyn Silber of the Birmingham Museums and Art Gallery, who alone were acquainted with my monuments elsewhere'. But, there was already a body of support for a Mason commission which was endorsed by the enthusiastic response to his retrospective at the City Museums and Art Gallery, *Raymond Mason. Sculptures and Drawings* (27 April - 18 June 1989).

Mason intended his work to be for the multitude in the city centre.

> I consider that the duty of the artist is to provide spiritual nourishment for the people. All my large sculptures have each demanded several years' work in order that everybody, young or old, cultured or not, can understand the subject sufficiently to reap the benefit of its aesthetics. Bluntly, it's beauty which engenders happiness.

Tess Jaray had already designed paving for Victoria Station and the entrance to the Stoke National Garden Festival – the latter curated by Vivien Lovell. The artist was originally employed by the NEC/ICC WAWP to work on the paving for the area outside Repertory Theatre with the aim of her being invited to join the City Architect's design team. She joined the team when this was absorbed into Centenary Square.

The Site Development Brief, 1988, described the creation of the as yet unnamed civic square as

> an opportunity to create an experience which is unique in its character to the City of Birmingham, and which will form an addition to the sequence of urban spaces found in the city centre … the square will possess its own unique qualities and characteristics.

Jaray's proposal for the Square was predicated on the notion that

Tess Jaray and members of the Planning and Architecture Team, *Centenary Square*, 1988-1991. Bird's eye view showing Raymond Mason's *Forward* © Birmingham City Council

Every aspect, each element, must function in its own right, for its own purpose, but still be part of the whole.

The paving, steps, seating areas, lighting, planters, railings, etc, designed with the help of Tom Lomax, were intended to 'contribute to this sense of wholeness'.

Ron Haselden was invited at PACA's suggestion, on the strength of his work for the Royal Centre, Nottingham. His neon sculpture, *Birdlife*, operated by computer programme, was designed for the entrance to the main mall of the ICC. He intended it to 'offset the bleakness of the building'.

An abstract tree form grows up through the 'aviary' [network of the steel construction of the building] bearing different species and origins of birds. The theme of migration and international travel symbolises to some extent the role of the Convention Centre (ICC undated).

According to David Patten, Lovell invited him

to make some response to the plans for ICC/Centenary Square.

Since 1983/4 I had been researching Birmingham's cultural history (to balance the common perception of it as being only a centre of mindless metal bashing) and had identified Baskerville as ... of interest. It was natural, therefore, to make a proposal based on Baskerville, as Centenary Square was the site of his 18th century works.

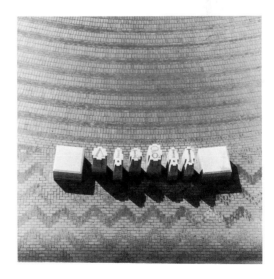

David Patten, *Monument to John Baskerville – Industry and Genius*, 1988-1991. Bird's eye view
© Birmingham City Council

Formally the piece is a direct quote from Baskerville artifacts designed as a robust structure on which site-users could sit or climb in pursuit of the range of activities necessary to support the traditional functions of a public square.

Lomax's fountain, *Spirit of Enterprise*, celebrates the industry, commerce and enterprise of Birmingham – the artist's response to the newly titled Centenary Square.

Tye's *Battle of the Gods and the Giants*, commissioned later and sited in 1993, is intentionally ambiguous. In the artist's statement of 1991 he described how

The work was conceived so as to exist entirely as 'presence':

Although a title was used for this sculpture ... the relationship between object and title evolved entirely as a poetic association ... The object was not asked to perform an illustration of the story referred to in the title ... The sculpture is not [intended] for any attempted association with Birmingham or the function(s) of the adjacent building (PACA undated).

According to the City Council's pamphlet, 'the cloud's meaning is open to interpretation by the spectator'.

The themes of the works were proposed by the artists, rather than being specified in their briefs. Three out of the five artists commissioned to work on Centenary Square – Mason, Patten and Lomax – chose themes associated with Birmingham's history and aspirations. (The WAWP intervened very little with the concept of the works.) Their only objections

Tom Lomax, *Spirit of Enterprise*, 1988-1991 © Birmingham City Council

appear to have been to Haselden's original proposal to have neon dogs racing across one of the bridges traversing the central mall inside the ICC. The site preparation and foundations were the responsibility of the site contractor through the Planning and Architecture Department.

Decisions about the final appearance of works rested with the artists. According to Patten

> There were several businesses interested in sponsorship, but this would have meant putting company credits or logos on the work which I felt would have been intrusive.

PACA's contract with the City covered selection procedures but not project management for the Jaray, Patten or Lomax commissions. The artists were responsible for overseeing manufacture and installation of their works, which, in some cases, required sub-contracting or collaboration. Sums allocated for their commissions included expenses. Mason thus paid for

> the cost of fabrication of the work, its transport from France, multiple journeys to Birmingham by my moulder and myself, a percentage to Marlborough Gallery.

Other expenses incurred by him were unexpected.

> A last minute decision that our special convoy lorry could not venture onto the square, despite our visits to Birmingham to decide the exact spot and signed the documents of the City Architects, entailed great expense for me by the hire of a giant crane to lift the work from the nearest thoroughfare. This meant a middle of the night job in rain and wind because the police would not allow this all-important artery to be blocked in day time.

Ultimately the artists had little control over the context within which their work was installed.

> Tess Jaray's paving design was originally 'zoned' to the west section of Centenary Square and surrounded by traditional civic paving. It was a long time after I had completed the Baskerville design process that [the Design team decided to extend Tess Jarray's paving] across the whole site. This obviously has a major impact on the Baskerville Monument and its relationship to the two neighbouring buildings – Tess's original solution accommodated these three items in a straightforward civic aesthetic, but the later spread of the paving creates a 'carpeting' effect on which the monument and buildings appear to 'bob'. By the time I knew of this change, it was too late to adapt the

Baskerville Monument because my budget and sub-contracting were finalised. In the end I had to let the piece 'bob' along with its architectural context! (Patten).

Impact

The social impact of public art is evident to anyone wandering around the city centre on a warm day. The discussion groups clustering round some of the sculptures, kids demanding to be allowed to climb on them and the deafening noise of camera shutters are all we need to convince ourselves of the social impact of public art. The cultural impact will only be fully known years from now, when the quality of what we have been doing can be truly assessed. What we know now is the blindingly obvious fact that what we have been doing has brought the arts very close to the top of the agenda of public debate in the press and on the local media, and also in the minds of ordinary people, many of whom now come to the City Centre just to see the art. The economic impact is much more difficult to define precisely, but common sense and simple observation show quite clearly that the 'concrete desert' image of Birmingham has been radically changed by our City Centre policies, including those for public art, and that this can only have a positive impact on the city's economy (Sir Richard Knowles, former Leader of the Council, Birmingham City Council).

There has been no formal evaluation, as such, of the Art in Centenary Square by either Birmingham City Council or PACA. But along with other public art projects in the city, it has been the subject of formal reviews within the City Council. The Director of the Museums and Art Gallery, for example, presented a report on *Public Art: the Management Process*, to the Joint ACE Sub-Committee in January 1991.

External bodies have judged Centenary Square according to their own criteria. As part of the BSRA, it was awarded the RTPI Silver Jubilee Cup (1991) for Planning Achievement.

The design and implementation of the Broad Street Redevelopment Area, which involved the creation of Centenary Square with its associated buildings, approaches and works of art, as part of the revitalization of the city centre, is an achievement of very high quality.

Centenary Square was shortlisted for the Art in Public Places category of the Arts Council/ British Gas Working for Cities Award, 1992.

On the basis of some of the press coverage, it appeared – in the short-term, at least – that Birmingham was regarded as having achieved several of its ambitions for Centenary Square. Writing in *The Times* (15.4.91) Richard Cork, for example, described how

> Bullied, polluted and throttled for decades by the city's obsession with traffic flow, the people of Birmingham are at last re-emerging from their subway-ridden oppression ... Nowhere more spectacularly than in the remodelled Centenary Square, an immense open space dedicated to the pedestrian rather than the car.

Birmingham's adoption of Percent for Art for the ICC was taken as showing the city to be 'pioneering' and culturally enlightened.

> Birmingham City Council has been first off the mark with a scheme for its new £90 million Convention Centre in the city centre. The budget for art is just short of £1 million ... With over £30 billion of new building in Britain (including the massive Canary Wharf, King's Cross and combined South Bank redevelopments) the potential for a renaissance in Britain's arts and crafts is enormous ... ('Guide to the Arts', *Sunday Correspondent*, 1990).

The Working for Cities judges credited the Art in Centenary Square with contributing to confidence in the public sector. *The Birmingham Post* and *Evening Mail's* sponsorship of the canalside commission, for example, was prompted by their attempt to encourage precisely that. 'Business in the city should combine with civic projects to make Birmingham a more attractive place.' Their parent company, Ingersoll Publications, also pledged funds to the same work on the basis of their involvement in the community. A research study commissioned by the City Council showed that in 1990, when the ICC and Centenary Square were under construction, the arts in Birmingham received an estimated £1.5 million of business sponsorship (The Arts Business 1991:12).

Centenary Square brought new life to the City, by definition. People now promenade in an area previously restricted to cars, which was dirty and dangerous. According to critics, the art in the Square has also 'enhanced' the ICC.

> What you see today, writ terrifyingly large, is the complete failure to design any new civic buildings of real architectural quality ... architects considered and rejected included Richard Rogers and Skidmore Owings and Merrill.

> ... it is the artists who have provided most of the redeeming features of the scheme (Amery 1991).

Images of the art in Centenary Square are used by businesses promoting their products and in press and media coverage of events in the city. In that sense they could be said to symbolise the new Birmingham.

Another indication of success might be that several of the parties overtly involved in the public art programme have met with professional acclaim elsewhere in the country. The City, for example, has been approached by a number of other local authorities, including various London Boroughs, Southampton, Preston and Oldham, for advice in setting up their own programmes. The artist, Tess Jaray, was subsequently commissioned to design Wakefield Cathederal's new precinct; Raymond Mason was invited to create a monument for the City of Birmingham, Alabama, USA to celebrate their vote for Civic Rights and PACA lead a consortium of public art consultants advising Cardiff Bay Development Corporation on its public art strategy.

However, as the public art programme proceeded, what the City identified as 'severe difficulties with the definition of roles, responsibilities and processes' were revealed (BCC 1991).

The management of the public art programme and its impact on those overtly involved

Problems with the management of the public art programme focused on Deanna Petherbridge's mural for the ICC. Although this was an isolated case, the implications of the incident directly affected the City Council's attitudes towards the employment of the agency and the artists.

Without giving notice to the artist or the agency, a series of plants on trolleys were installed in front of Petherbridge's mural. This was in compliance with the City Council's Licensing Laws, according to which designated drinking areas in the ICC had to be screened off from other public areas. The effect of the planters was to push viewers inside the building too close to the mural and obscure the view of it from outside the building – special lighting for which was included in the National Westminster Bank's sponsorship of the work. Petherbridge halted work on the mural. The City Council considered taking action against her for breach of contract; her proposed counter action was predicated on the need for the City to uphold the artist's moral rights, and focused on her objections to the derogatory treatment of her work.

In short a compromise was negotiated by PACA between the various parties involved. These included the artist, her solicitors, the City Council and its legal Department, the architects for the ICC, the Licensing Justices and their solicitors, the NEC/ICC management and its solicitors and the Licensees. The Arts Council and PACA's Trustees were also involved. The work was completed for the opening of the ICC in June 1991.

However, in November, a temporary exhibition of canal paintings, scheduled for three days, was placed immediately in front of the mural. Although, according to Diamond, the matter was immediately rectified, Petherbridge, a well respected writer, took the opportunity to describe the events in the national press, and raise questions about public art practice – the relationship between commissioners and artists in particular (Petherbridge 1991).

Following difficulties with previous contracts in January 1991, the Director of Museums and Art Gallery had already made several recommendations to the Joint ACE Sub-Committee with respect to the management of the City's public art programme. These included clarifying the client brief for the public art commissions and distinguishing more clearly between the City's client and contractual capacities; that the role of the ACE committee should be to ensure the City's policies are consistent and that the quality of the work is high; that the clients should define the brief and the precise role that public art plays in the project; that the client committee should be involved in the selection of the artist and the brief met; that a project controller should ensure the interests of the client committee and ACE Sub-Committee are met and that schemes are implemented on time and within budget and that the design process is undertaken by a multi-disciplinary design team with a team leader.

Following the opening of the ICC and Centenary Square, the Directors of the Museums and Art Gallery and Planning and Architecture articulated some of their concerns about working with public art agencies.

> The fundamental problem seems to be that the Agencies in this field inevitably find it difficult to balance their 'crusading' role on behalf of art and artists, with their responsibilities to their client [the City Council].
>
> The second problem is administrative ... When the Agency quotes for administering a given project, it has to make judgements about the time it will take. But artists are unpredictable, and the projects they create are often complex and unusual (which is why we employ them!). Problems do arise and the Agency can all too easily find that it is working at a loss. It does not have

reserves to call upon in such circumstances, and the fees it quotes are low by commercial standards.

Both these factors required active involvement in the management of the public art programme by the City's officers, who considered it important to reassess the conditions of their working relationship.

> It would, in our view, be worth making a distinction between that work to which the Agency can make a special contribution (identification of appropriate artists; running competitions) and that which would normally be better done in-house.

Despite PACA's very considerable experience it was noted that all the Council's public art work, up to that time, had gone to the same consultants.

Some individual officers in the City Council doubted the need for an agency. One, a former member of the Planning and Architecture Department maintained that 'the working relationship depends on the competence of the employing authority to design the brief ... you don't need an agency'.

The City and the Agency appear to have differed over the question of consultation. PACA consistently supported the notion of consultation. The Leader of the Council considered that while they might look to advice from various parties, it was the job of the elected Councillors 'to make the decisions'. However, the Directors of Museums and Art Gallery and Planning and Architecture acknowledged 'the value of arranging an appropriate form of public consultation'.

> We have in fact consulted with the public on all our projects, in whatever way is appropriate for the scheme concerned. We are always looking for better ways of doing so, and there is a particular difficulty with city centre projects where it is by definition difficult to identify a public with which to consult. More localised schemes can be associated with local residents or community groups in a way which is not possible on city centre sites (Diamond).

The General Manager of the ICC, where the staff had not yet been appointed and were, therefore, not represented in the WAWP, perceived consultation as a pragmatic issue. He emphasised

> the need to ensure that the operational needs of any proposed location are fully taken into account. There does seem to be room for improvement in

management techniques as to how to integrate design aspirations with practical reality.

According to one of the artists commissioned elsewhere in Birmingham, the public's 'visual illiteracy' had largely informed their response to the works – 'Blame the education system. They're not able to deal with innovative art'.

The issue of consultation in Birmingham is sometimes compounded with education, presumably in the sense of preparing the public for the commissioned works. In this sense, PACA proposed that 'knowing the community as well as decision makers is important. It would have been good to have had artists working in the community and in local schools.'

The issue of consultation was also closely related to the provision of community projects within Birmingham's public art programme. In 1989 PACA initiated the post of Inner City Public Art Officer, having negotiated joint funding from the Calouste Gulbenkian Foundation and the Economic Development Unit of Birmingham City Council. The establishment of this post was intended to balance the prestigious city centre public art commissions and to enable communities to improve the visual quality of their neighbourhoods; encourage in communities a sense of ownership of their local area; provide opportunities for people who do not normally have access to the arts to work with professional artists on quality visual art commissions and to involve in this process those who often have little control over their environment. Following cuts imposed on its spending, the City withdrew its funding of the post after two years. Up to that time 16 projects had been completed ranging from artists in residence through to artists' designs for a mobile library vans. The officer also gained the commitment of several City Council departments to work with artists.

The City's attitude towards working with artists is, in many ways, 'demanding'.

We try to recognise the full implications of 'public' art as a form which demands both high aesthetic standards and responsibility towards the receiving public and the site which is provided for its use (Diamond).

Birmingham had encountered difficulties

with artists being unable or unwilling to recognise that making art for public places imposes responsibilities on them and on us as clients which do not apply elsewhere. For much of the twentieth century art has functioned within

151

an environment of dealers, galleries and private collectors, where everything is arranged to meet the needs of art rather than anything else. In public places art has to deal with a whole range of practical issues and with the public as a whole, not just those who visit galleries.

Other problems pertained to the relationship between the artist, the architect and the site-user. With respect to the ICC, the Directors of the Museums and Art Gallery and Planning and Architecture felt that these needed

to be much more closely managed. Likewise contracts need to make it clear that the City Council can ultimately give no guarantees on the environment within which a work of art is to be placed, however desirable this may be.

Given that the City was responsible for the foundations and other technical details, they also proposed that

any engineering implications need to be identified and dealt with at a very early stage. Delays and additional costs were experienced on two of the ICC schemes because of engineering problems.

By comparison, Jaray's membership of the design team represented a model of good practice. As one of the design team put it

it was strategically useful as a bargaining point employing artists on the team and ... in raising the profile of the scheme and securing the Councillor's support.

The Directors of Museums and Art Gallery and Planning and Architecture believed that employing an artist in the team resulted in a

scheme which appears to work in every practical respect and which is also visually coherent and of very high artistic quality.

The working relationship was reputedly difficult at times. Jaray's appointment lead to the usurping of extant plans by the City's landscape architects, who eventually submitted formal objections to the planning committee. There were also practical difficulties. According to one of the team

Tess wasn't used to working with a team. She refused to compromise. Tom Lomax, who was trained as an engineer, was useful as a mediator and could identify real problems.

There were, apparently, some practical problems with her design concept. 'The engineers saw problems with the bond [of the lay out of the bricks] that you don't get with a herringbone lay. It is not able to withstand weight.' The architects thought that the pattern would be hard to achieve. Although the contractors persisted, there was a flaw in the variation of bricks.

> The inspiration was hers, the technical work and shaping of concepts ours ... The only arguments were over the basic design, walkways, planning, materials. The fact that there was no firm brief allowed the artist more freedom and more scope for difficulties.

For her part Jaray had felt that the team didn't want an artist, in particular her and she had to accommodate the City's change of the brief and 'fight every inch of the way'. A major issue that underlined her and Lomax's relationship with the team was that of assuming responsibility, not least towards the project and the public. On the one hand, they felt that the City 'unloaded responsibility on the artists'; on the other, they assumed certain responsibilities. 'To certain people it was only a job ... [whereas] as artists we upheld the part of the community.'

Some of the participating artists were ultimately critical of the programme as a whole. David Patten described the project as

> structured like an a la carte menu ... which precluded meaningful interaction because of the 'ego-needs' of key players. This was further compounded by the role of the City Museum and Art Gallery.

> In retrospect, I firmly believe that if the whole ICC/Centenary Square project had initially been approached conceptually (as opposed to a la carte!) this would have created opportunities for city-wide dialogue and partnerships would have enriched the final product and ensured a far greater public gain.

In terms of the City's development of its public art programme, different public art projects fall to different departments in the City Council. Whereas Centenary Square was the responsibility of Planning and Architecture, the redesign of Victoria Square fell to the Engineers, Recreation and Community Services. 'Although there were discussions with [them and they] had attended meetings and visited the site of Centenary Square, there was no direct carrying over of experience.'

The impact on those not overtly involved

One of the lessons of Centenary Square was that 'public art can be a high risk business in publicity terms'. The art at the ICC and in Centenary Square created considerable interest in the local media, in particular, both before and after its installation. Once Raymond Mason's sculpture *Forward* was erected in Centenary Square in summer 1991, public art became 'a major talking point in the city.' While some visitors to Birmingham are attracted by the recently sited public art works, others appeared to be less conscious of them. PSI's survey of users of the ICC showed that 48 per cent were unaware of the art in the ICC or Centenary Square. As Birmingham City Council anticipated, the public art programme did not specifically encourage users to the ICC (Appendix 4, p. 333).

Much of the press coverage reflected on Birmingham City Council's spending. In 1988 the proposed expenditure on art for the ICC was described with a sense of pride. *The Birmingham Post*, for example, reported: 'A dramatic £100,000 neon-tube sculpture will be the eye-catching feature at the main entrance to the mall' (2.6.88). In the event, the commission was £180,000 in total.

However, the City's past experience of the City Sculpture Project of 1972, led some journalists to associate the costs of art works with controversy. It was anticipated that Ron Haselden's 'modern sculpture' proposed for the ICC for one, would provoke the 'hottest debate since *King Kong* loomed over the city' (*The Sunday Mercury*, 6.11.88). This was a reference to the Nicholas Munroe sculpture which had been temporarily sited in Birmingham as part of the *Peter Stuyvesant Foundation City Sculpture Project* of 1972. Concern that the city should not make itself a laughing stock extended to Mason's *Forward*.

> It must be some kind of in-joke. It might mean Birmingham City Councillors were twerps to pay for it (*The Birmingham Post*, 7.6.91).

Despite the general consensus that pieces of public art had contributed to improving the environment and that all the decisions were made by the Councillors, including Conservatives, once the art works were in place, the spending on art was contrasted to the lack of spending on pressing social needs. Features frequently compounded issues of cost and aesthetics. One headline in *The Evening Mail* (6.2.92), for example, asked

> Good taste or a waste ... Would you pay £590,000 for these six works of art?

Other articles raised the issue of public accountability. The Conservative Councillor David Roy, was frequently cited to this effect.

> We have made some disastrous decisions on public art in Birmingham recently. I don't know how we managed to decide whether to accept some of this rubbish (*The Birmingham Post*, 11.6.91).

> If there was some system to let the public decide what they consider quality art ... I might have more sympathy with some of the ludicrous wastes of cash agreed by a small cabal of people – some of whom are unselected and thus unaccountable to the voters (*The Evening Mail*, 26.2.92).

The Birmingham Post also promoted the view that the city's public art was an indulgence – 'art for art's sake' (3.12.91). It further compounded issues of excessive spending and xenophobia. In an editorial entitled 'Spending has to stop' it described how

> For a City Council which has overspent by an estimated £50 million on the ICC, a mere £30,000 may seem like a drop in the ocean. But for the poll tax-payers of Birmingham, it is an added insult to the injuries already endured at the hands of a council which seems to delight in profligacy (30.7.91).

The Evening Mail and its sister paper, *The Birmingham Post* promoted Conservative councillors' objections to the quality of art commissioned so vigorously that they came to be regarded as party political by organs as diverse as *Arts Management Weekly* (July 1991) and *The Spectator* (August 1991).

One effect of these papers' coverage of the public art programme in Centenary Square and at the ICC was that all public art in the city became controversial. Once Victoria Square was redesigned, controversy shifted from the Mason to Gormley's *Iron Man*, despite its being a gift from the TSB to the city to mark the bank's relocation from London to Birmingham. Discussions about other public art projects in the city tended to focus around similar issues. *The Birmingham Post's* coverage of a sculpture, *Sleeping Iron Giant* sited in the Heartlands Redevelopment Area, for example, indicated that the work was regarded well by local residents.

> Before it came the place was just a rubbish dump. But now it's landscaped and it makes the area look a lot cleaner and tidier.

> I think its great. Our school unveiled the statue and we have been writing essays and making up legends about how it came to be there. But we know it has really come from the council.

But the paper's coverage also showed that residents thought that other services represented more of a priority.

I don't think they ought to spend that kind of money on art when schools are short of money (*The Birmingham Post*, 28.3.93).

Impact of Birmingham's regeneration

In 1992 Patrick Loftman and Brendan Nevin, of the Faculty of the Built Environment, the University of Central England, published a research paper challenging the success of Birmingham's urban regeneration. In particular, they questioned the benefits of the city's massive public sector spending in support of private sector interests. Their research has been discredited, particularly within the City Council.

Birmingham City Council claimed that it had created 2,000 jobs, generated visitor spending of £50 million and attracted new private investment into the city. Indeed, Sir Nicholas Goodison of the TSB cited Birmingham's cultural programme as one of the reasons for his company relocating there. The researchers, however, maintained that, like similar models of urban regeneration in the US, including Baltimore, Denver and St Paul, Birmingham had failed to address issues of social equity and had produced an inequitable distribution of benefits and costs. They cited research, carried out on both sides of the Atlantic, which claimed that disadvantaged city residents often fail to benefit in terms of quality employment or the use of facilities developed, and that deprived neighbourhoods and essential public services lose out in terms of the redirection of scarce public resources towards prestige projects.

Between 1986/7 and 1991/92, a figure equivalent to 30 per cent of Birmingham City Council's capital budget (as distinct from its revenue budget) was expended on transforming the appearance of the Central Business District (CBD) – an area comprising 2.6 per cent of the city. This capital sum was raised through European grant aid (30 per cent) and loans arranged through the National Exhibition Centre Co. According to Loftman and Nevin disadvantaged groups are effectively excluded from prestige developments such as the luxury hotels, new sports facilities, flagship arts and cultural facilities and shopping malls, etc. The jobs created are predominantly low-paid, low-status and largely part-time. Issues of equal opportunities in recruitment practices and employment within publicly funded initiatives have not been upheld due to government legislation. The extent of public subsidy to private sector businesses within the CBD has led to the local authority assuming private sector risk. The prestige model adopted by the City entailed opportunity costs which reduced local authority resources available to support much needed investment in deprived areas, and public services, such as pubic housing and education, depended upon by the most disadvantaged in the city.

Loftman and Nevin's research interested both the local and national press. Nick Cohen, for *The Independent*, reported that in the nine inner city wards, 31 per cent of adults were out of work; that Birmingham's schools required £200 million on repairs and modernisation; just 23 per cent of pupils were said to achieve five or more GCSEs at Grade C or above, equivalent to former 'O Levels'. The unemployment figures show that almost ten years of high profile projects have failed to boost the city's economy. The ICC was reported to have an operating loss of £6 million a year as well as costing the council £20 million in debt-repayment charges (Cohen 1993). As a news story it was made all the more topical by the fact that, as in a number of major cities in the US, Birmingham appeared to be rejecting its CBD-focused urban regeneration strategy. Loftman believed his findings were vindicated by the fact that

> in every US city where this policy has been tried it has failed. In each case, reforming administrations have now come to power promising to concentrate on basic services. Theresa Stewart's election is the first sign that this trend is now hitting Britain (Loftman, cited in Cohen, 1993).

The public art programme for Centenary Square and the ICC was necessarily implicated in these criticisms even though, as Diamond had pointed out, the public art programme in Birmingham received a high level of non-Council funding. 'Much of the programme has been funded by Europe or by sponsors, so the question of transferring funds to other Council purposes simply does not arise.' While there has been no evaluation of the contribution it made to employment or the generation of income in the city, the research of the consultants, The Arts Business into *The Cultural Economy of Birmingham* commissioned by the City Council in 1991 found that culture was less appreciated and valued in Birmingham than in other cities, such as Glasgow and Manchester. However, unlike the art in the ICC, the art in Centenary Square represents one aspect of the CBD-strategy which is publicly accessible. That fact, however, has not served to protect it from criticism.

Forward

Once the works at the ICC were in place, the papers tended to seek public opinion through vox-pop interviews and inviting readers to write in. In July 1991, for example, *The Evening Mail* organised a telephone poll of 6,000 people, 76 per cent of whom were reported to be in favour of moving *Forward* to 'Handsworth, Sparkbrook or anywhere'. By August, *Forward* had

> become the major talking point in the city. It is attracting people into the square who haven't been there for years. It's attracting people in the city to walk around and have a look at the new developments ... who haven't done it for years (Ed Doolan, *Tell Ed*, phone-in, BBC West Midlands, 7.8.91).

It was only in mid-1992 that 'public art phobia' shifted to Victoria Square.

Press reports about people's opinion of the Mason tended to reflect themes covered by the media itself. The relationship between the two appears to have been symbiotic. In June and July 1991 for example, correspondents to the *Birmingham Post* and *Mail* suggested replacing the Mason with William Bloye's sculpture of *Boulton, Murdoch and Watt*. Mason had, in fact, studied under Bloye at Birmingham School of Art. One writer proposed raising a subscription for the purpose. The following December *The Birmingham Post* revitalised the discussion by advocating to its readers that the Bloye should be moved (3.12.91 onwards).

By comparison with the Mason the smaller pieces in Centenary Square and the ICC attracted little or no response. PSI's research of passers-by in Centenary Square (Appendix 2, p.287) and users of the ICC (Appendix 4, p. 333) suggests that more people noticed *Forward* than any other piece. Many disliked it. By comparison, Mason's work had attracted almost unanimously positive reactions during his 1989 exhibition. The second most discussed piece was Lomax's *Spirit of Enterprise*.

The Mason was controversial for a variety of reasons. He was the city's 'most famous sculptor' and the theme of *Forward* was the motto of Birmingham. More pragmatic issues were the cost of his work – £275,000. Much of this sum was spent on materials and expenses incurred in its production. Mason himself felt that 'The £45,000 I earned for two and a half years work was my way of repaying a debt of gratitude to my native city'. People regarded the fact that *Forward* was constructed out of fibreglass as controversial. Other issues that contributed to the debate were the style of the figures, the fact that the sculpture was painted and that it was once vandalised. That the work was 'parachuted' overnight into a space that people already used was, in itself, evidently provocative. This, as indicated earlier, had been for practical reasons – so that the roads could be closed – but people interpreted it as representing civic embarrassment. 'No wonder they put it up in the middle of the night' (*The Birmingham Post*, 7.6.91).

The majority of letters published and the majority of passers by whom we interviewed responded negatively to the work. The colour was said to be 'awful', 'the shape ugly' and the' size wrong'. The sculpture was described as resembling 'a slab of rancid butter', 'a mould' and as having the 'appearance of an enlarged toy from the Far East – cheap and nasty.' The materials and the finish were particularly criticised.

Why it couldn't have been done in bronze or stone I'll never know (caller to *Tell Ed*, 7.8.91).

Fibreglass has no connection with Birmingham past, present or future.

Resentment about its appearance reflected on the Council's role as a 'patron'. One headline in *The Birmingham Post* referred to the imposition of its taste on the citizens – 'Jaundiced reactions to a yellow monster'. A letter to the paper complained about the lack of a democratic process in the Council's failure to consult the public. Comparisons of the work to Stalinist or Nazi art – 'Red Square, Birmingham B1' (*The Birmingham Post*, 7.6.91) referred as much to the process of its commission as to its formal resemblance to Socialist Realism.

'Common sense attitudes' featured in the reporting of several vox-pop features. '*Forward* fails the audit test', for example, recorded the attitudes of a group of managers in a local accountancy firm towards the Raymond Mason. Children's behaviour towards the work was regarded as a kind of critical barometer.

Perhaps the children who were in the square this weekend have found the solution. All afternoon they could be seen climbing all over it (*The Birmingham Post*, 23.7.91).

The same theme preoccupied callers to *Tell Ed*.

I'm highly disgusted every time I go because kids are actually being helped by the parents to get onto the statue.

Many members of the public responded badly to more city funds being spent on security, following vandalism of the work.

Perceptions of the artist's own attitudes also provoked hostility among those writing to *The Birmingham Post* and *Evening Mail* (1.7.91), in particular his suggestion

> that your editorial staff are unequipped to deal with this sort of art must surely encompass a large number of the population. What right does he have to be so patronising?

However public opinion about *Forward* was far from one-sided. *The Birmingham Post* published letters in support of the work, and the majority of callers to *Tell Ed*, a BBC West Midlands phone-in, on which Mason appeared in August 1991, said they liked it. Some thought that controversy itself validated *Forward* as a work of art.

> We look at Rodin's sculptures which were ridiculed at the time and are classics now.

Enthusiasm for the work was often bound up with civic pride. One phone-in caller, for example, described how

> each time I come home it's been almost a disappointment ... I was just amazed to see such beauty in Birmingham.

A 12 year old correspondent, writing to *The Birmingham Post* thought *Forward's* value lay in its references to the city.

> We hope the statue will not be removed because it represents the past and future of Birmingham city (23.7.91).

Other writers felt the same.

> Not just a simple picture of Birmingham through the ages but also our evolution,our coming to terms with change, our invention, our suffering, our survival, our hope, our contribution to mankind and so on (*The Birmingham Post*, 26.11.91).

It was important to several members of the public that the Mason was appreciated by foreign visitors to the city.

> As a Brummie, I was keen to hear the views of colleagues from other countries – and what I heard made me very proud ... The majority were impressed by this massive work of art (*The Birmingham Post*, 4.7.91).

People believed that the sculpture, if not the controversy associated with it, attracted many people to the city centre.

Such was my surprise that anything at all could elicit such passion in Birmingham that I made time to examine Raymond Mason's piece myself (*The Birmingham Post*, 12.12.91).

I keep saying, me and my Mum, we keep saying we must go into town ... just to have a look at it to see what it looks like in real life (caller to *Tell Ed*, 7.8.91).

Birmingham has benefitted phenomenally from the development of Centenary and Victoria Squares, and the city is a very much pleasanter place to be as a result of their existence. I walk across both fairly regularly, and seemingly whatever the weather, there are always people consciously looking at their surroundings. Little knots of people spend a lot of time looking at and physically encountering the sculptures ... Both squares have become places of leisured strolling, of sitting, talking, looking and playing. I have to conclude that people are genuinely deriving much pleasure and enjoyment from their experience of them and I don't think you can divorce their pleasure in the overall improvements from the role artists have played in them (Antonia Payne).

However some people had grave doubts as whether attracting people into the city centre signified *Forward*'s value as a work of art.

I really take exception to you saying that its alright, leave it there, it might not be good but it's bringing people in. You could have two dogs in fibreglass copulating. That'd bring people in. But it's tacky (Caller to *Tell Ed*, 7.8.91).

Some regarded it as more than a curiosity, as something that made them think.

You have to stop and look at *Forward* time and again to see it ever more unfolding; it is grand, startling, humble in turn (*The Birmingham Post*, 26.11.91).

I've been to Centenary Square to look at your statue more than once ... I think the more you go to have a look at it the more you can sort of see (Caller to *Tell Ed*, 7.8.91).

Improvements to Smethwick High Street, Sandwell, 1986-1990

Background

Improvements to shopping centres in the West Midlands
By the late 1970s both the social culture of local neighbourhoods and the livelihood of individual traders in the West Midlands were being disrupted by the development of supermarkets, out-of-town hypermarkets, discount warehouses, mini-markets, chains and purpose built shopping centres. In 1978, with funding from the Labour Government's Urban Programme, authorities in the region launched an initiative intended to stabilise or regenerate declining inner city shopping centres. The programme grew to become the most substantial in the country, doubtless reflecting the degree of investment required in what the 1981 census listed as one of the most deprived areas in the country.

The objectives of the West Midlands' County Council's Shopping Improvement Programme, articulated in 1985, were to

> assist with the stabilisation and retention of the district and neighbourhood shopping centres, in order that they may continue to serve the shopping needs of local inner city communities, with particular regard for low income and low mobility groups:
>
> assist with the retention and adaptation of centres, so that they can continue to provide a social and physical focus for inner city communities:
>
> demonstrate local authority commitment to inner city regeneration areas, by carrying out improvements in areas which have a high profile, and thereby help to inspire confidence in the future of the inner areas for businesses and residents alike (PSMRC 1988).

In order to achieve these aims, the programme sought to make the centres more visually attractive, stimulate shop owners to carry out internal improvements, improve the economic viability of the centres, make the areas more attractive to shopkeepers and shoppers, ensure a sound structural condition of the properties so that they could continue to serve their function, stimulate and complement other improvements being undertaken in adjoining areas, such as housing improvements, improvements to pedestrian safety and convenience and the removal of sources of danger and congestion.

The shopping centres themselves were a particularly emotive area.

As Rod Willman, who lead the Regeneration Section of the Planning Division of both the West Midlands County Council and, subsequently, Sandwell Metropolitan Borough Council (MBC) put it

> The shopping centres were ... seen by us not just as places to go shopping, but as the public face of the community.

Eligibility and range of improvements

Under the shopping centre schemes, only certain types of properties were eligible for improvements. Grant aid was not paid directly to the traders themselves, but provided funds for the local planning authority to carry out improvements. These comprised standard packages of structural and decorative work to the front elevation of shops – making good chimneys, roofs, brickwork, windows, doors and decoration, replacing shop sign fascia boards and providing or renewing damp proof courses. As the scheme developed in the West Midlands, the security of premises became increasingly important. Insurance companies were imposing substantial increases on premiums on shops in all inner city areas. In certain areas obtaining any insurance cover was contingent upon the installation of security devices, such as steel security shutters. These were installed in certain areas as part of the refurbishment schemes.

These external refurbishments were carried out under 'envelope' schemes – so called because they literally embraced whole blocks of shops. This process was intended to restore the original features of the buildings and achieve an overall consistency of design which would have a direct impact on the street scene. By 1984 these 'face lifting' schemes received 100 per cent grants since it was considered vital that improvements should not depend on the ability of shopkeepers to contribute.

Packages of improvements were also made to the area in which the shops were located. These included works to pavements, the provision of pedestrian crossings, street furniture, improvements to the street lighting, rear access for loading and unloading and off-street parking. In 1983 the scheme had been extended to incorporate improvements to the rear of properties. Owners and tenants were expected to contribute 50 per cent of the extra cost.

Typically consultations about shopping centre improvements were carried out by the local authorities with local traders and the community. The process usually involved the distribution of leaflets to shopkeepers outlining the proposals and inviting them to attend a public meeting to discuss them. The local authority officers' role was primarily to convince shopkeepers of the need to improve the fabric of their properties. The schedule of work was drawn up by their architects on the basis of individual inspections. It was then left to contractors, employed as a result of competitive tendering, to carry out the work.

In the early schemes the County Council attempted to take account of the preferences of individual traders. In the event, they exerted so strong an influence that, according to *An Evaluation of Urban Programme Funded Schemes in the West Midlands,* carried out by the Management Research Centre, Aston University (PSMRC) and published in 1988, they disrupted the schedule and diminished the impact of the finished work.

Smethwick

The improvements to Smethwick were initiated by the County Council in 1983. After its abolition in 1986, responsibility for the scheme passed to Sandwell MBC, which redeployed many of the County Council's staff. This ensured a some degree of continuity to the scheme.

In 1981, the government had identified Sandwell and three other West Midlands areas as among the 20 most deprived areas in Britain. At that time, Smethwick (population 17,476) had a higher incidence of unemployment, single parent and single person households, pensioners living alone, people lacking basic amenities, people of other than British ethnic origins and households without a car than was the average in the West Midlands, England and Wales. Comparisons between the 1981 and the 1991 *Census Area Profiles* of the shopping centre catchment area for Smethwick High Street (Sandwell MBC) show that although unemployment had fallen from 19 per cent to 17.3 per cent, the number of residents who were economically active had dropped from 59 per cent to 42 per cent. This may have been due in part to the ageing of the population. Fifty eight per cent of households were listed as occupied by pensioners. People still lacked basic amenities. The 1991 statistics showed that over 32 per cent of the households in the area had no central heating.

The area around Sandwell has historically attracted immigrants – from France, Ireland and Jamaica and more recently, Asia. The 1991 profile of the Smethwick High Street shopping centre catchment area showed that the number of residents from ethnic groups has risen to 38 per cent from 36 per cent in 1981. A total of 30.7 per cent of residents were from the Indian sub-continent. Another 7.3 per cent were black Caribbean and African.

Smethwick itself has attracted what Malcolm Harris, formerly Chief Planner, Sandwell MBC, described as a 'stigma which plays upon a dull and impoverished image and racial bigotry'. The loss of the Labour MP Patrick Gordon Walker's seat in 1964, for example, was largely put down to the slogan 'If you want a nigger for a neighbour, vote Labour'.

The need for improvements to Smethwick's shopping centre was particularly acute. The locality was already subject to a housing clearance programme. In 1983/84, one side of the High Street was demolished to clear the way for a new bypass. In one fell swoop it halved the number of shops and reinforced the effects of the recession by diminishing passing trade. It left the traders feeling 'downgraded', stranded and exposed. There was, according to the Town Artist, a general feeling that Smethwick had 'been destroyed by the planners'. As Roy McCauley, Planning Assistant in the Department of Technical and Development Services, Sandwell MBC and formerly with the West Midlands County Council, put it

> We basically had a single parade of shops that looked as if it ought to be on the sea front, but instead of the sea you were now exposed to noise of traffic roaring in and out of Birmingham. We didn't feel we had much of a chance of salvaging the situation.

Plan of Smethwick
High Street showing the
shops to be redecorated
© Sandwell Metropolitan
Borough Council

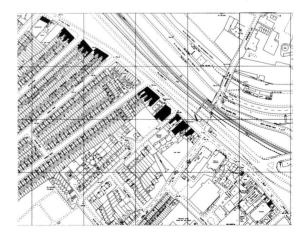

The planners realised that the traders on the fringe of the centre, who occupied the poorest properties, had little reason to be optimistic about their future prospects.

> Lots of the Smethwick traders down there are people who lost their jobs during the recession of the 1970s. They're first-time traders and it's their only lifeline ... They took over the shops deserted by the more traditional traders in Smethwick (McCauley).

The shops left in Smethwick reflect the changing demography of the area, in particular the development of the Asian retailing sector. *Shopkeepers' Surveys* of 1984 and 1986 revealed that nearly 70 per cent of Smethwick's shopkeepers were Asian (PSMRC 1988); the Town Artist estimated that by 1987 it was 'closer to 97 per cent'. The introduction of their businesses, which were oriented to the changing requirements of the community, doubtless helped to check the decline in the number of small independent traders. They were prepared to trade at low prices and although their individual prosperity may have been checked by intense competition, they contributed to the social culture of the community by offering services in marginal locations, often over long hours (PSMRC 1988).

Under the shopping centre improvement scheme, the shops in Smethwick were eligible for improvements to their front elevations, roofs and off-street parking. None of the traders opted to contribute to improvements to the rear of their properties. Grants were not available to owners of properties occupied by multiple chains, banks, building societies, public houses and political organisations, although they were invited to participate in the scheme at their own cost.

Traders whose shops had been demolished to make way for the bypass were compensated. In that sense the enveloping represented an indirect form of compensation for those left behind. But it hardly made up for the loss of trade. Officers in the County Council's Planning Department felt that Smethwick needed significantly more help than other shopping centres to stop it spiralling.

> Smethwick had gone further than any of the other centres. None of the others were so badly decimated. In Hay Mills we were enveloping the shops in advance of the road scheme, but in Smethwick we started during its construction, after established traders had already given up and moved out (McCauley).

The Council had planned to build an earth bank on the opposite side of the High Street between the shops and the new bypass. The traders objected to this proposal vehemently. The Town Artist, who by then was himself a Smethwick resident 'was getting the message from the traders that they really needed to advertise themselves ... to shout out that there was something worth making a detour for'. The standard improvements would hardly satisfy such needs. 'The decorations tended to look as though they'd come out of a catalogue. They lacked vitality. We were not particularly proud of how we presented the newly refurbished shops' (McCauley).

In the event the shops in Smethwick came to be distinguished from those in other centres by a decorative scheme, designed by Francis Gomila, the Town Artist, in consultation with the traders themselves.

Processes

Town Artist

Francis Gomila, formerly Town Artist in Peterborough, was one of two artists appointed in 1985 to work with the Landscape Department of West Midlands' County Council. He was initially employed for 12 months. His post was funded by West Midlands Arts which provided his fee and the County Council which provided materials in kind.

Both artists' posts were an adjunct to the County Council's Operation Green-Up. As a highways authority, the West Midlands had developed a scheme intended to improve the approaches to and the environment of the conurbation as a whole. It was based on European models and included landscaping, planting and the installation of street furniture. Whereas the other artist, Jeremy Waygood, was employed as part of the landscape team, Gomila's brief was to create 'features' and to work with the 'community' in Smethwick, which was one of Operation Green-Up's key target areas.

According to Gomila this brief was ill-conceived, not least because it had been formulated without consultation with the Planning Department. He was doubtful about how the community would perceive him and indeed how he would fit in. As one of the planners commented in retrospect, he was only part of the community 'in the sense that he was landed on it'.

Nevertheless, Gomila perceived himself as an agent of change. Although he maintained that the short-term, superficial brightening up of the environment with 'a substance as thin as paint' could 'be potent ... and inspire people to make changes', his interest lay in making 'a more substantial contribution to a longer term programme of urban renewal'.

> I had great hopes that public art could present some kind of hope in a fragmented community – not like a tranquilliser, but [in terms of] real action.

Gomila's initial 12 months were spent in developing contacts and relationships within the local authority and the community itself. In his own words, he wanted to 'provoke a dialogue' and 'raise awareness' of what could be achieved by an artist working in the context of urban renewal. During that time he 'established a base from which to launch this philosophy' and secured a commitment for the continued funding of the project. After four months he moved from his base in County Hall to the 18th century Toll House on the High Street, the one building left standing on the side of the High Street that had been demolished. This brought him into immediate physical contact with the local community.

During his first year Gomila completed murals and mosaics and organised a street festival – all of which involved the community. He also produced *Waiting for Halley's Comet?*, a sculpture which marks the Western entrance to the High Street. It was made shortly after the passing of Halley's comet in 1986. The comet is not expected to be visible from the earth for another 75 years.

Waiting for Halley's Comet? is made of steel (a reference to the industrial revolution) and comprises seven flat life size figures depicted holding hands and dancing in a circle. It is formally reminiscent of Matisse's *Joy of Life*, 1909. The circle surrounds an area in which a time capsule is buried. Members of the community were asked to suggest or donate items, representative of Smethwick in the 1980s, to be placed in the capsule. Contributions included Asian textiles, an Argos catalogue, a number one hit record, a dictionary of citizens' band radio terms, an AIDS information booklet, a packet of Black Country pork scratchings, a piece of jewellery, a copy of the *Sandwell Evening Mail*, a photographic history of Smethwick and a collection of modern coins. According to Gomila, 'there are also some small items of treasure, but I am not going to say what these are, because I think there should be a certain mystery to something like this.'

Malcolm Harris, Chief Planner at the time, described the work as celebrating 'the renewal of the area'. Gomila, on the other hand, refers to it as representing the general ambience of the times.

Everyone seems to be waiting for something – a job, a new house ... The return of Halley's Comet heralds a time of change ... What will Smethwick be like when the comet returns?

The work was reputedly disliked by the Chair of the County Council's planning committee, who considered it 'inappropriate'. This negative reception contributed to opposition to Gomila's post being extended, but in the event 'it slipped through the cracks during abolition. Sandwell was happy to see it implemented' (Willman).

Following the abolition of the West Midlands County Council, Sandwell MBC redeployed many of the County Council's staff and extended Gomila's post for a further four years with funding from the Urban Programme. It was hoped that the introduction of an artist to the refurbishment team, which comprised town planners, architects, landscape architects and private building contractors, would result in a 'new and fresh approach'.

We saw funding a community artist ... as fairly innovative. Although there are examples of artists being employed elsewhere, they are mainly in new towns (Willman).

The fact that he was formally contracted to West Midlands Arts ensured that Gomila could maintain his independence and

keep the planning department at arm's length ... Once he was free from Operation Green-Up, he was able to range over all sorts of improvements. That's why we deliberately called him the Sandwell Town Artist (McCauley).

Shopping centre improvements
Gomila perceived the refurbishment as the most important thing that had happened to the High Street and wanted to be involved in it. He approached Sandwell planning department with a proposal to work with the community in respect of the improvements. 'It was a last minute thing.' He hoped to

revitalise the street, both physically and psychologically, by encouraging a new attitude and confidence from the traders (Harris, undated).

For their part, the planners imagined he would 'give more flair to

Standard Jewellers, Smethwick High Street, before redecoration
© Sandwell Metropolitan Borough Council

Standard Jewellers, Smethwick High Street, after redecoration
© Sandwell MetropolitanB orough Council

Billingham Shoes,
Smethwick High Street,
after redecoration
© Sandwell
Metropolitan Borough
Council

what we usually had ... add some zest and vitality to a standard enveloping scheme – they don't often make a huge impact'. The team also viewed the artist as a potential intermediary between themselves and the shops' owners .

Gomila regarded everyone who had 'a stake in the High Street' – the traders and the shoppers – as his clients. His relationship with the traders was doubtless helped by the fact that he kept them informed about the progress of the improvements.

> They didn't know precisely what would happen to their properties or when ... so I found myself telling them.

The brief the artist set himself was to develop designs which would transform the dull and featureless face of the High Street and expose what he perceived as the 'richness' of the shops themselves. The 28 shops included in the scheme were run by traders from different cultural origins. They ranged from *Billingham's Shoes*, which had been in the hands of the same family since 1879, to comparative newcomers selling a variety of merchandise – foods from all over the world, Asian textiles and jewellery. In Gomila's words, they reflected 'a wealth of colour, exotic design and culture' – particularly in the context of the Black Country. It was precisely this aspect of the community he wanted to emphasise.

From November 1986, by which time the refurbishment was under way, Gomila developed a series of proposals for the decorations. Over a period of four to six months he discussed the ideas and the evolution of the designs themselves with individual traders. 'The time was important in allowing people to talk'. The traders knew the decorations would increase the visibility of their shops and wanted the designs to refer to the use of individual shops at the time. The development of the designs fostered a sense of competition between the traders as to what their designs would look like. Gomila also wanted to maintain the overall integrity of the blocks in which the shops were situated. He was forced to assume an essentially diplomatic role.

In his discussions with the traders, the artist explored matters which are rarely talked about, such as how the traders displayed their goods, their visual traditions and aesthetic concerns.

> It seems a simple question ... To allow people to choose between two colours – say black and white, is one kind of choice. But to allow people to choose any colour is quite ... different ... People need time to adjust and react to this, requiring different examples to access and evaluate:

> Given this choice, everyone is likely to respond differently, and this case was no exception – all the shopkeepers finding their level of participation. Some took an active part in projecting their image and pride in their trade. Others contributed by suggesting or producing actual designs for inclusion in the scheme, while others were quite simply happy to accept the majority decision (Gomila cited by Harris, undated).

Despite the fact that what Gomila was proposing could always be changed – literally painted out – the unusual nature of the designs unsettled officers in the planning department. They considered themselves responsible for the work at this stage. Never having seen 'anything like it before', they doubted that was what 'the traders said they wanted'. There was

> a general sense of disbelief that Francis was having the meetings with the community, despite his reassurances.

> We wanted a quality scheme that people would be proud of. The proposed designs seemed so outlandish. It raised questions about who is the arbiter of public taste... Had we the right to overrule in favour of a 'safer' scheme? We weren't sure about how you honour the spirit of participation with such an unusual outcome. It was our first encounter with artwork which challenged convention. Initially we couldn't believe it wasn't a flight of fantasy on the part of the artist (McCauley).

Ill at ease with the prospect of 'blindly commissioning something that the artist prescribed, when we would get all the flack', the officers needed convincing and went to the High Street to talk to the traders themselves.

Not surprisingly, the proposals met with even stronger reservations from elsewhere in the Technical and Development Services Department. There was a real fear that the proposals would bring ridicule to the authority. Some felt very strongly that this 'Asian' image was totally inappropriate for a Black Country high street. The main point of contention was that

> here you've got a Black Country Street with Victorian shops and you should not be changing the character of it in such a radical way. I suppose it was a conservation argument ... You should have respect for the original design. We had one or two sessions debating the issue, and agreed to disagree (Willman).

Although the decorations did not formally require planning permission, the officers directly concerned with the project wanted it to go to committee for a proper debate and formal decision.

> At the time, there was a real danger that the proposed designs would effectively be blocked by disagreements between officers. It was a bit of a tussle to get it to planning, but it gave the artist and the traders a chance to explain things. We like to keep our members informed of anything new. We thought that we needed to get them on our side. We'd already been converted. It would have been contrary to the spirit of democracy [not to] ... The next problem was how were we going to get it through committee (McCauley).

In the event, the final proposals for the High Street were presented at a public meeting attended by the traders and local councillors in March 1987. Councillors were divided between those who regarded the designs as 'frivolous' and those who believed that they would give pleasure and 'lift the community's spirits'. The proposals were supported by Councillor Ron Davies, then Chair of the Land and Town Planning Committee. In order to eliminate any doubts about the community's support for the project

> the traders stood up in committee and said that they wanted it. This was something almost unheard of in Sandwell. Trade had declined thanks to the County Council, and they needed this kind of promotion to survive (McCauley).

In the event, the politicians and the traders formed 'an unholy al-

liance', Objections were overruled. The planners went straight into implementing the scheme.

Davies' support for the scheme was fuelled by his own 'secret fan-
tasy' of Smethwick as the focus of the Asian music scene and the High
Street as a latterday Carnaby Street.

> As a local authority we were trying to encourage the Asian sweatshops to
> produce a better class of garment ... the High Street is where those sari shops
> are.

> We were looking for an Indian pop group that would have a number one
> record and would take off – the Asian Beatles. That was a dream. The fact of
> allowing ... the artist and all that, was part of the dream.

The decoration was applied to numbers 2-22, 86,90 and 92 High
Street, numbers 1-5 St Paul's Road, The Empire Theatre and the Princes
Cinema. During the refurbishment it became necessary to rebuild the
entire gable wall at 5 St Paul's Road. This gave Gomila the opportunity
to incorporate a design for a polychromatic brick 'tree of life' motif.

After the first phase was complete, Davies requested that the scheme
be extended to the rest of the street. This was achieved in 1989/90 when
the Council decided to carry out some remedial works to shops which
had been enveloped by the County Council three years earlier. Although
there was less scope for artwork on most of these buildings, this phase
nevertheless included designs for the Indoor Market, the Red Fort Social
Club and a tap on the ironmonger's shop.

The contractors tendering for the work had reservations and according to one of the planners, priced their work 'beyond what's reasonable,
just to avoid doing it'. In the event, the main contractors appointed were
A & R Astbury Ltd and Sandwell MBC'S Works Division. The designs
were transferred on to the walls by a newly established local firm of
signwriters, Four Images Ltd, whose estimates undercut those of the
others who tendered for the job. They had been trained on the Youth
Training Scheme and had set up business under the Enterprise Allowance Scheme. According to McCauley,'Francis gave them a kick start'. In
the event, the contractors initial hostility soon gave way 'to a remarkable
partnership and working relationship'.

> With the foreman taking the challenge the art scheme demanded on board,
> the workers followed, realising that the project provided an opportunity for
> them too, to be creative and show the extent of their skills. From Frank Evans,

the bricklayer, who built the 'Tree of Life' gable end, the carpenters who worked on the pilaster details, the painters, a small local firm of signwriters ... to the planners in the Council's Regeneration Section, who steadily tackled any obstacle:

The whole workforce worked as one creative team, sharing skills and solving design problems on the spot. By the end of the contract the feeling was not of finishing yet another refurbishment scheme but of completing a work of art:

One of the workers remarked 'I am so glad there are artists around ... life would be so boring otherwise' (Gomila cited by Harris, undated).

Fourth form pupils from Shireland High School were involved in the design and production of mosaics. The school had a 'very enthusiastic, energetic and creative teacher who wanted to involve the students' and who had worked with Gomila previously. The pupils designed the kicker panels under the windows of shops numbers 2-10 High Street. The work was carried out as part of life/social skills course. All the participants volunteered.

Kicker panels, Smethwick
High Street, designed by pupils
from Shireland High School
© Sandwell Metropolitan
Borough Council

As far as the artist was concerned, 'it was nice to get people who were already half-motivated'. Although the architects were unused to working with school children, the Planning Assistant thought it 'very important for me to make that kind of space'.

The regeneration of the High Street also involved Michelle Buckley, from the local YTS, who was on a training placement with Gomila. She spent three months designing and painting the mural on the hoardings around the Princes Cinema which had been closed since 1982. Her intention was

> to draw the public's attention to this beautiful building which could be saved from further decay and put to good use – especially by the young people of Smethwick, who have nowhere to go (Harris, undated).

The cost of enveloping the first phase of 20 shops was at an average of £14,500 per property. The total cost of transferring the graphic designs to the walls of the 34 properties in the two phases was £8,600 – an average of £253 per property. Shireland School's mosaics cost £400 to produce. £100 was spent out of the promotions budget for the enveloping scheme to celebrate the completion of the project.

Impact

The benefits of the decorative scheme to Smethwick High Street can be assessed from a variety of perspectives: from the points of view of those with an overt interest in the scheme – the artist, the planners, local councillors – and those with a stake in the High Street itself – the traders and shoppers.

Sandwell MBC has not carried out a formal evaluation of the scheme or in-depth analysis of the shops' turnover. Those involved are, however, aware of responses to it. 'It's stuff you pick up talking to people.'

In 1988 the Department of the Environment published an evaluation of the improvements to inner city shopping centres in the West Midlands (PSMRC 1988). Its evaluation of Smethwick High Street was based on research carried out before the decorative scheme was completed. It nevertheless contains observations relevant to this study, and is referred to below. During the course of research for this case study we carried out a series of short interviews with shopkeepers and shoppers in Smethwick High Street (see Appendix 2, pp. 287-288.).

Formal recognition of the scheme has largely come from external agencies. The West Midlands Branch of the Royal Town Planning Institute gave Sandwell MBC an award for having made a significant contribution to town planning in 1987/88. The scheme was also commended by the Art at Work Awards. Informally the Planning Assistant gives some six talks a year to students about the improvements, and answers a similar number of requests from other local authorities wanting to know how it was done. The scheme has attracted media attention.

Criteria

Sandwell's objectives, according to which the benefits of the scheme might be measured, were very specific.

> We virtually had an impossible task. We had to salvage the shopping centre which was spiralling (Willman).

The scheme was intended to boost trade and investment in the area.

> Public investment was largely justified as a means of pump-priming private investment, encouraging shop owners to do their own investing, encouraging others to stay in the centre ... public art was part of that (Willman).

The planners, by their own admission, had limited expectations of the decorative scheme. It was intended to symbolise the Council's investment in the centre.

> ... it has helped to demonstrate that investment has gone in ... I can only imagine that the positive effects [of the improvements] were increased by the obvious visual display of improvement (Willman).

Whereas the planners were concerned with 'getting the structure of the place in fine fettle', they could not attend to 'the more elusive thing of trying to get the spirit of the place back on course'. This was assumed to be within the capabilities of the artist. It was also expected that the scheme would improve the environment.

> Environmental improvement and improving the image of an area is one aspect of economic development. It helps to boost confidence. This is a fairly depressed industrial area. It is lacking – to a certain extent – in a quality environment. Public art is part of the image enhancement and confidence boosting process. It contributed to a cumulative impact – you can't disassociate the one from the other (Willman).

In the event, planners regarded both the enveloping scheme and the decorative scheme as successes.

> Given what [Smethwick's] been through, I think its been a major victory from stopping it from falling even more ... What would it have been like otherwise?

Shoppers and shopkeepers

Before the scheme was undertaken, surveys of shoppers carried out in Smethwick showed that between 1984 and 1986, as many as 30 per cent of white households in area had stopped shopping in the High Street.

Furthermore, there was a substantial fall in the purchasing of basics in Smethwick by households in socio-economic group E (state pensioners and widows, casual and low grade workers). However after 1986 the High Street became more prosperous. According to PSMRC, major factors to which this might be attributed were changes in the general appearance of the centre and in the range of shops. In Smethwick both were identified with the increase in Asian traders.

Responses to the decorations were always mixed. Although the decorative scheme initially provoked 'some adverse reactions from older, more traditional residents of Smethwick' as Willman observed, 'no one felt moved enough to organise any opposition to it'. A general dislike of the work may have been predicated on resistance to change *per se*. The majority of traders and shoppers doubtless compared the High Street to how it had been in the 1960s – a bustling, two-sided street.

> They don't want any changes from the good old days, when Smethwick was at the hight of the industrial revolution. People despise anything that brightens the place up ... [They] see the colours as the last nail in the coffin (Gomila).

Councillor Davies concurred

> Anything different, they seem to resent. Their minds have rusted with the process of aging. They have not kept up with what the new generation expects.

For their part, the planners supposed negative reactions were informed by 'a racist undertone'.

> People jump to the conclusion that if it's different it must be the new Asian community ... because Francis doesn't look Anglo-Saxon, they assume he's Asian... The scheme looked so alien, it must be to do with the Asian community.

Five years on attitudes remain much the same. Out of a random sample of Saturday shoppers surveyed at the bus stop on the High Street, only 20 per cent thought that the decorations improved the appearance of the shops and over half believed that the appearance of the shops was worse. However, their comments often referred to their perceptions of the shops in general – 'no decent shops', 'one can tell that they're not English shops', 'foreign looking', could be 'more up to date'. Some people thought that the shops in Smethwick looked scruffy, others that they looked 'different – brighter'.

Those overtly involved in the scheme, in particular the artist and the planners, who compared the street with how it had been in the early 1980s, regarded the decorations as having exerted a positive impact.

> I feel that the work on the High Street had this kind of power when it was created – had a sense of the High Street being reborn (Gomila).

> It's brought the place alive ... It has had an amazing visual impact. Yes, it has contributed to the general regeneration programme (McCauley).

By dint of visibly uniting the whole street, the scheme has had the effect of extending the centre.

> There certainly used to be vacant shops – especially in the end block by the Empire Theatre, which is very much off centre. You'd almost think that bit was in terminal decline, but its been brought very much into the centre by the painting scheme. It looks reasonably successful (Willman).

Not only has the scheme changed the look of the High Street, but it appears to have drawn the traders together to promote themselves collectively. When the scheme was newly completed, Gomila organised a street party for all the people who had 'been through it'. He did the same the following year. They were reputedly

> really good do's ... in a place that you would have imagined had lost its will to do anything ... Yes, we can celebrate coming from Smethwick. Yes, we can celebrate the shopping centre turning a corner (McCauley).

Following a break of three years

> what seemed to be really elusive was happening – the councillors and traders wanted to organise the carnival on their own (McCauley).

No other improvements in the West Midlands have been celebrated in that kind of way.

> Our improvements don't tend to unite anybody... We find [what's happened in Smethwick] very useful. We have helped to stimulate a collective spirit in a place – something which had always escaped us in the past. It never dawned on us how important it was (McCauley).

With respect to trade, those overtly involved in organising the scheme reported that trade was up. According to the artist 'some shopkeepers maintain that it has gone up something like 10-15 per cent. It has been considerable'. Councillor Davies believed that 'most traders are proud of their shops'. The shops themselves are said to be 'more market-able, desirable'. Few traders have moved away.

> The fact that the painting is lit up at night has made people enquire into the possibility of living here (Gomila).

> New traders have come in. The shop vacancy rate has dropped from 15 per cent down to 4 per cent and stayed there. This is significantly below the average for Sandwell (Willman).

The Prince's Cinema has reopened and the Empire Theatre has been refurbished as a Sikh temple.

Although over half the traders interviewed thought that the appearance of the High Street had improved – 'looks cleaner and better decorated' – one described it as a dead shopping centre, something to which the bypass and the lack of employment in the area had contributed. It could be that few traders can afford to move away. Five years after the improvements were made, the majority said that there was no increase in business.

Sandwell Metropolitan Borough Council
The Council clearly regards the decorations as a good investment.

> You spend £8,600 on an art work scheme and get ... a landmark for the borough ... and all the favourable publicity... The same sum would fund a little bit of landscaping or part of a paving scheme which would go unnoticed (McCauley).

The scheme focuses attention on the place. It is

> a very attractive feature of the town ... It reminds me of a child's cut-out, or Carnaby Street. Drivers, if they have anything in their souls, look along [the High Street], especially when its flood-lit at night (Davies).

> I would say, it has helped put the place on the map more than it was before ... There's something quite unique about it ... It's quite famous now – not a bad thing for a place like Smethwick which had quite a negative reputation. Its put the place back on course ... [The scheme] is a statement about Smethwick: 'Something is happening there' (McCauley).

The scheme has contributed to the official reconstruction of Sandwell's identity. In fact, Gomila's work features on Sandwell's promotional literature.

Sandwell Surprises, promotional brochure issued by Sandwell Metropolitan Borough Council, showing Francis Gomila's *Waiting for Halley's Comet?*, Smethwick High Street © Sandwell Metropolitan Borough Council

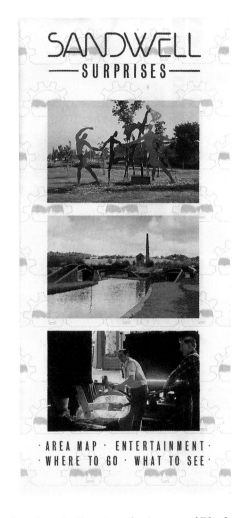

The scheme is generally thought of as challenging the image of Black Country industrial heritage, which currently informs so much of the region's promotion. In that respect, it stands in stark contrast to the monument to James Watt, one of the leading figures in the industrial revolution in Smethwick, sited at the top end of the High Street in 1983-4. Although Gomila's scheme might be thought of as referring to the canal heritage, it is more frequently associated with changing people's perception of the place. According to the artist, the work has contributed to the community's own sense of identity. They can now identify what Sandwell is about. Part of the power of public art is that it can change prejudices of what an area is like (Gomila).

According to the planners the scheme went beyond their expectations. 'Francis demonstrated just how much mileage there was ... he basically educated us.' They have used the same approaches that were tried on the High Street elsewhere.

> We now have the foundation to support subsequent work. We have expanded the area we operate in. We have examined how things can be done ... We now recognise the value of making time to talk to shoppers, traders, kids ... explaining why we're doing it and seeking their involvement (McCauley).

However, attitudes towards the decorations themselves and the employment of an artist remain fundamentally unchanged. The painting of the stark 1960s Windmill Precinct bright pink did not have the impact that had been anticipated. The proposal 'seemed to have the support of the traders. They gave it the thumbs up'. At the time of research, the painting was vehemently disliked. However the planners assumed that as the paint fades, the community will warm to it. Attitudes may change. According to Councillor Davies, 'We find they will appreciate it when it's done'.

Despite the planners' perceptions of the High Street scheme, Sandwell did not continue Gomila's funding beyond the life of the Urban Programme.

> It didn't score highly enough as a priority. Art is still seen as a bit of a luxury when it comes to it (McCauley).

> It was obviously a political decision. It's hard to argue with it. Which worthy scheme do you cut? Public art or the rape crisis centre? How do you trade these things off? (Willman).

The project did little to eliminate the prejudices held by the authority's officers against working with artists.

> When you announce that an artist is working on the design team – you get a really sharp reaction – they don't see the relevance (McCauley).

Even within the Planning Department, there is still a feeling that artists intrude in the design process.

> The artist is the lowest in the pecking order. Not respected at all. Yet people

from outside acknowledge his achievement more readily than those of the other design professionals who are involved.

People regularly use [the High Street scheme] as a bench mark for what they don't want. They feel justified in slagging anything new off (McCauley).

Five years after they were painted, the decorations are suffering the same lack of maintenance that affects most other enveloping schemes. The traders are not motivated to carry out routine maintenance repairs. Yet, although some new traders have taken over the properties, the decorations remain intact. According to the Planing Assistant, this may be 'partly because they can't afford anything better, partly because they don't want to destroy its unity'.

At the time of research Gomila was still based in the Toll House on Smethwick High Street, but worked on a consultancy basis – employed partly by Sandwell; partly elsewhere. His projects included those related to Tipton's City Challenge bid.

The future of public art in Sandwell is, however, becoming less secure. Sandwell Metropolitan Borough Council has a Percent for Art policy and its draft Unitary Development Plan stated that it would continue to encourage public art schemes. However, the Urban Pro-gramme is being wound up and the initial success of getting public art specifically incorporated in the successful bid for Tipton City Challenge does not appear to be being followed up with any strong commitment from the City Challenge Board.

As far as the planners were concerned the scheme was salutary. It forced them to become

aware of the limitations of bricks and mortar, which is important. There was a tendency to rush in. Something appears overnight. You rushed out, leaving them on their own again.

It raised questions about public responsibility.

Some people regarded the spending of that amount of money as an act of charity. But we had damaged livelihoods at the focal point of the community with the bypass.

More specifically, the Smethwick High Street scheme raised ques-tions about the long-term impact of such improvements. As PSMRC proposed, while the physical improvements to the shops in the West Midlands were important in the short-term, they were insufficient to safeguard their long-term future. The effects tended to tail off after a few years. The report recommended continuing intervention as necessary for small scale schemes in order to maintain the catalytic and confidence building effects. The artist and the planners agreed. McCauley, for example, maintained

> there is a need to do more to change the spirit of the place. The recommendations of the research [PSRC] emphasised that these schemes were worthwhile – but that there needs to be a sustained layer of support for these shopping centres.

For his part, the artist was

> interested in the fatigue principle. How can you sustain people's interest? It will take 20 years of investment to reverse the blight. Public art should be seen in that context ... I believe in the long-term.

> Perhaps it [the decorative scheme] shouldn't be kept. If you are unemployed – continuously disenfranchised – it must be difficult to live in a festival town.

> I get the feeling that the project has been seen as a bit of an experiment that has probably run its course.

6 Yorkshire and Humberside

The Chantreyland Sculpture Trail, Graves Park, Sheffield
1989-1990

Background

90 days in 89: A season of new art in Sheffield
In summer 1989, Sheffield Contemporary Arts Trust (SCAT), an artists' association, organised a three month long festival of the visual arts in collaboration with Sheffield City Council's (SCC) Arts Department. The festival, called *90 Days in 89*, ran from 3 June to 3 September.

SCAT was formed to set up exhibitions for and by Sheffield artists, and had already organised two exhibitions of its members' work in temporary spaces. In 1987 they organised *Witness*, followed in 1988 by *InterCity*, a collaboration between artists in Sheffield and Birmingham. It has since been involved in many projects which have taken place in public spaces. *90 Days in 89*, however, remains SCAT's largest project to date. It included the work of over 100 artists working in the City.

The festival represented what David Alston, Deputy Director of Arts, SCC, referred to as 'a series of enthusiasms'. For Barbara Cole, then Chairperson of SCAT:

> Apart from the obvious desire to have new works seen, the over-riding ambition of SCAT members, is that everybody should have the opportunity to experience and enjoy art in all its forms and to benefit from the experience (SCAT, undated report).

The City Art Galleries were, 'as a matter of policy', concerned to 'build up links with artists in the locality'. Alston described the authority's attitude in the *90 Days in 89* programme.

> This season of new art in Sheffield is about visibility – perhaps the hardest thing for any artist to achieve, so limited are the possibilities for showing work in our society as a whole ... For many artists with self-commitment the possibilities of showing work are few. The gallery system itself has a

185

conditioning effect, in that it sets up certain expectations ... Gallery spaces encourage the production of gallery art, or a gallery public.

Over the last few years, in a determined effort to overcome these unspoken 'rules', artists in Sheffield have self-organised to find new ways of making contact with the public in an uninhibited way. They have provided a refreshing challenge to the so-called threshold fears of people coming into contact with art.

The Arts Department has welcomed these past ventures and sought to be supportive in various ways ... *90 Days in 89,* as a season, must be judged ... as a starting point for future seasons of new art in perhaps increasingly diverse and unconventional locations.

The Department also had an art administrative agenda.

The project brings a 'breath of fresh air' to sculpture in the urban environment which is long overdue in many of our cities in Britain. It was during the great Victorian era that sculpture really found a place in municipal parks. There was a tradition of placing sculptures that commemorated certain events, or indeed official dignitaries. In recent years sculpture has either moved indoors or has been sited within the concrete urban environment. This sculpture project in Sheffield is different, it revives some of the old traditions but places it a modern context (Alston, undated B).

Alston hoped that the collaboration between SCAT and the Arts Department would have several advantages, not least that it would represent a more effective use of public money, give more people the chance to see artists at work and 'advance the cause of public art'.

The festival took place all over the city. The majority of events were held at the Graves, the Mappin and the Ruskin Art Galleries and Graves Park, all of which are administered by the City Council. Other venues included schools, arts venues, a hospital, a day centre, a shopping centre, a community centre and a play scheme. Artists opened their studios to the public.

90 Days in 89 embraced a range of activities – crafts, painting, sculpture, installation, mixed media, video, documentation, residencies and placements, an exchange exhibition with artists in Scarborough and an artmart. Some events specifically focussed on women's issues and Aids. To complement the festival of new art the Graves Art Gallery showed a major survey of *British Art 1890-1980,* which was purchased for the nation under the terms of Sir Francis Leggatt Chantrey's bequest and was on loan from the Tate Gallery. Chantrey (1781-1841), was a highly prolific and prestigious sculptor, who was born and buried locally.

The Art in the Parks Programme

The Art in the Parks Programme was held in Graves Park and Weston Parks, in which the Mappin Gallery is situated. However, the main focus of the activities was in Graves Park.

Graves Park is the largest in Sheffield. Situated in Norton, on the outskirts of the city, it covers some 300 acres. It was given to the city in 1926 by Alderman J.G. Graves. The park has been administered by the Recreation Department of SCC together with the Rare Breeds Centre and the Norton Nursery, also a gift of Alderman Graves, since 1988. The combination of all three is known as Chantreyland.

The Recreation Department's interest in the Art in the Parks programme stemmed from its plans for marketing the parks in Sheffield, the development of Chantreyland in particular. It set up a Chantreyland Project Group which, on the basis of a survey carried out in March 1989, proposed enhancing the park and improving its overall image. Priorities included signage, car parking and toilets. Since the implementation of the Group's plans required sponsorship, they perceived the Art in the Parks programme as being to their advantage 'in making a case for funding'. It was deemed

> very appropriate in the vicinity of the great sculptor's birth, [that] this unique sculptor/artistic project has been born (Sheffield Recreation Department, undated).

The group was also attracted by the notion that the artists 'would be addressing environmental issues'.

The Recreation Sub-Committee became formally involved with the project at a relatively late date. On 11 May (some three weeks before the festival started) they responded to a request from David Alston to assist with appropriate services and site accommodation at Graves Park and Norton Nurseries. This enabled the project to take place. They also allocated funding towards the marketing of the programme from the outdoor promotions budget, assumed responsibility for the maintenance of the sculpture, and made timber available to the artists in kind.

In line with the overall objective of the festival to show art in places where it is not normally shown, Art in the Parks was conceived 'as an

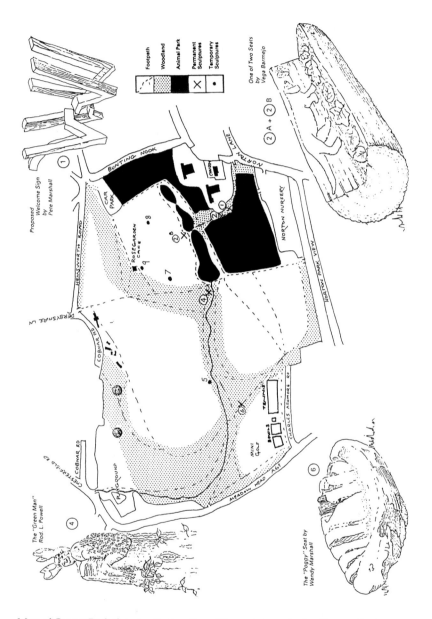

Map of Graves Park showing the location of the sculptures in the Chantreyland Sculpture Trail from the promotional brochure issued in 1989 to mark its opening. © Recreation Department, Sheffield City Council

alternative to indoor venues'. The public was intended to 'discover' artists 'working at various points throughout Graves Park on sculpture, and other artistic projects of their own devising'.

On the completion of their works, a 'mini-sculpture trail' would be set up in the park over a weekend, which would 'give the public a chance to experience a sculpture trail at first hand. We will be inviting them to make comments and recommendations for what they would like to see in the future.' It was not anticipated at this early stage that the trail would be permanent (but see p. 200).

In financial terms, the Art in the Parks programme in Graves Park constituted a major feature of *90 Days in 89*. It was allocated £8,300 out of a total budget of £21,300 – 40 per cent of the total spend. The programme was funded and supported by the Henry Moore Sculpture Trust (£2,000), Sheffield City Arts Department (£4,500) and the Recreation Department (£1,800).

Processes

Twelve artists were involved in making art in Graves Park. Eight artists had placements, and four were commissioned.

Those with placements – sculptors, a potter and a water-colourist – worked in the park for between 2 to 15 days. They worked in full view of the public and ran workshops intended for public participation. Work by Barbara Cole, Susan Stockwell, Sally Harper, Karen Scott, David Mayne, Edmund de Waal and Vic Brailsford (whose work had been carved at the Fargate Shopping Centre) were temporarily included in the trail. They were employed at the rate of £50 per day.

The four artists who were commissioned to make permanent pieces were Vega Bermejo, Wendy Marshall, Pete Mountain and Rob Powell. They also worked on site. All these works were commissioned by Sheffield Arts Department. Each artist received £1,000, a fee which included any costs and expenses involved. The work was expected to take a month. According to SCAT, payments were made according to guidelines recommended by the Arts Council.

The artists who participated in the Art in the Parks programme were effectively 'self-selecting'. All the artists who wanted to work in the park were accommodated, except for two who wanted to work together on one piece of work for a fee of £2,000, which was beyond the budget. The majority wanted to make temporary, as opposed to permanent, works.

> It was just a Sheffield thing. Not very many artists were interested. They were probably deterred by the idea of working in wood or making something functional (Bermejo).

All the artists, in principle, were 'concerned to make contacts with the general public'. Some – Bermejo and Powell, for example – were keen to gain professional experience. For Powell, 'It was my first commission as a professional artist'. Bermejo wanted to make a work which she knew would be sited. She also wanted to earn the money.

There was no brief, as such, for the artists to work to. They had no contracts. They were, however, bound to use timber which had been cut down, died or which would have had to be removed from the park.

The project was essentially artist-led, with some debate between the Recreation Department and the Arts Department about the nature of permanent features in the park and their functional ends.

As the festival publicity put it, they were expected to devise their own projects 'with a keen eye on the environment'.

> There was no formal process of vetting ideas. We had total confidence. The sums were so small, there was no way we could intervene (Alston).

However, the artists all tended to work with an eye to the context. Bermejo, for one, assumed that the works should be 'in harmony with the park' and that considerations would have to be paid to the safety of the public. She, nevertheless, assumed that her ideas would be appropriate as a matter of course. In the event, three out of the four commissioned artists made functional works. Two made seats, one made a sign.

The sites were chosen by the artists in conjunction with the Recreation Department. The latter wanted the works spread out through the park and sited along familiar routes. The artists' reasons for selecting particular sites were idiosyncratic by comparison.

Powell walked around the park to find a site. 'They told me about trees designated to be cut down – Dutch Elm Disease.' In the event, he selected 'a 12 foot stump which stands by the entrance of woodland'. He was already 'preoccupied with the conflict between urban and rural cultures', the ancient past and the notion of a collective unconscious. He was also interested in stories about the park itself. His piece, *The Green*

Rod Powell, *The Green Man*, 1989
© Christopher Callow,
Sheffield City Council

Man, derived from green issues and the story of the Celtic God of the woods. 'I played on the qualities of a half-human tree – half-man, half-tree.'

> During my time in the park there was a sighting of a ghostly figure of a green man. I didn't know about it. I was working on ley lines, on old burial sites, Celtic remains.

> They drew up a quiz on the Parks Department with questions about *The Green Man*.

Bermejo chose sites for her two benches along main routes through the park: one by the duck ponds; the other, overlooking meadows. She chose the 'biggest pieces of wood' she could from Abbey Lane Mill and decorated the benches with carving that refers to their settings. One has

Vega Bermejo, *seats*, 1989
© Christopher Callow, Sheffield
City Council

ducks and lilies and the other, a basset hound chasing butterflies – a
reference to dog-walking in the park.

Wendy Marshall's idea for what she referred to as a 'poggy' bench

came from a childhood word from Rotherham meaning someone's favourite
place. A place where you feel at ease with yourself. A place where you might
go to find some peace of mind.

I wanted the shape to have quite powerful proportions and yet have a gentle protective feel to it. To invite onlookers to sit in its lap. The site was chosen because it evoked these kinds of feelings. Even though it was close to a path it has a quality of being secluded – of being cossetted by the banking and the woods ... The site chosen to construct the bench overlooked a dried up stream and a waterfall.

In constructing the work, Marshall selected curved tree trunks from the City Council sawmill in Ecclesall Woods. These were cut to size and arranged tightly in the hollow that had been cut in the bank.

A grab arm lorry and several members of the tree felling gang manoeuvred the heaviest logs into position. The upright logs were baked with roofing felt and sealed with tar based glue to afford some protection from rotting. Once positioned the logs were scalloped out with a chainsaw. Nails were then driven into the back of the logs to grip the concrete in which the structure is embedded. The earth was then replaced around the tips:

Chainsaw and chisel marks were removed with various power sanding tools. Finally the bench was oiled several times (Marshall, Artist's Report, SCAT, undated report).

The Recreation Department relandscaped the area after the bench was concreted in. They

organised a group of conservation volunteers to build sweeping woodland steps down to the bench and lay woodland paving at its base. The paving took on the feel of a pool reflecting the rhythms of the bench.

Wendy Marshall, *The 'Poggy' Bench*, 1989 © Christopher Callow, Sheffield City Council

Pete Mountain also worked with wood from the Ecclesall Woods saw mill. It was proposed that his work, a six foot high sign reading 'Welcome', should be placed on the approach to Parkway – the main link road between the M1 and the city centre. However, planning permission was refused. It was agreed that the sign should be erected at the entrance to the park. He carved the piece on site during the weekend of the Sheffield Show.

The sculptures were introduced to the public in two ways. The festival itself was advertised. According to Bermejo, posters were 'stuck up all over town', there was 'good press coverage', 'well over a thousand sculpture trail leaflets were distributed during the Sheffield Show'.

The leaflet has a map of the trail and information about Graves Park, Chantrey and Chantreyland. It shows the sites of the commissioned pieces, the proposed site for Pete Marshall's *Welcome Sign* and the four temporary pieces. In the park itself, there was a map showing where artists were working and information boards 'so that the public could read about each artist'. The sculptures were, however, primarily introduced to the public by the artists themselves.

Impact

The Chantreyland Sculpture Trail was not formally evaluated by either the Henry Moore Foundation (as funders) or the Recreation Department. However the Arts Department and SCAT (which 'actively practices a policy of self-assessment') both produced reports on *90 Days in 89*, which review the festival as a whole and the Art in the Parks programme in particular. The SCAT report also contains individual reports by the artists who participated in the programme.

The criteria

The criteria by which the trail might be evaluated are those articulated by SCAT and the Arts Department as constituting their ambitions for the project. They included the promotion of work by Sheffield artists, enabling the public 'to experience and enjoy art' in the open, challenging the public's 'fear of art', encouraging them 'to have a go' and make art themselves, heralding 'future seasons of new art in diverse and unconventional locations' and making effective use of collaborations between different agencies and the spending of public money.

In general terms the artists deemed the festival as a whole, and the Art in the Parks programme, a success.

90 Days in 89 has been a challenging exhibition of art, breaking down the barriers between artists, curators and galleries. The exhibition presented a changing face of work by artists from a variety of disciplines ... An artmart exceeded all expectations in encouraging the public to purchase art.

Artists took up the challenge of taking on new roles as promoters, curators and co-ordinators and filled every venue in Sheffield.

Events such as the work undertaken by the Graves Park artists for the Sheffield Show were considered of great importance in fulfilling SCAT'S policy of community access (Introduction SCAT, undated).

Overall, the Graves Park part of *90 Days in 89* was of great benefit to the artists, each of whom has received financial backing and support from all the groups involved in the furtherance of their careers (Cole and Brailsford, SCAT, undated).

The Chantreyland Sculpture Trail and the public
There was no detailed investigation of how the Chantreyland Sculpture Trail impacted on the public, either before, during or after the Sheffield Show.

The survey into the Recreational Use of Parks in Sheffield, carried out in March 1989 by the Department of Geography and Recreation Studies, Staffordshire Polytechnic provided a profile of the visitors to Graves Park. The user profile of Graves Park largely conforms to national trends.

Over 50 per cent of the park users – the people most likely to follow the trail – are women, aged between 21 and 45. (This includes those visiting the park with children.) Over 52 per cent are employed, 11 per cent retired, 4 per cent unemployed. The majority of people who visit the park (57 per cent) go to walk, with or without a dog. Supervising children, watching and playing sport and visiting the rare breeds centre are also popular activities. The survey showed that visitors particularly like the size of the park, 'its natural look' and its 'open space'. The majority of the park users are local. They walk to the park and visit it regularly. (Over 33 per cent go to Graves Park once a fortnight. Slightly less go once a week.) Once in the park, they stay for longer than the average visitor to other Sheffield parks. Nearly 45 per cent of visitors stay between two and three hours.

The survey also showed that relatively few of the Graves' users were actively interested in looking at art. Whereas 75 per cent used the authority's libraries and swimming pools, less than 40 per cent visited galleries. In this respect, at least, the Art in the Parks programme could be said to have made art accessible to a non-gallery going public.

There is no record of the number of people who saw the sculpture trail, or of those for whom seeing art in the open was a new experience. Some 63,262 people were recorded as having visited the galleries during the festival. In his Summary Report, David Alston pointed out that the numbers of participants in the workshops and residencies, those passing the artists in the park or the artist working at Fargate could only be estimated. They would inevitably 'represent existing, new and potential audiences for the visual arts'.

The impact of the sculptures
Little was known about the impact of the work. Few, if any, members of the public partook of the Recreation Department's invitation to suggest sites for benches. The public's interest in the artists themselves was taken to be synonymous with the impact of the work.

It was generally reported that the majority of the public 'were interested and enthusiastic about the work going on in the park' (SCAT, undated). One artist's impression was that they 'were appreciative of our presence (Powell, SCAT, undated). This was confirmed by the fact that they 'regularly passed favourable comments', 'they were interested in the ideas behind what I was doing', by 'letters from the public, the press. Verbally. Yorkshire Arts and the galleries all came around.' Another assumed that because the public talked to her about her work, it was well received.

What SCAT regarded as a relatively low incidence of vandalism suggested that few people took exception to the works. The artists' association reported that 'of the twelve artists' work in Graves Park ... only one piece was subjected to persistent vandalism'. This was a temporary piece. However, with the exception of Powell's *Green Man*, all the permanent commissions were subject to some degree of vandalism. There were attempts to move one of Bermejo's benches, which was subsequently set in concrete.

Not all the so-called vandalism was perceived as destructive.

Bermejo, for example, regarded names being gouged out on the back of one of her benches as 'a sign of success'. According to Alston, the

> key to why the works are still there [is because] ... the public were involved in their making of the works ... the artists were engaged with the public.

In some cases the public appeared to make gestures of encouragement to the artists. While Marshall was working, she reported that 'each morning ... the loose logs she puts on to cover the bench have been cleared off, all ready for her to get started'. Four years on letters written to PSI suggest that members of the public still hold the sculptures in affection.

> They really are very refreshing and add greatly to my enjoyment when dog walking. The thoughtful use of wood is particularly good in the Graves Park area as it is so wooded, and they are attractively situated.

> My friend and I often walk in Graves Park and we always include at least one of the sculptures on our route. We find them excellent and evocative.

Press coverage

The artists considered the trail to have been well covered by the local media. According to Berjemo, 'the only response at the time was in the papers and they were quite positive'.

The newspaper coverage of the trail effectively described the organisers' intentions. Even in the case of Ian Cooper's *Vulcan* which was added to the trail in 1990, the press reported the Recreation Department's aspiration for it to 'be seen daily by hundreds of people who might never think of going into a gallery. What better way to encourage a growing interest in art?'

Newspaper coverage of the trail was largely determined by specific sets of interests, which might be classified as novelty value, anecdote and chauvinism.

Brailsford referred to 'the shock of the new' reflex which not only determined responses to herself – 'a female stone-carver' – but to Wendy Marshall, in particular. 'If you go down to the woods today, you're in for a big surprise. For a Sheffield sculptress is making her impression on a city park with a chain saw' (*The Star*). Elsewhere, Marshall was described as 'wielding her chain saw with ease'. Other works making up the trail were cast as novel and humorous. Cooper's *Vulcan* was described as 'a sculpture that can definitely grow on you'. It was 'being carved from a live tree badly buffeted by a January storm'.

The sculptures were sometimes cast as the focus of human interest stories. One headline about Rob Powell's carving of *The Green Man* from a scaffolding tower read 'Artist defies heights of fear'. The story focussed on the artist overcoming vertigo.

> I didn't realise what it was like working so far off the ground ... Doing chain saw work up here is terrifying and I think it must be the most frightening thing I have ever done.

One woman was described as having 'watched the half-man, half-tree figure emerging over the weeks. Her alsatian dogs have enjoyed the process too, coming away with a good chunk of wood every day' (*The Star*, 22.8.1989).

Chauvinism also featured in the press coverage. The vitality of Sheffield's visual arts scene was praised over and above the quality of the work produced. Robert Clark, writing in *The Guardian* (5.7.1989), described *90 Days in 89* as far surpassing

> in organisation and general liveliness any similar survey I've seen in other cities.

> Since no selection has been made ... all artists getting roughly equal space, it gives a fascinating cross section of what's going on. Not all the work's astoundingly original of course, but the refreshing thing is it covers a variety of approaches and most of which is highly committed.

> For me, since I live in Sheffield, it's an encouraging experience to feel that all this dedicated creativity had been bubbling away through the city.

In general, the papers reported the public's 'warm affection' for the works that made up the trail. Compared to other case studies, there was little correspondence about it. This may reflect the fact that the work was not controversial. A writer to *The Star* singled out *The Green Man* for comment, as a 'clever and imaginative work which obviously required considerable researching in its concept'. According to the artist, 'Only one man didn't like it. He said if Henry Moore saw it he would turn in his grave.' Marshall's bench was reported to be a favourite with joggers. 'One jogger was so impressed with the bench he even wrote a couple of poems about it.'

A year later, when Ian Cooper was commissioned to add one piece to the trail, *The Star* described the trail as 'highly-acclaimed – now billed as one of Sheffield's top tourist attractions' (13.8.1990). Four years after the trial opened the works still appear to be held in affection. Alston speculated that this is because they were 'ultimately about the care of the environment'. Visitors to the park concurred.

> As a regular walker in Graves Park, I would like to say how delightful I found the sculptures there. They really are very refreshing and add greatly to my enjoyment when out walking.

> Many people do not get the opportunity to visit a gallery to see sculptures, so I think Art in the Park is an excellent idea.

In personal terms, the artists perceived their work as possessing qualities over and above the general criteria for the programme. Powell, for example, regarded the trail as a

> great public strategy for any Council. Generally people feel councils don't care. But here, it was good to see the Council doing something.

Marshall regarded her work as a 'small part' of a more general move towards a new spirit 'of optimism in Sheffield' itself.

> We are bringing ourselves out of the slump we were in a few years ago. There seems to be an arts renaissance going on in the North, and for once it is getting more fashionable to be positive and to concentrate on the nice things in life (*Sheffield Telegraph*, 2.3.1990).

How the experience of the Chantreyland Sculpture Trail has impacted on the work of those involved

Arts Department

In his Summary Report, David Alston identified the potential *90 Days in 89* had established in terms of cultural and economic developments in Sheffield. These particularly pertained to the sculpture trail. In his terms, the festival had demonstrated

> a lively but undernourished cultural base in the city ... The financial base for projects needs developing. This means realistic timescales and funding strategies ... The role artists can play in the local economy is signalled here.

The programme had demonstrated that there was a 'need for art in public places in the city'. This necessitated 'a need to build bridges with other council departments to carry forward the idea of promoting art'. In this respect

The combined Arts, Artists and Recreation effort to create Art in the Parks should be seen as providing the initial momentum for an extended art involvement in Graves Park and the Round Walk. Recreation's business plan is addressing this issue.

The festival as a whole had provided 'experience for artists and administrators' which could 'be built on'. While he thought that 'SCAT may have confirmed itself as a viable art organisation in Sheffield', it inevitably faced 'the problems of any unpaid voluntary organisation. How can it set its activity on a professional basis? How can it build up its membership across generations of artists working in the city?'

Recreation department

According to Alston, the development of the sculpture trail considerably influenced certain members of the Recreation Department. One individual, for instance, 'came cold to the project, and became a passionate advocate for the work'. Even as the artists were at work on the Art in the Parks programme, the Recreation Department was looking to develop the trail in the future. On 24 June, *The Star* reported the Department's Marketing Officer's intention to look

for further funding for the next year and hopefully that will be enough to create a major permanent sculpture trail.

If it does take off we don't have to limit ourselves to just one trail.

In the event, the Chantreyland Trail, which was not intended to be permanent, has become so.

There have been two developments since the trail opened. In Spring 1990, the Recreation Department made a former park keeper's lodge in Glen Howe Park available as a studio. At the time of research, it was occupied by Vic Brailsford, who was involved in the Art in the Parks project. Under the terms of a special lease, drawn up by the Public Art Officer in Sheffield, the artists occupying the lodge do so on the condition that they give the council works of art for the park in lieu of rent.

In summer 1990, the Recreation Department commissioned a further sculpture, *Vulcan*, from Ian Cooper to add to the trail. The work was carved from a storm-damaged tree. At this point, a spokesman reported that the department was looking for business sponsorship for 'its biggest challenge to date – the transformation of five nearby elms into living sculpture'.

Despite its enthusiasm and support for the Art in the Parks, Alston has criticised the Recreation Department for being 'unselective and exploitative'. The artists' criticisms of the project concur.

However, given the changes in personnel in the Recreation Department none of the proposed developments has taken place. Nevertheless, the draft UDP proposals for improving Sheffield's open spaces include enhancing their 'visual attractiveness', which may include the placing of more sculptures. Graves Park is prioritised as one of the spaces requiring attention.

Artists

Despite SCAT's stated policy of 'community access' and desire to 'involve the public', the artists tended to assess the impact of the Art in the Parks programme project in their own terms. Several of the artists, including those who worked on temporary pieces, regarded it as a positive experience.

> I was very grateful for the opportunity to work in public. It was my first commission in Sheffield (Powell).

> It's a very positive thing being accepted in your home town. It was useful. I am now stone carving rather than wood carving. I have done several public art projects in Sheffield (Bermejo).

> Taking part in this project was a very positive experience for me (Marshall).

> I ... spent the time concentrating on my own work ... I found the three weeks at the park enjoyable ... produced a piece of work I was reasonably happy with, started another and generated ideas for many more pieces. It was good to have a number of artists working there at the same time and interesting to see the development and working practices of others as well as having them there for 'moral support' (Mayne, SCAT, undated).

Four years later, Powell is still attached to the work. He stated that he 'wouldn't go back to see it. I would love to rework it ... I have done another Green Man since.' He was 'surprised at the amount of people. I got hoarse from talking during the first two days.' He thought 'it was great'. In general, artists found that as a result of working in public they needed more time to complete their commissions than had been allocated for in the budget. Marshall spent eight weeks working, Bermejo, five.

Some artists regarded contact with the public as having benefited the work (as opposed to the work benefiting the public).

> The warmth and support of the community of park users who frequent the area around the site is woven into the work (Marshall).

Other artists saw the contact with the public as intrusive. Bermejo, for example, commented on the fact that

> Progress was slow due to frequent interruptions by the public. I, therefore ... had the other [bench] delivered to my studio.

> Working in public is extremely demanding due to PR work and can retard processes drastically. Wearing headphones sometimes helps.

It was significant that Brailsford should have referred to working in public as being 'for advertisement reasons'. It suggests that she confused the promotion of the programme with making opportunities for the public to have access to the work.

In some respects, the artists appear to have felt put upon. The amount of work that SCAT found itself involved in

> got out of hand. The scale of the galleries' programme created a huge workload and it cannot be overemphasised that too much of the workload fell on a few individuals ... relying on their good will and commitment (Introduction, SCAT, undated).

This may have reflected on the management and organisation of SCAT itself. Brailsford remarked that 'SCAT has about 120 members, only 20 of whom do anything'.

More specifically, the artists complained about the conditions of their employment. There were no contracts. It was unclear where final responsibility lay. Although it was understood that the Recreation Department was supposed to maintain the sculptures, the artists expressed some doubt as to whether the pieces were being protected from rotting, despite their having given the department instructions about this. (On inspection, some of the pieces were growing fungus.)

The artists' payment was reported as having been 'greatly delayed due to an industrial dispute'. SCAT put this down to 'lack of good communications between SCAT Treasurer and SCC Arts Department'.

Powell felt there was insufficient technical support from the Recreation Department. He had to buy in his own scaffolding out of the fee he was paid. The City Council would not lend him the equipment and firms were unwilling to hire to him, since it would be left up in the open while he was working. 'The Parks Department would not take it down each night.' The artists were not covered by council indemnity. 'The fact that there was an 18 foot drop on one side of the site was my risk.'

In general the artists felt that the 'question of publicity is obviously one of the items to be placed on future agendas' (SCAT, undated). The Recreation Department's failure to publish a leaflet about the Art in the Parks until the last weekend, or to produce sufficient details in advance of the workshops, frustrated the artists. David Mayne, for one, decided not to run any workshops.

> People had to know in advance so that they could bring basic tools with them in order to participate and as there had been no information in the parks (about my work) ... it was a waste of time, in my view, to attempt to run any workshops.

Another difficulty was that, with respect to the general publicity for the festival, some artists felt that the 'Recreation and the Arts Departments always put themselves first. Sometimes they never mentioned the artist's name' (Bermejo). Letters to the *Star* from members of the public complained that an article about the trail had not 'referred to any of the sculptors who have participated in the success of the trail'. One writer suggested that 'further encouragement be given to the sculptors who are contributing, by publishing not only the description of their work, but naming them'. Another wanted to know 'what other enterprises they may be engaged upon'.

Alston also proposed that sustaining publicity during the extended period of the Visual Arts festival was a major problem. Although he maintained that the 'local coverage was good in the press and on radio, which sustained the publicity momentum, SCAT felt that insufficient attention was paid to the art that had been made and the fact that the event was the result of 'a body of artists working on their own initiative'. Alston reported that the artists were disappointed by the lack of national coverage. For their part, they thought that

> the success, therefore, of the project in Graves Park, while maintaining a high profile through the odd news items or local radio programme, could have been much greater (SCAT, undated).

The Silkstone Heritage Stones, Silkstone

Background

In 1987 a group of eight residents of Silkstone and Silkstone Common, near Barnsley, South Yorkshire, came together to prepare a survey of the parish inspired by the Parish Maps Project. This had been initiated by the environmental organisation, Common Ground. The group had no contact with Common Ground itself, but were recruited – by word of mouth – through the Community Action in Rural Environment scheme (CARE), which had been set up by the Countryside Commission in association with Barnsley Metropolitan Borough Council (BMBC) and ten rural parishes to the west of Barnsley.

The Parish Maps Project was launched by Common Ground in 1987 (see Chapter 1, p. 29). It was intended to encourage people to recognise what they value in their locality – 'what features combine to make it different and distinct from another'. As its title suggests, the project encouraged the making of maps – by environment, parish, women's, community, arts and schools' groups among others. These were conceived as a means to inspire 'us to look again at our surroundings and to discuss and discover new ways of ensuring that ordinary, but well loved features are looked after'. According to Common Ground, many groups' maps represented 'the beginning of an ongoing manifestation of active caring for their place' (Common Ground, 1991). The Silkstone group's map was no exception.

Membership of the residents' group, which is now formally constituted as the Silkstone Heritage Stones Project, has changed very little since 1987. It includes two housewives, a local planning officer, countryside officer, an environmental consultant, architect, retired miner, and someone employed in the health service. They are all aged 35 and over, and have been resident in the village from between six and 74 years. Two group members also belong to the Roggins' local history group, so-called after an area in Silkstone.

The group's original intention was to produce a map of the parish which is historically well documented – indeed there are several references to it in the Doomsday Book. They found that few of them knew where the village boundaries were. Only one boundary marker had survived out of a number shown on maps dating back to 1850. The group decided to reinstate the stone markers, and proposed that this should be done in the traditional form of simple carvings, bearing the parish emblem, which would be produced in the Conservation Workshop (a local Community Programme initiative).

At the time the proposal for the markers was conceived, the group's discussions tended to focus on the absence of collective memory and the village's loss of identity. Little remained of its historic buildings, ancient monuments, hedgerows or evidence of its industrial past. What was once a thriving mining area had become 'a sanitised community for other businesses and industrial areas. Most of the hard edges have been rubbed away over the past 20 years leaving attractive topography and woodland, but rather banal buildings and architectural features.' As one of the group put it, 'Silkstone was becoming like Slough or Woking'.

Their plans for the boundary markers, consequently, developed into a more ambitious scheme to commission individually designed sculptures to mark the 16 points at which roads and rights of way cross the parish boundary. It was proposed that each stone would depict different aspects of life in Silkstone and its history – its characters, legends, facts and 'important features of village life'. This change came about through the introduction to the group of a young sculptor who had been born and lived in the parish. His membership of the group prompted the development of the project in the form in which it came to be realised.

The Silkstone Heritage Stones Project was formally launched in 1989. Its objectives, as defined in its constitution, are 'for the public benefit' and 'to promote civic pride in the parish'. It seeks to re-instate boundary markers around the parish in the form of sculptures depicting the heritage, myths and legends of the parish; to use such sculptures as an educational facility to promote awareness in the parish of the heritage and the environment of the parish; to investigate the geography, history, natural history and architecture of the parish, and to encourage the preservation, protection, development and improvement of features of historic and public interest in the parish. To quote one member of the project:

> Hopefully it will encourage some people to look beyond their immediate surroundings, ask questions about the village and perhaps see the value of maintaining the special character of an area.

The project is based on community involvement of various kinds.

Groups and individuals contribute ideas and practical help related to fund-raising, design, and associated events. The group had always intended that the stones should be used by schools as an educational tool, and the two primary schools in Silkstone and Silkstone Common were encouraged to participate. In 1990 a Parish Festival 'celebrated the parish in words, music, dance, environment, heritage, history and enjoyment'.

The project's first meeting was in January 1989. Its first major event was the unveiling and blessing of the first Heritage Stone in 1989 attended by about 250 people.

In early 1993 the anticipated cost of the project, as a whole, was £30-35,000. The first four stones cost in the region of £7,500. Financial support and encouragement has come from a variety of local and national sources, all of which has a different interest in the project. The Parish Council, for example, supports local initiatives. It originally supported the project because it wanted to see parish life enriched and was interested in the prospect of local educational benefits. Other local funders include the Howard Walker Trust, a local charity: CARE which supports local community initiatives and Pawson Brothers of Morley, which provided stone by way of sponsorship in kind, worth an estimated £5,000.

Sponsorship is raised for particular stones. BMBC, for example, funded the project in connection with its support for the trans-Pennine Dove Valley Trail; the York & Lancaster Regimental Association and the Barnsley Branch of the Regimental Association provided support for another stone which recalls a regiment based in the area.

National organisations have supported the Silkstone Heritage Stones Project in their capacity of supporting environmental projects. They include UK 2000 and Shell Better Britain. Funding has also come from the Silkstone Huskar group, Mr Ownsworth, the Lang Charitable Trust, Yorkshire Arts, *The Barnsley Chronicle*, British Rail and the Polar Motor Company Barnsley Ltd. The Ford UK Conservation Award, which the project won, was worth some £8,000.

Responsibility for the project is independent of its financing. The design of the sculptures is the responsibility of the commissioned artist, the management of the project, that of the group. No public art agency has been involved because 'we preferred, at the time, to keep the project local'.

Processes

At the time of writing four stones had been commissioned – three by Tony Slater, *The Railway Stone, The Huskar Stone* and *The PALS Stone,* and one by Lorna Broughton – *The Balloon and Miller Plaque.* Julia Barton was commissioned to make a design for *The Beacon Stone.* This has not yet been realised. Slater and Broughton were both resident in Silkstone at the time of their commission. Barton's Featherstone relief had won an Arts Council/British Gas Award. The selection of artists remains 'constantly under review'.

The Railway Stone and *The Huskar Stone* were both commissioned in April 1989, completed in July and sited by the September of the same year. *The Ballon and Miller Plaque* was commissioned in June 1991, completed in September and sited in October 1991. *The PALS Stone* was commissioned in September 1991. At the time of writing, it had not yet been sited.

The Railway Stone was the first to be sited. It is situated along a public footpath which is part of the Dove Valley Trail and follows the track of an old railway used for hauling coal from the colliery. The sculpture represents an engine driver and fireman at either end of a bench which is carved to depict a steam engine. The stretch of railway line, which opened in 1880 and closed in 1981 was, for a while, used by the most powerful locomotive to run on British tracks – the London and North Eastern Railways's No 9999, *The Garratt.*

The Huskar Stone is sited in a field off Moor End Lane, a mile south-east of Silkstone Common. It recalls a colliery disaster of 1838 when 26 local children aged between seven and 17 died in a flash flood in the

Tony Slater, *The Railway Stone,*
1989 © Christine Boyd,
The Yorkshire Post, 1993

Tony Slater, *The Huskar Stone*, 1989
Silkstone Heritage Stones, winner of
the Ford Conservation Award 1990,
organised by the Conservation
Foundation

nearby Huskar pit. The disaster led to a government enquiry and helped to secure the passing of Lord Shaftesbury's Act banning the employment of women and children in mines. The sculpture, which is eight foot high, represents waves of water flooding the mine with a child's face – mouth open – facing upwards.

The Balloon and Miller Plaque refers to events that took place at Blacker Green Lane, where the stone is sited. The balloon referred to was one which landed near the site in 1853 having been used as part of a demonstration about the fall of Sebastopol. The balloonist, in fear of his life from the throng which gathered around him, offered an individual in the crowd 10/- to pack his balloon up and deliver it to the station.

Local legend has it that the miller was a 19th century resident of Silkstone Cross. It was his habit to release the Blacker Green dam sluice gate and gallop back to his mill in an attempt to beat the water.

The PALS Stone was intended to be erected alongside the main A628 road to Barnsley, on the site of a First World War Army Camp built to house volunteers who joined the Barnsley PALS Unit, part of Lord Kitchener's Army. The stone shows four embracing figures – comrades helping each other – at the top of a turret. Images of a soldier and a boy scout refer to the fact that the camp is now a scouts and guides camping ground. Silkstone Old Hall is also represented on the stone. The image of a bird recalls the local legend about a buried crock of gold, protected by a black hen. The stone is currently on display at Elsecar Heritage Park, where the artist had a studio.

The most contentious proposal to date is for a *Beacon Stone* to be sited on Champney Hill, the highest point in Silkstone. It is to bear the parish emblem of a miner's lamp and horseshoe, and to be used for local events and European celebrations to mark the village's twinning with St Florent des Bois in the Vendee. It might also create a public open space and picnic area. However, a local farmer and other residents on the road approaching the site have objected to this potentially spoiling the area.

Other Heritage Stones are proposed, including one to be sited at Norcroft Bridge, which has associations with Dick Turpin and the Packhorse Inn. This was used as a billet by Cromwell's men who desecrated the church. Another stone has been proposed for Waggonway Bridge, used for coal traffic between Silkstone and Cawthorne canal basin; another near Knabbs Lane, where King Charles was said to have hidden. One more might form a central marker in the village with a parish map showing the location of all the stones.

Themes for potential commissions are discussed within the group and at parish meetings. Contributions are often made by local historians and artists. Works are intended to express what are tantamount to common values.

Group members photograph potentially suitable sites and investigate their viability with respect to the ownership of the land, leasing, the precise location of the historical events represented, visibility from the road, the placing of the works, public access, the scale and individual characteristics of the proposed sculptures.

Briefs and contracts

The group prepares a brief for each site which specifies the physical size and theme of the works to be commissioned. Artists prepare preparatory drawings, and develop their proposals in consultation with members.

Contracts are drawn up between the project, landowners and artists, following advice from the Yorkshire Sculpture Park and solicitors. The contracts with artists – Commission Agreements – refer to payment, the storage and insurance of the works, educational projects ('public and schools workshops, demonstrations before work commences and during the actual carving') and a subsequent Contract of Sale. This includes details about the group's responsibility for the transport of the work and repairs. No mention is made of maintenance or insurance (Appendix 7, pp. 357-359).

The group's contracts and licences with landowners refer to maintenance and repair, damage to property, conditions of access, fees, notice of termination of agreement, photographic copyright and acknowledgement of siting. Deaccessioning has been considered in order to provide for the maintenance and insurance of sculptures in the future (see Appendix 7, pp. 359-362).

Introduction to the public

The project is introduced to the public through public meetings, schools and broadcasts and publicised gatherings. The first Heritage Stone, *The Railway Stone*, was unveiled in September 1989 at a ceremony which included a blessing, talks, displays about the railway and the project, and refreshments. Children from the two local primary schools buried a 'time capsule' in the foundations of the piece.

Impact

At the time of writing, three Heritage Stones had been sited – *The Huskar Stone*, *The Railway Stone* and *The Balloon and Miller Plaque*.

The project has been assessed formally by various award making bodies. It won The Times/RIBA Award (1991), the Yorkshire Rural Community Council, Village Ventures (1990), the Ford United Kingdom British Conservation Awards, Heritage Category and the UK Conservation Project of the Year (1990). The criteria by which it was assessed by the Conservation Foundation included

> Need. Does the project address a real need for conservation? Dedication. How much effort, enthusiasm and skill has been shown by those working on the project? Originality. Does the project demonstrate an original approach to conservation, a new way of tackling an old problem, or does it offer a solution to a new problem? Benefit. How much does the project need to win one of these awards and how would it benefit from such a win?

The stones were always intended as educational. One of the two local primary schools uses them regularly. Silkstone Common Junior and

Infants School is situated near *The Railway* and *Huskar Stones*. *The Huskar Stone* is not used as the object of school outings because it is located on a farmer's land off a road which has no pavement. Visits with 30 children or more represent a safety risk. According to the headteacher, most of the children are familiar with the stone. Not only is it about children, but it appeals to their 'morbid fascination'. *The Railway Stone*, however, is used in the context of history teaching, particularly with regard to Victorian transport.

The Silkstones Heritage Stones Project was described in the House of Lords by Baroness Lockwood as an example of regional participation and enjoyment in the arts (*Hansard*, 15.5.1991). It received widespread news coverage in local and national papers, particularly after winning the Ford Award. The project has also been covered by such specialist press as *Heritage Outlook* and *Architects Journal*. There has, however, been little critical writing.

Ford UK located the project as belonging to the tradition of

> European stone monuments which started in pre-Christian times. Though sites like Stonehenge and Carnac are not generally considered to have been primarily intended to convey information about contemporary lifestyles to future generations, that is nevertheless the role they fulfil. It is hoped that in a similar way the Silkstone Heritage Stones will provide a lasting record to a way of life unique to this small South Yorkshire village.

An article in *The Times*, however, described the Heritage Stones in the context of a secondary tradition of 'vanity' stone circles, which were fashionable among wealthy landowners from the 18th century onwards and were built by the local unemployed. Precedents in Yorkshire include those at Ilton, near Masham and Bierly Hall, Bradford (Winpenny, 1991).

Criticism of the project has, however, come from nearer home. *The PALS Stone* which still remains to be sited was felt to bear insufficient resemblance to the artist's proposals. Members of the group are undecided as to whether it should be formally shown.

Local responses to the Heritage Stones have been mixed. The project has been discussed and debated in public meetings. Reaction has varied from warm support to deep hostility. This is reflected in the public's response to the enquiry. The project evidently attracts support in principle. According to one villager, 'the small committee is to be commended for their commitment, there is much apathy'. Other correspondents to PSI described themselves as understanding and appreciating

> the philosophy behind the project ... There is obviously educational value in the project, especially beneficial in a schools context.

However, they were

> less convinced that the sculptures erected to date help to create a unique local identity. You might be surprised how few local villagers know where they are located, what they represent or how many found them less than artistic. Moreover unfortunately they have attracted vandalism.

> I have to tell you that the vast majority of the people in this parish are opposed to the erection of heritage and other such boundary stones, and that this opposition is based on experience and not on a prejudice based on any ill-considered or unreasoned approach.

> Heritage or boundary stones have been erected around the borders of our parish for sometime, gathering resentment, ridicule and abhorrent obscene graffiti, and their presence is ill regarded by the vast majority of this community's inhabitants.

'Strong local reaction' was elicited, in particular, by the most recent proposal to erect a beacon. This was shelved, following a heated parish meeting and the council's support for the local inhabitants.

> I trust that no sculpture will be erected in the future without the fullest consultation in advance on any documented plans.

> There exists a wide opposition to the erection of the stones we already have, and the placing of any further structures.

> Further attempts to place additional stones in the parish as well as private land, have been successfully rebutted and I'm sure this will be the attitude if similar monuments are suggested in future, unless the nature of these objects is radically overhauled.

Opposition to the project seems to be largely predicated on the appearance of those stones erected to date.

> We have no objection to Heritage Stones marking boundaries in Silkstone Common as was agreed in 1991 by Silkstone Parish Council. But we do object very strongly to our heritage being ruined by (such) monstrosities as the *Beacon Stone* (which) the Heritage Stone Group tried to site in a very prominent position.

Members of the local community also object to these works' intrusion into their daily lives.

We have a very large sculpture park, approximately three miles away. If you wish to display your work there, we will go and see it! What we don't want is to have to walk past it every day of our lives. It's not everybody's idea of art and at Bretton Park we have the choice.

It was suggested that the project had exceeded its own brief.

We don't think there is any more to discuss about these projects. The parish council made it quite clear after many such meetings, that the original plan was for boundary stones to mark boundaries and that is what they should do.

And the appearance of the sculptures is considered out of keeping with their context.

In my own opinion, small stones inserted into dry stone walls would be one acceptable alternative. Perhaps equally acceptable would be free standing stones of modest size (under a metre in height) and simply inscribed, and lacking the radical appearance of some misplaced Aztec monstrosity, such as this village has witnessed in recent years! Totem poles look perfectly in place within an Indian encampment but not sheltering beneath the lea of a weeping willow in a quiet English meadow!

One correspondent, at least, was concerned to point out that this was not a philistine response.

Ours are old established villages which have undergone a rapid expansion, being favoured by beautiful rural views and entirely surrounded by green belt, we have become a very desirable place to live. Consequently, this is reflected in the price of properties within our boundary, and we therefore have a large proportion of residents who can fairly be regarded as well educated and rather middle class. What I'm trying to say is this, if there are philistines in our community, they will be likely to be in a minority.

The parish council's attitude towards sculpture is not restricted to the Silkstone Heritage Stones Project. They also forbade the siting of a sculpture privately commissioned in remembrance of a local postmaster, which depicts a child and a dog. It is now on display in the Yorkshire Sculpture Park.

The experience, if not the evaluation, has informed the subsequent work of the group. One member described the Ford Award, in particular, as having given them confidence. 'Some of the more hostile reactions from local people have served to remind us of the need to proceed with great caution on matters of leases and contracts.' The future of the scheme in Silkstone seems bound up with the membership of the parish council.

A Light Wave, Westgate Station, Wakefield, 1985 -1988

Background

In 1985 the sculptor Charles Quick approached Graham Roberts, then Advisor on Art in Public Places for Yorkshire Arts Association, based at the West Yorkshire Metropolitan County Council, to propose a sculpture for Wakefield Westgate Station.

Quick, who lived in Leeds, had been commuting to Wakefield District College where he taught on a part-time basis. The derelict state of a bay siding alongside the main platform at Wakefield Westgate Station, disused since Beeching's reforms to the railways in the 1960s, made such an impression on him that he proposed an artwork which would improve the general environment and serve as a 'landmark' for Wakefield itself.

In September 1985, Roberts convened a meeting at Wakefield Westgate Station to discuss the proposal with the Station Manager and British Rail Regional Architect. They approved the proposal in principle, which was then passed to the British Rail Board Environment Panel for comment and authorisation.

British Rail

Physical environment
British Rail had been explicitly concerned with the physical environment (its land, property and architectural heritage) since 1977, when it established a panel to advise the Board on such matters. Its policy of improving the visual environment was part of a wider concern to be seen to be acting in a socially and environmentally responsible manner.

British Rail's environmental policy (like its health and safety policies) was corporate-led by the Board and applied to each part of its business. Its programme of improvements to the visual environment was manifest in a number of ways – cleaner buildings, landscaping, improved pas-

214

senger amenities and a more focused approach to design. At the time, the programme was overseen by Jane Priestman, Director of Architecture, Design and Environment, British Railways Board. It was led, in a practical sense, by David Perry, the Board's Environment Manager, who worked with regionally-based British Rail architects. 'Art on the Railway' constituted one aspect of these improvements.

Community Unit

In 1988 the Community Unit, a department of the British Rail Board, took responsibility for the 'desirable, rather than essential' improvements to the visual environment and amenities – aspects of British Rail's operation which do not directly generate income.

> With some 11,000 miles of railway and over 2,400 stations, railway lands and properties impact widely in the national landscape … We recognise that the aspect of some of our property may still remain less than pleasing. We recognise the value and importance of environmental quality. Our stations are 'gateways' to the communities whose names they bear; they are often the first impression for the visitor – and first impressions are important. Equally, railway lanesides reflect the landscape to which they contribute and of which they are a part.

> Quite simply, as we strive to meet the increasingly stringent financial targets imposed upon us by central government, so some areas surplus to our business needs may lie disused – even derelict … Some stations are unstaffed, giving free reign to vandals and graffiti … (British Rail, *Community Partnership*).

Partnership

The Community Unit sought to approach

> its environmental problems in a constructive way. As we continue our policy of investing in the upgrading of our stations and in providing better facilities for our customers, so we also offer to share with local communities the cost of further enhancing the railway scene – to the extent in some cases of matching the community contribution £-for-£. Our object is to involve local communities in improving the aspect of what is, in truth, their Railway. It is a policy of community partnership (British Rail, *Community Partnership*).

The concept of partnership had existed within British Rail since 1979. By 1986 when it published its partnership statement, British Rail had carried out some 400 projects with a variety of agencies including local authorities, civic groups, environmental organisations, the Manpower Services Commission, development agencies and the private sector. In addition to commissioning works of public art on railway property, projects had included improvements to station forecourt areas with paving and new planting, the repainting of bridges in bright colours, improvements to amenities for passengers (disabled passengers, in particular) and upgrading the appearance of tenancies in the arches of railway viaducts.

Schemes were selected on the basis of a mixture of financial, environmental and political considerations – the benefits that a scheme might bring to an area, the potential for future business development and the scope for extending partnerships.

> In declining inner-city areas, environmental regeneration is seen as a valuable precursor to economic recovery and job creation. Elsewhere pride in the local station is an expression of civic pride and community confidence. For the private sector, partnership is a lasting way of establishing a corporate presence within the community. And in human terms, the value of partnership in creating job and training opportunities for the unemployed is widely recognised (British Rail, *Community Partnership*).

Public art

In 1986 two members of the environment panel, Sir Hugh Casson and Simon Jenkins, who also played a part in siting *The Arch* in Kensington Gardens, together with David Perry, then Secretary to the panel, prepared a policy statement for the Board with respect to art. It coincided with what Perry described as their 'euphoria' following British Rail's first major public art commission at Brixton, which had been conceived in association with substantial urban programme investment in the station area following the riots.

The Board's policy was adopted and published as *Art on the Railway*. Its guiding principle was the desire for environmental improvement.

> British Rail recognises the value of art as a means of enhancing the environment of the railway. Art contributes distinction and visual enrichment. It is also a tangible expression of quality and care.

Art on the Railway's aims were to

> encourage art and craftworks of integrity and imagination both on and within our stations and properties.

It sought to pursue such projects

in partnership with external bodies representative of the community or business interest with a view to jointly acquiring or commissioning new artworks on the railway and is willing in most cases to contribute towards the costs involved.

In 1986/7, before committing itself to *A Light Wave*, British Rail had allocated over £93,000 to public art commissions – some 5 per cent of its corporate annual allocation of £2m for environmental partnerships. This sum generated at least matching external funding, producing well over £186,000 for art.

City of Wakefield

British Rail's interest in the proposed project for Wakefield was partly due to its interest 'in establishing local confidence in partnership generally'. Its concern with environmental improvement complemented that of the City of Wakefield, which Graham Roberts had approached for the provision of resources. The city's interest in the project was prompted by the opportunity to carry out an enhancement of the station which involved little structural change and which would assist the image of Wakefield by 'tidying up' the area.

Wakefield's campaign *Lighting the Green Fuse* was launched in Spring 1987. It was intended to revitalise the district's environment and create interest in the proposed Wakefield Groundwork Trust. Like British Rail's Community Partnership programme, it was primarily concerned with the creation of an attractive environment, not only for people to live and work in, but to enable the district to compete with other areas for industrial and commercial investment.

Everyone should be able to live and work in a pleasant environment. Traditionally this may not have been attainable, but changes in industrial processes and higher standards of development make this a practical long-term objective. There is a marked disparity in environmental quality through the district. If this imbalance could be redressed significant progress would have been made towards securing an attractive environment for everyone.

The environmental quality of an area relates directly to that area's image. It is this image which plays a vital role in attracting industrial and commercial activity. Wakefield has to compete for new jobs with places that are blessed with environmental qualities that it does not have and areas that have not suffered two centuries of industrial development. To compete on anything approaching an equal footing, Wakefield's image should reflect a vigorous programme to enhance the industrial urban environment and to promote careful husbandry of its significant natural and historical environmental resources (City of Wakefield, undated).

Quick's proposal provided them with a way of not only 'enhancing' the station, but also of improving the environment of a commercial area.

Public Arts
The third organisation involved in the commission of *A Light Wave* was the public art agency, Public Arts. Following the abolition of West Yorkshire Metropolitan County Council in 1986, the district council and Yorkshire Arts agreed to fund an agency, Public Arts, with Graham Roberts as its director. It was established as a charity in 1986, 'dedicated to innovative environmental improvement through the use of art'.

For the City of Wakefield's Planning Department the partnership had distinct advantages. According to Jonathan Hall, Assistant Head of Planning Services, Development Control, working with the agency enabled the city to receive specialist services in an area of agreed development and remain at arm's length from the commission.

Audiences
Each of the parties involved in the project identified different constituencies for the work. British Rail and City of Wakefield, for example, both referred to 'the community'. For British Rail this embraced the community whose name the station bore, visitors to that place and passengers passing through and using the station. Another audience comprised those for whom jobs or training opportunities might be created as a result of a project. For the City of Wakefield, the community comprised those who live and work there or those who wish to relocate or do business there. Public Arts' promotional information, on the other hand, alluded to the community as a body of people who would, by definition, inform the public artworks created. This included the station staff.

> We work closely with local communities and local businesses in the North of England to ensure that new public artworks are a unique reflection of local interests and aspirations and serve to generate a sense of place and community (Public Arts, promotional literature, undated).

The artist was more specific. He referred to his work as being seen by 'British Rail travellers between Kings Cross and the North of Britain by day and night'. He wished to 'engage with a wider audience' and 'involve as many people as possible in making art'.

Funding

Yorkshire Arts initially made an award of £250 from its Art in Public Places fund to enable the artist to produce a scale working model of the sculpture to present to British Rail Environment Panel.

The proposal was taken up by the panel who agreed to match pound for pound any funds which Public Arts, as the artist's agent, could generate. By July 1986 the budget for the project was estimated at £18,000. British Rail offered 50 per cent (£9,000) from its Corporate Environment Fund. The Planning Committee, City of Wakefield MDC allocated £4,000. It was also agreed that the costs of all environmental and site preparation works were not to exceed £9,000, a figure quoted by the British Rail Area Civil Engineer in November 1985.

However it subsequently emerged that this was an underestimate, based on a misunderstanding of the size of the sculpture and the scale of the site preparation required. By December 1986, the budget for the project as a whole was calculated at £35,000. British Rail increased its contribution to £17,500. Funds were raised from the Chippindale Foundation (£2,250), set up in memory of Sam Chippindale which supports artistic endeavours. Roger Suddards, a trustee of the Foundation described his interest in supporting the work as being 'to change people's attitude to sculpture ... to show them that it is not strange and remote'. Yorkshire Arts provided £2,000 and several local companies gave 'in kind'. Ellis & Booth Ltd, timber merchants based in Huddersfield and seven other wood suppliers, whom they persuaded to do so, donated 2,500 feet of homegrown Celpruf treated softwood for the construction of the sculpture which they treated free of charge. Stain was supplied by Sadolin (UK) Ltd. The project was also granted an award of £3,500 from the government's Business Sponsorship Incentive Scheme. Landscaping material and the hire of plant were included in the project budget.

The education programme was initiated and funded by Public Arts as a separate item.

Responsibility for the work

British Rail's formal agreement with Charles Quick and Public Arts was issued in 1987. It specified each party's responsibilities.

The artist was commissioned to create the work described in the schedule (Appendix 7, p. 366) for the agreed fee of £4,000. This included all the expenses he might incur in connection with the work. The artist was also expected to indemnify the Board against any action relating to the originality of the work.

As agents, Public Arts, for a fee of £1,000 (out of British Rail's £17,500) was responsible for

a) commissioning the Artist to undertake the work

b) overseeing and managing the progress of the work

c) obtaining any further funding found necessary to complete the work and its installation

d) managing and accounting to British Rail for the funding of the commission and making whatever payments were necessary for its proper execution

e) assisting the Board in generating publicity for the work (*Agreement*, p. 362).

On completion of the work and payment to the artist, the property and copyright of the work, all the preparatory and working documents and drawings, passed to British Rail.

The artist also drew up a maintenance schedule for the work (Appendix 7, p. 367) for which the Board accepted responsibility. Its policy determined that

> for practical reasons, artworks on the Railway must require minimum after care. Alternatively, the Board must be assured that responsibility for any necessary maintenance is accepted by an established authority capable of undertaking that commitment. For this reason also, British Rail prefers artworks of a permanent or semi-permanent nature, comprising materials that are intrinsically durable and vandal resistant (British Rail, *Art on the Railway*).

It was standard practice for works of art to be regarded as part of the normal infrastructure of the railway and, as such, to be a local civil engineering maintenance responsibility. Any costs arising would be debited to the relevant business sector (in this case, InterCity) in line with

usual spending on structural maintenance. British Rail Board made its original funding commitment contingent on that principle.
Were the work to be damaged

> the Board does not undertake to execute its restoration or repair. If, after consultation with the Artist, the Board decides that restoration/repair is feasible at an acceptable cost, the Board will give the Artist the option to conduct or supervise the restoration on terms and to a schedule to be agreed, at the expense of the Board (*Agreement*, p. 364).

British Rail also agreed that

> while the work is on site ... no attempt will be made to obstruct the public's clear view of the work (*Agreement*, p. 362).

It also assumed the right to 'sell, lend or otherwise part with possession of the Work' (*Agreement*, p. 365) or 'remove the Work prior to the expiry of the minimum period specified', having undertaken

> at its own expense to take all reasonable steps in an endeavour to transfer the Work to an alternative site in England, Scotland or Wales as may reasonably be agreed with the Artist (*Agreement*, p. 365).

Unusually, at the instigation of the artist, the sculpture had a contractually agreed limited lifetime.

> After the work has been on site for 10 years the Board shall consult with the artist to determine whether or not the work shall remain on site, be relocated elsewhere or be dismantled (*Agreement*, p. 362).

Originally this was suggested with regard to the life expectancy of the electronic timer, but there were other concerns. Quick regarded the project as creating a site for sculpture and did not wish to monopolise it. He was also aware that the environment might change to such a degree that the work would no longer be appropriate. For its part, British Rail wished to establish the principle articulated by the Environment Panel that works of art should not necessarily be considered 'immovable' and that Art on the Railway should present a changing vista.

Processes

British Rail's stated policy, as articulated in *Art on the Railway*, was to

> respond positively to original ideas for new artworks of creativity and imagination that are appropriate in the context of the Railway environment.

The details Roberts sent potential funders in 1985 included the following proposal by the artist for *A Light Wave*.

> The sculpture titled *A Light Wave* will be sited along the entire length of one of the platforms at Wakefield Westgate Station, which has for some time been disused but is directly adjacent and in full view of the main line platform. This area will be renovated, including some structural alterations, the major one being the infilling of the old disused trackwell and the levelling off of the whole area. The finished result will be to change an unattractive, disused and derelict site into a creative and visually stimulating one:

> The sculpture will consist of 7 large wooden blue structures leant against the back wall of the platform and totalling 150 feet in length. This will be combined with a line of lights running through the inside of all the structures and controlled by an electronic timer. During the hours of darkness the sculptures will be lit. Only one light will be on at any one time and will change in sequence appearing to move along the line of structures, lighting their interiors as well as causing lines of light and shadow to move across the exterior surfaces of the sculptures and walls. It is a sculpture that can be viewed equally as well from the platform as from the carriage window of a train in the station. This is because it has been designed so that the sculpture will be placed on a bed of railway ballast, raising it slightly.

> The sculpture has been designed to use materials that are sympathetic to this particular environment and are synonymous with the traditions of the railways, as well as incorporating modern technology.

The only refinements described in the schedule appended to the agreement were that the sculpture would be featured in a 'landscaped setting'. One key area of the council's involvement was the erection of a fence adjoining the sculpture, with an area planted out behind to the specification of a landscape architect from the Planning Department. This was included as the setting of the work evolved to complement it and to ensure the removal of unsightly features along the rest of the platform length.

Values and relevance to site

Quick had already temporarily constructed the work on a smaller scale, during his 1985 sculpture residence at the Henry Moore Centre for the Study of Sculpture, Leeds City Art Gallery. He wanted to 'make a piece that would announce itself as a piece of sculpture, which would express its three-dimensionality', which 'needed an audience to pass by', and which was a 'response' to the site.

> My main concern is in creating sculpture that derives its identity from a specific site and its encompassing environment, that it is constructed in, and for. The work is a direct response to the cultural and physical facets of a particular location (Charles Quick, cited in Public Art's *Briefing Notes for LEAS' Art Advisors*, undated).

Quick described the work as relating to railway sleepers and the rhythms of railway architecture and structures. He credits 'the support and advice of the local and regional engineers of British Rail' as playing a major part in the successful completion of the work. However his conception of the work was at variance with that of British Rail's regional officials, as misunderstandings over the details of the site preparations revealed. The problem was one of internal communications within British Rail, particularly between its architects and civil engineers.

In preparing the original estimate, the Area Civil Engineer had assumed that the preparations would be for a 'statue type of thing'. He had not anticipated what he subsequently described as 'some form of monster more than 50 yards long' which would require the infilling of 'two thirds of the bay platform' – 'not a small section'. The major costs involved would be those incurred in transporting to the site 900 tons of rubble for infilling the trackbed, providing concrete decking across a railway under-bridge, sandblasting the walls, creating access to the foundations, providing top soil, dense ground cover planting and removing the existing platform fence. The revised estimate for these preparatory works was in excess of £38,000.

The correspondence generated by the revisions to the budget reveals something of the regional officials' attitudes towards the proposed sculpture. In the Area Civil Engineer's opinion, for example, carrying out work to the rear wall was 'for aesthetic reasons, to highlight the proposed sculpture'. Aesthetic reasons were not sufficient to merit expenditure from his budget. The scheme represented a distraction from the 'proper' business of British Rail.

> I do not now intend to do anything further for this scheme until specific detailed proposals are available in at least drawing form. I regret I do not have the staff to continue this type of exercise when the operating railway continues to cry out for attention.

In view of the extreme pressure on local maintenance budgets within British Rail, Perry has suggested that 'this view was not, perhaps, unreasonable for someone who had ultimate local responsibility for the integrity and safety of the railway'.

The regional Intercity Manager, who had not only recently been appointed and had not hitherto been involved in the proposals, did not see 'what benefit would accrue to the Intercity business' from the sculpture and was, therefore, 'not prepared to support the expenditure of £38,000 on this project'. Priestman observed

> British Rail generally has an engineer's mentality. They don't see the need for aesthetic improvement. There is clearly a need for education.

The issue of planning permission did not arise. As Perry pointed out, 'British Rail does not, I believe, require planning consent for construction that is wholly within its property and not visible from outside.' For its part, Wakefield would have only been concerned with a construction which was technically considered development, as opposed to 'tidying up', and which might, therefore, require permission.

Community Industry

The council arranged for a small workforce from its partnership programme with Community Industry to prepare the ground and assist the artist on site. Community Industry is a youth training scheme, set up to offer disadvantaged young people opportunities for training and personal development. It received an annual budget for materials from Planning Department, City of Wakefield to work on conserving buildings in the public realm. The Community Industry team spent longer than anticipated on site. In the event, a team of eight young people with one foreman worked for three months. During that time, the make up of the team changed many times as individuals' training periods expired.

The artist

A Light Wave was Quick's own initiative and he was committed to seeing the project through. He was already on site by the time British Rail's agreement was issued. His contribution outweighed what the contract demanded of him.

After the project was threatened by revisions to the estimates for the site preparation, Quick designed the support for the sculpture and re-thought access, and made alternative proposals for the environmental works, which were approved by British Rail's Civil Engineer. These were 'at a substantial saving' to British Rail's proposals, and made the project financially and practically viable.

The engineers had, for example, not wanted the bridge under the trackwell covered in rubble and suggested concrete decking. Quick proposed constructing a permanent scaffolding structure which would produce a cost effective way of protecting it permanently with the top soil and crushed stone on top, leaving the access hatched for inspection. He also proposed hiring a bulldozer and driver to dig up the old track bed further down the disused line and move it to the trackwell. One hundred tons of topsoil and 200 tons of crushed stone were delivered to Wakefield prison's car park, situated behind the railway line from where it was lifted to the site using large, mechanical dumper trucks. As Project Manager, Quick was involved with the site work from the end of June 1987 to December 1988. During that time he constructed the work. He was required to indemnify British Rail against liability in respect of himself or three assistants crossing the line.

Quick also largely negotiated the 'in-kind' sponsorship, with the help of Keith Ellis of Ellis & Booth (subsequently Ellis Ventures Ltd), writing about 50 letters to national and local firms. Quick had formerly bought his timber from Ellis & Booth. Two or three years earlier it had commissioned the sculptor to produce a sculpture which still stands on its premises.

Introduction to the public

The project was introduced to different constituencies in different ways. Quick had spent a week in an empty shop in the Ridings Shopping Centre where the proposals and maquette were on show to the public. He perceived his task as informing the public about the project. Public Arts referred to the same exercise as 'public consultation'.

The artist subsequently talked to the public informally on site. At that time the working model of *A Light Wave* was displayed in the ticket hall together with some information about what was taking place. Information was provided in poster cases on both platforms at Westgate Station which had photographs documenting the work at different stages. These posters remained up for a year.

A formal education programme, intended to complement the project, was organised by Public Arts, targetted at 'groups of young people, school children and the public'. It was scheduled from October to December 1987 and planned to coincide with the artist working on site. The programme largely comprised tours, discussions and workshops and a public lecture by the artist.

Quick, who has spent half his working life teaching sculpture at various levels, was committed to the education programme. Like many arts organisations constituted as charities, Public Arts is concerned to develop the educational potential of projects. The education programnme for *A Light Wave* was managed by Lorraine Cox, who had previously been involved in education at the Ikon Gallery, Birmingham.

Public Arts specifically devised a package for schools, which was targeted through Local Education Authorities advisors in Spring 1987, two academic terms before work was due to take place. The package was intended to allow participants to 'appreciate the improvements to the station' as they were taking place. Cox hoped it would be fun for the participants to witness 'such dramatic changes taking place to a small station'.

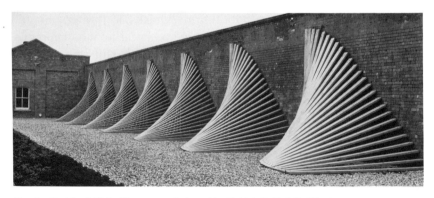

Charles Quick, *A Light Wave*, commissioned by British Rail © Public Arts

It was proposed that in October, groups should take guided tours of the station. The tours, which would last approximately 30 minutes, would be led by a member of the Public Arts staff and would comprise 'viewing the site preparations' and the model of the sculpture. The theme of 'Improving our Environment' was to form the basis for discussion. In November groups could make a follow-up visit to the station during the construction of the sculpture. The subject of the discussion would expand to encompass 'The role of the artist in a public place'. The artist would be available to answer questions after the tour. In December, groups would make a final brief visit (lasting 20 minutes) to the station followed by a half-day workshop led by the artist. On this occasion groups would view the finished sculpture and discuss its contribution to the environmental improvement. The workshop, held in Unity House, Westgate, was intended to give participants a further insight into the artist's approach to sculpture 'to get a better sense of what was being done by doing it themselves'. They built wooden structures, learned about light shadow and movement, considered formal aspects of the work such as tension, balance, rhythm and light and worked collaboratively to build a large construction at the end of the day.

In the event six classes, with pupils aged between eight and 12 years, used the education programme to which British Rail also contributed. As part of their experience, they were given platform tickets and met a rail guard.

Unveiling and switching on

In January 1988 the sculpture was unveiled by Michael Palin, of 'Monty Python' fame. He was, at the time, Chairman of Transport 2000 (a public transport pressure group). British Rail supplied a commemorative plaque to mark the event.

The unveiling was followed by a luncheon at Wakefield Town Hall for sponsors, local councillors and many of those immediately involved. The 'switching on' ceremony was followed by a celebration for 100 people at a pub near the station, most of whom had been involved in the project. The cost was met jointly by British Rail and the Wakefield City Council.

Charles Quick,
A Light Wave,
commissioned by
British Rail.
A night time view
© Graham Sykes

Dissemination of information

Despite the scale of *A Light Wave* less information was produced about it by those overtly involved than had been intended. It was not covered by *Intercity Magazine*, available in first class carriages on trains. British Rail had intended publishing a brochure about the work, as it had for the Sue Ridge mural at Southampton Station and the Alex Belechenko glass column at Reading Station. However the take up of these relatively expensive brochures was minimal and British Rail considered the money better spent on other art commissions elsewhere on the railway. The piece has, however, subsequently featured in a number of official British Rail publications.

Impact

A Light Wave was not formally evaluated. According to Bob Scriven, formerly of the Planning Department, Wakefield MDC, 'it is not normal procedure for the Planning Department to evaluate projects. It normally just moves on.' Although the authority had not commissioned the work, it was concerned to see that it was completed within the parameters set.

> It saw the work as contributing to the better image of the district in the eyes of the visitor to Wakefield and those passing through.

Priestman wondered 'which British Rail department would evaluate it? InterCity, PR ... ?'

The public

According to Cox, responses to the work were not monitored and no record of them exists. Quick recalls the majority of the public having a positive attitude to the proposals for the work.

> The reaction of Wakefield people who spoke to me has been very good, and a lot of them told me the site has been derelict for about 20 years.

Yorkshire Television's 'vox pop' recorded one passenger who regarded the sculpture as 'marvellous. Let's have sculptures on all our stations.'

Roberts suggested that the general 'response to the work was manifest in lack of response'. Scriven suggested that although its impact was 'not great ... it did offer an interesting surprise for passengers'.

The only vandalism to the work appears to have been unintentional and was caused by someone trying to ride a bicycle up it.

Press coverage of the project was prompted at various points: when money needed to be raised to realise the proposals; when schools visited the site and at the time of the unveiling ceremony. According to Quick the project was reported 34 times in the national and local press between April 1986 and March 1990, in addition to its coverage by local radio and television and inclusion in books.

There was little that was contentious about the reporting. It was described as 'a landmark', as 'turning a derelict site into sculpture'. The tone of much of the coverage was good humoured 'Wakefield makes waves [by] giving sculpture a platform', 'Tripping the light fantastic', 'Charles waves the green flag'. Variations of 'The sculpture now standing ...' were popular.

A small minority of articles were critical and typically raised such issues as modern art as a 'con' and the cost of the work. In the early stages of the commission the artist was reported as having been 'promised £9,000 for the project by British Rail' and being 'confident about raising the remaining £10,500'. It was later described as 'a £27,000 sculpture' or as 'costing around £30,000'. There was little acknowledgement of British Rail's support for the project. Although the Planning Department 'never had anybody moan about the Council wasting public money', after the work's unveiling *The Wakefield Express* published a poem questioning its cost – particularly in the light of British Rail increasing the cost of its fares and perceptions as to a decrease in its standards of public service. Other issues raised were its status as a work of art; the degree of environmental improvement granted by the sculpture and the authoritarianism implied by the imposition of the work on the public.

Making Waves over Sculpture

Oh! A sight of the Westgate Wave
Is bound to make you feel sick,
When you think how our struggle to save
And the cost of this thing by Charles Quick.

More than thirty thousand nicker
For seven large fans in a line,
And making electric light flicker
Over this stack of Corsican pine.

To justify what's been spent
They'd have the public believe,
It's environmental improvement
But it just makes you want to heave.

And up go British Rail fares,
And up go my local rates,
But it seems as if nobody cares
When highest authority dictates.

All you electricians should note.
And joiners from far and wide.
You're wasting your time when you quote
There are better paid jobs on the side.

If you're a British Rail shunter
There's a lot of money to make.
Just set yourself up as a sculptor
And get a big slice of the cake.

For the cost of this so-called art
Is more than those bricks at the Tate
And honest, all joking apart,
Why does modern art create hate?

A traditional flower display
Is fragrant and colourful too,
Such a pleasure to see each day
Instead of wood planks painted blue.

A train in this siding once stood
When they catered for our needs,
Do you remember how we all could
Go to Bradford, and not via Leeds?

FILFUZ, (Anti avant-garde letting off steam),
The Wakefield Express, 22.1.1988.

Over six years after its unveiling, PSI found that attitudes towards the sculpture were mixed. One Friday morning we carried out an on the spot, random survey of over 40 people at Westgate Station plus members of the station staff.

The majority of people interviewed used the station regularly, and had done so for five years and over. Slightly under 20 per cent of those interviewed had 'never thought about it' or professed not to have noticed the sculpture. Opinions about the sculpture varied enormously. Some disliked it, others 'loved it'. Some thought it was scruffy, others found it 'imaginative' and 'effective'. One thought it resembled the sea. 'It's nice when you go past in the train', 'nice at night'. Over 50 per cent of those surveyed remembered the station before the sculpture was erected. Most of them thought it had improved the station by adding interest. 'It lifted the station a bit into the twentieth century.' It makes it 'different to other stations'. 'It makes it look like someone cares, that someone has bothered.' One commuter remembered that it 'initially got people interested, but now it's taken for granted'. Station staff concurred. It had tidied up and lightened a dark corner of the station. However they were frustrated by its lack of maintenance. 'The light bulbs blow and it can take ages before they are replaced.'

Those overtly involved
According to Quick, over 30 different groups – organisations, companies, British Rail departments – and individuals worked on the project.

Unfortunately it has not been possible to trace any of the young people Community Industry involved in the construction of *A Light Wave*. There is consequently no way of assessing how they benefited through the creation of jobs or the skills they acquired. The artist and planning officers have suggested that the Community Industry team was reliable and committed, that they were very proud of *A Light Wave*. They got their photos into the local papers and a day in London. 'Better than digging ditches'. The scheme enabled Community Industry to be involved in a different type of work experience.

It has not been possible to discuss the project with the teachers involved in the education programme.

For the sponsors, Roger Suddards, a trustee of the Foundation, felt that 'it was wonderful to be involved ... I am very impressed by the work. I believed it was a beautiful thing and that it did beautify the station, which could have been left to rot forever.' Other than that there was 'not a lot to say'. Articles about the work appeared in trade press, such as *SupaTimba News*, Winter 1987. Keith Ellis of Ellis Ventures Ltd regarded it as a worthwhile involvement.

> It showed some of the products which we sell in a most unusual way, it precipitated the refurbishment of Wakefield Station, and improved the image presented to both locals and travellers passing through on the main line route.

Roberts regards the subsequent environmental improvements to the station as directly accountable to the success of *A Light Wave*. In December 1987, British Rail commissioned Quick to design another sculpture for the station. *Lightspray* was intended to complement *A Light Wave*. Made of blue metal, it was placed on the wall of the down-side of the footbridge stairwell. It was unveiled in September 1989, by which time more of the station had been renovated. As a result of these and improvements to passenger facilities, Westgate was awarded British Rail's Best Station Awards in 1989 and 1990.

The sculpture changed the image of Wakefield from the point of view of rail travellers. Hall observed

> It's very critical, even to the people who don't get off at Wakefield, that they begin to appreciate that they are going through Wakefield. That is what the sculpture did above anything else. People remember it. Wakefield station is no longer the one after Peterborough, Doncaster and the rest. It is the one with the funny sculpture.

Its lack of maintenance raises questions about British Rail's attitude. Quick carried out some maintenance to the work during the year after its completion, partly to iron out some design problems with the sequencing.

He regards the maintenance of the sculpture as having become less of a priority. It is 'never going to be able to compete with the maintenance or the running of the railway or the continuous reorganisation and cost cutting. So I think there will always be problems.'

From the point of view of financial development, the employment of an artist made good economic sense.

> Unlike the landscape architects, the artist can always beg free materials. In this sense, public money is like seed funding. The rest – the lion's share – comes from outside.

Subsequent developments

Their involvement in *A Light Wave* appears to have influenced the subsequent work of each of the parties. For Hall, the project set the context for subsequent public art projects in the borough.

> The Wakefield station scheme allowed me not to have to take the big jump from promoting environmental improvement to promoting public art ... It provided a good starting point to talk about public art overtly rather than surreptitiously ... It set a context to be 'more up front' about putting public art into the general environmental campaign ... It paved the way for us to be able to do the others. It created a formula which we developed. Work on *A Light Wave* also demonstrated the advantages of working with an agency 'at one remove from the council. We are able to set up a way of administering the projects at arms' length.' Wakefield's subsequent public art projects have been carried out in collaboration with Public Arts. In particular, they have developed closer relationships with the communities involved through consultation, workshops, schools' visits and residencies. In Featherstone, for example, the community's attitude towards a proposed mural was researched in various ways including public meetings, door knocking, talking to shop owners and meetings with the Town Council. In this case, consultation established what the community did and did not want.

Cox thought in retrospect that Public Arts should have provided more information while the artist was working on site, including a photograph of the artist and a update of what was going on.

> But in retrospect, although information was presented. whatever else had been done would never have been enough due, I think, to the nature and activity of the public there.

For her the experience of working on the project informed subject education work carried out in her present capacity as Public Art Officer, Thamesdown Borough Council.

A Light Wave also offered Wakefield the opportunity to develop its partnership with British Rail. 'The contacts we made with British Rail did no harm.' The Capital Line project was set up in 1990 by a partnership consisting of Wakefield MDC Planning Department, British Rail and West Yorkshire Passenger Transport Executive, supported by Wakefield Groundwork Trust and Countryside Commission. Its objective was to improve the quality of the environment adjacent to the Leeds to London railway line through Wakefield District.

> The principles behind Capital Line are exactly the same as those behind the sculpture. A huge number of people pass through that sliver of the district ... [We wanted to] present the district as a more attractive place in which to live and work (Hall).

The project also heralded a change in Wakefield's attitude towards artists. Quick had

> all the support I needed from Public Arts, more importantly I had a huge amount of support from the British Rail architects and civil engineers which enabled the project to be completed.

However Wakefield felt that for the artist to run the education programme, contribute to raising sponsorship and manage the site was more than could reasonably be expected. In subsequent projects, the artists were better supported.

For Quick,

> the project provided me with a national profile within the field of public art practice and I have been involved in more than 16 commissions at some stage. I have continued to be involved in permanent and temporary work in galleries and in public since then. Since 1990 I have been an Associate Senior Lecturer at the University of Central Lancashire with responsibilities for aspects of the Public Art programme on the BA Hons Fine Art Course.

The announcement in 1992 that British Rail would be privatised might, in the long run, open up considerable potential for the development of art and design features. According to David Perry, there is 'little hope for British Rail's arts policy'.

References to Part 2

ACGB, *Henry Moore at the Serpentine. 80th Birthday Exhibition of Recent Carvings and Bronzes*, The Serpentine Gallery, Kensington Gardens, 1 July – 8 October 1978, Arts Council of Great Britain, 1978.

Alberge, Dalya, 'The Profit and the Pleasure Principle', *The Independent*, 1990.

Alston, D.A. [A], *90 Days in 89. A Summary Report*, (unpublished and undated).

Alston, D.A.[B], *Art in the Parks 1989 – Sheffield. Briefing Notes for News Editors*, (undated).

Amery, Colin, 'There is no frozen music here', *Financial Times*, 1991.

The Arts Business, *The Cultural Economy of Birmingham* (Draft), Birmingham City Council, 1991.

Arts Council British Gas Awards, *Working for Cities*, 1992.

BBC, *Masters of the Universe. The Men who Rebuilt the City*. Transmitted BBC2, 1993.

Bianchini, Franco, 'Alternative Cities', *Marxism Today*, 1991.

Birmingham City Council (undated A), *Birmingham: A Celebration of Success*.

Birmingham City Council (undated B), *Public Art in Birmingham*.

Birmingham City Council, Department of Recreation and Community Services (undated C), *Birmingham City Council Arts Strategy. Summary of Aims*, (unpublished).

Birmingham City Council, Joint Arts Culture and Economy Sub-Committee (1990), *Joint Report of Chief Executive, Director of Recreation and Community Services, Director of Library Services, Director of Museums and Art Gallery and Director of Development: An Arts Strategy for Birmingham*.

Birmingham City Council (1991), *Report of the Director of Museums and Art Gallery to Joint Arts, Culture and Economy Sub-Committee: Public Art. The Management Process*, (unpublished).

Birmingham City Council (1992A), *Report of the Director of Museums and Art Gallery to Joint Arts, Culture and Economy Sub-Committee: Public Art and The Image of Birmingham*, (unpublished).

Birmingham City Council (1992B), *Joint Report of the Director of Museums and Art Gallery and Director of Planning and Architecture to Joint Arts Culture and Economy Sub-Committee and Planning Committee: Public Art Policy Review*, (unpublished).

Bostock, Jonathan P., *The Future of Birmingham: The Business View*, Bostock Marketing, 1990.

British Railways Board, *Community Partnership with British Rail*, (undated).

British Railways Board, *Art on the Railway. A Policy Statement*, (undated).

British Railways Board (1987), *Agreement between Charles Quick, Public Arts and the British Railways Board*, (unpublished).

Broadgate Estates, *Broadgate Live*, 1992.

1991 Census, *Area Profile: Smethwick High Street Shopping Centre Catchment Area*, 1991.

Chave, Anna C., 'Minimalism and the Rhetoric of Power', *Arts Magazine*, 1990.

City of Wakefield Metropolitan District Council, Planning Department, *Lighting the Green Fuse* (undated).

Cohen, Nick, 'Renaissance that never was'. *Independent on Sunday*, 1993.

Common Ground, *The Parish Maps Project*, leaflet, 1991.

The Conservation Foundation, *10th Ford British Conservation Awards 1982-1991. Details*, (undated).

DEGW, *Post Occupancy Evaluation of One Broadgate and Five Other Buildings* (unpublished), 1988.

Farrington, Jane and Silber, Evelyn, *Raymond Mason: Sculptures and Drawings*, Lund Humphries in association with Birmingham City Museum and Art Gallery, 1989.

Harris, M.W., *Shopping Centre Improvements: A New Approach. Smethwick High Street, June 1986-1987*, Sandwell Metropolitan District Council, (undated).

Hillier, Ben, Grajewski, Tadeusz, Jones, Liz, Jianming, Xu and Greene, Marguerita, *Broadgate Spaces: Life in Public Places, Bartlett School of Architecture*, (unpublished), 1990.

International Convention Centre, Birmingham, *Art at the International Convention Centre, Birmingham*, ICC, (undated).

International Convention Centre, Birmingham/Birmingham City Council, *Art in the City: Public Art Programme. An invitation from the Lord Mayor of Birmingham*, ICC, (undated).

Kay, Tess, *The Recreational Use of Parks in Sheffield: A Report of User Surveys Conducted in Selected Parks on Sunday 12 March 1989*, Department of Geography and Recreation Studies, Staffordshire Polytechnic, (unpublished), 1989.

LDR/HLN Consultancy, *Pedestrian Movement and Open Space Framework*, City of Birmingham, 1988.

Loftman, Patrick and Nevin, Brendan, *Urban Regeneration and Social Equality: A Case Study of Birmingham 1986-1992*, Research Paper no. 8, Faculty of the Built Environment, University of Central England in Birmingham, 1992.

Mason, Robert, *The Broadgate Experience*, Department of Architecture, University of Edinburgh, (unpublished), 1993.

Petherbridge, Deanna, 'Writing on the Wall', *The Independent*, 1991.

Public Sector Management Research Centre, *Improving Inner City Shopping Centres: An Evaluation of the Urban Programme Funded Schemes in the West Midlands*, PSMRC, Aston University for the Department of the Environment: Inner Cities Directorate, HMSO, 1988.

Quick, Charles, *Proposal for 'A Light Wave'*, (unpublished), 1985.

RSD (1990), *Broadgate: Paintings and Drawings 1989-1990 by Robert Mason*, Rosehaugh Stanhope Developments plc, 1990.

RSD (1991), *Broadgate and Liverpool Street Station*, Rosehaugh Stanhope Developments plc, 1991.

RSD(1992), *Art at Broadgate*, Rosehaugh Stanhope Developments plc, 1992.

Rimmer, Hilary, Webster, Nick, Bissell, Bob and Bartlam, Norman, *Student Information Pack, International Convention Centre*, Birmingham, 1991.

Roberts, Marion, Marsh, Chris and Salter, Miffa, *Public Art in Private Places: Commercial Benefits and Public Policy*, University of Westminster, 1993.

SCAT Annual Report, *90 Days in 1989: A Season of New Art from Sheffield*, Sheffield Contemporary Arts Trust, (unpublished and undated).

Serra, Richard with Weyergraf, Clara, *Richard Serra Interviews etc, 1970-1980*, Hudson River Museum, 1980.

Sheffield Recreation Department, *Chantryland Sculpture Trail*, leaflet, (undated).

Sorr, Robert, 'Titled Arc: Enemy of the People?', *Art in America*, 1985.

Stanhope Properties plc, *Collaborative Development. Employment and Training Initiatives in Local Communities*, (undated).

Strong, Sir Roy, *Ministering to the Arts, Part 111: 'Opening the Door'*, BBC Radio 4, 1992.

Upton, Christopher, *The Past, the Present & Future: A Commemorative Book for the Opening of the International Convention Centre*, Birmingham City Council, 1991.

Urban Design Division, Department of Planning and Architecture, Birmingham, *Broad Street Redevelopment Area: Fact Pack*, 1992.

Weyergraf-Serra, Clara (ed.), The Destruction of 'Tilted Arc': Documents, MIT, 1991.

Winpenny, David, 'In ever decreasing circles', *The Times*, 1991.

PART 3

Observations
Implications
Policy Issues &
Recommendations

Introduction

Part 3 draws together the main findings of this enquiry and considers what implications they might have for the policies and practices of permanent public art.

It is divided into two chapters. Chapter 7 makes a series of observations about the commissioning, siting and reception of public art. Issues raised in each sub-section refer to implications which should be considered in respect of the formulation and evaluation of policy. Chapter 8 contains a series of operational recommendations which draw on the above. These are addressed to those in arts funding bodies, local authorities and others directly concerned with the formulation and evaluation of policies pertaining to art in the public sector.

7   Observations and implications

The works which constitute the case studies were selected precisely because of the significant differences between them (p. 77). The fact that certain similarities, nevertheless, exist between them has enabled several observations to be made. These pertain to the commissioning, production, siting and reception of public art and the theoretical assumptions that inform them. They also draw on issues raised in the focus group discussions and other interviews. These issues are couched in the form of questions. Who is public art for? What it is supposed to do? Why is it like it is? How is it perceived by the public? And, finally, how is it evaluated?

Who is public art for?

The nature of the relationship intended between works of public art and the public was rarely articulated in the case studies. Yet the concept of public art suggests an art of the public, one which is commissioned on the public's behalf or one which is subject to democratic processes.

The majority of works examined as case studies were described as for the wider community – local residents as well as international visitors. By definition, such audiences are geographically defined. However, geographical associations *per se* may be insufficient to elicit people's interest in works of public art. Some of the case studies were contextualised within the complexity of interests of the community as a whole. Although not excluding other groups, they directly referred to relatively small individual groups within the community – the residents of Silkstone (p. 204), the traders and some of the shoppers of Smethwick High Street (p. 162) or passengers on the Leeds to London line (p. 214). It follows that public art works may, conversely, effectively exclude certain groups. Prestige projects sited in proximity to areas of urban deprivation may, for example, highlight the interests of one community over and above those of another and thereby reinforce extant social divisions.

The case studies suggest that professional interests usually prevail in the initiation and management of public art works, and that it is comparatively rare for people not professionally engaged in the visual arts to be involved in these processes. However the fact that a work is initiated from within the community does not guarantee that it is considered to represent the broader community, as *The Silkstone Heritage Stones* illustrate.

The public was usually assigned a relatively passive role. The two case studies which included practical contributions by the public (Smethwick High Street and Silkstone), involved children working in the context of a school education programme.

It also appeared that the public is more likely to be informed about proposed commissions than consulted. Smethwick presents the most detailed example of public consultation of all the case studies. It is not surprising, therefore, that the processes by which the public might be consulted about public works of art are not highly formally developed.

Public art is conceived as being in the public interest – implicitly capable of improving people's quality of life, empowering or educating them. But given that it does not necessarily actively involve the public, it follows that it may be paternalistic. Whereas in the past such an art might have promoted what were regarded as social, civic or national virtues (such as heroism, leadership and achievement), current public art practice is more likely to be informed by the individual artist's interests.

The tenets of much art education and art practice almost uniquely encourage artists to work within their own terms of reference and to aspire to 'artistic integrity'. This is reinforced by many art world practices, such as the conventions of exhibiting. The conditions of public funding are frequently intended to protect the artist from having to comply with a wider set of requirements. Either because of, or in spite of these conventions, artists (or art administrators on their behalf) occasionally complained about the terms and conditions of their employment and the treatment of their work.

This raises questions about whose interests should be prioritised with respect to the commissioning or patronage of public art and whether it is desirable that those involved in the initiation and commissioning of public art elicit the views of the community. If so, how might these most accurately be represented?

What is public art supposed to do?

Intentions for the case studies – what it was hoped they would achieve and why and whom they were for, were rarely formally articulated.

In general terms, they reflected several categories of aspiration for public art commissions and were conceived as contributing to urban regeneration and local distinctiveness. They were seen as improving the environment, representing a financial investment and serving as the focus for partnerships or such mechanisms as Percent for Art. The case studies also embraced the creation of opportunities for artists and for the public to enjoy and appreciate art.

Aspirations for the case studies inevitably reflected the interests of the different constituencies involved. For their part artists might be interested in generating income, for the opportunity to work on a larger scale on their own terms and to further their careers; agencies wished to secure commissions and develop their reputations; developers, to attract tenants; local authorities, to create a sense of local distinctiveness, improve the quality of life for local residents and the environment and support the arts and so on. The interests of the public, who were not usually overtly involved in the case studies, were less clearly represented.

The works themselves were consequently required to reflect several sets of interests. Raymond Mason's sculpture *Forward* in Centenary Square (p. 128), for example, simultaneously sought to represent civic aspirations and function as an autonomous work. This raises questions as to how many interests individual works of public art can effectively serve, not least if these are in any way contradictory.

The case studies were often informed by certain assumptions. Artists' contributions were, without exception, presumed to be inherently educational. In some instances (Centenary Square for example) they were assumed to be instinctively capable of solving problems conventionally faced by other professional groups (such as planners, landscape architects, architects) and understanding the interests of the public. They were often credited with occupying a central, catalytic and decisive role in working collaborations although other professional groups involved did not necessarily subscribe to that (again as in Centenary Square or in the Broadgate development).

Why is public art like it is?

Among the various conditions likely to influence the production of public art, the case studies highlighted the following:

Professional relationships
The parameters of the relationships between people directly involved in the case studies were not always clear. This is exemplified by the roles assigned to, if not assumed by, artists.

Although at Broadgate for example, artists were deliberately treated similarly to other contractors, in the majority of case studies artists were generally assigned a more privileged position. Whatever their reputation or experience, the value of artists' involvement is largely taken as 'a given', and they were granted a higher degree of autonomy than other professionals alongside whom they worked. Why this should be the case, and why artists should be regarded as capable of serving wider interests than other professional groups is rarely questioned.

Responsibilities
The precise lines of responsibility among those directly involved in the commissioning of the case studies were often ambiguous. Artists may or may not have wished to be credited as sole authors, and agencies may or may not have wished their contribution to appear independent of their clients, the commissioners. Questions of responsibility may be further complicated by agencies' divided loyalties between the artist and their clients, the commissioners.

Selection of artists
None of the work examined in the context of the case studies involved open competitions. Several artists whose work was included among the case studies were self-selecting in that they had been involved in the initiation of the projects themselves (for example, Smethwick High Street and Westgate Station). Some had little or no previous experience of working in public places.

Artists who were selected had either entered limited competitions or were directly invited (as at Broadgate, Centenary Square and Silkstone). Some had national and international reputations, others were chosen for extra-artistic characteristics such as local connections. Equal opportunities were not a major factor in any of the case studies.

In fact an overall impression to be gained from the case studies was that there is a functional relationship between the scale of a purchaser or commissioner's aspirations for the work, the size of the budget, the status and reputation of the artist. Put simply, the greater the artist's reputation, the more prestigious the project and the bigger the budget. In this sense major projects reflect the interests of the art world and the scale of the aspirations of patrons. What is less clear is the relationship between the scale of the fee and the value to the public of the work produced.

Agreements

The majority of case studies were formalised by agreements between the artists, commissioners and agents. In some cases a brief for the work was also agreed. The details of these are often relatively ambiguous, and thereby allow the artist greater flexibility. It may be assumed to be the artist's prerogative to extend the brief as much as possible.

The agreements pertaining to the case studies (see Appendix 7, p. 348) contain clauses about originality, acceptance, planning and other consents or approvals, installation, care and maintenance, delivery, assembly, ownership, risk and insurance, payments, copyrights, conditions pertaining to a breach or termination of agreements, rights, obligations, liability, removal or sale. They may also include clauses which refer to educational provision, the life expectancy of the commissioned work, the role of the agency and acknowledgements.

However, the existence of agreements did not necessarily prevent matters from going wrong. In Silkstone, for example, the appearance of one work constituted a matter of dispute between the artist and the commissioners which at the time of writing remains unresolved. This was not the case with commissions at Broadgate for instance, for which agreements were only issued after receipt of a maquette made to scale.

Maintenance clauses were not always fully respected (for example at Westgate Station. This may ultimately be self-defeating in that an unmaintained work may detract from the quality of the visual environment rather than improve it. Dissatisfied artists are unlikely to take legal action to safeguard the care and conservation of their works, not least because of the cost involved or the damage to their reputations.

Commissioning and consultation

In all the case studies the theme, content and appearance of commissioned works were proposed by artists who were more or less constrained by briefs issued by the commissioning body or their representatives (as, for example, at Broadgate: Appendix 7, p. 348).

To be commissioned – to receive an order for the production of a work – implies similarities between the processes of design and artistic creativity. But since artistic merit is often associated with 'freedom', the avoidance of constraints implied by commissioning is considered desirable among some artistic constituencies. Ironically, some of the artists employed in the Chantreyland Sculpture Trail in Sheffield who were not issued with briefs or contracts, lamented their absence. Artistic autonomy was generally considered to be of major importance to all constituencies involved.

Different conditions of funding public art imply different relationships. Commissioning is distinct from patronage (the disinterested support, promotion or encouragement of an artist) or sponsorship (a form of corporate promotion administratively regarded as analogous to advertising).

The case studies suggest that the public sector (as represented in Centenary Square, Smethwick and Sheffield) is less likely than the private sector (for example at Broadgate) to intervene in the production of works. This may reflect functional differences between the two sectors. The private company, Broadgate Properties, was driven by clear objectives. Work they commissioned such as *Fulcrum* had to fulfil specific functions, such as a meeting place and a landmark (see Appendix 6, p. 344). By comparison local authorities appear to have less overtly determined the works they commissioned. There may be several reasons for such differences. Planning Officers are discouraged from involving themselves in decisions about aesthetic matters; works commissioned by partnerships, including those forged between different departments within the same authority and those intended to serve the interests of numerous groups within the community or the administration itself. Local authorities may wish to be perceived as patrons of the arts offering opportunities to artists.

Siting

Artists were not usually instrumental in determining the sites for commissioned works (for example, *The Arch* in Kensington Gardens, at Broadgate or in Centenary Square, Birmingham). However, their initiation of projects tended to be prompted by the potential of particular sites (for instance, Smethwick High Street or Westgate Station in Wakefield). Few if any of the case studies conceived as discrete objects dominate their contexts. This implies that public art is conventionally perceived, if not conceived, as an accessory to the wider context.

The majority of case studies, were, to a greater or lesser extent, site-specific, in that the works were conceived for and determined by particularities of the location. The widespread practice of 'site-specific' work raises questions about the nature of artists' responses to sites, particularly if they adopt a formal approach rather than one which is informed by the history and associations of the place. This raises questions about the value of artists' responses to places and how they shape the 'meaning' of particular places.

Planning permission

Some case studies were granted planning permission, others did not go to planning committee. By definition the granting of planning consent carries certain implications. At Broadgate the granting of permission implied – albeit through association – that the authorities involved endorsed the work. In another example, Smethwick High Street, it was used as a procedural device to enable officers to formalise decisions.

How is public art perceived by the public?

Eliciting responses from the public is generally regarded as the last stage of the complete public art process and, therefore, desirable. This holds even if responses are negative. Paradoxically this can be construed as pre-empting the need to act on criticism. In Graves Park (the Chantreyland Sculpture Trail), the artist interpreted a small act of vandalism – people carving their names on a public art work – as indicative of the success of the work.

As is sometimes the case with contemporary art, there was little evidence of considered criticism by either members of the public or the press about the respective merits or qualities of individual works of public art. As with contemporary art certain preoccupations were common, such as the cost of the works; for example whether or not they had been funded by the local public – as was the case in Smethwick – their appearance and finish and whether they were a 'con'. These issues raise political and philosophical dilemmas: should the cost of public art works be borne by the public purse when insufficient funds are being committed to such public services as housing, health care and education? (In the case of work privately commissioned for Broadgate one member of the public proposed that a sculpture was a waste of material resources. The implication was that better use could have been made of it.)

Some of the more prestigious case studies which had received considerable media coverage (such as *the Arch* or the artworks in Centenary Square) suggest that public attitudes have a symbiotic relationship with media coverage. Public responses were either often informed by or had stimulated media interest. Responses were often determined by certain expectations of art. These were implicit rather than explicit and were, therefore, rarely articulated. These included the assumption that art is manifest in objects *per se*, as opposed to city spaces (none of those surveyed identified the paving of Centenary Square as art); it should be attractive, appropriate, inoffensive and give pleasure rather than being 'challenging' or stimulating; it should be figurative rather than abstract or conceptual; its value should be represented by the material from which it is produced – bronze, for instance, rather than fibreglass. In some cases people's response to works they disliked was to demand that they be removed elsewhere (see, for example, Centenary Square), or to regard children clambering over them as somehow judgemental as in the case of *the Arch*. These popular paradigms are rarely consonant with those of the professionals engaged in the promotion of public art. Works that are popularly admired may be denigrated by professionals who blame deficiencies in the education system. This implies a lack of respect for the public's attitude.

The received wisdom of professionals engaged in public art is that the public may grow to appreciate public art works in the long-term on the basis of familiarity. A survey carried out in respect of the longest standing case study (*the Arch*) suggested that this was not necessarily so. By the same token, messianic promoters of public art sometimes suggest that the burgeoning of public art outside the gallery may contribute towards the creation of new audiences for art. We found no evidence to support this.

Information and interpretation

It was significant that little information about the public artworks studied was made available to the public beyond the formal education programmes and initial dissemination of information. At the time of writing, published material had been produced for three out of the seven case studies; Broadgate, Centenary Square and the Chantreyland Sculpture Trail. The amount of information and depth of interpretation provided for these varied.

This reflects the broader problem whereby little information or interpretive material about contemporary art in particular is provided, even by institutions in the public sector. There are various pretexts for this, such as the notion that works should be left to speak for themselves; that forms of mediation may be detrimental to audiences' direct experience of art or that works are open to any form of interpretation. That logic suggests that the provision of art *per se* is regarded as constituting a public service and that merely making art physically accessible is considered synonymous with encouraging a wider understanding and appreciation of art.

How is public art evaluated?

None of the case studies examined had been subject to formal, written evaluations by those involved. Some people interviewed during the course of research proposed that public art is unquantifiable, asking how public response could be measured, and suggesting that judgements about quality are ultimately subject to historical processes, as in 'great art stands the test of time'.

Given that the objectives of case studies were rarely clearly articulated, it follows that the criteria according to which works might be formally evaluated tended not to be identified. Nor were there any processes by which the opinions of different constituencies or tiers of local, regional, national or international influence might be considered or compared.

Some of the case studies had been judged by award-making bodies. But this was according to their own terms of reference.

In certain case studies, the objectives cited were self-fulfilling. These included the creation of opportunities and the forging of partnerships between different local authority departments or other bodies. These were to do with administrative processes and had little to do with matters pertaining to the art itself.

Assertions about the qualities of projects were often made in the short-term, on the basis of visible evidence, and in terms of their qualities as visual art. Such observations may bear little relationship to the long-term social or economic impact of the work. They make no allowance for the ways in which a work's symbolic value may shift according to changing social, cultural, economic or political conditions. It was often the case that little distinction was made between the aspirations for and the actual impact of those projects studied. In short, claims made for public art were frequently unsubstantiated.

Comments: art in public places, public art and modernism

All the case studies were conceived in relation to diverse, traditional European practices such as architectural embellishment and the placing of sculpture in the landscape. They were also conceived within, or in reaction to, the Western theoretical context of Modernism. Many of the works examined uphold notions associated with Modernism: that of the artist as a free, instinctive spirit, privileged as a special, creative individual who is the producer of unique work of individual expression whose meaning he or she determines. Such notions are particularly problematic, especially in relation to public art. One way of looking at this is suggested by Charles Harrison and Paul Wood. In *Art in Theory 1900-1990: An Anthology of Changing Ideas*, they describe Modernism as having determined the values attributed to art throughout much of the 20th century. According to its tenets, art is both an autonomous practice, and

> an exemplary realm. What might be done, seen, experienced within this realm would have a critical bearing on the actual conditions of social existence but only in so far as art maintained a moral independence from these conditions.

According to Harrison and Wood the theoretical tradition of Modernism is essentially maintained in tension with the various forms of what they identify as Realism 'according to which the practice of art constitutes a form of participation or intervention in the social process'. This theory maintains that art represents the interests of a wider social group and that it refers to the circulation of ideas in the world which the artist practises.

Public art, as the case studies in this report suggest, is typified by such tensions. They are manifest in the contradictory expectations of artists and the public; between works conceived as art in public places, community art and art developed in consultation with the public; arguments for and against public consultation; compromise and artistic integrity; the assumption that art speaks for itself as opposed to requiring interpretation; the difficulties implicit in conceiving of art as a public service or of the artist having a social function; the notion that public art is unmeasurable, and so on.

To suggest that these positions might be represented by the alternative practices of art in public places and community art would be to oversimplfy. Although they appear to be fundamentally incompatible, in practice they often coincide. Few of the case studies are entirely uncompromising. For example, Raymond Mason's *Forward* in Centenary Square, which seeks to represent the people of Birmingham, was produced according to the artist's own terms of reference rather than in consultation with the people themselves.

The frequency of such contradictions and dilemmas has shaped the recommendations in the following chapter.

8 Policy issues and recommendations

The following policy issues and recommendations draw on the observations recorded in Chapter 7. They address matters pertinent to the range of professional interests represented in the field of public art and could be implemented in both the public and private sectors through conditions of funding.

Intentions

There should be a greater openness as to how decisions are made, who makes them and for what reasons. The intentions and values which inform the funding, commissioning, siting and reception of a work of public art should be clearly articulated at the outset:

- Who is it for?
- What it is supposed to do?
- How will it meet those objectives?
- What kind of relationship is it expected to have with the public?
- How long is it expected to remain in place?
- What is it going to be like and how will it be evaluated?

The conditions implied by funding should also be made explicit – whether the proposed work is a commission or the object of patronage or sponsorship; whether it is required to fulfil a brief and what the anticipated roles and responsibilities of the various protagonists are.

Such declarations of intent should not only prevent the interests of one constituency dominating those of another during the production of the work, but should ultimately inform the subsequent evaluations of the project.

Responsibilities and accountability

The respective roles and responsibilities of all those overtly involved should be agreed at the outset and specified in contracts or agreements. This will serve to establish clear lines of accountability.

The precise nature of an artist's anticipated contribution should be determined – albeit as a member of a design team, sole author, project leader, site manager, advisor, animator, educator, etc.

Selection of artists

Funders should consider the implications of how artists are selected – by invitation, open competition, limited competition, self-selection – and whether they want to embrace some element of risk, or would prefer knowing precisely what to expect. In short, do they regard their relationship with the artist as that of a commissioner or a patron?

Funders should consider the relative skills and experience of artists. If they require artists to work with people in the community for example, they may wish to consider their ability to communicate with members of the public, in addition to those with whom they will have to develop a professional relationship such as architects, planners and so on.

Professional development

All those overtly involved in commissioning and producing public art need to understand what is required of them, what to expect of other constituencies involved – in short, to comprehend the pragmatic and theoretical issues that pertain to promoting contemporary art within the public realm.

Building on what has already been achieved, further professional development with respect to such issues should be provided for all the constituencies involved. Artists, for example, may require training in practical matters such as estimating for and managing the time spent on commissions; assessing and meeting the expectations of commissioners or solving problems rather than working intuitively.

Planners may need to develop their knowledge, understanding and confidence about art and to assess what can reasonably be expected of artists in respect of such functions as public consultation and the value of their contributions to the built environment. In both cases such training could form part of their basic qualifications.

Consultation

Depending on its objectives, the commissioning of permanent works of public art – in particular within the public sector – should be subject to consultation.

Proposed commissions should be introduced to and discussed with the public and/or professional groups likely to be involved (ie the users of a building) with the intention that their views be respected and represented in the final work. This would not only serve to reinforce the consideration of precisely who particular public art projects are intended for and whose interests they should serve, but would contribute to the public's understanding of and appreciation for the works themselves.

The depth of such consultation, the methods to be employed (see *Evaluation* below), the use to which it might be put and the sample of the public to be consulted should be agreed at the outset. These should form part of the Agreement.

Agreements

All commissions should be formalised by legally binding agreements and briefs which protect all the parties involved, including intermediaries. Such agreements should specify the requirements of the commission, allocate functions and responsibilities, uphold the rights of those involved and guard against potential contention. They should also refer to consultation and evaluation.

Currently little stigma attaches to commissioners failing to maintain works. Agreements should serve to reinforce the obligation, if not guarantee maintenance clauses being respected. Agreements should also refer to the anticipated life of the work (for example, Appendix 7, p. 362).

Information and interpretation

It should be required that information about public artworks is made easily available to the public beyond any formal education programme and initial dissemination of information. This particularly applies to work in the public sector, where standard practice dictates that works displayed in galleries or museums have labels and extended captions.

At one level such information should include declarations about how decisions are made, who makes them and for what reasons. At another level, the information and interpretation should also be provided about the works themselves. This should be conceived in relation to the context within which the work is located (be it a civic square or rural track); the potential audiences for the work (be they local residents or international tourists); the appropriate form (for example, leaflets as opposed to information panels) and the value of particular kinds of information and interpretation (dates; medium; interpretation of the work by members of the local community in addition to, or instead of, the artist's intentions). The form and content of the information provided may refer to the findings of consultations (see above).

Evaluation

Formal evaluation and the monitoring of projects in the short, medium and long-term by funders or other responsible bodies, will contribute to respect for the claims and particular qualities of public art.

Criteria for evaluation, based on the stated intentions and objectives of particular public art projects, should be established at the outset. The methodology and timescale according to which evaluation is carried out should also be agreed at that stage.

The ways in which public art works are evaluated may vary according to the criteria for individual works, the conditions of their funding and the contexts within which they are located. They may refer to the quantitative or qualitative impact of the work, how many people it attracts and how it influences their perception of the place where it is located and so on.

The methods involved in such evaluations may be similar to those employed in this enquiry, namely, random surveys of members of the public; postal surveys of specific constituencies (such as tenants at Broadgate), on the spot interviews (as with the traders of Smethwick High Street or passengers at Westgate Station, Wakefield) or focus group discussions with professional groups and in-depth interviews with particular individuals.

The period of time over which such evaluations might be carried out should refer to the anticipated life of the work. The short-term impact of a work with an expected life of ten years, for example, might refer to the first six months, the medium term to between two and four years and the long term to five years or more.

The outcome of such evaluations should be used to inform subsequent work by those involved. They should contribute to respect for public art and its development in the future. The funding of public art projects within the public sector should be contingent upon evaluations of previous projects by those involved.

Bibliography

ACGB *Art into Landscape: Prize-winning and other entries in a competitive schemes for the development of open spaces*, Serpentine Gallery, Arts Council of Great Britain in co-operation with the Royal Institute of British Architects, the Institute of Landscape Architects and the *Sunday Times, 1974.*

ACGB *Art into Landscape: An exhibition of schemes to enliven public spaces.* Prize-winning and selected entries from the second competition organised by the Arts Council of Great Britain in co-operation with the RIBA, the Landscape Institute and the *Sunday Times*, Serpentine Gallery, Arts Council of Great Britain, 1977.

ACGB *Henry Moore at the Serpentine: 80th Birthday Exhibition of Recent Carvings and Bronzes*, Serpentine Gallery and Kensington Gardens, 1 July – 8 October, Arts Council of Great Britain, 1978.

ACGB *Art into Landscape: Prize-winning and selected final-stage proposals for sites in England, Scotland and Wales*, Serpentine Gallery, Arts Council of Great Britain, 1980.

ACGB *Percent for Art.* Report of a Steering Group established by the Arts Council of Great Britain with the Council of Regional Arts Associations, the Welsh and the Scottish Arts Councils, 1990.

ACGB *Percent for Art: a review*, Arts Council of Great Britain, 1991.

ACGB *A Creative Future: the Way Forward for the Arts, Crafts and Media in England*, coordinated by the Arts Council of Great Britain on behalf of the English Arts Funding System, HMSO, 1993.

ACGB *Art for Whom?* Serpentine Gallery, Arts Council of Great Britain (undated).

ACGB *An Urban Renaissance: The role of the arts in urban regeneration. The case for increased public and private sector co-operation*, Arts Council of Great Britain (undated).

ACGB *An Urban Renaissance: sixteen case studies showing the role of the arts in urban regeneration* (undated).

al-Khalil, Samir, *The Monument: Art Vulgarity and Responsibility in Iraq*, Andre Deutch, 1991.

Apgar, Garry, 'Redrawing the Boundaries of Public Art', *Sculpture*, 1992.

The Arts Business, *The Cultural Economy of Birmingham*, Birmingham City Council, 1991.

Arts Council & British Gas Awards, *Working for Cities*, 1992.

(–), 'Introduction', *Art-Language. The Journal of Conceptual Art*, May 1969.

Association of District Councils, *Towards Unitary Authorities: Arts and Entertainment*, (undated).

Atkinson, Terry, 'Concerning Interpretation of the Bainbridge/Hurrell Models', *Art-Language. The Journal of Conceptual Art*, February, 1970.

Audit Commission, *Local Authorities, Entertainment and the Arts*, HMSO, 1991.

BBC, *Masters of the Universe. The Men Who Rebuilt the City* (transmitted BBC2, 2.1.1993).

Bailey, Trevor and Scott, Ian, *Rural Arts: A discussion document for the Calouste Gulbenkian Foundation*, Calouste Gulbenkian Foundation, 1989.

Banfield, Edward C., *The Democratic Muse: Visual Arts and the Public Interest*, Basic Books, New York, 1984.

Banham, Mary and Hillier, Bevis, *A Tonic to the Nation*, 1976.

Barrett-Lennard, John, 'Public Art, Public Space, Public Access ...', *Praxis* 5, 1989.

Barrett-Lennard, John, *Working in Public*, Artspace Visual Arts Centre, Woolloomooloo, 1992.

Batchelor, David, 'Under the Canary', *Frieze* 5, 1992.

Beardsley, John, *Art in Public Places*, Partners for Livable Places, Washington DC, 1987.

Beck, Anthony, 'The Impact of Thatcherism on the Arts Council', *Parliamentary Affairs 42, 3*, 1989.

Biancini, Franco, 'Urban Renaissance? The Arts and the Urban Regeneration Process' in MacGregor and Pimlott, 1990.

Biancini, Franco, 'Alternative Cities', *Marxism Today,* June 1991.

Biancini, Franco, Fisher, Mark, Montgomery, John and Worpole, Ken (1988), *City Centres, City Cultures: The Role of the Arts in the Revitalization of Towns and Cities*, Centre for Local Economic Strategies, Manchester, 1988.

Biancini, Franco and Parkinson, Michael (eds), *Cultural Policy and Urban Regeneration: The West European Experience*, Manchester University Press, 1993.

Bicknell, Sandra and Farmelo, Graham (eds), *Museum Visitor Studies in the 90s*, The Science Museum, 1993.

Birmingham City Council, *Public Art in Birmingham*, (undated).

Booth, Peter and Bloye, Robin, 'See Glasgow, see Culture', in Biancini and Parkinson, 1993.

Bordieu, Pierre and Darbiel, Alain, *The Love of Art: European Museums and their Public*, Polity, 1991.

Bostock, Jonathan P., *The Future of Birmingham: The Business View*, Bostock Marketing, 1990.

Braden, Sue, *Art and People*, Routledge, 1976.

Brighton, Andrew, 'Philistine Piety and Public Art', *Modern Painters*, 1993.

British Railways Board, *Art on the Railway. A Policy Statement*, (undated).

Cabinet Office, *Action for Cities*, Cabinet Office, Department of the Environment, Department of Trade and Industry, 1988.

Carey, John, *Intellectuals and the Masses: Pride and Prejudice among the Literary Intelligentsia 1880-1939*, Faber & Faber, 1992.

Cembalest, Robin, 'The Ecological Art Explosion', *ARTnews*, 1991.

Chapman, David and Larkham, Peter, *Discovering the Art of Relationship: Urban Design, Aesthetic Control and Design Guidance*. Research Paper 9, School of Planning, Faculty of the Built Environment, Birmingham Polytechnic, 1992.

Chave, Anna C., 'Minimalism and the Rhetoric of Power', *Arts Magazine*, 1990.

Clay, Grady, *Close-Up. How to read the American City*, Pall Mall Press, 1973.

Coffield, Frank, *Vandalism and Graffiti: The State of the Art*, Calouste Gulbenkian Foundation, 1991.

Cohen, Nick, 'Renaissance that never was', *Independent on Sunday*, 1993.

Collard, Paul, *Arts in Inner Cities*, The Office of Arts & Libraries (unpublished), 1988.

Common Ground, *The Parish Maps Project*, leaflet, 1991.

Common Ground, *An Introduction to the deeds and thoughts of Common Ground,*1990.

Conway, Hazel, *People's Parks. The Design and Development of Victorian Parks in Britain*, Cambridge University Press, 1991.

Countryside Commission, *Enjoying the Countryside: Policies for People*, 1992.

Crosby, Theo, *Let's Build a Monument*, 1987.

Cutts, Simon et al., *The Unpainted Landscape*, Coracle Press, Graeme Murray Gallery and the Scottish Arts Council, 1987.

Davies, Peter and Knipe, Tony (eds), *A Sense of Place*, Coelfrith Press, 1984.

Delafons. J., 'Design Control – the American Experience', *The Planner 77*, no 40.

Dempsey, Andrew, 'Introduction', *Outdoor Sculpture*, Arts Council of Great Britain, 1967.

Department of the Environment and the Welsh Office (1983), *Town & Country Planning Act 1971: Planning Gain*, DOE Circular 22/83, 1983.

Department of the Environment and the Welsh Office (1985), *Aesthetic Control*, DOE Circular 31/85, 1985.

Department of the Environment and the Welsh Office (1992), *Planning Policy Guidance: General Policy and Principles*, 1992.

Dix, Gill, *Resources for Urban Areas: historical and current context*. Briefing Paper 003, Policy and Planning Unit Arts Council of England, 1993.

Dormer, Peter, 'Lipstick on the face of a gorilla', *The Independent*, 1992.

Everitt, Anthony, 'Homage to the arts', *The Insider*, no 13, 1992.

Feld, L., O'Hare, M. and Schouster, J.M.D., *Patrons Despite Themselves: taxpayers and arts policy*, New York University Press, 1983.

Fisher, Mark and Owen, Ursula (eds), (1987). *Whose Cities?*, Penguin 1991.

Garnham, Nicholas, 'Concepts of Culture: Public Policy and the Cultural Industries', *Cultural Studies 1*, 1987.

Glasgow City Council, *The 1990 Story: Glasgow Cultural Capital of Europe*, 1992.

Greenwich Mural Workshop, *Murals in London Since 1971* (undated).

Griffiths, Ron, 'The Politics of Cultural Policy in Urban Regeneration Strategies', *Policy and Politics*, 21, 1, 1993.

Harding, David, 'Some Developments in Art Education in the UK with Reference to Public Art, *Art Monthly*, no 9, 1986.

Harris, M.W., *Shopping Centre Improvements: A New Approach. Smethwick High Street, June 1986-1987*, Sandwell Metropolitan District, (undated).

Harrison, Carolyn and Burgess, Jacqueline, 'Qualitative Research: An Open Space Policy', *The Planner*, November 1988.

Harrison, Charles and Wood, Paul (eds), *Art in Theory 1900-1990. An anthology of changing ideas*, Blackwell, 1992.

Harvey, David (ed.), *The Urban Experience*, John Hopkins University Press, 1989.

Heartney, Eleanor, 'What's missing at Battery Park?', *Sculpture*, November-December, 1989.

Heath, Jane (ed.), *The Furnished Landscape; Applied Art in Public Places*, Bellew Publishing, the Crafts Council and the Arts Council, 1992.

Hewison, Robert, *The Heritage Industry, 1992.*

Hillier, Ben, Grajewski, Tadeusz, Jones, Liz, Jianming, Xu and Greene, Marguerita, *Broadgate Spaces: Life in Public Places*, Bartlett School of Architecture (unpublished), 1990.

Hughes, Gordon, 'Measuring the Economic Value of the Arts', *Policy Studies 9*, no 3, 1989.

Hunter, I.A., *Environmental Sculpture Practice as a Contribution of Landscape Achitecture*, PhD dissertation, Manchester Polytechnic (unpublished), 1991.

International Convention Centre, Birmingham, *Art at the International Convention Centre, Birmingham*, ICC, (undated).

Isles, Chrissie, 'The Role of Controversy in Art', *Confrontations*, Projects UK and Tyne and Wear Museums Service, 1987.

Jackson, Peter, *Maps of Meaning: An introduction to cultural geography*, Unwin Hyman, 1989.

Jarvis, Bob, 'The Lost Art of Town Planning', *Urban Design Quarterly*, 1992.

Johnson, Diana, *The Arts in Rural Areas*, Discussion Document 39 National Arts & Media Strategy, Arts Council of Great Britain, 1991.

Johnson, Diana, *Pride of Place: The Arts in Rural Areas*, Arts Development Association, 1991.

Jones, Peter Lloyd, *Manifesto*, Art and Architecture, 1989.

Jones, Susan, (ed.), *Art in Public. What, why and how?* AN Publications, 1992.

Keens, William, Owens, Pam, Salvadori, Danni and Williams, Jennifer (eds), *Arts and the Changing City: Agenda for Urban Regeneration*, British American Arts Association 1989.

Kelly, Owen, *Community, Art and the State*, Comedia, 1984.

King, Angela and Clifford, Sue (eds), *Introduction to the Thoughts and Deeds of Common Ground*, Common Ground, 1990.

Lauf, Cornelia, *Snakes and Ladders. The archive of Dr. Willi Bongard.* Artscribe, November - December, 1990.

Lewis, Justin, *Art, Culture and Enterprise: The Politics of Art and the Cultural Industries,* Routledge, 1990.

Lingwood, James, (ed.), *New Works for Different Places: TSWA Four Cities Project,* TSWA, 1990.

Loftman, Patrick and Nevin, Brendan, *Urban Regeneration and Social Equality: A Case Study of Birmingham 1986-1992,* Research Paper no. 8, Faculty of the Built Environment, University of Central England in Birmingham, 1992.

MSS Marketing Research Ltd., *Arts 93: Audiences, Attitudes and Sponsorship,* Clerical Medical and ABSA, 1993.

MacGregor, Susanne and Pimlott, Ben, *Tackling the Inner Cities: The 1980s Reviewed, Prospects for the 1990s,* Clarendon Press, 1990.

Marriage, Helen, 'Critical Times', *Frieze,* 5, 1992.

Martorella, Rosanne, *Corporate Art,* Rutgers University Press, 1990.

Miles, Malcolm, *Art for Places,* Winchester Press, 1989.

Morland, Joanna, *New Milestones: Sculpture, Community and the Land,* Common Ground, 1988.

Mulgan, Geoff, *The Public Service Ethos & Public Libraries,* Comedia Working Paper 6: The Future of Public Library Services, 1993.

Mulgan, Geoff and Worpole, Ken, *Saturday Night or Sunday Morning: From Arts to Industry – Forms of Cultural Policy,* Comedia, 1986.

Myerscough, John, *The Economic Importance of the Arts in Britain,* Policy Studies Institute, 1988.

Nairne, Sandy and Serota, Nicholas, *British Sculpture in the Twentieth Century,* Whitechapel Art Gallery, 1981.

Netzer, Dick, *The Subsidized Muse: Public Support for the Arts in the US,* 1978.

Peacock, Sir Alan and Cameron, Dr Samuel, *The Socio-Economic Effects of the Arts,* Discussion Document 4, National Arts & Media Strategy, Arts Council of Great Britain, 1991.

Petherbridge, Deanna, 'The Town Artist Experiment', *Architectural Review,* 1979.

Petherbridge, Deanna, 'Sculpture up front: A look at sculptural commissions', *Art Monthly,* no 43, 1981.

Petherbridge, Deanna, 'Art & Architecture: Digest of selected papers from a conference held at the Institute of Contemporary Arts, London during 27 and 28 Feburary 1982', Supplement to *Art Monthly,* no 56, 1982.

Petherbridge, Deanna (ed.), *Art for Architecture: A Handbook on Commissioning,* Department of the Environment, HMSO, 1987.

Petherbridge, Deanna, 'Writing on the Wall', *The Independent,* 1991.

Phillips, Patricia C., 'Public Art. The Point in Between', *Sculpture,* 1992.

Pickvance, Ronald, 'Introduction', *Contemporary British Sculpture,* Arts Council of Great Britain, 1960.

Planning Inspectorate (21 May 1992), *Retention of a Public Sculpture "undated 1986" (the Shark)*, Reference APP/G3110/A/91/184337.

Public Art Consultancy Team, *The Strategy for Public Art in Cardiff Bay*, Cardiff Bay Development Corporation, 1990.

Public Art Forum, *The Public Art Report: Local Authority commissions for art in public places*, 1990.

Public Sector Management Research Centre, Aston University, *Improving Inner City Shopping Centres: An Evaluation of the Urban Programme Funded Schemes in the West Midlands for the Department of the Environment*, Inner Cities Directorate, HMSO, 1988.

Punter, John V., 'The Privatisation of the Public Realm', *Planning, Practice and Research* 5 (3) 9, 1990.

RSD, *Art at Broadgate*, Rosehaugh Stanhope Developments PLC, 1992.

Relph, E., *Place and Placelessness*, Dion Ltd., 1976.

Research Surveys of Great Britain, *Report on a Survey on Arts and Cultural Activities in GB*, Arts Council of Great Britain, 1991.

Robb, Denis, *Results of Research into the Contemporary Visual Arts*, Arts Council of Great Britain, 1992.

Roberts, Marion, Marsh, Chris and Salter, Miffa, *Public Art in Private Places: Commercial Benefits and Public Policy*, University of Westminster Press, 1993.

Rogers, Richard and Fisher, Mark, *A New London*, Penguin, 1992.

Salker, Douglas and Glymour, Clark, 'The Malignant Object: Thoughts on Public Sculptures', in Glazer and Ilea, *The Public Face of Architecture: Civic Culture and Public Spaces*, The Free Press, 1987.

Schuster, J.Mark Davidson, 'Government Leverage of Private Support: Matching grants and the problem with "new money",' *The Cost of Culture: ACA-Arts Research Seminars*, 1989.

Schwendenwein, Jude, 'Breaking Ground: Art in the Environment', *Sculpture*, 1991.

Seattle Arts Commission, *A Planning Study for Seattle Art in the Civic Context*, Seattle Arts Commission, 1984.

Senie, Harriet, *Contemporary Public Sculpture: Tradition, Transformation and Controversy*, Oxford University Press, 1992.

Sennett, Richard, *The Use of Disorder*, Penguin, 1970.

Sennett, Richard, *The Fall of Public Man*, Cambridge University Press, 1977.

Sennett, Richard, *The Conscience of the Eye, The Design and Social Life of Cities*, Faber & Faber, 1991.

Serra, Richard, 'Tilted Arc Destroyed', *Art in America*, 1989.

Serra, Richard with Weyergraf, Clara, *Richard Serra Interviews Etc, 1970-1980*, Hudson River Museum, 1980.

Shaw, Roy et al., 'Sponsorship and the Arts Supplement', *The Political Quarterly* 61, no 4, 1990.

Sheffield Recreation Department, *Chantreyland Sculpture Trail*, (undated).

Shiller, Herbert I., 'Corporate Sponsorship: Institutionalised Censorship of the Cultural Realm', *Art Journal*, 1991.

Shoard, M., *This Land is our Land*, 1987.

Sowder, Lynne and Braulick, Nathan, *Talkback-Listen: the Visual Arts Program at First National Bank 1980-1990*, edited by Ferguson, Bruce, Swingle, Jane and Conaway, Kobi, Winnipeg Art Gallery, 1989.

Strachan, W.J., *Open Air Sculpture in Britain*, Zwemmer and Tate Gallery Publications, 1984.

Storr, Robert, 'Tilted Arc': Enemy of the People?', *Art in America*, 1985.

Stote, Sally, *Think Rural, Act Now*, Arts Council of Great Britain, 1989.

Sudjic, Deyan, *The 100 Mile City*, Flamingo, 1993.

Taylor, Michael, 'The Art of the Environment', *The Planner*, 1991.

Townsend, Peter (ed.), *Art within Reach*, Art Monthly and the Arts Council of Great Britain, 1984.

Tucker, William, 'Notes on sculpture, public sculpture and patronage', *Art International 183*, no. 940, 1972.

Upton, Christopher, *The Past, the Present & Future: A commemorative book for the opening of the International Convention Centre*, Birmingham City Council, 1991.

Weyergraf-Serra, Clara (ed.), *The Destruction of 'Tilted Arc': Documents*, MIT, 1991.

Whitechapel Art Gallery, *Art for Society: Contemporary British Art with a Social or Political Purpose*, 1978.

Whyte, William H., *City: Rediscovering the Center*, Doubleday, 1988.

Williams, Jennifer, Bollen, Hilde, Gidney, Michael and Owens, Paul, *The Artist in the Changing City*, British American Arts Association, 1993.

Williams, Raymond, *Culture and Society, 1780-1950*, 1958.

Willis, Paul, *Moving Culture: An enquiry into the cultural activities of young people*, Calouste Gulbenkian Foundation, 1990.

Willmott, Peter and Hutchison, Robert (eds), *Urban Trends. A Report on Britain's Deprived Areas*, Policy Studies Institute, 1992.

Wright, David, *A Strategy for Public Art Development in the Eastern Region*, Eastern Arts Board, 1992.

Wright, Patrick, *A Journey through Ruins. A Keyhole Portrait of British Postwar Life and Culture*, Flamingo, 1993.

APPENDICES

Appendix 1

Those consulted

Members of the Steering Committee

Paul Filmer, *Goldsmiths College*
Caroline Foxhall, *West Midlands Arts Board*
Felicity Harvest, *West Midlands Arts Board*
Alan Haydon, *formerly of Arts Council of England*
Robert Hutchison, *formerly of Policy Studies Institute*
Amanda King, *London Arts Board*
Sandra Percival, *Public Art Development Trust*
David Perry, *British Railways Board*
Caroline Taylor, *Yorkshire & Humberside Arts Board*

With thanks to: Marjorie Allthorpe-Guyton

Focus Group participants

Those participating in a Focus Group at Policy Studies Institute, July 1992
Eileen Adams, *Freelance education consultant*
Sue Clifford, *Common Ground*
Tim Eastop, *formerly of the London Borough of Hammersmith and Fulham*
Liz Kessler, *Freelance consultant*
Tamara Krikorian, *Cywaith Cymru. Artworks Wales*
John Maine, *Lewisham 2000*
Graham Roberts, *Public Arts*
Pru Robey, *London Arts Board*
David Wright, *Eastern Arts Board*

Those participating in a Focus Group organised by the Association of Business Sponsorship for the Arts (ABSA), December 1992
David Blackburn, *Blackburn Associates Ltd*
Robert Dufton, *ABSA*
Gordon Edington, *BAA plc*
Dorothy Griffiths, *London Electricity plc*
Ron Parsons, *English Estates*

David Perry, *British Railways Board*
Christopher Pulline, *ABSA*
Colin Tweedy, *ABSA*

Those participating in London Regional Focus Groups

Leaders of local opinion
Robin Clements, *LPAC*
Richard Cork, *The Times*
Theo Crosby, *Pentagram Design Ltd*
Maggie Ellis, *Open Air Productions*
Steve Hearne, *Goldsmiths College*
Bob Jarvis, *South Bank University*
Baj Mathur, *Harrow Heritage Trust*
David Powell, *Freelance consultant*

The Artistic Community
Paul Collett, *London Borough of Camden*
Richard Deacon, *Artist*
Sally Freshwater, *Artist*
Jane Heath, *Freelance consultant*
Carol Kenna, *Greenwich Mural Workshop*
Dhruva Mistry, *Artist*
Paul de Monchaux, *Artist*
Virginia Nimarkoh, *Artist*
Daniel Sancisi, *Space Explorations*

Those participating in West Midlands Regional Focus Groups

Leaders of local opinion
Terry Grimley, *The Birmingham Post*
Charles King-Farlow, *Public Arts Development Agency*
John Peverley, *City of Birmingham*
Councillor Rene Spector, *City of Birmingham*

The Artistic Community
Chris Bailey, *formerly of Wolverhampton University*
Robin Campbell, *Photo Call*
Graham Fagen, *Artist*
Dave Hirons, *Mid-Warwickshire College of Further Education*
James Holyoak, *Artist*
Juginder Lamba, *Artist*
Vivien Lovell, *Public Arts Commissions Agency*
Antonia Payne, *Freelance consultant*

Claire Stracey, *Midlands Contemporary Art*

Those participating in Yorkshire & Humberside Regional Focus Groups

Leaders of local opinion
Narendra Bajaria, *Sheffield City Council*
Peter Downey, *Sheffield Hallam University*
Dave Kennedy, *Community & Enterprise*
Andy Kerr, *City of Wakefield Metropolitan District Council*
Elizabeth Norman, *Sheffield Hallam University*
David Patmore, *Sheffield City Council*
Councillor Michael Pye, *Sheffield City Council*
Mary Sara, *Yorkshire Evening Post*

The Artistic Community
Gail Bolland, *United Leeds Teaching Hospitals, NHS Trust*
Brian Holland, *Sheffield Contemporary Arts Trust*
Roger Standen, *Design Dimension*
Mike Stubbs, *Hull Time-Based Arts*

Planners
Sarah Collings, *Durham County Council*
Lester Hillman
David MacDougall, *City of Dundee District Council*
Anna Parfitt, *Planning and Design Services*
Gillian H Spiers, *West Lothian District Council*

Individuals interviewed for the case studies

The Arch, Kensington Gardens
Baroness Birk, *formerly Parliamentary Under Secretary of State for the Environment*
Sir Nigel Broakes, *Trafalgar House*
The Rt Hon Lord Callaghan of Cardiff, *formerly Prime Minister*
Joanna Drew, *formerly of Arts Council of England*
Sue Grayson Ford, *formerly of Serpentine Gallery*
Nigel Green, *Department of National Heritage*
Lady Kennet, *Friends of Hyde Park & Kensington Gardens*
Sir Robert Marshall, *formerly of Department of the Environment*
David Mitchinson, *Henry Moore Foundation*

Art at Broadgate, Hackney and the City of London
Fraser Borwick, *London Borough of Hackney*
David Blackburn, *formerly of Rosehaugh Stanhope Developments PLC*
Brian Carter, *Arup Associates*

Stephen Cox, *Artist*
Peter Foggo, *Peter Foggo Associates*
Robert Mason, *Artist*
Ray Michael, *London Borough of Hackney*
Peter Wynne Rees, *Corporation of London*
Richard Serra, *Artist*
Jenni Walwin, *formerly of Broadgate Estates*
Roger Whiteman, *Skidmore, Owings and Merrill*
Barry Winfield, *Broadgate Properties PLC*

With thanks to: Katie Dodds, *Broadgate Properties PLC*; Rob Harris, *Stanhope Properties PLC*; Jackie Kinnear, *Rosehaugh Stanhope Developments (Holborn) PLC*; Bill Malcolmson, *Peter Foggo Associates*, Julie Richmond, *Broadgate Estates PLC*

Art in Centenary Square, Birmingham
Barry Cleverdon, *International Convention Centre*
Nigel Davies, *Birmingham City Council*
Michael Diamond, *Birmingham City Council*
Ron Haselden, *Artist*
Tess Jaray, *Artist*
Councillor Sir Richard Knowles, *Birmingham City Council*
Tom Lomax, *Artist*
Vivien Lowell, *Public Art Commissions Agency*
David Lucas, *Birmingham City Council*
Raymond Mason, *Artist*
David Patten, *Artist*
Deanna Petherbridge, *Artist*
Bill Reed, *formerly of Birmingham City Council*
Anthony Sargent, *Birmingham City Council*
Tessa Sidey, *Birmingham City Council*
Jane Sillis, *formerly Public Art Commissions Agency*
Geoff Wright, *Birmingham City Council*

Improvements to Smethwick High Street, Sandwell
Councillor Ron Davies, *Sandwell Metropolitan Borough Council*
Francis Gomila, *Artist*
Val Jones, *Shireland School*
Roy McCauley, *Sandwell Metropolitan Borough Council*
Rod Willman, *Sandwell Metropolitan Borough Council*

Chantreyland Sculpture Trail, Graves Park, Sheffield
David Alston, *Sheffield City Council*
Vic Brailsford, *Artist*

Vega Bermejo, *Artist*
David Cooper, *City of Sheffield*
Ben Haywood, *The Henry Moore Sculpture Trust*
Rod Powell, *Artist*
Paul Swales, *Sheffield City Council*

With thanks to: Brian Holland, *Sheffield Contemporary Arts Trust*; Sylvia Pybus, *Sheffield City Council*; John Sutton, *Trafford Metropolitan Borough Council*

Silkstone Heritage Stones, Silkstone
David Bannister, *Silkstone Heritage Stones Project*
Mr. Evans, *Silkstone Common Junior & Infants School*
Mr. Flemming, *Silkstone Junior & Infants School*
Councillor A. A. Hampshire, *Silkstone Parish Council*
Paul Swales, *Sheffield City Council*

'A Light Wave', Westgate Station, Wakefield
Lorraine Cox, *formerly of Public Arts*
Keith Ellis, *Ellis Ventures Ltd*
David Frost, *City of Wakefield Metropolitan District Council*
Jonathan Hall, *City of Wakefield Metropolitan District Council*
Ralph Hirst, *Community Industry*
Ian Hurst, *InterCity*
David Perry, *British Railways Board*
Jane Priestman, *formerly of British Railways Board*
Charles Quick, *Artist*
Graham Roberts, *Public Arts*
Bob Scriven, *formerly of City of Wakefield Metropolitan District Council*
Roger Studdards, *Trustee, Chippendale Foundation and Public Arts*

With thanks to: Clive Gossop, *Westgate Station, Wakefield*

Individuals consulted

Will Alsop, *Alsop, Lyall and Barnett*
Anthony Beck, *University of Liverpool*
Franco Biancini, *De Montfort University*
Peter Booth, *University of Strathclyde*
Walter Bor, *Freelance consultant*
Robert Breen, *Art in Partnership*
Richard Broadhurst, *Forestry Commission*
Stephen Burrows, *Crafts Council*
Richard Burton, *Ahrends, Burton and Koralek*
Henrietta Buttery, *Countryside Commission*

Dr Alan Clarke, *University of North London*
Sarah Collings, *Durham County Council*
Prof Michael Ellison, *The Landscape Institute*
Steve Field, *Dudley Metropolitan Borough Council*
Anthony Gormley, *Artist*
Lester Hillman
Jean Horstman, *formerly of London Arts Board*
Ian Hunter, *Projects Environment*
Caroline Kaye, *formerly of ABSA*
John Barrett Lennard, *Freelance consultant*
Richard MacCormack, *RIBA*
David MacDougall, *City of Dundee District Council*
Helen Marriage, *formerly of Canary Wharf*
Malcom Miles, *British Health Care Arts Centre*
Sarah Parfitt, *Planning & Design Services*
Dr Marion Roberts, *University of Westminster*
Miffa Salter, *University of Westminster*
Phillada Shaw, *Freelance consultant*
Gillian Speirs, *West Lothian District Council*
Sally Stote, *Arts Council of England*
Alistair Warman, *formerly of Arts Council of England*
Ken Warpole, *Comedia*

With thanks to: Anthony Tyson, *The Planner*

Contributors to surveys

Public Art Agencies
Art in Partnership
City Gallery Arts Trust
Common Ground
Cywaith Cymru: Artworks Wales
Freeform
Jeremy Hunt Associates
Projects Environment
Public Arts
Public Art Commissions Agency
Public Art Development Trust
Raku Works Sculptural Arts
Scottish Sculpture Trust
Sustrans

With thanks to: Artists Agency; Arts Resource; Platform

Art dealers
Phillip Belcher, *Christie's*
Edward Horswell, *The Sladmore Gallery*
William C.M. Jackson, *William Jackson Gallery*
Madelaine Ponsonby, *New Art Centre*
James Rylands, *Sotheby's*
Petronilla Silver, *Contemporary Art Society*
Leslie Waddington, *Waddington Galleries*

With thanks to: John Sankey, *The Society of London Art Dealers*

Local authorities

London Boroughs
London Borough of Barking and Dagenham
London Borough of Barnet
London Borough of Bexley
London Borough of Bromley
London Borough of Camden
London Borough of Croydon
London Borough of Ealing
London Borough of Enfield
London Borough of Greenwich
London Borough of Hammersmith and Fulham
London Borough of Haringey
London Borough of Harrow
London Borough of Havering
London Borough of Hounslow
London Borough of Islington
London Borough of Lambeth
London Borough of Lewisham
London Borough of Redbridge
London Borough of Richmond upon Thames
London Borough of Southwark
London Borough of Tower Hamlets
London Borough of Waltham Forest
London Borough of Wandsworth
Royal Borough of Kensington and Chelsea
Westminster City Council

Development Corporations
London Docklands Development Corporation

City Councils
Birmingham City Council
City of Bradford
Hereford City Council
Hull City Council
Leeds City Council
Sheffield City Council
Stoke-on-Trent City Council
City of Worcester
City of York

Metropolitan Councils
Barnsley Metropolitan Borough Council
Metropolitan Borough of Calderdale
Doncaster Metropolitan Borough Council
Dudley Metropolitan Council
Kirklees Metropolitan Council
Sandwell Metropolitan Borough Council
Solihull Metropolitan Borough Council
City of Wakefield Metropolitan District Council
Wolverhampton Metropolitan Borough Council

County Councils
Hereford and Worcester County Council
North Yorkshire County Council
Shropshire County Council
Staffordshire County Council
Warwickshire County Council

Borough Councils
Boothferry Borough Council
Cleethorpes Borough Council
East Yorkshire Borough Council
Glanford Borough Council
Great Grimsby Borough Council
Harrogate Borough Council
Holderness Borough Council
Newcastle-under-Lyme Borough Council
North Warwickshire Borough Council
Nuneaton and Bedworth Borough Council
Redditch Borough Council
Tamworth Borough Council

District Councils
Bridgnorth District Council
Bromsgrove District Council
Cannock Chase District Council
Hambleton District Council
Malvern Hills District Council
Oswestry District Council
Richmondshire District Council
Ryedale District Council
Selby District Council
South Herefordshire District Council
South Shropshire District Council
South Staffordshire District Council
Staffordshire Moorlands District Council
Stratford-on-Avon District Council
Warwick District Council
Wrekin District Council
Wychavon District Council
Wyre Forest District Council

Public Art Officers and Artists in local authorities
Robin Campbell, *City of Swansea*
Iain Cartwright, *Oldham Metropolitan Borough*
Peter Cole, *Borough of Newport*
Lorriane Cox, *Borough of Thamesdown*
Paul Drake, *Gloucester City Council*
Tim Eastop, *formerly of London Borough of Hammersmith & Fulham*
Steve Field, *Dudley Metropolitan Borough Council*
Rosy Greenless, *Southampton City Council*
Julia Isherwood, *London Borough of Haringey*
Michael Johnson, *Basingstoke & Deane Borough Council*
Branda Oakes, *City of Swansea*
Carolyn Primett, *Lancashire County Council*
Karen Stevens, *Bristol Development Corporation*
Paul Swales, *Sheffield City Council*

Public art course leaders and university staff
Chris Bailey, *formerly of Wolverhampton University*
Andrew Brighton, *formerly of Kent Institute of Art & Design*
Faye Carey, *Chelsea College of Art & Design, The London Institute*
Chris Crickmay, *University of the West of England*
Paul Easchus, *Central Saint Martins College of Art & Design, The London Institute*

Ronnie Forbes, *Duncan of Jordanstone College of Art*
David Harding, *Glasgow School of Art*
Alan Humberstone, *Coventry University*
Eric Moody, *City University*
Jane Riches, *University of East London*

Planning course leaders
Michael Biddulph, *University of Liverpool*
Bob Jarvis, *South Bank University*
Robert Marshall, *University of Sheffield*
Philip E McGhee, *Heriot-Watt University and Edinburgh College of Art*
Alan Prior, *Heriot-Watt University and Edinburgh College of Art*
Dr J.V Punter, *University of Reading*
Dr S.M Romaya, *University of Wales College of Cardiff*
Jack Wawrzynski, *University of Manchester*

Arts funding agencies
National Funding Agencies
Rory Coonan, *Arts Council of England*
Tony Ford, *Crafts Council*
Alan Haydon, *formerly of Arts Council of England*
Amanda Loosemore, *Welsh Arts Council*
Seona Reid, *Scottish Arts Council*

Regional Funding Agencies in England
Hugh Adams, *Southern Arts Board*
James Bustard, *Northern Arts Board*
John Buston, *East Midlands Arts Board*
Carline Collier, *South East Arts Board*
Caroline Foxhall, *West Midlands Arts Board*
David Kay, *Southern Arts Board*
Amanda King, *London Arts Board*
Valerie Millington, *South West Arts Board*
Pru Robey, *London Arts Board*
Amanda Ryan, *Eastern Arts Board*
Virginia Tandy, *formerly of North West Arts Board*
Caroline Taylor, *Yorkshire & Humberside Arts Board*

With thanks to: Paula Campbell, *Arts Council of Northern Ireland;* Richard Cox, *South East Wales Arts Board;* D LLion Williams, *North West Wales Arts Board*

Appendix 2

Interview schedules and topic guides, questionnaires and surveys

Schedules and topic guides

Schedule for assessing the case studies

Origination

i) What prompted the work to be commissioned?

ii) Which constituencies were involved in the conception of the commission? What was the nature of their involvement, and at which stage did they become involved?

iii) For whom was the work intended?

iv) How was the work funded?

v) Where does final responsibility lie?

Expectations

i) What did the different constituencies hope to gain from the commission?

ii) What informed those aspirations?

iii) What roles were the work's 'public' ascribed?

Process

i) How were decisions made about the theme, contents and appearance of the work?

ii) On what basis was the artist selected? What was the nature of his/her personal engagement or commitment to the project?

iii) Whose values was the work to express? Where did these originate? On whose authority were they articulated?

iv) In what sense was it considered specifically relevant to its location?

v) How were decisions made about the siting of the work, and its introduction to the public?

vi) How was it introduced to the public?

vii) What steps were taken to ensure that the criteria of the funding bodies were met?

Evaluation

i) Has the work been evaluated? By whom? How?

ii) How has the work, or the circumstances of its location, impacted on the public?

iii) Have the different constituencies' opinions towards the work shifted? If so, in what ways? What has informed them?

iv) What symbolic values does the work hold for different constituencies?

v) Has the question of deaccessioning been raised? If so, in response to what circumstances?

vi) How has the evaluation informed
   a) the subsequent work of the commissioning agency or the individuals concerned, and
   b) their perceptions of their responsibilities?

Topic guide for ABSA focus group

Origination

What has prompted businesses to invest in public art?

For whom are such works intended?

How are such works funded? Is Percent for Art used?

Are commissions or purchases made and administered by businesses themselves, or do they employ agencies?

Expectations

What do businesses hope to gain by investing in public art?

What informs those aspirations?

Process

How are decisions made about the theme, contents and appearance of the work?

On what basis are artists selected?

Whose values are works to express?

In what sense are works considered specifically relevant to their location?

How are decisions made about the siting of works and their introduction to the public?

Is it considered necessary, or desirable, for statements of intent or interpretations to be provided?

What steps are taken to ensure that the businesses' criteria are met?

Evaluation
Are works formally evaluated? By whom? How?
How have works, or the circumstances of their location, impacted on the public?
Have opinions towards public art works shifted? If so, amongst whom and in what ways?
What symbolic values are attached to the works?
Have questions of deaccessioning been raised? If so, in response to what circumstances?
Has the experience of particular works informed businesses' subsequent investment in public art?

Topic guide for regional focus groups
1. Definitions of public art
What do you consider constitutes public art? What aspect of it is public?

2. The impact of public art
What are the social, cultural or economic benefits of public art?

3. Commissioning, siting and consultation processes
Given its siting in public places, should public art comply with certain criteria
– for example, types of subject matter, style, political neutrality, intellectual accessibility?
Whose interests should works in public places express?
Should responsibility for commissioning works for public places be assigned to particular professional groups?
Should there be formalized processes of public consultation, community or education programmes?
Are there circumstances in which public art should be deaccessioned?

4. Funding
Who should take the lead in commissioning public art?
How might the public funding of public art be justified in respect of other services?

Topic guide for discussions with planners
1 Definitions of public art
What do you consider constitutes public art? What aspect of it is public?

2. *The impact of public art*
What are the benefits of public art to planning?

3. *Commissioning, siting and consultation processes*
Given its siting in public places, should public art comply with certain criteria
– for example, types of subject matter, style, political neutrality, intellectual
accessibility?
Whose interests should works in public places express?
Should responsibility for commissioning works for public places be assigned
to particular professional groups?
Should there be formalized processes of public consultation, community or
education programmes?
Are there circumstances in which public art should be deaccessioned?

4. *Funding*
Who should take the lead in commissioning public art?
How might the public funding of public art be justified in respect of other
services?

Questionnaires

Questionnaire to public art agencies
1. When was your organisation set up?

2. What was its original impetus?

3. What is its mission? Has it changed over the years? If so, how?

4. How is it, or has it been, been funded?

5. Please give some idea of the scope of the organisation's work by way of
    examples of projects.

Questionnaire to art dealers
1. Can you estimate how much public art has been sold or commissioned
    in recent years? Who are the main purchasers?

2. Have the patterns of sales or commissions of public art varied? If so, how?

3. Do those developments parallel changes in the art market in general?

4. Would you say that the commissioning and/or display of works in
    public places has influenced the market for a particular artist's work?

Questionnaire to chief executives in local authorities

The Benefits of Public Art and Improvements to the Visual Environment

Your name and position ....

Department ....

Full title of local authority ....

Address ....

....

....

....

Telephone and extension ....

Definitions

The term 'public art' is used here to refer to the commissioning or purchasing by local authorities of permanent sculptures, murals, street furniture, paving and other embellishments in public places. It does not refer to the funding of art organisations, touring exhibitions, loans, temporary works or festivals.

'Partnerships & collaborations' refer to financial or other forms of alliance with bodies outside the local authority.

The Benefits of Public Art and Improvements to the Visual Environment

POLICY AND PRACTICE

1. **Has your authority commissioned any public art since January 1988?**

    Yes .... ☐   No .... ☐

    IF YES, please append a list of the principal works.

2. **Does your authority have a public art policy or a policy for making improvements to the visual environment which embraces public art?**

    Yes .... ☐   No .... ☐

    IF YES, when was it adopted by the full Council? (please give month and year)

    ....

    IF NO, please proceed to question 5.

3. **Is that policy described in any of the Council's official planning documents?**

    Yes .... ☐   No .... ☐

    IF YES, please give the name and date of the document.

    ....

    It would be helpful if a copy of the relevant section could be sent.

4. **Is the Council's public art policy being implemented?**

    Yes .... ☐   No .... ☐

5. **If your authority does not have a policy for public art or if that policy has not been implemented in practice, is this due to (please tick one or more boxes):**

    a lack of financial resources .... ☐

    a lack of specialist staff .... ☐

    a lack of appropriate opportunities .... ☐

    uncertainty as to its benefits .... ☐

    it being early days .... ☐

    other (please give details) .... ☐

    ....

FRAMEWORK

6. **Does any particular department within the authority have overall responsibility for public art?**

   Yes .... ☐   No .... ☐

   IF YES, please name the section and the department or directorate within which it is located.

   ....

7. **Have any other departments been involved in commissioning public art works?**

   Yes .... ☐   No .... ☐

   IF YES, please name the departments or directorates within which they are located.

   ....

   ....

8. **Does your authority have a written strategy, framework or directive which determines how public art is commissioned?**

   Yes .... ☐   No .... ☐

   IF YES, please attach.

9. **Does the authority employ a specialist public art officer or agency with respect to public art?**

   Yes .... ☐   No .... ☐

   IF YES, please attach a description of their responsibilities or brief.

   ....

   Is the post financed solely by the authority?

   Yes .... ☐   No .... ☐

   IF NO, is it funded in partnership with:

   the Arts Council .... ☐

   the Regional Arts Board .... ☐

   Other (please name) .... ☐

10. **Does the authority currently have a budget for public art?**

    Yes .... ☐   No .... ☐

IF YES, is it (please tick one box):

up to £25,000 .... ☐

£25,000 - £100,000 .... ☐

£100,000 - £250,000 .... ☐

in excess of £250,000 .... ☐

11. Has the authority's commissioning of public art involved partnerships with any external bodies?

Yes .... ☐   No .... ☐

IF YES, with whom?

the private sector .... ☐

other organisations in the public sector .... ☐

Have these been funding partnerships?

Yes .... ☐   No .... ☐

Or did they involve collaborations of another kind?

Yes .... ☐   No .... ☐

Please specify ....

....

PERCENT FOR ART

12. Do you have a Percent for Art policy?

Yes .... ☐   No .... ☐

IF YES, please state when it was adopted by the Council (please give month and year).

....

Does it pertain to:

commissions or purchases of permanent works .... ☐

time-based or temporary works .... ☐

resources (for instance, artists' studios or material banks) .... ☐

community or educational involvement .... ☐

Thank you for taking the time and trouble to answer this questionnaire.
Please return the completed questionnaire to:
Sara Selwood, Policy Studies Institute, 100 Park Village East, London NW1 3SR

Questionnaire to public art officers in local authorities with particular reference to their posts

1. When was your post set up, and to which department it is attached?

2. What was its original impetus?

3. Has its mission changed over the years and if so, how?

4. How is it, or has it been, funded?

5. Please give us some idea of the scope of your work by way of examples.

Questionnaire to public art officers in local authorities with particular reference to Percent for Art

1.i What is your authority's policy with respect to Percent for Art?

1.ii Does it pertain to land over which the authority has planning control; local authority land being sold for development or the authority's own capital programme?

1.iii Does percent for art feature in any of your authority's official planning documents? Please give examples.

2.i How many percent for art projects have been, or are being, carried out in your authority?

2.ii Of these, how many are local authority developments and how many private developments?

3.i How is Percent for Art defined within the terms of those projects? Does it, for example, represent a specific percentage of the total cost of the development agreed at the outset, or is the percentage calculated retrospectively?

3.ii What is your target percentage?

3.iii Does the percentage pertain to commissions of permanent works; time-based or temporary works; resources (such as artists' studios or materials banks); community or educational involvement?

4.i Do you operate a system of pooling funds from Percent for Art? If so, how is it organised?

4.ii Are you considering operating such a system?

5.i What structures and procedures exist to ensure that your Percent for Art policy is carried out?

5.ii Are these funded by the local authority or does the Percent for Art agreement include an allocation for administration costs?

6. Last but not least, what do you perceive as the future for Percent for Art?

Questionnaire to public art course leaders and university staff
Please send us details about any course or courses you teach which are devoted to public art or which have a substantial public art component.

1. When did it start?

2. How did it come about?

3. What are its objectives?

4. What does it comprise?

5. How many students does it attract?

Questionnaire to planning course leaders
I would be very grateful if you could give me some details about the courses you run, in particular what aspects of design and aesthetics are taught to students and how such components of the course are assessed.

I would also be very interested to know if public art is covered and if so, how. Is it in the form of site visits, seminars or projects?

Questionnaire to arts funding agencies

1. How are you currently approaching public art and Percent for Art?

2. What do you identify as your priorities in these areas?

3. How would you describe the nature of your relationship with the public art agencies, local authorities and the private sector?

4. Has the organisation's attitude towards public art changed over the years and, if so, how?

Questionnaire to users of Kensington Gardens

1. Are you a regular park user? YES [ ] NO [ ]
   Why have you come to the park today?
   to walk [ ]
   exercise [ ]
   get some fresh air [ ]
   to visit the Serpentine Gallery [ ]
   Other:

2. Are you interested in art, in particular modern art? YES [ ] NO [ ]

3. Has the white sculpture by Longwater attracted your attention?
   YES [ ] NO [ ]
   If YES, why?

4. Did you know that it was by Henry Moore? YES [ ] NO [ ]

5. Do you think knowing who the artist is makes any difference to what you think about the piece? YES [ ] NO [ ]
   Why?

6. Have you got anything you would like to add about the sculptures in the park generally, or the Henry Moore in particular?

7. Is there an example of a piece of public art that you particularly like?
   Thank you for answering these questions

Age of interviewee	Male [ ]	Occupation:
20+ [ ]	Female [ ]	
30+ [ ]		
40+ [ ]		
50+ [ ]		
60+ [ ]		

Questionnaire to passers by in Centenary Square

1. Do you live in, or near, Centenary Square? YES [ ] NO [ ]
   If NO, are you a visitor?   YES [ ] NO [ ]
   Where from?
   Are you a tourist [ ]
   Are you on business? [ ]?

2. Why are you here today?

3. How do you find the ambience of Centenary square and the area around it, particularly by comparison with how it used to be?
   Is it better [ ]   the same [ ] worse [ ] In what ways?

4. Has any of the art in the square captured your attention in particular?
   YES [ ] NO [ ]
   If YES, which and why?

5. Have you got anything you would like to add about the art in Centenary Square or in Birmingham generally?
   Thank you for answering these questions

Age of interviewee	Male [ ]	Occupation:
20+ [ ]	Female [ ]	
30+ [ ]		
40+ [ ]		
50+ [ ]		
60+ [ ]		

Questionnaire to traders in Smethwick High Street

1. Was your business here before the decorations to the shop front were painted?   YES [ ] NO [ ]

2. Do you think that by comparison with how it used to be, the distinctive appearance of the High Street and the area around it is
   better [ ]   the same [ ] worse [ ] In what ways?

3. Do you think that in comparison with other local shopping centres it is
   better [ ]   the same [ ] worse [ ] In what ways?

4. Do you think that the decorations, as opposed to the improvements generally, have made any difference to trade
   Is there more [ ] less [ ] business?
   Are the people shopping different [ ]

5. Given that they were painted several years ago, do you think that the decorations ought to be
   kept as they are [ ] repainted the same [ ]
   repainted differently [ ]

6. Is there anything else you would like to add about the decorations?
   Thank you for answering these questions
   Name of interviewee
   Name and number of shop

Questionnaire to shoppers in Smethwick High Street

1. Do you live in, or near Smethwick? YES [ ] NO [ ]

2. Do you regularly shop here?   YES [ ] NO [ ]

3. Do you still notice the decorations to the shops?   YES [ ] NO [ ]

4. How do you find the appearance of the High Street and the area around it in comparison with how it used to be?
   better [ ]   the same [ ] worse [ ] In what ways?

5. How do you find the appearance of the High Street and the area around it in comparison with other local shopping centres?
   better [ ]   the same [ ] worse [ ] In what ways?

6. Do any parts of the decorations attract you in particular?
   YES [ ] NO [ ] Which parts and why?

7. Is there anything else you would like to add about the decorations?
   Thank you for answering these questions
   Age of interviewee   Male [ ]   Occupation:
   20+ [ ]   Female [ ]
   30+ [ ]
   40+ [ ]
   50+ [ ]
   60+ [ ]

Questionnaire to travellers at Westgate Station, Wakefield

1. Do you use this station regularly? YES [ ] NO [ ]
   Do you, or are you travelling locally   YES [ ] NO [ ]
   or on the main Intercity London/Leeds line YES [ ] NO [ ]

2. How many years have you been using this station?
   Do you remember it before the sculpture was unveiled (1988)?
   YES [ ] NO [ ]

3. What do you think about this station, in particular in comparison to others that you use?

4. What do you think about the sculpture in the siding?
   (Prompt) In comparison with how it used to be?
   (Prompt) have you any comments to make about sculpture installed in railway stations or in other public places ?

5. Can I ask you for some details about yourself?
   Age:
   20+ [ ]   Male [ ]
   30+ [ ]   Female [ ]
   40+ [ ]
   50+ [ ]
   60+ [ ]
   Do you live in or near Wakefield?   YES [ ] NO [ ]
   Do you work in the locality   YES [ ] NO [ ]
   or are you visiting?   YES [ ] NO [ ]
   What is your reason for being here today?
   Thank you for answering these questions

Surveys

Survey of tenants at Broadgate

New Developments in Cities:
Broadgate, London

The Policy Studies Institute, Britain's leading independent social research organisation, is examining attitudes towards environmental improvements and new developments in cities. The results of its research will be published in a report in 1993.

Broadgate is one of the case studies. We are particularly interested in finding out about tenants' attitudes to the environment that has been created there.

We would be very grateful if you would complete this form and return it, in the attached stamped addressed envelope, to:

> Sara Selwood
> Associate Research Fellow
> Policy Studies Institute
> 100 Park Village East
> London NW1 3SR

by Easter.

*   *   *   *   *   *

How do you find the general ambience of the public spaces at Broadgate?

Very pleasant ☐   Pleasant ☐   Unpleasant ☐

Is there anything you particularly like or dislike about them? Please give details.

Are you aware of the sculptures at Broadgate?

Yes ☐   No ☐

Do you think they contribute:

    a feature ☐

    an atmosphere of quiet or escapism from the ☐
    hustle and bustle of the everyday world

    an irritant ☐

Do any capture your attention especially? Which one/s and why?

Which factors encouraged your company to take up tenancy at Broadgate:

the design and construction of the offices ☐

Broadgate's location ☐

good transport links ☐

good business opportunities ☐

the general ambience of the public spaces ☐

*   *   *   *   *   *

We are interested in finding out more about your opinion of the enviornment at Broadgate. Would you, or another representative of your company, be willing to participate in a discussion. This will take place at Broadgate on 12 May.

Yes ☐   No ☐

If yes, please complete the following:

Name ....

Title ....

Company ....

Address ....

....

Type of business ....

Telephone ....

Fax ....

I would prefer to participate in a discussion group:

at lunchtime ☐

in the early evening (after 5 pm) ☐

Thank you for taking the time and trouble to complete the form.

Survey of users of the International Convention Centre

New Developments in Cities:
The International Convention Centre and Centenary Square, Birmingham

---

The Policy Studies Institute, Britain's leading independent social research organisation, is examining attitudes towards environmental improvements and new developments in cities. The results of its research will be published in a report in 1993.

We are interested in learning what organisations who have used the International Convention Centre think about the environment of the centre itself and Centenary Square.

We would be very grateful if you would complete this form and return it, in the attached stamped addressed envelope, to:

Sara Selwood
Associate Research Fellow
Policy Studies Institute
100 Park Village East
London NW1 3SR

by the end of April

*   *   *   *   *   *

What was the nature of the event you organised at the International Convention Centre:

Annual General Meeting ☐   Product launch ☐   Conference ☐
Other (please write in) ☐

....

How many people attended: under 25 ☐   250-500 ☐
25-50 ☐   500-1,000 ☐
50-100 ☐   over 1000 ☐
100-250 ☐

How did you find the general ambience of International Convention Centre?

Pleasant ☐   Not particularly pleasant ☐   Unpleasant ☐

How did you find the general ambience of Centenary Square?

Pleasant ☐   Not particularly pleasant ☐   Unpleasant ☐

292

During you visit were you aware of works of art in the International Convention Centre and/or Centenary Square?

Yes ☐   No ☐

If yes, did any capture your attention especially? Which, and why did you find them interesting?

Did the presence of the artworks encourage your organisation to use the Convention Centre?

Yes ☐   No ☐

It is possible that, at a later stage, we may wish to ask for your opinion in further detail. Would you be willing to help us?

Yes ☐   No ☐

If yes, please complete the following:

Name ....

Title ....

Company ....

Address ....

....

Type of business ....

Telephone ....

Fax ....

Thank you for taking the time and trouble to complete the form.

Appendix 3

Analysis of surveys of local authorities

Summary of previous surveys about local authorities and public art

Since the Public Art Forum's (PAF) *Public Art Report* was published in 1990, there have been various published and unpublished reviews about the dissemination of pubic art. They have tended to focus on the number of local authorities committed to public art and Percent for Art in particular.

Public Art Report

The Public Art Report is one of the most comprehensive surveys to date. It was based on research carried out in 1988, the year that the Arts Council launched its Percent for Art campaign and set up its Steering Group.

The survey was carried out among the 513 local authorities in England, Scotland and Wales. Approximately 55 per cent responded. Returns were made from a variety of local authority departments including Education, Libraries, Planning, Arts & Entertainments, Architecture, Tourism, Recreation & Leisure, Museums & Art Galleries, Marketing, Legal, Administration and Chief Executives Offices. Some authorities returned more than one form. The information they contained was often contradictory.

In preparing this summary, we reanalysed 277 returns (one per authority). The survey indicated that less than six per cent of local authorities had policies pertaining to the commissioning of public art. While 34 per cent had been involved in the commissioning of public art, only five per cent had budgets specifically allocated to public art. Less than three per cent had already adopted or were implementing Percent for Art policies, less than five per cent were considering doing so.

These figures show no direct correlation between authorities having policies and the allocation of budgets for public art. Several described not being able to allocate specific funds to public art because their budgets had been frozen. The majority appeared to fund their public art commissions *ad hoc*. Nine per cent voluntarily cited the sources from which they funded public art commissions. Of those, nearly 50 per cent drew on funds allocated to environmental improvements, including urban programme monies. Twelve per cent referred to Planning; 12 per cent to Leisure and 12 per cent to Arts and Entertainments budgets. Eight per cent referred to Architecture. Individual authorities had drawn funds from Housing and Public Works.

Several authorities described needing to produce a formal visual arts policy as a prerequisite to a public art policy, a proviso which was not restricted to the returns from departments primarily concerned with the visual arts. Other authorities did not perceive public art as necessarily allied to visual arts but as falling within the wider remit of environmental improvements.

The Public Art Forum's research listed 333 works known to have been commissioned between 1984 and 1988. This excluded the 100 small works commissioned by Swansea City Council.

Arts Council

Percent for Art. Report of the Steering Committee, 1990 listed 40 local authorities and agencies in England, Scotland and Wales 'understood to have adopted Percent for Art at committee level, in local plans or building policies'. This represents less than eight per cent of the total number of authorities and Urban Development Corporations (UDCs). Percent for Art was defined as 'the method by which a proportion of the capital costs of building and environmental schemes is set aside for commissions'.

The Visual Arts Report in the Arts Council's *Annual Report* for 1989/90 cited 50 local authorities and two UDCs as having adopted Percent for Art, bringing it up to just under ten per cent.

In 1991 the Arts Council carried out an informal, unpublished review of English local authorities' committment to public art through the major Public Arts Agencies and Regional Arts Associations. Returns revealed that 26 local authorities and development corporations had adopted public art policies and that 49 expressed 'a serious interest' in public art. Further evidence of local authorities' commitment to public art might be demonstrated by their employment of specialist officers. The Arts Council's *Percent for Art: A Review* of 1991 lists eight local authority public art or Percent for Art officers.

Regional Arts Boards

West Midlands Arts Board
In 1991 West Midlands Arts Board sought to compile a list of local authorities' Percent for Art initiatives in the region, partly in response to the Arts Council's enquiries, partly in anticipation of the present report. As was the case with the Public Art Forum (PAF) research of 1989, returns came from a variety of departments within the local authorities. Out of 41 authorities contacted, 68 per cent responded. Of those 22 per cent had adopted a Percent for Art policy as against 77 per cent who had not. About 22 per cent had plans to develop one.

Details from West Midlands do not allow comparisons to be made between the numbers of local authorities with a policy and the numbers who had comissioned public art. One borough with a Percent for Art policy, however, admitted to having no mechanism by which it could be put into action.

Some of the West Midlands returns gave reasons for authorities adopting Percent for Art strategies. They include the quality of the built environment, increasing public access to and awareness of visual arts, stimulating economic regeneration, developing positive identities for different areas of the borough.

Eastern Arts Board
In preparing *A Strategy for Public Art Development in the Eastern Region* for the Eastern Arts Board (1992), David Wright surveyed 62 local authorities. Of the 81 per cent which responded, 46 per cent had commissioned works of art. Another 18 per cent had a Percent for Art policy but not all these had commissioned work. Fifty per cent of authorities had no policy, although 22 per cent were considering adopting one.

University of Westminster
In 1993 Marion Roberts, Chris Marsh and Miffa Salter of the University of Westminster published *Public Art in Private Places: Commercial Benefits and Public Policy*. Its objectives were 'to investigate the commercial bene-

fits of provision of public art to private sector investors and developers' and 'to consider public policies which promoted such provision'. The research team undertook two postal surveys of local planning authorities in England and Wales – the first in 1991, the second in 1993. By combining the two, they achieved an overall response rate of 80 per cent.

There was a response from 42 per cent (152) of the authorities, which stated that they had a public art policy. A further 23 per cent were considering adopting such a policy. Of those respondents with policies, 63 per cent (96) had implemented them. The London Boroughs (57 per cent) and the Metropolitan Councils (64 per cent) were the most likely to have policies. Of those 60 per cent had written them into their Unitary Development Plans.

Reasons for local authorities encouraging the provision of public art included civic pride and the promotion of local artists. Less frequently cited was the desire to enhance the commercial viability of a scheme 'because the public like it', or the wish to patronise the arts and for planning gain.

The mechanisms through which authorities implemented their policies included 106 agreements, sponsorship of local artists and funding of art centres, the development of planning briefs, environmental art, community based projects, hospital/health initiatives, civic art, residencies, educational programmes, roadside projects and business park installations.

Westminster categorised the works that had been provided as sculpture, murals, fountains, tiling/painting, street furniture, signage and specialist fittings, such as clocks. Free standing sculpture was most commonly cited and was identified in 48 per cent of the responding authorities. Research identified 750 public art works as having been installed over the past decade (582 in the public sector; 176 in the private sector).

Observations

The picture that might be constructed from these surveys does not provide an accurate view of the development of public art or Percent for Art since 1988, although it may indicate some general trends.

In 1989 for example, PAF indicated that less than six per cent of authorities in England, Wales and Scotland had public art policies; in 1992 Eastern Arts recorded 18 per cent within its region; in 1993, University of Westminster showed 42 per cent of authorities in England and Wales as having policies.

The surveys generally reveal a discrepancy between local authorities adopting policies and commissioning works. According to PAF in 1989, 34 per cent of local authorities had commissioned public art. In 1992 Eastern Arts showed that 46 per cent of its local authorities had commissioned works. Both suggest that the number of those commissioning public art outweighs the number of those with policies. In the case of PAF's research this was at a ratio of 6:1; in the case of Eastern Arts, it was at 5:2. The University of Westminster's report does not distinguish between commissioning works and implementing policies.

The figures also show an increase in the numbers of authorities with Percent for Art policies. In 1989 PAF reported less than three per cent, in 1990 the Arts Council registered eight per cent rising to ten per cent; in 1991 West Midlands Arts recorded 22 per cent. The University of Westminster does not specify numbers. The position is, however, made complex by the fact that certain departments within authorities may adopt policies and others not. For example, at the time of writing Birmingham Libraries had a Percent for Art policy, whereas other departments did not.

The figures also suggest that more authorities are considering adopting Percent policies. In 1989, PAF gave this as under five per cent of authorities; in 1991 and 1992 West Midlands Arts and Eastern Arts suggested 22 per cent were considering Percent for Art policies. This figure is consistent with the University of Westminster's findings, which were that 23 per cent were considering adopting public art policies.

Local authorities have numerous reasons for adopting policies towards public art, many of which reflect the tenets of the Arts Council's campaigns in particular. According to Roberts and Salter (1992) 80 per cent of local authorities were familiar with the Arts Council's Percent for Art Campaign. Policies are essentially aspirational. They refer to the quality of the built environment, the desire to increase public access to and awareness of visual arts, stimulate economic regeneration and develop positive identities for different areas of the borough. They are also determined by the political will to foster civic pride. Other reasons given are more pragmatic. They range from promoting local artists to providing planning gain.

These aspirations need to be considered in relation to the reasons why local authorities do not adopt policies or fail to implement those that they have. PAF, the University of Westminster and West Midlands Arts' surveys all had some returns which cited the provision of public art as not being in the public interest. Some authorities cited lack of finance and resources as reasons for not adopting or implementing policies, not least the downturn in the construction industry. A smaller number articulated the problem of having no mechanism by which such policies would be put into action.

Analysis of survey of Chief Executives in London, the West Midlands and Yorkshire and Humberside

In Autumn 1992, PSI undertook a postal survey of local authorities' Chief Executives in the three regions on which the case studies for this report were based. The questionnaire is in Appendix 2, p. 281.

The survey represented an attempt to construct a more comprehensive picture of local authorities' attitudes towards public art and Percent for Art than could be deduced from the findings of extant surveys (Appendix 3, p. 294). It sought to find out how many local authorities had a public art, if not a Percent for Art policy; how many commissioned art; why they had adopted policies and – conversely – why they had either not adopted policies, or had not implemented those that they had.

Following the summary, the survey is presented in three main sections:

1. The number of returns
2. Commissions
   - The number of authorities which have commissioned public art
   - Types of public art commissions
   - Conditions that pertain to the commissioning of public art
     - authorities with budgets for public art
     - authorities employing specialist pubic art officers
     - partnerships
3. Public art policies and their implementation
   - Adoption of policies
   - Policy statements

- Authorities with plans to adopt public art policies
- Percent for Art policies
- Implementation of public art policies
- Authorities with no policy

A list of those authorities which participated in the survey is in Appendix 1, pp. 273-275.

Summary

Approximately 53 per cent of the authorities surveyed have commissioned public art. The majority of those are in metropolitan areas (the London Boroughs, City Councils and Metropolitan Borough Councils).

Policies

Forty eight per cent of authorities have a public art policy. These are mostly authorities in metropolitan areas. District and Borough Councils are the least likely to have policies. The majority of their policies is stated in Unitory Development Plans.

Twenty eight per cent of authorities have a Percent for Art policy. The majority (50 per cent) refer to commissions or purchases of permanent works.

A number of authorities were in the process of developing public art policies. Fourteen per cent described themselves as doing so.

Although 64 per cent of authorities that commission public art have a policy, we found that 36 per cent of those who commission do not. The majority of public art policies is articulated in statements of commitment to a Percent for Art policy.

Authorities in metropolitan areas are the most likely to implement their policies. But, having a policy is no guarantee that an authority will commission art. About 32 per cent of policies were not implemented. The most frequent reasons for policies not being implemented, and for authorities not adopting policies are the lack of financial resources, the lack of specialist staff and it being 'too early'. The lack of written strategies describing the processes by which an authority might go about commissioning work may also be a contributory factor. Only nine per cent of authorities have such strategies.

Budgets
Twenty one per cent of authorities have budgets for public art. However many of these do not commission works. In fact only 40 per cent of those who commission art have budgets. There is no uniformity as to who spends these budgets or how they are allocated.

Specialists
Twenty one per cent of local authorities surveyed employ a specialist public art officer or agency, in other words 40 per cent of those who commission public art. There is no uniformity among authorities' employment of specalist staff. The majority of authorities which appear to be the most prolific commissioners of public art employ specialist officers or consultants.

Partnerships
The majority of local authorities (59 per cent) enter into partnerships with external bodies when commissioning public art. All of those who commission prolifically are involved in such partnerships.

Responsibility with authorities
Within authorities themselves, planning departments and those concerned with environmental, economic and technical matters are more likely to be responsible for commissioning public art or being involved in such commissions than departments concerned with the arts, recreation, leisure or community services.

Public art policies tend to reflect certain local authority functions. These include 'enviromental improvements', 'entertainment and cultural facilities', 'general policies', 'conservation and design', 'community needs and services', 'arts and tourism' and 'tourism and leisure'.

Definitions
Definitions of what constitutes public art are similarly determined. They largely refer to 'enhancing the public environment'. In metropolitan authorities in particular, public art is strategically employed in 'environmental improvements' and the 'regeneration of depressed areas'.

> Public art can take many forms: sculpture for internal or external sites, decorative iron work, terrazzo flooring, street furniture (seating, lighting, planters etc), murals, mosaics paintings etc.

Public art is also taken to refer to landscaping and tree planting. It follows that the majority of permanent commissions described by authorities appear to be 'environmental features'. These include street furniture, decorations, embellishments, paving, features and landmarks.

Number of returns

A total of 106 questionnaires were sent to authorities in London, West Midlands and Yorkshire & Humberside. A list of those authorities which returned questionnaires is attached at the end of this section.

Of these 74 per cent (79) returned questionnaires. This represents the total percentage subsequently referred to.

Table 1   Authorities which returned to the survey

	Received	Sent out	Per cent returned
Region			
London	34	26	76
Midlands	42	31	74
Yorkshire & Humberside	30	22	73
Authority			
London Boroughs	25	33	76
Development Corporations	1	3	33
City Councils	9	10	90
Metropolitan Borough Councils	9	11	82
County Councils	5	7	71
Borough Councils	12	16	75
District Councils	18	26	69

Note   The Royal Boroughs, Westminster City Council and the City of London are included in the category 'London Boroughs'.

The commissioning of public art

Fifty three per cent of the authorities surveyed have commissioned public art since 1988, the date research was carried out for the *Public Art Report* (Appendix 3, p. 294).

Authorities in metropolian areas are the most likely to commission public art (see Table 2). Given the kinds of work commissioned, this may reflect public art being used to aid urban regeneration.

Table 2   Authorities that have commissioned public art since January 1988

	Commissioned art		Not commissioned art	
	n	(%)	n	(%)
Region				
London	16	(61)	10	(38)
West Midlands	17	(55)	14	(45)
Yorkshire and Humberside	9	(41)	13	(59)
Total	42	(53)	37	(47)
Authority				
London Boroughs	15	(60)	10	(40)
Development Corporations	1	(100)	0	
City Councils	7	(78)	2	(22)
Metropolitan BC	6	(67)	3	(33)
County Councils	4	(80)	1	(20)
Borough Councils	3	(25)	9	(75)
District Councils	6	(33)	12	(67)

Types of public art commissioned

It was not PSI's intention to audit the amount of public art that has been commissioned by local authorities, although authorities were asked to append lists of their principal works.

Several authorities listed touring or temporary works which they had commissioned, residencies and spending on museums and galleries. These were not, however, necessarily distinguished from permanent commissions. Furthermore, many examples cited appear to have been speculative or forthcoming projects, rather than those already carried out. Some commissions were not located in what we understand to be 'public places' for the purposes of this report (see Introduction).

The examples of public art commissions described had not always been carried out exclusively by artists. Several involved the community and local schools in their design and development.

Types of public art commissions varied from authority to authority. They ranged from landscaping and street furniture to murals and sculpture. Each authority describes work it has commissioned differently. 'Environmental improvements' for one authority include 'hard and soft landscaping', whereas for another, 'environmental sculptures' constitute 'seating, railings and play structures'. Fountains, and sun dials are variously referred to as street furniture or sculpture. Sometimes only the titles of the works were given. It proved impossible to present a statistical analysis of such types and no attempt has been made to do so. However, in crude terms, the majority (over 50 per cent) of the examples of permanent commissions could be categorised as 'environmental features'. These include works classed as street furniture, decorations, embellishments, paving, features and landmarks. Approximately 30 per cent of all public art reported commissioned is described as sculptures or statues; the remaining 15 per cent are murals. This may reflect the fact that planning departments and those concerned with environmental, economic and technical matters are more likely to commission public art or to be involved in such commissions than departments concerned with the arts, recreation, leisure or community services. Precise details of commissioning departments have proved difficult to calculate because of the divergent internal organisation of local authorities. Consequently no table has been provided.

The conditions that pertain to the commissioning of public art

On the basis of authorities' own lists of projects it appears that those in metropolitan areas, particularly the London Boroughs, City Councils and Metropolitan Borough Councils have commissioned, or have been involved in commissioning, the largest number of works.

No attempt has been made here to quantify the numbers of commissions generated by particular authorities, or to compare them. Descriptions of projects were often ambiguous. Authorities use different criteria for listing commissions. Some included works of art funded through Percent for Art, whereas others did not. Some may have referred to several works by different artists under one project heading.

The authorities listed in Table 3 appear to have been involved in the greatest number of public art commissions – none in less than six projects since 1988. Table 3 shows that all these authorities are involved in partnerships; that 75 per cent have a public art policy and employ specialist staff. Only 25 per cent have budgets. (These details are further examined in Tables 5, 9 and 12.) By comparison, authorities which have commissioned no public art are less likely to have budgets (only four per cent had), policies (17 per cent), specialist staff (nil per cent) or partnerships (17 per cent) (see Table 4).

Table 3   Characteristics of authorities that describe the most public art projects

	Budget	Policy	Specialist staff	Partnerships w. external agencies	Percent for Art
London Boroughs					
LB Croydon	no	no	no	yes	no
LB Hammersmith & Fulham	yes	yes	yes	yes	yes
LB Tower Hamlets	no	yes	no	yes	anticipated
LB Waltham Forest	no	yes	no	yes	anticipated
Development Corporation					
Docklands Development Corporation	no	no	yes	yes	no
City Councils					
Birmingham City Council	yes	yes	yes	yes	no
Hull City Council	no	no	yes	yes	no
Sheffield City Council	no	yes	yes	yes	yes
Metropolitan Councils					
Dudley MC	yes	yes	yes	yes	yes
Sandwell MBC	no	yes	yes	yes	yes
Doncaster MBC	no	yes	yes	yes	no
City of Wakefield MDC	no	yes	yes	yes	yes

Table 4 **Characteristics of authorities which have not commissioned any public art**

	Budget	Policy	Specialist staff	Partnerships with external agencies
London Boroughs				
LB Camden	no	yes	no	no
LB Hounslow	no	yes	no	no
LB Redbridge	no	no	no	no
LB Wandsworth	no	no	no	no
RB Kensington and Chelsea	no	no	no	no
City Councils				
Stoke-on-Trent City Council	no	yes	no	no
Metropolitan Councils				
Barnsley MBC	no	no	no	no
MB of Calderdale	no	yes	no	no
Solihull MBC	no	no	no	no
Borough Councils				
Boothferry BC	no	no	no	no
East Yorkshire BC	no	no	no	yes
Glanford BC	no	no	no	yes
Harrogate BC	no	no	no	yes
Newcastle-under-Lyme BC	no	no	no	no
North Warwickshire BC	no	no	no	no
Tamworth BC	no	no	no	no
District Councils				
Bridgnorth DC	no	no	no	no
Bromsgrove DC	no	no	no	no
South Shropshire DC	no	no	no	no
South Staffordshire DC	no	no	no	no
Staffordshire Moorlands DC	no	no	no	yes
Stratford-on-Avon DC	no	no	no	no
Wrekin DC	yes	no	no	no

Authorities with budgets for public art

Overall only 21 per cent (17) of local authorities surveyed have specific budgets for public art. However, these are not necessarily spent on the commissioning of public art. Only 40 per cent (17) use their budget for this.

Having a budget cannot be taken to indicate that an authority actively commissions public art. District Councils, which are the second least likely to commission works (see Table 2), are more likely to have specific budgets than other authorities, albeit small budgets of under £25,000. Conversely (as Table 3 implies) not having a budget may not necessarily inhibit commissioning. Sandwell MBC, which has been prolific in its commissioning of public art, has no specific budget. Its funding of commissions at an average of between £25,000-£100,000 per year has been possible through various Urban Programme budgets. Works commissioned include shop improvements, as at Smethwick High Street and decoration of major structures such as bridges, etc.

Table 5   **Local authorities' budgets for public art**

	A	B	C	D	None
Region					
London	3	0	1	–	22
West Midlands	4	3	1	–	23
Yorkshire & Humberside	5	–	–	–	17
Total	12	3	2	0	62
Authority					
London Boroughs	3	0	1	0	21
Development Corp.	0	0	0	0	1
City Councils	0	1	0	0	8
Metropolitan BC	1	1	0	0	7
County Councils	1	1	0	0	3
Borough Councils	2	0	1	0	9
District Councils	5	0	0	0	13

CODE
A   Up to £25,000
B   £25,000-£100,000
C   £100,000-£250,000
D   £250,000 plus

There are no standard procedures as to how budgets are allocated. At the time of research the London Borough of Lewisham had a budget of £100,000-£250,000 entirely allocated to one project. The City of Birmingham spends £10,000 on new works and £90,000 on maintainance. Kirklees Metropolitan Council's budget of up to £25,000 is used as an investment to pump-prime other funding. Its major works are funded through individual project budgets via Percent for Art. Other authorities contribute funding to projects managed by other bodies. Holderness Borough Council, for example, which has a budget of up to £25,000, contributed to Gateway Europe, a three year project to develop and promote cultural tourism in Humberside.

Authorities employing specialist public art officers
Twenty one per cent of local authorities employ a specialist public art officer or agency. This represents 40 per cent of those who commission public art.

There is no uniformity among authorities' employment of specalist staff. The Docklands Development Corporation employs consultants on a project basis. Leeds City Council has 'a close relationship' with the public art agency called Public Art based nearby in Wakefield. Kirklees Metropolitan Council has a contractual agreement with the same agency, which advises on the suitability of particular types of commission for agreed locations, methods of selecting artists for commissions, the appropriate level of fees to be paid to artists etc. Cleethorpes seeks advice from the Public Art Officer in another authority. Other authorities employ a range of specialists. At the time of research, Birmingham City Council, for example, employs a Public Art Conservator, a Public Art Officer and the local public arts agency (see p. 136).

Whereas some authorities, such as Nuneaton and Bedworth Borough Council depend on curators in the Borough's Museum and Art Gallery, others have specialist officers whose only remit is public art. Although these posts tend to have different titles (such as Public Art Officer, Percent for Art Advisor, Arts Development Officer) and they may be attached to different directorates or sections, their remits have much in common. They are generally employed to identify opportunities for the commissioning of art for the built environment, to enable local communities to participate in and have better access to contemporary public art and craft, create opportunities for artists, identify possibilities for external funding and sponsorship, encourage debate about the value of public art, maintain a database of artists and craftspeople and to promote and assist the establishing of Percent for Art policy (see below, p.319).

More unusually Dudley Metropolitan Council employs an artist whose job is to create public artworks as well as to commission public art from other artists in consultation with the local community. His work is overseen by the Planning and Architecture Department.

Table 6   Employment of specialist public arts officer or agency

	Arts officer/ agency	How financed
Region		
London	6	Partnership with commissioning body
		RAB
		LA
West Midlands	5	LAs
		RAB/ LA depts/ private developers
		DOT, DOE, EEC
Yorkshire & Humberside	6	ACGB/ RAB
		LAs
		RAB
		Urban Programme
Total	17	
Authority		
London Boroughs	6	
Development Corp	-	
City Councils	4	
Metropolitan BC	5	
County Councils	1	
Borough Councils	1	
District Councils	-	

There appears to be some ambiguity among authorities about what constitutes the employment of specialists. The London Borough of Harrow, for example, stipulated that it did not employ a specialist public art officer or an agency. Its public art programme which has a policy and a budget is, nevertheless, administered by a independent trust. Similarly Sandwell depends heavily upon the former Smethwick Town Artist for advice and expertise. At the time of research his studio accommodation was still supported by the Metropolitan Borough Council.

Partnerships
The majority of local authorities (59 per cent) have commissioned public art in partnerships with external bodies.

Table 7   Number of local authorities which have entered into partnerships with external bodies in the commissioning of public art

	n	(%)
Authority		
London Boroughs	14	(50)
Development Corp	1	(100)
City Councils	6	(66)
Metropolitan BC	6	(66)
County Councils	4	(80)
Borough Councils	7	(58)
District Councils	18	(50)

Note: The percentage refers to the total number of local authorities of that type surveyed.

Most of those partnerships are with other bodies in the public sector or with a combination of both public sector and private sector organisations. London has the highest number of authorities with solely private sector partnerships.

Table 8   Partnerships involved in the commissioning of public art

	Public sector		Private sector		Both	
	n	(%)	n	(%)	n	(%)
Region						
London	2	(14)	6	(43)	6	(43)
West Midlands	9	(50)	5	(28)	4	(22)
Yorkshire & Humberside	5	(36)	2	(14)	7	(50)
Total	16	(35)	13	(28)	17	(37)
Authority						
London Boroughs	2	(15)	5	(38)	6	(46)
Development Corp.*	-		1	(100)	-	
City Councils	1	(17)	1	(17)	4	(67)
Metropolitan BC	1	(17)	1	(17)	4	(67)
County Councils	4	(100)	-	-	-	-
Borough Councils	5	(71)	1	(14)	1	(14)
District Councils	3	(33)	4	(44)	2	(22)

*   Only in case of temporary public art

Table 9   Types of partnerships

	n	(%)	Type of funding partnership
Region			
London	11	(79)	Acted as agents
			Grants and sponsorship
			Advising private sector
			Work with Housing Association to set up
			consultation leading to commissions
West Midlands	12	(67)	Work with community organisations
			Design and construction
			Negotiations re. locations and support in kind
			Schools, artists residencies
			Consultation
			Involvement with local schools and colleges
			Joint adoption of Arts Strategy with Shropshire
			Assistance with schemes
Yorkshire	12	(86)	Materials, subsidised agency rate
			Advice, specialist knowledge
			Training iniatives, education initiatives,
			giving in kind etc
			Exhibitions, publicity
			Advice on specialist subjects
Total	3	(76)	
Authority			
London Boroughs	10	(77)	
Development Corp	1	(100)	
City Councils	6	(100)	
Metropolitan BC	5	(83)	
County Councils	1	(25)	
Borough Councils	5	(71)	
District Councils	7	(78)	

Note: Percentages are of those with partnerships

Public art policies and their implementation

Adoption of policies
Metropolitan areas (the London Boroughs, City Councils and Metropolitan Borough Councils) are the most likely to have policies concerning public art, whereas District and Borough Councils are the least likely.

Although 64 per cent (27) of authorities that commission public art have a policy, 36 per cent (15) of those who commission have not.

Conversely, 32 per cent of those with a policy do not commission art (see Table 13).

Table 10   Authorities with a policy/policies

	Have a policy		Designated in official planning documents		No policy	
	n	(%)	n	(%)	n	(%)
Region						
London	17	(65)	17	(65)	9	(35)
West Midlands	12	(39)	6	(19)	19	(61)
Yorkshire & Humberside	9	(41)	7	(32)	13	(59)
Total	38	(48)	30	(38)	41	(52)
Authority						
London Boroughs	17	(68)	17	(68)	8	(32)
Development Corp	-		-		1	(100)
City Councils	6	(67)	5	(55)	3	(33)
Metropolitan BC	7	(78)	7	(78)	2	(22)
County Councils	3	(60)	-		2	(40)
Borough Councils	2	(17)	1	(8)	10	(83)
District Councils	3	(17)	-		15	(83)

Policy statements

The majority of authorities with a public art policy (48 per cent) state their policy in their Unitary Development Plan. 28 per cent of authorities have Percent for Art policies.

Authorities conventionally publish their strategies for Percent for Art alongside their public art policies. For example, Dudley's strategy for the implementation of its Percent for Art policy appears in its Unitary Development Plan (UDP). The London Borough of Hammersmith and Fulham's Implementation Plan is contained within its 'Public Arts Strategy'.

Table 11 Where policies are stated and the frequency of Percent for Art policies

	UDP		Percent for Art		Other
	n	(%)	n	(%)	
Region					
London	16	(94)	11	(65)	Hammersmith Public Arts Strategy
					Strategy for Building the Arts – Harrow 2000
					Lewisham: a plan involving art in the Town Centre
West Midlands	1	(8)	7	(58)	Local Plans
					Sandwell Arts Development Plan
Yorkshire	6	(67)	4	(44)	Kirklees Cultural Strategy
					Cleethorpes Seafront Action Plan
Total	23		22		

Note: Percentages are of the total who have policies. Not all those with policies described them.

In several authorities, public art policy is not 'overtly' described in their official planning documents. In Cleethorpes Borough Council's documents, the term 'features' is used ambiguously to refer to public artworks. While Redditch Borough Council has no specific policy on public art, allusions to it are implicit in most Amenity Design Briefs.

Authorities' adoption of public art policies may or may not be relatively straightforward. In the London Borough of Lewisham, which adopted Percent for Art in 1984, support for public art evolved without the need for further formal approval. In the London Borough of Hounslow, Percent for Art was dropped from the original UDP (deposited in July 1992) after complaints from developers that this was not in line with government recommendations.

Policies themselves may reflect the interests of funders or the strategic concerns of the authority. For example Sandwell Metropolitan Borough Council's programme is largely funded by Urban Programme grants. Its 'Arts Development Plan' is based on the recommendations contained in *Putting the Art back into Sandwell* written by a team of arts consultants commissioned in 1989. It prioritises the enviromental benefits of the arts and emphasises their importance in the regeneration of the area. *Kirklees Cultural Strategy* (consultancy report) refers to a 'Cultural Quarter', a new development in an area of Kirklees. It proposes that the development should be characterised by a commitment to the inclusion of artists and craftspeople from different ethnic communities.

Authorities with plans to adopt public art policies
Nearly 14 per cent of authorities surveyed described themselves as in the process of developing policies which pertain to public art.

Yorkshire

- Barnsley Metropolitan Borough Council was in the early stages of producing an arts and cultural industries policy.

- Boothferry Borough Council was developing an 'Arts Strategy'.

- The Metropolitan Borough of Calderdale was developing a 'Cultural Policy' which will include recommendations about adoption of public art and Percent for Art.

- East Yorkshire Borough Council states that certain proposals include a public art element.

- Great Grimsby Borough Council was in the process of considering Percent for Art.

- Hull City Council was in the process of developing a public art policy.

West Midlands

- Bridgnorth District Council's recently appointed Leisure Services Officer hopes to develop a public art policy.

- Malvern Hills Distrcit Council will include public art in Local Plan due for deposit in 1993.

- Shropshire County Council was developing a 'County Arts Plan 1993-1996' due for committee approval March 1993.

- South Herefordshire District Council was considering a public art element as part of draft District Plan.

- Wrekin District Council was developing its 'Arts Strategy' which goes to committee in the Spring.

Percent for Art policies

Of the 28 per cent of authorities with a Percent for Art policy, (see Table 11) the majority (50 per cent) refer to commissions or purchases of permanent works.

Local authorities may, however, implement Percent for Art without adopting a formal policy. Birmingham is one such authority.

Table 12   **What Percent for Art policies pertain to**

	A		B		C		D		Date implemented
	n	(%)	n	(%)	n	(%)	n	(%)	
By region									
London	3	(27)	-		1	(09)	2	(18)	1988 1989 1990 1992(x2) 1993(x2)
West Midlands	6	(86)	3	(43)	3	(43)	5	(71)	1992 1993(x2)
Yorkshire	2	(50)	-		-		1	(25)	1988 1990 1991
Total	11	(50)	3	(14)	4	(18)	8	(36)	

CODE
A   Commissions or purchases of permanent works
B   Time-based or temporary works
C   Resources (artists' studios, material banks etc.)
D   Community or educational involvement

Note: Percentages refer to the total number of authorities in the region with a Percent for Art policy (see Table 11). Totals refer to the percent of all those with a Percent for Art policy.

Implementation of public art policies

Public art policies are more likely to be implemented in urban areas. Reasons for them not being implemented are lack of financial resources, lack of specialist staff and its being 'early days'.

Table 13   Implementation of policies

	Implement policies		Do not implement policies	
	n	(%)	n	(%)
Region				
London	11	(65)	6	(35)
West Midlands	8	(67)	4	(33)
Yorkshire and Humberside	7	(78)	2	(22)
Total	26	(68)	12	(32)
Authority				
London Boroughs	11	(65)	6	(35)
Development Corp	-		-	
City Councils	4	(67)	1	(16)
Metropolitan BC	7	(100)	-	
County Councils	2	(67)	1	(33)
Borough Councils	1	(50)	1	(50)
District Councils	1	(33)	2	(67)

Some of those authorities that implement public art policies only do so partially. The London Borough of Richmond upon Thames, for example, stated that its policy is implemented 'where possible'; Leeds City Council is implementing its 'slowly'; Wolverhampton Metropolitan Council's policy is implemented 'in part'. Those that do not implement their policies blame the lack of financial resources, lack of specialist staff and its being 'early days'. Nuneaton and Bedworth Borough Council, for example, which has a Museum and Gallery budget of between £100,000 and £250,000, cited lack of funds as a problem with implementation. Sandwell Metropolitan Borough Council pointed out that implementation 'depends on the enthusiasm, foresight and determination of a limited number of officers'. Cleethorpes doubted that its 'partial' policy would ever be accepted as a 'blanket' policy. Consequently, it is introducing it 'subtly' through development and refurbishment.

Table 14 Reasons why policies are not implemented, slowly or in part

	A	B	C	D	E	F
Region						
London	4	3	3	-	2	DOE clamp down on Per cent for Art Lack of internal coordination To be developed
West Midland	3	2	-	1	2	Political uncertainties (change in political power) Awaiting arts 'audit' report
Yorkshire	2	2	-	1	2	Members would not accept as 'blanket' policy
Total	9	7	3	2	6	
Authority						
London B.	4	3	3	-	2	
Dev. Corp.	-					
City C.	1	1	-	1	2	
MBC	1	1	-	-	-	
County C.	1	-	-	1	1	
Borough C.	-	-	-	-	-	
District C.	2	2	-	-	1	

CODE
A   Lack of financial resources
B   Lack of specialist staff
C   Lack of appropriate opportunities
D   Uncertainty as to benefits
E   Early days
F   Other

It may be that the absence of written strategies determining how public art is commissioned is a contributory factor to authoritities not implementing policies. Only 9 per cent of local authorities have such strategies.

Table 15 **Authorities with written strategies determining how public art is commissioned**

	Has strategy		No strategy	
	n	(%)	n	(%)
Region				
London	2	(08)	24	(92)
West Midlands	4	(13)	27	(87)
Yorkshire & Humberside	1	(04)	21	(95)
Total	7	(09)	72	(91)
Authority				
London Boroughs	2	(08)	23	(92)
Development Corp	-		1	(100)
City Councils	2	(22)	7	(77)
Metropolitan BC	1	(11)	8	(89)
County Councils	2	(40)	3	(60)
Borough Councils	-		12	(100)
District Councils	-		18	(100)

Of those submitted Birmingham City Council has the most thorough strategy for the commissioning of public art. It defines the role of artists in the design and implementation of development and refurbishment schemes and covers that of the client and the ACE sub-committee. It also defines the brief, processes regarding the selection of artists, how projects should be controlled and the design process (p. 128). By comparison the London Borough of Southwark has a code of practice for Percent for Art but states that it is 'not used much, each project is taken separately'.

Authorities with no policy
The reasons why authorities do not have public art policies are the same as the reasons why they do not implement the policies they have (see Table 14) – lack of financial resources, lack of specialist staff, 'early days'.

Table 16   Why authorities have no policy

	A	B	C	D	E	F
By region						
London	4(44)	2(22)	2(22)	3(33)	3(33)	In process x2
						Not a LA
West Midlands	8(42)	7(37)	4(21)	3(16)	8(42)	Local political environment
						Not aware of need
						Ad hoc approach
						In process
Yorks & Humb.	5(38)	3(22)	-	2(15)	3(23)	In process
Total	17(41)	12(29)	6(15)	8(19)	14(34)	
By authority						
London B.	3(37)	1(12)	2(25)	3(37)	3(37)	
Dev. Corp	1	1	-	-	-	
City C.	1(33)	-	1(33)	-	2(67)	
Metr. BC	1(50)	1(50)	-	1(50)	1(50)	
County C.	1(50)	1(50)	-	-	1(50)	
Borough C.	5(50)	2(20)	1(10)	1(10)	3(30)	
District C.	5(33)	6(40)	2(13)	3(20)	4(27)	

CODE
A   Lack of financial resources
B   Lack of specialist staff
C   Lack of appropriate opportunities
D   Uncertainty as to benefits
E   Early days
F   Other

NOTE: Percentages are of those without a policy

Analysis of survey of specialist public art officers in local authorities with particular reference to Percent for Art

In 1988 the Arts Council launched its Percent for Art campaign. It was targetted at local authorities and Urban Development Corporations which were legally obliged to provide a 'visually attractive environment'. This was followed by the Report of the Percent for Art Committee in 1990. Although the Arts Council officially supported the notion of Percent for Art legislation, rather than lobbying for a mandatory scheme, the campaign disseminated information and sought to pursuade bodies to adopt Percent policies.

This survey was carried out in October 1992, four years after the Arts Council had recommended that local authorities should adopt Percent for Art. It was carried out among specialist public art officers employed in local authorities and UDCs. Its intention was to examine their attitudes to Percent for Art, to see whether authorities had adopted Percent for Art policies and, if so, what conditions pertained to them? How many Percent for Art projects had been carried out in those authorities and were they located in the public or private sectors? How was Percent for Art defined and administered.

The survey, which follows the summary, is divided into six sections

- Percent for Art policies
- Projects
- Working definitions
- Pooling
- Administration
- Future

Summary

Policies

Of those authorities whose officers responded to the survey, 50 per cent had adopted a Percent for Art policy. These did not necessarily apply to all an authority's activities.

Although the precise details varied, different authorities' policies had much in common. They were largely driven by the benefits that might accrue to the authority; they generally implicitly presumed that Percent for Art referred to art in public rather than private places. In all cases they pertained to land over which the authority has planning control, local authority land being sold for development and the authority's own capital programme.

The policies themselves feature in wide range of development and planning documents. In some cases, authorities' adoption of a formal Percent for Art policy was due to follow the ratification of these documents.

Projects

The majority of authorities – both with and without policies – were, in theory, open about what Percent for Art might apply to. In practice, Percent generally pertains to permanent, usually site-specific, works. The majority of examples cited were of street furniture.

In authorities with Percent for Art policies completed projects were more or less equally balanced between the public and private sectors. Authorities with the longest standing policies, however, recorded a significantly higher proportion of public to private projects.

Working definitions

Those without formally adopted policies reported no Percent for Art projects (as opposed to public art projects).

Of those authorities with Percent for Art policies, none operates a strict percentage. Flexibility is generally deemed essential in reaching what are necessarily voluntary agreements. It may also render up more than the Arts Council's recommended one per cent. There were no formalities about the stage at which percentages were agreed.

Pooling

While authorities with Percent for Art policies recognised the merits of pooling, only one operated a public art fund. Respondents doubted that the authorities would have an acceptable system for pooling.

Administration

Public art officers are generally responsible for overseeing that policy is implemented. Few had formal procedures for doing so and at least one had encountered difficulties coordinating all the parties involved. Few of those authorities anticipating adopting policies had considered such problems.

The future

Although Percent for Art was considered to have been strategically useful, some officers thought that it had become impractical.

Percent for Art officers felt that they would be under pressure from their authorities to generate income from Percentages. The implications of enforced Percent for Art policies were also worrying. It was still viewed with suspicion by many District Planning Officers, who feared it would inhibit developers from moving into their area. It would also encourage the production of mediocre works. The only authorities which supported mandatory Percent for Art were those that had not yet formally adopted policies themselves. They believed it would not only contribute to quality of life in the authority, but that it was synonymous with the authority having a progressive attitude.

Survey

Returns
Of the 19 specialist officers mailed, we received returns from 10, in other words 53 per cent.

Percent for Art policies
Fifty per cent of the authorities in which the specialist officers were employed had Percent for Art policies. Their policies had been adopted between 1988 and 1991. Thirty per cent were in the process of adopting policies. One was developing a three year public art programme before 'taking stock'; two had public art policies which had been put into the draft UDP but which had not yet been ratified. The logic was that such ratification would produce a policy, rather than a formally adopted policy informing the UDP.

The nature of the policies themselves varied. They generally implicitly presumed that Percent for Art referred to art in public places rather than on private property. It was in that sense that one authority encouraged 'Percent for Art' as one component of achieving a better environment. Another specifically targetted 'key sites in the central area and important town and village centres elsewhere'.

Policies were also guided by the principle of attracting money to the arts.

> In future development, redevelopment and improvement schemes carried out by the Borough Council, proper consideration is given at an early stage of planning to a percentage of the overall cost of the development being made available for the arts ... in similar schemes carried out by the private sector, the officers should advocate the benefits of the Public Arts Policy and seek to obtain an involvement in and/or contribution from developers for the arts.

One authority described it as an 'essential part of the policy that the money is not from an arts budget'.

Percent for Art policies do not necessarily apply to all the authorities activities and may only pertain to particular committees. They are, however, largely determined by the benefits that might accrue to the authority. One authority asserted that Percent for Art

i) ... makes the best use of financial resources by allocating a percentage of the overall scheme at the planning stage

ii) it can be applied to both the public and private sector

iii) it establishes a minimum base line of expenditure of public art

iv) it secures funds which are in proportion to the scale of the development

v) it ensures the proper integration of artworks at the development stage

It can bring a wide range of benefits to the City and assist the Council in fulfilling its City Strategy:

The City's adoption of the scheme would also make it eligible to apply for other sources of funding eg. the 'Art for Architecture Award' administered by the Royal Society of Arts and Department of the Environment.

All the authorities which had adopted Percent for Art applied it to land over which the authority has planning control, local authority land being sold for development and the authority's own capital programme. Those that had not yet adopted policies intended that it should cover all development opportunities.

Percent for Art policies feature in a wide range of development and planning documents including local plans, draft city plans, economic plans, City Strategy for Leisure, draft UDPs, submissions and negotiations of planning documents, major planning briefs, marketing packages for sale of land, 106 agreements and annual reports.

(Under the Town & Country Planning Act 1990, Section 106 – formerly the Town & Country Planning Act 1971, Section 52 – authorities may consider artworks in relation to the external appearance of a building and its surroundings and moreover, according to Robert Carnwath QC's advice to the Arts Council, encourage them [ACGB 1991: 81].)

Authorities which proposed adopting policies referred to the inclusion of references to Percent for Art in their draft UDPs and forthcoming public art policy and plans. Adoption of a Percent for Art policy was contingent upon ratification of these documents.

Projects

Of those authorities with policies, officers cited between seven and 14 projects having been completed with more in progress or coming on line. One estimated having 'anything up to 12 awaiting easing up of recession'. Completed projects were more or less equally balanced between the public and private sectors. One authority reported having had four of each, one had seven of each, another listed four public to three private developments. The two authorities with the longest standing policies recorded a significantly higher proportion of public to private projects – one, 2.4:1; the other 1.8:1. In the latter, plans for the future referred to three private and one public sector projects.

There are, however, problems about distinguishing between public as opposed to private projects, not least because private Percent for Art projects may be instigated, advised on or managed by the public sector. By the same token, many projects are jointly funded.

Authorities without formally adopted policies reported no Percent for Art projects (as opposed to public art projects) – certainly 'none that we are aware of to date'.

Working definitions

Of those authorities with Percent for Art policies, none operates a strict percentage. Flexibility is generally deemed essential in reaching what are necessarily voluntary agreements. Officers regard that flexibility as advantageous. One reported having secured a range of percentages for various projects spanning 0.25 per cent to five per cent. Another cited achieving a percentage as high as six per cent. These substantially exceed the one per cent recommended by the Arts Council.

Although authorities were not asked to distinguish between percentages on public and private developments, one commented that the authority's own projects have rendered between 0.55 per cent and one per cent. Another observed that the percentage is often much greater in the publicly funded schemes than in private schemes.

There were no hard and fast rules about when percentage had to be agreed, although one officer referred to 'the rule of thumb' which is 'to start as early as possible' and in collaboration with planners and other relevant officials. Legal and Valuers'. Authorities described negotiating at different stages – the time of land sales, planning applications and when planning permission was being granted. As one commented, percentages negotiated at such times 'are not necessarily a true percentage', referring to the Arts Council's paradigm of one per cent to be agreed at the outset of the development.

Authorities without policies could only speculate about prospective percentages. One specified it would not be less than one per cent, although they would be open to negotiation on each project. Another had not sought to 'calculate' it in any formalised way. One reported that a previous spend had depended on the needs of the project and the goodwill of the developers and architects, implying that Percent would follow suit.

All the responding officers took the Art Council's recommended one per cent as a standard target, but each had various provisos. For one officer, one per cent represented a minimum and ten per cent a maximum target. Another took a pragmatic line.

> In difficult times we negotiate for what we deem to be a reasonable contribution. These negotiations concentrate on the amount of money rather than on a percentage basis.

Others regarded the notion of a target as irrelevant.

> We don't have one, although one per cent is mentioned in the scheme. Achieving what is appropriate is more desirable that a percentage sought for the sake of it.

> As a policy we encourage Percent for Art as one component of achieving a better environment. The amount of money to be spent, as a percentage of the capital costs is not discussed as we are only interested in the visual impact the development will have.

In the case of the latter, the contribution to the environment was described as the sole criterion, not the amount of money secured.

Authorities without policies were unable to identify what their target percentage would be. It was largely presumed that the matter would be open to negotiation.

The majority of authorities with policies were, in theory, open to the notion that Percent for Art could 'cover anything'. Permanent works were only one aspect of what policies might allow for. One authority's policy described the breadth of its approach:

i) the purchase, design and production of art and craft works on and off the site of the development, refurbishment or landscaping scheme

ii) the promotion and development of projects including exhibitions of proposed public art works, artists residencies in design teams, communities and schools and presentation to developers, architects and landscape designers

iii) the provision of arts facilities eg. artists' studios

iv) the commissioning of both permanent and temporary artworks

However in practice it appears that Percent for Art most often pertains to permanent, usually site-specific, works which may or not be described as sculptures. No examples of other completed Percent for Art projects were cited. In one authority five out of ten projects comprised furniture, street furniture, paving, metal work and stained glass. In another authority ten out of 17 included furniture, paving, street furniture and signage.

Responses from authorities without policies were ambiguous. One believed that funds should be flexible enough to tailor spending to 'project/community needs'.

Pooling
Of those authorities with Percent for Art policies, one operated a public art fund

> which consists of money accrued from a percentage of the Percent for Art contribution and other sources. This fund is used to respond to local initiatives as opposed to development-led work.

Another gave an isolated example of pooling, resulting from

> a planning application by BT, where 0.25 per cent of the capital cost (£15,000) was employed on other sites with BT's agreement.

One authority with a Percent for Art policy stated outright that it had no plans for a pooling system. Others recognised its merits, indeed one had already included the idea in its Percent for Art scheme.

> It could be an answer to the Council's shrinking funds. If the Authority no longer has its own schemes or very few, then the emphasis will shift to planning gain. In the content of the Authority's policies it would be desirable to locate works/projects strategically rather than where the development happens to be. A pool would provide the solution.

The drawback of a pooling scheme, was that

it would be difficult to pursuade developers of the benefits. Sponsorship has, in our experience, been extremely difficult.

One officer doubted that his authority had an acceptable system for pooling.

None of the authorities without policies had plans for pooling. Two considered it would be an 'acceptable mechanism for delivering art'. One considered it 'inappropriate'. One understood it to refer to pooling sums from various departments within the Council.

Pooling is clearly seen as a way of reinforcing central control. One authority with a public art policy, which is primarily funded by Leisure Services, is establishing a fund to provide an incentive to the private sector. In practice it should match funding for public art pound for pound and tops up Percent for Art projects in both the public and private sectors.

Administration

Public art officers employed by the authority are generally responsible for overseeing that the policy is carried out: 'we are constantly monitoring the programme'. In some cases, the survey revealed some ambiguity about precisely how this is done. 'We probably need a procedure, but I'm not sure what it would be.'

Working procedures vary from authority to authority, department to department. However certain patterns are more or less common. In one authority, for instance, the public art officer works with the Planning Department

> to identify schemes. However it is largely reliant on Councillors at the planning committee, planning officers, landscape architects and other Council officers to identify potential projects and contact the public art officer.

In another

> the planning applications list is circulated, the policy is raised by colleagues ... Individual local authority schemes are discussed at team level and by Design and Area Co-ordination sub-heads. A Public Art Panel, chaired by the Chair of Planning, meets to review progress, select artists, etc and to prioritise future work.

Once a percentage is agreed the public art officer may assume responsibility for the project, depending on whether a developer or a department within the authority itself is involved. In one authority the money is given over to the Public Arts Unit, which is then responsible for ensuring that the work is undertaken and for managing the project throughout its development.

The success of this system depends heavily on the Council's well-developed corporate staff network.

Elsewhere, the co-ordination 'between legal services, planning, environmental design and Public Art and the sculptors carrying out the work' was regarded as problematic.

Of those authorities without a policy only one anticipated working procedures 'as an issue that needs to be carfully addressed'. They presumed that the implementation of Percent for Art policies would require 'clear guidelines on when and how it should be applied'. Others either implied that the procedures they employed for conventional public art would apply, or that the principles laid out in draft policy documents would suffice.

In two authorities, both the Percent for Art scheme and the officers' posts are funded internally. However, one officer doubted that this would last for long.

At the moment there is no allocation for administration costs from the percentage. However, it is likely this will change in the future.

In principle, authorities require Percent for Art to generate income:

Percent for Art does allow for a percent of the percent to cover administration costs incurred by the City Council.

One officer's post was supported by contributions from the Arts Council and the RAB. Any time spent working for an outside developer, architect or public body is currently charged for. Although as a member of the Planning Department no charges are made for City Council projects, he anticipated that this might 'be open for discussion in the future'.

Authorities without policies were divided between whether Percent for Art should be the funding responsibility of the local authority or whether 'an allocation for administration costs' should be charged within the Percentage raised.

The evident ambivalance about whether or not public art officers should be self-supporting may reflect their dual responsibilty for advocating Percent for Art, and advising or managing projects.

The future of Percent for Art

Some officers imagined that they would develop, if not refine, processes already in operation.

> We intended to continue to develop our 'pooling' approach to enable us to respond to local people's initiatives.

> We also aim to continue to develop and improve our processes of commissioning – ie. public consultation and education programmes.

Others suggested that officers could continue to use Percent for Art to provide 'opportunities' for the creation of more artworks, to increase 'quality of life' within the community, and to unite artists and architects.

> With government legislation for Percent for Art ... careful guiding and monitoring, such a policy has the capability of breaking down the barriers between architecture and art and enhancing urban and rural environments.

However these aims are shared by conventional public art programmes. Several officers (employed in authorities with and without policies) doubted that Percent for Art was the most effective way of achieving those ambitions.

> I feel too much rides on Percent for Art rather than the more general ... public art.

Some were less than optimistic about the futue of Percent for Art.

> Percent for Art has had its day. It ... fulfilled a useful function in the debate ... and has encouraged many, both in the public and private sector, to think analytically about our environment and embark upon arts-led projects which have had social as well as artistic benefits.

Others thought it had become impractical.

> In the current recession one per cent of capital costs is not a small amount and not a realistic proposition for many schemes.

Even in larger developments

> One per cent yields an infinitesimal amount for art as to be almost non-existent ... Consequently, I'm beginning to feel that Percent for Art might be leading us up a cul-de-sac, an irrelevance.

One described how

> The concept of Percent for Art is viewed with suspicion by many District

> Planning Officers ... as a policy which will put developers off moving into their area.

Other officers perceived Percent for Art as increasingly strategically useful.

> In the current financial climate, I think there will be more emphasis on Percent for Art and, in particular, planning gain.

Despite their desire to provide more public art, officers were sceptical about the effect their promotion of Percent for Art might have. Some worried about the aesthetic and environmental implications of enforced Percent for Art policies.

> My concern is that uninteresting, anonymous office developments will be 'decorated' by artworks.

> Public art should be located where it is needed, not just where the development happens to be.

> The notion of a defined 'Percent' for Art ... marginalises the benefits which can be gained from integrating public art (including crafts) into developments at the earliest stage ... 'let's stick some art into this' approach.

Although no mention was made of deaccessioning (removing works of public art), there was a fear that Percent for Art would generate too much permanent public art. One officer thought that temporary projects should be promoted as a way of preventing cities becoming 'crowded with artwork ... the broad range of eligible uses [is] the potential salvation of Percent for Art. Otherwise it will become stale and unattractive'. Another proposed that the focus should shift away from the art *per se* to 'the environmental contribution. [It] may well prove to be a more realistic aspiration.'

The majority of authorities which believed Percent for Art should be made mandatory were those that had not yet formally adopted policies themselves. One imagined that Percent for Art

> should be made mandatory as the quality of the public realm adds to the quality of life.

Another associated it with authorities' displaying forward thinking.

> Those authorities with foresight and a progressive attitude will continue to commit themselves ... If we are to make any great moves forward, Percent for Art might need to be made mandatory.

Appendix 4

Analysis of surveys relating to case studies

Survey of tenants at Broadgate

In March 1993 PSI carried out a survey of the 85 tenants, sub-tenants and retail tenants at Broadgate. We received 41 returns (48 per cent). Of those who made returns 56 per cent did so anonymously. The remaining 44 per cent was divided equally between the three categories of tenants who make up the population at Broadgate: 17 per cent tenants, 12 sub-tenants, 15 per cent retail tenants. Their business interests ranged from banking, stockbroking, property and the law to health, men's fashion, catering and newsagency. No distinction has been made between them in the following analysis. The survey questionnaire is reproduced (Appendix 2, p.290).

The 75 per cent of tenants who responded found the general ambience of the spaces 'very pleasant'; 25 per cent 'pleasant'. However, the ambience of the spaces had not been a major factor in attracting tenants to Broadgate.

The majority (83 per cent) had been encouraged to take up tenancy at Broadgate because of its location. 51 per cent were attracted by the design and construction of the offices; 44 per cent by the prospect of good business opportunities; 36 per cent by good transport links and 27 per cent by the general ambience of the public spaces.

Particular likes or dislikes about the public spaces were expressed by 56 per cent. The most commonly cited preferences were for the open spaces, including the waterfeature, the terraces and the seating, which gave respondents a 'feeling of freedom' and 'relaxation'. The leisure activities, including the arena and the shops were also cited, as was the 'greenery', including the trees.

By comparison, there were few 'dislikes'. Most complaints referred to the lack of care of the grass and plants and to the wind in the spaces between the buildings. One respondent specifically objected to the Richard Serra sculpture.

All the respondents were aware of the sculptures. About 66 per cent regarded them as a feature, 'a conversation point'; 29 per cent as contributing to 'an atmosphere of quiet and escapism from the hustle and bustle of the everyday world'; 12 per cent found at least some of them 'an irritant', and five per cent particularly so.

Approximately 71 per cent of respondents commented on sculptures that had captured their attention particularly. Out of 13 works sited in public spaces, only six were mentioned. The majority – 34 per cent – referred to the Botero, *Broadgate Venus* (on Exchange Square); 20 per cent to Segal's *The Rush Hour* (Finsbury Avenue Square) and 20 per cent to Serra's *Fulcrum* (sited between Broadgate Circle and Liverpool Street Station); ten per cent to Flanagan's *Leaping Hare on Crescent & Bell*; seven per cent to Corbero's *The Broad Family* (at the entrance to Exchange Place) and five per cent to the water feature in Exchange Square.

As a general observation it could be said that the Corbero, Cox and Flanagan provoked little comment. Corbero was liked for its humour ('the feet poking out from under one of the blocks'); the water feature was deemed 'relaxing' and 'peaceful'; the Flanagan gave the 'feeling of movement'. It was liked because of its 'original theme and design', and because 'it is not as abstract as most of the sculptures at Broadgate'.

The Segal was particularly appreciated for its 'life-like' qualities. Respondents referred to it as 'the people' or 'commuters'. They found it 'relevant' largely because it related to their own experience: 'just how I feel sometimes, 'it mirrors bustling commuters', 'it captures so precisely the look of people on their way to work'. One respondent who found it 'very pleasing' referred to it as 'the downtrodden'.

Botero attracted a divergent range of opinion, as already mentioned. It was referred to as 'the big Bhudda' and 'the fat lady'. A few comments about it were essentially academic. It reminded one respondent, for example, of '17th century Old Masters'. However, the sheer 'size' of the sculpture and its 'fatness' captured most peoples' attention. Those who liked it, liked its sensual qualities – 'voluptuous, wonderful', 'she reminds me of my childhood sweetheart'. One woman particularly liked it because 'it makes everyone sitting nearby feel slim'. But it was more disliked than liked. Respondents were quite categorical about their feelings towards the sculpture. They found it 'gross', 'somewhat repulsive', 'quite revolting' and 'awful. It cannot be avoided, an unpleasant feature.'

No one expressed a liking for the Serra, although one respondent thought it was of a 'good scale'. Some evidently have difficulty in bringing themselves to refer to it as a sculpture. They alluded to as an 'item', 'boiler plates', 'slabs of steel'. This may have been reinforced by the fact that 'it is used as a late night urinal'. Several objected to the rust. 'It looks a mess'; 'I would have [the sheets] sand blasted and painted'. Others found it 'out of keeping with the general positivism of Broadgate'.

Survey of users of the International Convention Centre, Birmingham

In March 1993, PSI surveyed those organisations which had used the International Convention Centre, Birmingham (ICC). The questionnaires were mailed out by the ICC. 50 completed ones were returned. The questionnaire is reproduced (Appendix 2, page 292).

Of those who identified themselves, organisations had travelled to the ICC from as far afield as Edinburgh, Cardiff and the home counties. They included a government department, trade associations, learned societies and various professional groups representing boat builders, chiropractors and industrial conglomerates among others.

The majority (68 per cent) had used the ICC for conferences. Eighteen per cent had used it for their AGMs, the rest for a variety of events including launches, annual dinners, awards and conventions. The 50 events had attracted up to 29,000 to the centre, the majority (88 per cent) attracting from 100 to over 1,000 people each. Without exception the organisers had found the ambience of the ICC pleasant. However eight per cent had not found the ambience of Centenary Square 'particularly' so.

A majority (52 per cent) were aware of works of art at the ICC and in Centenary Square. None had been encouraged to use the ICC because of the presence of art works there. However one respondent reported that these had 'contributed to the general satisfaction'.

Twenty six per cent of respondents had had their attention drawn to particular works. With three exceptions (the 'water sculpture'; 'posters of visiting musicians and conductors' and 'the glass mosaic') all remarked on Raymond Mason's *Forward*. Although the majority were non-committal, over 30 per cent of those who commented on it disliked the work. They found it 'inappropriate', 'horrid', out of keeping with the 'high quality of the rest of the square'. None identified the paving or the street furniture in the square as art.

Appendix 5

Analysis of survey of arts funding bodies

Background

Between November 1992 and June 1993 PSI surveyed the arts funding bodies – the national funding bodies such as Arts Council of Great Britain, the Crafts Council, the Welsh Arts Council, the Scottish Arts Council, the Arts Council of Northern Ireland, and the Regional Arts Boards (RABs) about their attitudes towards public art. The survey was carried out in the form of letters addressed to Chief Executives, with the exception of the Arts Council of Great Britain, where copies were sent to the Senior Officer responsible and his predecessor.

In 1988 when the Art Council launched its Percent for Art campaign, it did so with the support of all the above organisations. However, since 1988 the policies and the operations of these organisations have changed considerably. Any overview of the development of arts funding bodies' attitudes to public art and Percent for Art has to take such changes into consideration.

In 1989 the Wilding Report, *Supporting the Arts*, commissioned by the then Minister for the Arts, proposed improving accountability for the public money spent by Regional Arts Associations (RAAs). It pointed to a lack of coherence between the national funding bodies and the RAAs in particular with regard to the formulation and delivery of policy and to their unwieldy structures and processes. Although Wilding's recommendations were not introduced as such, the RAAs and the national funding bodies have been, and indeed continue to be, under review. In October 1991, 10 new RABs took over from the 12 RAAs. At the time of this survey they were undertaking a four year plan. Between the time of research and the publication of this report, some had begun to revise their policies towards public art.

Summary

Attitudes and priorities at the time of research

All 15 of the arts funding bodies surveyed were currently involved in the promotion of public art, although the degree and the nature of that involvement varies.

None described having specific formal policies about public art. As many as 33 per cent of the agencies reviewed, were currently reviewing or intending to review, their approach to public art. This represented a priority.

Some 80 per cent of arts funding agencies promoted public art through advocacy, including advocacy of Percent for Art. For the majority this constitutes a priority.

Arts funding agencies were more likely to perceive their role as contributing to the public art 'infrastructure' than being directly involved with public art provision. Fifty three per cent gave grants towards projects, usually to encourage new developments and partnerships. The explicit support of public art intended to make a positive contribution to the environment and of the crafts were minority interests.

Relationship with public art agencies

Nearly 50 per cent of the agencies described working 'very closely' with the regional public art agencies. Nearly all those had or were devolving their commissioning services to specific agencies.

Thirty three per cent of funding agencies specified that they had no formal relationship with public art agencies. Thirty three per cent of RABs in England had no public art agency in their regions.

Relationship with local authorities

All the funding agencies were involved with local authorities to a greater or lesser extent, both in respect of their general advocacy for public art and Percent for Art in particular.

Nearly 50 per cent of funding agencies financially supported local authorities' promotion of public art. They did so in different ways. Some provided advice about public art for local authorities in the form of publications, seminars and day 'events'.

Relationship with the private sector
In principle arts funding agencies extended their advisory service to the
private sector free of charge. In practice several reported having 'no
direct relationship with the private sector'.

Changing attitudes
As their concern to review their priorities suggests, several agencies felt
the need to revise their attitude to public art and develop strategies
towards its promotion. Some were beginning to doubt the effectiveness
of advocacy, especially after the Arts Council's active campaigning for
Percent for Art finished. Several wished to improve specific aspects of
public art practice.

Many needed to use their money strategically and were investing in
projects with long-term benefits rather than one-off commissions.

Current approaches to public art

For several funding agencies their current approaches and their priorities
were synonymous.

All 15 of the arts funding bodies surveyed are currently involved in
the promotion of public art, although the degree and the nature of their
commitment varies considerably.

None described having formal policies for public art as such. One,
Yorkshire & Humberside Arts, referred to the fact that it had 'no formal
written policy'. West Midlands Arts was intending to develop one in
1994/5.

Thirty three per cent of these agencies had reviewed, were currently
reviewing or intended to review their approach to public art. This had
led to one already setting up a new public art agency. Another agency is
planning to establish a Public Arts Unit in the future.

Fifty three per cent of agencies promote public art through advocacy.
A further 26 per cent referred specifically to their advocacy of Percent for
Art.

Funding bodies were more likely to advocate support of public art
than support it directly themselves. Fifty three per cent gave grants
towards projects. These tend to be small grants intended 'to encourage
good practice' and to serve as an investment to attract other funders. East
Midlands Arts, for example:

seed fund only the design stage of the commission. In special circumstances where the commission is under £3,000 we can offer a grant to the total cost. This is particularly in the case of a new body funding a commission where further developments could take place.

The Arts Council of Northern Ireland described a 'tripartite' model of funding from local funds, private sponsors and BSIS scheme.

Whereas some agencies fund projects through a specific art form scheme, such as Eastern Arts's 'Art in Public Places Scheme', others funded projects through corporate strategies. At West Midlands Arts, 'project applications are ... made to either the New Work and Productions or the Community Projects schemes'.

Funding agencies are more likely to perceive themselves as strengthening the public art 'infrastructure' than as directly involved in public art provision. It is to this end that they fund training and professional development for artists and administrators and support public art agencies and local authority posts. Thirty three per cent have devolved their own commissioning services to revenue clients – Scottish Arts Council to Art in Partnership; Welsh Arts Council to Cywaith Cymru Artsworks Wales; London Arts Board to Public Arts Development Trust; West Midlands Arts to Public Arts Commissions Agency. Eastern Arts recently set up Commissions East. South West Arts is proposing to set up a Public Arts Unit as 'an advocacy and developmental arm of South West Arts'. In addition, Yorkshire & Humberside Arts supports Public Arts as a regional agency. The majority of directors of these public art agencies were formerly arts officers or consultants employed by the RAAs/RABs themselves. Several agencies fund more than one public art agency. Northern Arts listed seven. Nearly 40 per cent financially support local authorities' public art programmes. Funding a variety of agencies is one way in which Yorkshire & Humberside, for example, believes 'good quality public arts can be developed'. The Arts Council of England funds Public Art Forum ('as the collective professional body') and 'bids for increased funds for both the existing infrastructure as well as specific project activity'. Strengthening the public art infrastructure is fundamental to strategies that RABs, in particular, were developing for the future. Southern Arts is currently developing a strategy with environmental agencies.

Priorities

Whereas some funding agencies identified their priorities as synonymous with their current approaches, others articulated their priorities in terms of their aspirations. In this sense, their priorities were either synonymous with strategies they were currently devising or those that they would devise in the future. The priorities of those agencies which were currently reviewing their policies were less clear.

Of those which identified their priorities, some 66 per cent specifically referred to their advocacy of art in public places and Percent for Art. Only one agency referred to its advocacy of Percent for Art as opposed to public art.

Although it may have been implicit in the majority of responses, only two agencies specifically described their intention to encourage art in public spaces as being to make a positive contribution to the environment. The Arts Council of Northern Ireland referred to it as having 'a powerful and persuasive effect on a city's image'. The Arts Council of Great Britain described one aspect of its advocacy as being

> to encourage a wider context in which public art can be developed. This embraces the broader understanding of a quality environment, including architecture, planning, landscape and the role of visual arts and artists in this process.

The London Arts Board was prioritising art on public transport and urban programme boroughs and those who had bid for City Challenge funds. Such priorities are necessarily restricted to RABs with urban authorities. Three RABs (Eastern Arts Board; Southern Arts and South East Arts Board) have no urban local authorities within their remit (Dix 1993: 4).

Thirty three per cent prioritised developing the infrastructure for public art. One agency was developing strategies intended

> to establish long-term structures for the advocacy and management of public art projects in the South West including the potential for a 'public art network' of South West Arts, public art consultants, arts organisations and artists' groups [and] to provide advice on public art initiatives.

Others supported the infrastructure by maintaining their support for public art agencies and local authorities. West Midlands Arts, for example, prioritised 'those authorities where existing levels of work and expertise are threatened by funding cuts'.

Others emphasised training. South West Arts, for example, prioritised the provision of

> training and support for artists to enable them to define their roles and equip them for working in the public domain.

Some prioritised the provision of information on regional artists, regional and national public art projects and public art practice in general. The Crafts Council is developing its slide index of crafts works into a nationally available electronic picture bank.

Agencies were bound by what was financially possible. As Yorkshire & Humberside Arts put it, their priorities include developing 'a diversity of approaches within available resources'. The Arts Council of Northern Ireland, on the other hand, promotes public art initiatives on the basis of 'the theory that the arts can no longer be seen as a cost to be borne, but rather that they repay handsomely any investment in them'.

Southern Arts was concerned to develop new opportunities for the development of crafts within public art. The Crafts Council believes there were 'many opportunities in commercial organisations'.

Several agencies describe reviewing and research as a priority. East Midlands Arts's priorities are to undertake research into present policies employed by local authorities and gather information on other supporters of public commissions. South Eastern Arts' priority was to review what could be achieved in this region, bearing in mind that the RAB 'has neither an agency nor member of staff with a special responsibility for developing art in public places'.

Funding agencies' relationships

Public art agencies

Nearly 50 per cent of the agencies surveyed describe working 'very closely' with the regional public art agencies, albeit as a result of devolving their commissioning service to them and supporting them as revenue clients. The Crafts Council, which described its relationship with public art agencies as 'reasonable', felt that there was some prejudice among them against promoting the crafts as opposed to fine art.

Thirty three per cent of the funding agencies specified that they currently have no formal relationship with public art agencies.

Thirty three per cent of the RABs in England specified that they have no public art agency in the region. None were adverse to working with public art agencies. South West Arts may employ 'a wide range of agencies' to undertake project management for its forthcoming Public Arts Unit. East Midlands Arts 'research will recommend the best scenario for us in this respect – whether to link up with a particular agency, employ an individual on a consultancy basis or set up a new agency'.

Local authorities

All the funding agencies are involved with local authorities to a greater or lesser extent in respect of their general advocacy for public art, Percent for Art in particular. In the case of the Crafts Council this relationship is usually via RABs.

Nearly 50 per cent of funding agencies financially support local authorities' promotion of public art, West Midlands Arts through 'local finding agreements' and Eastern Arts through its 'Art in Public Places scheme'.

Some agencies fund public art posts in local authorities. North West Arts, for example, funds posts in Oldham and Lancashire; Northern Arts in Gateshead, Middlesbrough and Northumberland; Yorkshire & Humberside Arts, Sheffield and Humberside. Three of these were also supported by the Arts Council – Lancashire, Sheffield and Humberside. Others fund particular aspects of local authority development. The London Arts Board, for example, focuses on urban renewal schemes in city challenge and urban programme areas.

Less than 30 per cent specifically described providing publications, seminars and day 'events' for local authorities. The Scottish Arts Council, for one, has

> currently two members of staff who are involved in ongoing advocacy and current promotion. They are also working closely with the Convention of Scottish Local Authorities (COSLA) at the moment, to produce model policy and good practice guidelines which will assist member organisations in the development of Percent for Art policies.

Although funding agencies generally implied that their relationship with local authorities was 'very healthy', one, in particular, described itself as 'rather sour about the plethora of local authority public art policies and the lack of any tangible projects in many of them'.

The Private Sector

The advice available to local authorities is, in principle, also available to the private sector free of charge.

Sometimes arts funding agencies' relationships with the private sector are predicated on tripartite partnerships with local authorities. This is the case with South East Arts for instance.

In practice several reported having 'no direct relationship with the private sector'. Only North West Arts described itself as working independently of the private sector:

> To my knowledge we have not funded any projects with the private sector and at present we have no strategy for doing so.

Although it was concerned to reclaim public spaces, the London Arts Board deliberately focussed on local authorities rather than the private sector because they doubted that individuals were in a position 'intellectually or emotionally to transform places'.

One agency, South West Arts, which was developing a range of strategies, described their relationship with the private sector as 'changing' (see below).

Changes in attitude

Given changes in personnel and the transformation of RAAs into RABs it is difficult to trace the development of arts funding agencies' attitudes towards public art.

While the Crafts Council maintained that their attitude had not changed much over the past few years, other agencies evidently felt the need to make changes. This is largely due to the increased scale and diversity of public art practice, changes in local authorities' policies and financial stringencies, the loss of impetus of the Percent for Art campaign, the advent of the contract culture and, in one instance, changes in the personnel of the regional public art agency.

The need for change was sometimes articulated in general terms.

> Certainly, a few years ago public art was seen as a priority here. My view is that I would wish to analyse the concept. I feel the need for questioning the foundations of the idea; but also for a more focused approach to our involvement..

> I think you will find that there has been a considerable change in attitude to

the subject of 'public art', resulting in a more critical approach and a questioning of the value of the Percent for Art as a doctrine (South Eastern Arts).

Other agencies referred to the pragmatic effect of financial cuts on their service.

One of the main differences is our approach to funding. We are rarely even able to top up funding packages now. We generally only grant aid where there is a forward move in favour of the development of new materials, new partnerships and things of that kind (Southern Arts).

We are trying to use our money strategically and are looking for projects with long term benefits rather than one-off commissions (North West Arts).

The fact that South West Art's proposed Public Art Unit is to function within the arts boards trading company implies that it is expected to generate income.

Given the change to fewer and larger RABs, Eastern Arts's constituency has expanded. It now physically covers 7 counties and 65 rural and urban authorities, making it the second largest arts board outside London. Officers, consequently, have less time to be involved in individual projects: 'how often can we service projects or sit on panels?'

Some agencies are looking to make established practices more effective. The Arts Council of England, for example, expressed doubts about how effective advocacy had been.

Public art is still regarded as the icing on the cake ... [There is still] a lack of understanding about the concept of integrated practice that contributes towards overall quality of environment.

They also noted room for improvement in the quality of public art and the detrimental effects of making artistic compromises, which are often called for in partnerships.

Other agencies identified specific areas of public art practice for improvement. Yorkshire & Humberside Arts, for example, described needing

to do more to advocate the correct use of contracts, maintenance agreements and the long-term responsibilities for art works.

Some agencies recognised the need to change their own strategies and procedures. South West Arts envisaged providing a contractually agreed service for their funding authorities.

> We are moving to establish a contractual arrangement which would specify the range of services South West Arts, as a whole, will offer in return for the local authority subscription. It is likely that public art advocacy and policy development work will remain free, but this has yet to be clarified. We are currently establishing guidelines for the private sector that will probably involve a scale of charges relating to the nature of the work.

Others had reached the point of needing to develop new frameworks within which they might support public art more effectively.

> It is probably fair to say that our attitude towards art in public spaces has changed with regard to the nature and scope of the projects/organisations we now support. When there was very little development in this area ... we were naturally keen to assist whenever possible and were not unduly concerned by opportunities or commissions which sprang up through opportunism rather than anything else. However, now that this whole area is far more diverse and widely practised, we are keen to encourage developments which occur within some sort of strategy/context (Scottish Arts Council).

Appendix 6

Interview with Richard Serra

Some time after his exhibition at the Saatchi Gallery, London (September 1986-July 1987) the American artist, Richard Serra was commissioned to make a sculpture, *Fulcrum*, for Broadgate. He was the only artist invited to work for the site in the early stages of the development. It meant collaborating with the architects, engineers and developers and agreeing a location for the work. This interview took place at the Serpentine Gallery, London, in October 1992.

Question: What was your response to the invitation to make the sculpture?

I said 'absolutely'. Broadgate had just begun. They didn't really know exactly how the art was going to be placed, or where. They asked me to come in at the very initial stages and talk with people from Arup construction.

There was one walk down area they wanted to make either five, six, seven or eight sided, adjacent to the opening of the rink, where they thought it would be possible to make a sculptural inclusion. They asked me if I thought it would be possible to work there.

I started to ask what they thought would be the projected scale of the buildings and what height I would need to hold mass and load and volume, and to have the piece function both as a place to collect people – for people to walk into, through and around – and also to act as an entrance beacon. We talked about campanile and we talked about how sculptures and artifacts of those kinds had functioned in piazzas and at the ends of intersections or whatever. I came to the conclusion that the piece needed a certain height – 40 feet or so, or higher; it needed a certain width; it needed the potential to collect people and act as a conduit, a place where people could walk into or locate, meet or gather.

It also needed to present art as art. Not just to be subservient to some projected populist notion of satisfying or enhancing or decoration or being used as application. To tell you the truth, these people were very open in that they had no misconceptions about what a work of art ought to be They didn't tell me that I had to satisfy an aesthetic agenda – so to speak – which I thought was fairly liberated on their part. Nor did it seem to me that they were interested in having a work of art function as a symbol of their liberalism. The work wasn't going to be coopted by the context. Every frame is going to have its ideological overtone, [but] it didn't seem to me that the context of the stock exchange was going to be so overpowering in its physiognomy that anything that you put there was going to be used as decor. There really was a possibility of making a piece of work as art and having people reflect on sculpture as sculpture and think about the continuity of what sculpture was and what possibilities might become.

Having said that, we went ahead and proposed a piece 55 feet high with five plates which you can enter into. We presented a model of one inch to a foot, in other words 55 inches. We talked to all the engineers, developers and architects. It had to pass their board. As I recall, the only alteration they asked was that the openings to walk into the volume, which is probably about 24 feet across and that you can collect in, were about three and half feet and we opened it up to about five feet. That was the only objection they had. They thought that if the entrances were too tight the piece would be too claustrophobic. They were worried about who knows what – molestations, or whatever. That seemed something I could live with. We opened it up to five feet.

There are always initial readings – probably to do with the traffic flow, how people use pieces, how people understand scale. There are a lot of formal readings. But there are [also] reflective meanings and readings that change over a period of time. It's very difficult to understand how they're going to change. They could be the caprice of political instigation. Works of art can be used as scapegoats for people pushing political agendas. Dialogue can be diverted to censorship. There are a lot of ways that art is misused or misinterpreted by people who want to used it as a political football.

Works which appear as decor or embellishment usually are just badges of corporate awareness. For the most part, they don't enter into any kind of controversy at all, because – why bother? They're harmless and in that sense they're almost useless as art. To tell you the truth – a lot of applied art and decoration is being bandied about as what's needed. It masquerades under the guise of art for the people.

What you have, in the USA, is architects who, rather than giving the percent to painters and sculptors, take it upon themselves to interact with the needs of what they think ought to be presented to the public. You get Phillip Johnston at the AIT building doing a 25 foot high gold-leaf figure of Mercury, which is just a mediocre pastiche from the Greek tradition. It doesn't look like anything more than a playful stage set. That's where that money went. Then you have somebody like Michael Graves doing a cornucopia of economic prosperity in terms of fruit bubbling out of the front of a building. The most banal stuff you've ever seen. You have someone like Frank Geary pacifying the public with gigantic fish in Barcelona and Tokyo. Everyone smiles at that. Yet serious sculptors are denied the possibility of those interventions because the architects are coopting the money. You have somebody named Robert Ventui decide, in a very cynical way, that he's going to make a symbol for a house for the elderly by putting up an enormous stainless steel TV antenna on top of the building which is non-functional – as a sign to signify an old peoples' home, I find that cynical. But that also parades as a post-Modernist signature for context. When you have these kinds of signs either serving capitalist interests or symbolic interests, they enter into the dialogue. Given the contextual frame, two things happen. Either they're emptied of any references they might have, because they're appropriating them from history – so the signs and symbols are completely misused. Or, there is some cynical, capitalistic gesture to give people what they already know, but not telling them anything that they need to know but don't quite understand. So it's really playing into the *status quo*, under the guise of being a populist. And, basically, what that does is it deprives artists from their invention and it deprives the language of art its rightful extension.

Question: What do you think of the work in relation to the other pieces of sculpture at Broadgate?

I think from what I've said, some pieces really affirm the ideology or decorate the place – I am sure you could point to those. You could also say that some pieces in their size or character are insignificant because you could pass them by and you wouldn't worry about them. They are not going to present any problem to anyone. Then there are other pieces that take on the potential of their media and try to deal with their own language in relation to the context in a way whereby the sculpture can speak of itself as sculpture.

Question: What is the sense of your piece there?

I am very pleased with the sense of my piece there. I like the work very much. I think it really collects a volume of space and gives some definition to that entrance there. In some sense it exposes the quality – good or bad – of the buildings.

Question: Was that your intention?

Works of art, by comparison, always do that. And it's up to the dialogue that they enter into to either affirm or expose, I think. That's not the fault of the work of art. But I think that I am interested in that dialogue. Often people become very startled that that dialogue exists because it's something that they had not anticipated. I think that works of art (if they are worth their salt) have the potential to do that. I do not think that there is something wrong with that dialogue. I think it's a very healthy dialogue.

Question: Presumably, some people would prefer not to have such truths exposed?

Well, I guess the safest solution is the most paranoid context. We could put a policeman in front of every door but it would probably be better to put an art-work in front of every door.

Question: Is that why people prefer 'corporate baubles' to serious works of art – because they're safer?

Safer. Yes, and that's paranoid. That's secure *status quo* paranoia. In fact I think it's a whole appropriation of the post-modern ... It speaks of a kind of nostalgia for the 'good old days' when art was better and more meaningful. But it is really about a paranoia about the willingness to accept that art is continuous language and unexpected use is always going to take it somewhere else. Really, for a culture to grow it must deal with its sculptors, painters and architects at the extension of their invention and accept that. Rather, they bring in the nostalgia for the past and say, you know, 'here we have another Greek revival' – or whatever, 'another equestrian rider'.

Question: What do you think the developers hoped to gain by commissioning you? Since the commission was made at the time of the *Tilted Arc* case your work must have represented a considerable risk.

I think that, with them, it is a gamble. And I think Lipton was smart enough to go to museum directors and to the Saatchi Collection. I think that my work there captured his imagination – so did the catalogue – to the point that he was willing to risk the controversy that might accrue from building a big Richard Serra. And, to tell the truth, I think he is a very tolerant person, a very understanding person, not only in relation to building but architecture. He builds with a lot of very good architects. He builds with both Rogers and Foster here. And I suspect that Venturi, he also builds with. And I think he understands aesthetic extension and he understands the potential to even fail. Very few people are like that. I don't think he thought it would just be a feather in his cap. I think he really believes that you have to go with what you ascertain to be, maybe even potentially, the most radical. And, you know, I will give him credit for that. On the other hand, he certainly backed conventional work that was already ascertained as being of a certain quality.

Appendix 7

Agreements

Agreement and schedule agreed between Broadgate Properties, a commissioned artist and his representative © Broadgate Properties PLC

THIS AGREEMENT is made on xxx day of xxx 1993

BETWEEN:-

(1) xxx ("the Artist") and his representative, xxx ("the Representative") together hereinafter called "the Supplier": and

(2) Broadgate Properties Phase Company whose registered office is at xxx ("the Client").

WHEREAS

A. The Client wishes to purchase a sculpture by the Artist for installation at xxx ("the Site").

B. The Artist has conceived a unique sculpture of xxx ft in height.

C. The Artist has submitted to the Client a maquette and drawings of the proposed sculpture and the Client has approved such drawings. The proposed sculpture as represented in such maquette and drawings listed in the Schedule ("the approved drawings") shall be "the Sculpture" for the purposes of this Agreement.

NOW IT IS AGREED as follows:-

1. The Client will endeavour to obtain all planning and other consents and approvals required by statutes, regulations and bye-laws as may be necessary in connection with the installation of the Sculpture at the Site ("the necessary consents") and the Client shall notify the Representative when the same have been obtained or when, even though the same have not been obtained, the Client nevertheless wishes the Supplier to proceed under Clause 2.

2. If the Client notifies the Representative under Clause 1, the Supplier shall pre-fabricate the Sculpture (including all connections, bolts, shims, flanges required to assemble the Sculpture on site) in accordance with the maquette and approved drawings in a good and workmanlike manner using materials of good quality. The choice of the steel quality will be under the personal supervision of the Artist.

3. The Supplier shall provide to the Client in good time an estimate of the weight of the Sculpture and such other details, drawings and calculations as may be required by the Client to enable the base to be designed and the necessary consents obtained. The Supplier will provide instructions for the care and maintenance of the Sculpture.

4. The Client will procure the design and construction of the base and be responsible for reinstating the paving following assembly and completion of the Sculpture at the Site.

5. The Supplier shall, at his own cost, arrange for delivery of the Sculpture to the Site and for its assembly and completion including any welding, paint-work or other work necessary. The Client will provide cranage, including arranging road closure and access equipment, labour therefore, and coordination for the unloading and assembly.

6. Property in the Sculpture shall pass to the Client upon completion of the Sculpture. Risk of loss or damage to the Sculpture shall remain with the Supplier until the completion at the Site and the Supplier shall insure the Sculpture against all risks of loss or damage thereto prior to completion and shall, when requested so to do by the Client, produce documentary evidence of such insurance to the Client. The Client will provide drawings of the base to the supplier who shall satisfy himself and confirm to the Client that the connections are suitable for the Sculpture.

7. The Sculpture shall be delivered, assembled and completed on or before 8 weeks from the Client's notification to the Representative under Clause 1.

8. The Client shall pay to the Representative for the supply and installation of the Sculpture, the price of £xxx plus VAT payable as follows:-
   1/3 of such sum upon completion of this Agreement
   1/3 of such sum upon delivery of the Sculpture to the Site
   1/3 upon completion of the Sculpture

9. Copyright in all designs for and in the Sculpture shall remain with the Artist; property in the approved drawings and any drawings provided under Clause 3 shall remain with the Artist. Neither the Artist nor the Representative shall make any copies of the Sculpture or reproduce or permit to be reproduced in any form whatsoever without first obtaining written approval from the Client.

10. The Client shall be fully entitled under a royalty-free exclusive licence to use the Sculpture and the approved drawings and to reproduce the same by way of photograph or copy in any brochure or other material or publication for publicity and marketing purposes.

11. If the Supplier shall be in material breach of any of his obligations under this Agreement and shall fail to remedy the same (if capable of remedy) within 14 days of the date of any notice from the Client to the Representative, specifying the breach and requiring its remedy, then the Client may, by notice in writing to the Representative, forthwith terminate this Agreement and be entitled to recover the Supplier all loss and/or damage thereby arising.
    If the Artist shall die or be incapacitated before delivery of the Sculpture then either party may, by notice in writing to other, forthwith terminate this Agreement and the Client shall be entitled to recover from the Supplier any amounts paid on account of the price prior to the date of termination, but neither party shall otherwise have any liability to the other whatsoever in connection with this Agreement.

12. The rights, obligations and liabilities of the Artist and the Representative are joint and several. This Agreement shall be governed by and construed in accordance with English law and the parties submit to the non-exclusive jurisdiction of the English Courts. All notices may be served on the Representative at the Supplier's address.

13. Any notice or approval or disapproval under this Agreement shall be given in writing.

Payment by the Client to the Representative under Clause 8 shall be complete discharge of the Client's obligation to the Supplier under this Agreement.

Signed by the Artist: xxx

Signed by the Representative xxx

Signed by the Client: xxx

THE SCHEDULE

The maquette and approved drawings are:

1. Steel maquette approximately 2 ft high

2. SOM drawing reference xxx showing location, size and outline configuration

3. Two photographic representations by xxx of xxx

Note: These accurately represent the size, location, configuration and colours of the sculpture in general terms. They are not precise "blueprints" of the detailed construction nor do they include minor modifications resulting from discussions with the District Surveyor.

Commission for a major sculpture for Centenary Square. © Birmingham City Council

CONDITIONS OF CONTRACTS FOR NATIONAL EXHIBITION CENTRE (COMMISSIONED ART)

1. DEFINITIONS

    In these conditions the following words shall have the meaning herein assigned to them:

    The words 'NEC' shall mean the National Exhibition Centre Limited whose registered office is situated at xxx.

    The words 'the Agent' means Public Art Commission Agency of xxx.

    The words 'the Artist' shall mean xxx of xxx.

    The words 'the Council' shall mean the Birmingham City Council acting through the Director of Museums and Art Galleries.

    The words 'the Work' shall mean the work of art details and location of which are set out in the Brief.

    The words 'the Brief' shall mean the brief annexed hereto which shall form an integral part of this Agreement.

    The singular shall include the plural and vice versa.

    The masculine shall include the feminine and vice versa.

2. SCOPE OF THE WORK

    NEC hereby commission the Artist to undertake and carry out the Work.

3. SALE OF WORK

    It is agreed that upon completion and installation of the Work on site and payment to the Artist of the agreed Fee as specified in Condition 8.1 (or payment as specified in Section 9 in the event of termination) property in the Work shall pass to the Council.

4. COPYRIGHT AND REPRODUCTION OF RIGHTS

4.1 Copyright in the Work (and in any preliminary designs, models or drawings including those submitted under Condition 4.4) shall remain with the Artist.

4.2 The Artist undertakes that he will not make or authorise the making of any copy of the Work save that the Artist will have the right to make a limited number (not exceeding six in number) in any material of smaller copies of the work for private sale (and not, so far as the Artist or his agents are able to procure, for public exhibition) provided these are no more than one third of the size of the Work itself and credit given on the copies to the Council as commissioner of the Work.

4.3 The Council and the Agent shall each be entitled, after consulting the Artist (unless he is unavailable) and without further payment to make or authorise to be made any photograph of the Work and to include or authorise the inclusion of the Work or any such photograph of the Work (or of any preliminary models designs or working drawings submitted by the Artist under Condition 4.4) in any publication or film, video or television broadcast which is inteded to advertise, promote or record the making of the Work or the project of which it forms part, subject to Condition 15.2. For the avoidance of doubt this right does not extend to the sale to the public for profit of any item of merchandise incorporating a photograph or image of the Work.

4.4 The Artist will as soon as practicable following the installation of the Work provide the Council with a finished maquette of the Work which shall identify the Artist as the creator of the Work (either on the maquette itself or the base to which it is attached) and which shall thereafter become the property of Birmingham Museums and Art Gallery. In addition, the Artist will also give a right of first refusal to Birmingham Museums and Art Gallery for the purchase of any additional preparatory drawings and/or models, and shall make available copies of such documentary material as may be deemed reasonably necessary by the Director of the Museums and Art Gallery for the completion of his historical record of the project. The Artist will also (at no cost to the Artist) provide the Agent with a set of slides of the Work and such other documentary material as may be agreed.

5. LIAISON AND ROLE OF AGENT

5.1 The Artist shall maintain close liaison with the Agent throughout the progress of the Work and shall make whatever visits to sites and attend any meetings to discuss details of the Work at the request of the Agent as are reasonably necessary.

5.2 In addition the Agent will be responsible for liaising between all parties in connection with all arrangements for site preparation and installation and transportation of the Work to the site in its finished state.

6. CARE AND DILIGENCE

The Artist shall exercise all reasonable skill care and diligence in undertaking and carrying out the Work.

7. INSURANCE

7.1 The Artist will bear any risk of loss or damage to the Work (whether in completed or uncompleted state) in the course of fabrication, wherever situate, until the Work is installed on site.

7.2 The Council will ensure that the Work is insured after installation against loss or damage from unusual risks up to the valuation recommended by the Agent.

8. FEES AND COSTS

8.1 In consideration of the creation and sale of the Work by the Artist NEC agrees to pay the Artist the total sum of £xxx which agreed total sum shall be paid in the following instalments:

Stage 1 £xxx upon the signing of this Agreement (£xxx development fee already paid)
Stage 2 £xxx on or before 30th September 1989
Stage 3 £xxx on or before 31st March 1990
Stage 4 £xxx on or before 31st May 1991
Final Stage £xxx on installation

8.2 The Artist agrees to create the Work for the agreed sum, which (unless otherwise agreed in writing) is deemed to include all expenses borne or to be borne by the Artist in connection with the Work except where such expenses are caused as a direct result of additional requirements or conditions being imposed by the NEC or the Agent or their agents or sub-contractors or as a result of completion installation or delivery of the Work being delayed for reasons outside the Artist's control.

8.3 The amounts contained in Clause 8.1 above do not include Value Added Tax, which will be added as appropriate in accordance with current legislation.

8.4 The Work is to be completed and installed by the Artist by the respective dates specified in the Brief. These completion dates shall however be extended for such period of time as the Artist may be prevented by reason of illness, accidental damage or fire flood or other hazard or other cause outside the control of the Artist (including for this purpose any acts omissions or requirements of NEC or the Council or their agents or subcontractors) from completing or installing the Work.

8.5 The Artist will keep the Agent informed of progress with the Work and if at any time the Artist considers that the Work may not be completed by the specified time, the Agent will be informed immediately.

9. TERMINATION OF AGREEMENT

9.1 It is acknowledged that the Commission can only be terminated by NEC if the project of which the Work forms part is cancelled for unforeseeable reasons in which case NEC may terminate this Agreement by written notice to the Artist, who will thereupon be entitled to receive or to retain payment for all work done in pursuance of this Agreement up to the date of such notice accruing on a daily basis, and shall further be entitled to be reimbursed for all additional expenses he or his agents or sub-contractors may have incurred on a full indemnity basis. The Artist will retain ownership of the Work and shall be free to complete the Work and sell the same to any third party.

9.2 If the Artist should die before completing the Work, the Artist's successors in title will be entitled to receive or to retain payment for all work done by the Artist in pursuance of this Agreement, together with such further sums as may be considered reasonable in the circumstances and be agreed between the parties. The Council shall own the uncompleted Work but will permit the Work to be completed by the foundry who are responsible for fabrication provided this can be done to the reasonable satisfaction of NEC.

9.3   NEC may terminate this Agreement by notice in writing if the Work has not been completed and installed by 12th June 1991 (or such later date as extended under Condition 8.4) but in such event the Artist shall be entitled to retain any fees received prior to the date of termination and the Artist shall retain ownership in the uncompleted Work and shall be entitled to complete and sell the Work if he so chooses.

10.   ORIGINALITY
The Artist warrants that the Work will be original and will fully comply with the Brief.

11.   TRANSPORT AND INSTALLATION
The Artist or his authorised agents will arrange at his own cost and in consultation with the Agent all necessary transport of the Work, both during the making of the Work and for its delivery to the site, and installation of the Work on site.

12.   DELAYS FOLLOWING COMPLETION OF THE WORK
If the Work cannot be delivered to site and/or installed by reason of a delay to the project of which the Work forms part or for any other reason outside the control of the Artist, NEC agrees to arrange for storage of the Work at its cost and to reimburse the Artist for any reasonable out-of-pocket expenses incurred by the Artist as a result.

13.   SITE PREPARATION AND INSTALLATION
Save where otherwise provided in the Brief:

13.1 The Council will be responsible at its own cost and in consultation with the Artist and the Agent for the preparation of the approved site for the Work, including foundations.

13.2 The Artist will give not less than eight weeks notice to the NEC and to the Agent of the anticipated completion date for the Work.

13.3 The Artist will, at no additional charge, be present at, and make his expertise available to NEC and the Agent during the installation of the Work.

13.4 NEC will afford the Artist and his or her authorised agents access at all reasonable times to the approved site for the Work.

13.6 The Artist will liaise as necessary with the Agent in all matters concerning site preparation and installation.

13.7 NEC will be responsible for ensuring that all necessary planning consents and approvals of any statutory authority or the site owner has or will be obtained for all costs associated therewith.

14.   MAINTENANCE AND DAMAGE TO THE WORK

14.1 Prior to installation of the Work, the Artist will advise the Agent and NEC in writing of the required maintenance for the Work.

14.2 Upon installation of the Work the Work shall form part of the Council's Public Art

Collection and as such the Museums and Art Gallery will be responsible for ensuring the future inspection, insurance, maintenance and cleaning of the Work.

14.3 Subject to Condition 14.4 if the Work is damaged and after consultation with the Artist, the Council decides that restoration or repair is feasible at an acceptable cost, NEC will give the Artist the option to conduct or supervise the restoration or repair on terms and to a schedule to be agreed, at the expense of the Council or NEC.

14.4 Where the Work requires restoration or repair by reason of defects in workmanship or materials within 12 months of installation, the Artist shall be responsible for carrying out the necesary restoration or repairs at his cost. This obligation shall be without prejudice to the period of guarantee provided by the foundry responsible for the fabrication of the Work, as specified in the Brief.

15. MORAL RIGHTS, ATTRIBUTION & ACKNOWLEDGEMENT

15.1 As soon as possible following installation of the Work, the Council undertakes to place on the Work or on the plinth to which it is attached (at its cost) a suitable plaque, with wording to be agreed with the Artist, describing the Work and its subject, and naming the Artist and any funding agencies or sponsors.

15.2 NEC, the Council and the Agent will at all times acknowledge and identify the Artist as the creator of the Work including all occasions on which the Work or any drawings, designs or maquettes or models are exhibited in public or a visual image of the Work broadcast (or copies or a graphic work representing the Work) or of a photograph of it are issued to the public.

15.3 NEC and the Council undertake not to intentionally alter, adapt, modify or destroy the Work (or consent to others doing the same), or do anything (or consent to others doing anything).

15.4 If any alteration adaptation or modification of the Work takes place after installation and whether intentional or accidental and whether done by NEC or others, the Work shall no longer be represented as the work of the Artist unless the Artist otherwise consents in writing.

15.5 The provisions of this Condition 15 shall be in addition to and without prejudice to any of the Artist's rights or remedies under Sections 77 to 84 (inclusive) of the Copyright Designs and Patents Act 1988.

16. REMOVAL AND SALE

16.1 NEC and the Council confirm that the Work is intended to be available for public exhibition on the specified site for an indefinite period. However NEC reserve the right to remove the Work for temporary periods should this be required for maintenance or structural reasons or other good cause.

16.2 If for exceptional and unavoidable reasons the Work needs to be removed permanently, the Council undertakes at its own expense to endeavour to find an alternative site acceptable to the Artist and to resite the Work there, if the Artist so requests. If however no agreed alternative site can be found, NEC will ensure that the Work is stored by the Museums and Art Gallery until a suitable alternative site can be found.

16.3 The Council will notify the Artist in advance if it intends to sell the Work and will offer the Artist the first right to purchase the Work. NEC will in any event notify the Artist of the name and address of any new owner and will include in any contract with a new owner comparable obligations regarding maintenance and repair and moral rights.

17. ADDRESSES

The Artist undertakes, during the currency of the Commission, to notify the NEC and the Agent in writing of any change in his or her address, including the address of his or her studio, within seven days of that change occurring.

18. VARIATIONS

No variations or additions to these Conditions or the Brief may be made without the written permission of all parties.

19. GENERAL

19.1 In the event of any conflict between the terms of the Brief and these Conditions, the latter shall prevail.

19.2 The Artist shall have no liability or responsibility for the acts or omissions of site-contractors or employees or agents of NEC the Council or the site-owner.

19.3 This contract is personal to the Artist who may not assign any part of his obligations without NEC permission (not to be unreasonably withheld) except that the Artist may sub-contract the fabrication of the Work or any part of it to Haligon S.A. provided the Artist remains responsible for complying with these Conditions.

19.4 NEC warrants that it has the authority of the Council to enter into this Agreement and to give the undertakings and representations on the part of the Council herein contained.

20. DURATION

This Agreement is binding upon the parties, their assigns and all other successors in title.

21. PROPER LAW

This Agreement is governed by the law of England and Wales and many only be amended by further written agreement signed by all the parties.

22. DISPUTES

Any disputes under or arising from this Agreement may be referred at the instance of either party to an independent expert nominated by the Chairman for the time being of Public Art Forum (or other expert agreed between the parties) who shall use all reasonable endeavours to effect a solution acceptable to all parties and may make recommendations according to what he considers fair and reasonable in the circumstances of the case. Such referral shall be without prejudice to the right of any party to take legal proceedings at any stage.

SIGNED

xxx (The Artist)

xxx (for and on behalf of) (NEC)

Designation: Director-Finance & Administration, Company Secretary

ARTIST'S BRIEF
Artist: xxx
Address: xxx
Client: NEC Limited, Birmingham B40 1NT

Description of the Artwork:
Figurative sculpture cast in stratified resin, armed with cortone steel and treated with polyurethane paint. The form and subject-matter of the sculpture are described in xxx's notes on 'A Monument for Centenary Square' and further detailed in a maquette which was accepted by Birmingham City Council's NEC/ICC Committee and the commission confirmed on 3 February 1988.

Brief:
- To design, manufacture, deliver and install the sculpture described above.
- The plinth should be integral to the sculpture.
- The design should function fully in 3 dimensions and be capable of being appreciated by an observer approaching from any angle.

Durability:
The fabrication and materials, including plinth and fixtures, should be fully durable for outdoor siting, especially in relation to:
- load capacity, fracture and impact resistance
- water-proofing
- frost-proofing
- heat resistance
- effects of sunlight
- flame-proofing, including cigarette burns

Detailed specifications and guarantees covering the above headings must be supplied by Haligon Studios and the Artist for both the fabrication and the paint/colour/sealant finishes. Where specifications are published in French, translation to English must be supplied.

As the sculpture is for installation in the UK, all materials used in the sculpture must meet British Standard Safety regulations.

Location:
As detailed in appended plan.

Graffiti Resistance:
The sculpture must be protected by a suitable high-performance graffiti-proof coating of proven quality. Specifications for the coating must be supplied prior to its application for verification.

Foundations and Fixtures:
Details of specifications for foundations and fixtures must be supplied by the Artist or his Agent to Public Art Commissions Agency by an agreed date. The Agency will pass on instructions/specifications to Centenary Square Design Team (City Architects Department) for implementation.

Completion:
The sculpture must be completed by end of March 1991, and must be installed by mid-May 1991, the exact date to be agreed between the Artist, his Agent (Marlborough Fine Art), Public Art Commissions Agency (the art consultants), and the client.

Liaison:
The artist to liaise, through the Public Art Commissions Agency, with the Centenary Square Design Team (including its consultant artist Tess Jaray), led by City Architect's Department, over integration of the sculpture into the overall design.

Commission agreement between the Silkstone Heritage Stones Project and a commissioned artist © Silkstone Heritage Stones Project

COMMISSION AGREEMENT
This AGREEMENT is made the twentieth day of November, 1990 between xxx (THE ARTIST) of xxx and The Silkstone Heritage Stone Group (THE COMMISSIONERY) of xxx by which we agree as follows:

1.   COMMISSION
The Artist agrees to complete on or about xxx (1) unless circumstances beyond his/her control render this impossible, the following proposed work(s) of art ("The Works"):
DESCRIPTION (2)   xxx
DIMENSIONS   xxx
MATERIALS   xxx

2.   PAYMENTS
(a)   In consideration for creating the Work(s) the Commissioner agrees to pay the Artist the sum of £xxx (including VAT)(3) in the following instalments:
     (1)   One third upon signing this Agreement and
     (2)   one third when the Artist notifies the Commissioner that the Work(s) is/are two-thirds completed and
     (3)   one third when the Artist notifies the Commissioner that the work(s) is/are completed.

     For these purposes, the Artist shall notify the Commissioner in writing and shall permit him/her or his/her authorised agents, upon reasonable notice, to inspect the Work(s).
(b)   Subject to Clause 6 of this Agreement, the Artist shall retain the title of the Work(s), and all rights therein, upon payment of the final instalment.

3.   That the artist satisfies the Commissioners that he has adequate insurance cover to meet all aspects of this commission.

4.   ACCEPTANCE
It is understood that the Artist will use his/her aesthetic skill and judgement to create the Work(s), and that the Commissioner agrees to accept the completed Work(s) unless he/she

can show that the Work(s) was/were not executed substantially in accordance with the description agreed by him/her under Clause I of this Agreement.

5.   ACCESS
The Commissioner shall arrange for the Artist to organise, in association with the Group, public and schools workshops/demonstrations before work commences and during the actual carving. Prior arrangements to be made with the Artist.

6.   SALE
Upon completion of the Work(s) both parties shall sign the Contract of Sale (a copy of which is attached hereto).

7.   The Artist agrees to store and insure the finished work until sited in the Parish of Silkstone.

8.   TERMINATION
The Commissioner may terminate this Agreement at any time upon giving written notice to the Artist, who shall be entitled to receive or retain payment for all work done in pursuance of this Agreement up to date of receiving such notice. In the event of termination, title of the Work(s) and all rights therein, shall be retained by the Artist.

9.   PROPER LAW
This agreement shall be governed by the Law of England and Wales and may only be amended in writing by both parties.

10.   ARBITRATION
Any dispute shall be referred to an arbitrator to be nominated by Yorkshire Arts in accordance with the provision of the Arbitration Act 1950 or any Statutory modification or re-enactment thereof for the time being in force.

SIGNED
xxx (The Commissioner)
xxx (The Artist)

CONTRACT OF SALE BETWEEN THE SILKSTONE HERITAGE STONES PROJECT AND A COMMISSIONED ARTIST

THIS AGREEMENT is made the xxx day of xxx BETWEEN xxx (hereinafter called "the Artist") of the one part and THE SILKSTONE HERITAGE STONES PROJECT represented by xxx (hereinafter called "the Buyer") of the other part.

WHO HAS AGREED to purchase the xxx (hereinafter called "the Work") subject to the following terms and conditions:-

1.   Property in the Work will pass to the Buyer on payment of the final invoice.

2.   The Artist warrants that the Work is original and that no replica of it has been or will be made by her.

3. Copyright is retained by the Artist and the Buyer agrees to acknowledge the Artist as creator of the Work at all times.

4. The Buyer has inspected the sculpture on completion and agrees that the Work is completed to his satisfaction.

5. The Buyer will take reasonable care of the Work and will not intentionally alter damage or destroy it or permit others to do so.

6. The Buyer shall allow public access to the Work at all reasonable times in accordance with the provisions contained in the Licence with the Landowner.

7. The Artist agrees to store and insure the completed Work on behalf of the Buyer until such time as it is sited in the Parish of Silkstone in the County of York to include all liability for damage destruction or injury to anybody or anything howsoever arising from the Work.

8. The Artist agrees to ensure that the Work is safely installed on site to the satisfaction of the Buyer. All costs incurred in site preparation removing the Work to the site and installation will be borne by the Buyer.

9. The Work shall remain in the position in which it has been sited by the Artist unless it is unavoidable to move it.

10. All risk of damage destruction or prejudice in any way whatsoever to the Work shall pass to the Buyer and in the event of repair being necessary the Buyer shall give the Artist the option to conduct or supervise any restoration work or repairs on terms to be agreed.

11. The Buyer will not sell lend or remove the Work without first notifying the Artist who will keep the Buyer informed of any changes of address and whose consent will not unreasonably be withheld.

12. This Agreement shall be governed by the Law of England and Wales.

SIGNED AND DELIVERED as a deed by the said) xxx in the presence of:-) xxx
SIGNED AND DELIVERED as a deed by the said) xxx in the presence of:-) xxx

DRAFT AGREEMENT BETWEEN THE SILKSTONE HERITAGE STONES PROJECT AND A LANDOWNER

THIS AGREEMENT is made the xxx day of xxx BETWEEN xxx of xxx (hereinafter called "the Landowner") of the first part and xxx of xxx being the duly elected xxx of THE SILKSTONE HERITAGE STONES PROJECT (hereinafter called "the Group") of the second part.

W H E R E A S:-

1. The Landowner is the owner of the parcel of land described in the schedule hereto which includes the line of The Silkstone Parish boundary.

2. The Group are desirous of siting a Heritage Stone on the said parish boundary line.

IT IS HEREBY AGREED:-

1. That the Landowner his heirs and assigns grant permission to the Group for the siting of a Heritage Stone on the aforesaid parish boundary line

2. The Heritage Stone shall be the sole property of the Group or their Trustees in perpetuity

3. The Group or their Trustees shall be responsible for any damage, destruction or injury to anybody or anything however arising from the siting of the Heritage Stone.

4. The Group or their Trustees shall be responsible for all maintenance and repair of the Heritage Stone and the Landowner shall allow all reasonable access to the Group or their Trustees, servants, agents and licensees to carry out such works of maintenance and repair.

5. The Group or their Trustees shall be responsible for any damage caused to the Landowner's property by the actual siting of the Heritage Stone and undertake to reinstate such damage.

6. Public Access – to be negotiated but details to be included in Agreement.

7. The Group or their Trustees retain the sole right to all images of the Heritage Stone photographic or otherwise and any use of such images by the Landowner without prior consent in writing of the Group or their Trustees shall be deemed to be a breach of this Agreement.

8. The Landowner shall take all reasonable precautions to prevent damage to the Heritage Stone.

9. The Landowners agreement to the siting of the Heritage Stone will be duly acknowledged in any publicity connected with the Heritage Stone so far as the Group can ensure this.

LICENCE BETWEEN THE SILKSTONE HERITAGE STONES PROJECT AND A LANDOWNER © THE SILKSTONE HERITAGE STONES PROJECT

THIS LICENCE is made the xxx day of xxx BETWEEN (1) xxx ("the Landowner) and (2) SILKSTONE HERITAGE STONES PROJECT ("the Society") represented by xxx of xxx and xxx of as signatories ("the Licensee")

W H E R E A S:

(1) A sculpture owned by the Society with its associated foundations has been constructed on land described in the First Schedule hereto ("the site")

(2) The sculpture has been erected at the request of the Society under the supervision of a competent person. Insofar as it has been able the Society has taken all reasonable precautions to have the sculpture safely erected

(3) The Landowner had agreed to grant to the Licensee on behalf of the Society the Licence hereinafter contained

NOW IT IS AGREED as follows:-

1. Subject to the provisions of the next succeeding clause and to the observance and performance by the Licensee of the conditions and obligations specified in the Second Schedule hereto the Landowner hereby grants to the Licensee.

(a) license to retain the sculpture at the site

(b) access for the Licensee its representatives and the general public to the site across the adjoining land of the Landowner as suitably defined by the Landowner

2. This licence shall continue subject to termination as provided in clause 6 below for the period of five years from the date hereof and thereafter from year to year until determined.

3. The Licensee shall pay to the Landowner the annual licence fee of One pound (if demanded) on the first day of January in each year.

4(a) The general public shall be permitted to visit the site and use the defined access way for the purpose of examining the sculpture at all reasonable times.

(b) The Licensee may visit the site at all reasonable times in addition with workmen and equipment to maintain and carry out any necessary repairs to the sculptures that may from time to time be required to keep it in a safe condition and repair any damage at its discretion.

5. The Landowner may add to or vary the said conditions and obligations from time to time as he may consider reasonable for the protection of his adjoining property and may vary the accessways to the site in the course of good management of his adjoining property by notice in writing to the Licensee.

6. The Landowner may determine this licence without prejudice to any claim he may have against the Licensee in respect of breach of any of the provisions of the licence.

(a) by not less than three months notice in writing expiring at any time after the date specified in clause 2 hereof or

(b) by not less than fourteen days notice at any time if the Landowner is required to do so by any legally constituted statutory body.

7. The Landowner's use and enjoyment of his adjoining property and all his activities whether carried on by him or by persons authorised by him shall take preference over the permission hereby granted and the Licensee shall not be entitled to exclusive possession or occupation of the site nor shall the Licensee be entitled to any compensation in respect of any interference with the permission hereby granted.

8. The Licensee agrees to indemnify the Landowner for any damage sustained to the site as a result of the removal of the sculpture.

9. The Licensee will indemnify the Landowner from any claim brought by a member of the public arising from any injury sustained by the general public arising from any injury sustained as a result of the unsafe state of the sculpture and agrees to maintain public liability insurance.

10. The term "Licensee" shall be deemed to include all persons who are members from time to time of the Society according to its constitution.

11. This licence shall be binding on the successors in title of the Landowner and on the Society respectively.

AS WITNESS the hands of the parties hereto the day and year first before written

THE FIRST SCHEDULE above referred to (The Site)

THE SECOND SCHEDULE above referred to (Conditions and Obligations)

The Licensee shall if required by the Landowner erect on the adjoining land of the Landowner nearest to a public road a notice addressed to the general public incorporating the following conditions:-

(a) Not to enter the site except by the roads or tracks designated by the Landowner.

(b)   Not to light fires on or near the site or the adjoining land of the Landowner.

(c)   To refrain from smoking on or near the site or the adjoining land of the Landowner.

(e)   Not to take any dogs onto the site.

(f)   To take all reasonable care not to distub any game birds or their nests or eggs.

(g)   Not to leave any litter.

(h)   To warn the general public that they visit the site at their own risk.

SIGNED AND DELIVERED as a deed by the said xxx in the presence of xxx.
SIGNED AND DELIVERED as a deed by the said xxx in the presence of xxx.
SIGNED AND DELIVERED as a deed by the said xxx in the presence of xxx.

Agreement between the British Railways Board, the commissioned artist and his agents

BRITISH RAILWAYS BOARD
PUBLIC ART COMMISSION & SALE AGREEMENT

THIS AGREEMENT is made this xxx day of xxx 1987 BETWEEN xxx (herein referred to as 'the Artist') of xxx and xxx (herein referred to as 'the Agent') of xxx and THE BRITISH RAILWAYS BOARD (herein referred to as 'the Board')

1   Commission

1.1   The Agent hereby commissions the Artist on behalf of the Board to undertake the following work of art and/or craft – a sculpture in a landscape setting xxx and more particularly described in the Schedule hereto – (herein described as 'the Work') to be located in accordance with Clause 1.4 at xxx.

1.2   The Artist hereby agrees both to undertake the Work and to complete it to the satisfaction of the Board by xxx.

1.3   After the work has been on site for 10 years the recipient shall consult with the artist to determine whether or not the work should remain on site, be relocated elsewhere or be dismantled.

1.4   The Board agrees that whilst the work is on site that no attempt will be made to obstruct the public's clear view of the work.

2.   Sale

2.1   It is agreed that upon completion of the Work and payment to the Artist of the agreed sum property and copyright in the Work, together with all preparatory and working documents and drawings, shall pass to the Board.

3.   Fees and Costs

3.1   In consideration of the creation and sale of the Work by the Artist, under the Commission of this Agreement, the Board agrees to pay to the Agent upon commission the total sum of £xxx which is inclusive of the Agent's fee of £xxx

3.2   The Artist agrees to create the Work on behalf of the Board for the agreed fee of £xxx, which is deemed to include all expenses borne or to be borne by the Artist in connection with the Work. The Agent shall arrange with the Artist a schedule for payment of the agreed sum.

3.3 The amounts contained in Clause 3.1 above do not include Value Added Tax and the Board accepts responsibility for the payment of any VAT which may be properly levied on those amounts.

3.4 In consideration of the payment of the agreed Agents fee specified in Clause 3.1 hereof, the Agent undertakes to
   (a) commission the Artist to undertake the Work
   (b) oversee and manage the progress of the Work
   (c) obtain any further funding found necessary to complete the Work and its installation
   (d) manage and account to the Board for the funding of the Commission and make whatever payments are necessary for its proper execution
   (e) assist the Board in generating publicity for the Work

4. Termination of Agreement

4.1 The Board, or the Agent acting on behalf of the Board, may, upon reasonable grounds for so doing, terminate this Agreement by written notice to the Artist and the Agent, who will thereupon be entitled to receive or to retain payment for all work done in pursuance of this Agreement up to the date of such notice, together with such further sums as may be considered reasonable in the circumstances and be agreed between the Parties.

4.2 If the Artist should die before completing the Work, his successors in title will be entitled to receive or to retain payment for all work done by the Artist in pursuance of this Agreement, together with such further sums as may be considered reasonable in the circumstances and be agreed between the Parties.

4.3 If (a) due to the Artist's illness, or (b) due to damage by fire, flood or other hazard to the Artist's residence or studio or any other place where the Work is temporarily housed, or (c) due to any other cause outside the control of the Artist, the Work cannot be completed by the date specified in Clause 1.2 above, the Artist will be entitled to receive or to retain payment for all work undertaken in pursuance of this Agreement up until the date of commencing his illness or to the date of the occurrence, together with such further sums as may be considered reasonable in the circumstances and be agreed between the Parties.

4.4 If the Work cannot be completed for any reason, the Board reserves the right without further payment beyond those sums specified in Clauses 1-3 of this Section to take possession of all work as might then exist.

5. Originality

5.1 The Artists warrants that the Work will be original and will indemnify the Board and its successors in title against all damages losses charges and expenses in respect of all or any actions brought against the Board or its successors in title relating to the originality of the Work.

6. Acceptance

6.1 The Artist will use his aesthetic skill and judgement to create the Work in accordance with the agreed description and design set out in the Schedule annexed to this Agreement, and the Agent and the Board agree to accept the completed Work in accordance with the terms of this Agreement unless either the Agent or the Board can show that the Work was executed not in accordance with the agreed description and design or that the Work is not Original or that it has not been completed by the date specified in Clause 1.2 hereof. If the Work is not accepted by the Board for any reason all monies paid by the Board shall be refunded to the Board within 28 days of the Board giving notice that the Work is not acceptable.

7. Copyright and Reproduction

7.1 The Artists undertakes that he will not make any copy or take any photographs of the Work nor perform any act which would be in breach of or result in the breach of the Board's copyright in the Work without the prior consent in writing of the Board, which consent the Board undertakes will not be unreasonably withheld.

7.2 The Board and the Agent shall be entitled, without consulting the Artist and without further payment to him, to make or authorise to be made any photograph of the Work and to include or authorise the inclusion of the Work or any such photograph of the Work or any preliminary designs and working drawings in any record, publication, film, video or television broadcast.

8. Transport

8.1 The Artist undertakes to arrange at his own cost and in consultation with the Agent all necessary transport of the Work, both during the making of the Work and for its delivery to the approved site.

9. Site preparation and Installation

9.1 The Artist will give not less than four weeks notice to the Board and to the Agent of the anticipated completion date for the Work.

9.2 The Artist will, at no additional charge, be present at, and make expertise available to the Board, during the installation of the Work.

9.3 The Board will afford the Artist and his authorised agents access at all reasonable times to the approved site for the Work, upon completion of a suitable form of Indemnity.

10. Maintenance and Damage to the Work

10.1 Upon completion and hand over of the Work, the Artist will provide to the Board a maintenance schedule for the Work.

10.2 The Board will be responsible for the future maintenance of the Work.

10.3 If the Work is damaged, the Board does not undertake to execute its restoration or repair. If, after consultation with the Artist, the Board decides that restoration/repair is feasible at an acceptable cost, the Board will give the Artist the option to conduct or supervise the restoration on terms and to a schedule to be agreed, at the expense of the Board.

11. Acknowledgement

11.1 As soon as conveniently possible following installation of the Work, the Board undertakes to place near the Work a suitable plaque or other form of display, with wording agreed with the Artist and the Agent, describing the Work and its subject, acknowledging the Agent, and naming the Artist and any Sponsors.

11.2 The Board and the Agent will at all times acknowledge the Artist as the creator of the Work.

12. Removal

12.1 Upon written notice to the Artist and the Agent, the Board may for any good reason remove the Work prior to the expiry of the minimum period specified in Clause 1.4 hereof. In the event of removal under the terms of this Clause the Board undertakes at its own expense to take all reasonable steps in an endeavour to transfer the Work to an alternative site in England, Scotland or Wales as may reasonably be agreed with the Artist.

13. Addresses

13.1 The Artist undertakes, during the currency of the Commission, to notify the Board and the Agent in writing of any change in his address, including the address of his studio, within seven days of that change occurring.

13.2 The Board will take all reasonable steps to notify the Artist and the Agent if it intends to sell, lend or otherwise part with possession of the Work, and such notice will include the name and address of the person/institution which it is intended should acquire the Work. Where the Board notifies its intention to sell the Work, the Artist may offer to purchase the Work by notice to the Board's Secretary not later than 14 days after the date of the Board's notice of its intention to sell.

14. Duration

14.1 This Agreement is binding upon the parties, their assigns and all other successors in title.

15. Proper Law

15.1 This Agreement is governed by the law of England and Wales and may only be amended by further written agreement signed by all the parties.

16. Arbitration

16.1 Any dispute under or arising from this Agreement will be referred to an independent arbiter appointed in accordance with the provisions of the Arbitration Act 1950 or any statutory modification or re-enactment thereof for the time being in force.

SIGNED xxx (The Artist)
(for an on behalf of) xxx (The Agent)
(for and on behalf of) xxx (The Board)

SCHEDULE

Specification of the Work

TITLE
A Light Wave

DESCRIPTION - A Sculpture in a Landscaped Setting

(1)   The Structure
The structure consists of planks of wood of equal lengths lent against the wall. Beginning from a horizontal position each one leans a few inches higher up the wall until the final one stands vertically. This progression forms one element, it is then repeated 7 times along the entire length of the back wall to form the sculpture. Each element ties in with the spaces between the buttress walls projecting from the back wall, leaving 1 complete space empty at either end of the platform.

(2)   The Lighting
Along the base of the back wall a line of 500 watt light bulbs inside weatherproof covers would be equally distanced apart. During the hours of darkness the light sensitive switch turns on the lights. Only one light will be on at any time. The whole sequence will take approximately 45 seconds. The interior of each structure is lit in turn, light escapes from the gaps in the structure causing lines of light and shadow to move across the exterior surfaces of the sculpture and the wall.

DIMENSIONS

(1)   The structure: 150' in length
                          14' in height
                          14' in depth
(2)   The planted area: 150' in length
                          10' in width

MATERIALS
Timber (9" x 2" in 14' lengths) stained and weatherproofed.
Galvanised fixings.
Armoured cable.
Lights (21 500 watt) installed in waterproof covers.
Electronic timer with light sensitive switching.
Topsoil and vegetation.

A Light Wave Sculpture at Wakefield Westgate © British Railways Board

MAINTENANCE SCHEDULE

1. The Timber Structure

1.1 Individual planks that sustain irreparable damage should be replaced as soon as practicable with new planks, and it is recommended that a small supply of ready-stained timber be maintained for this purpose.

1.2 Every three years (commencing Spring 1994) the timber structure should be washed down and given one coat of blue stain on all facing surfaces. (Care must be taken to avoid spillage of stain onto the crushed limestone and onto the rear wall.)
USE SADOLIN CLASSIC 4/ BLUE STAIN (See attached data sheet)

2. Lights and Electronic Timer

2.1 Defective bulbs should be replaced promptly.
USE 500 WATT 240 VOLT TUNGSTEN HALOGEN LAMP FITTINGS
USE HARVEY HUBBELL QUARTZLITER WIDE ANGLE FLOODLIGHT QL500
SERIES (Data sheets attached)

Access to the inside of individual structures is via the sixth plank from the left. The base plate securing nuts should be removed and the plank lifted on the hinged bracket at the top.

The light fitting has a simple spring clip catch.

IT IS IMPORTANT THAT THE POSITIONING OF THE LAMPS IS NOT ALTERED.

The timer control comprises four elements:

1. enclosure holding power supply
2. enclosure holding micro-electronic timer
3. enclosure holding 21 MCBs
4. photo-electric cell (mounted on external wall) (Data sheets attached)

If a fault occurs in elements 1 and 2 of the timer control, then it is recommended that repairs should be carried out by the manufacturer, Charles Quick.

3. General Maintenance of the Sculpture Site

3.1 Regular clearing of litter from in and around the sculpture is required.

3.2 The planted area must be kept free from weeds and litter, and any dead plants promptly replaced.

Charles Quick